ELIZABETH R

'It will be impossible for anyone to finish this
book without an enhanced picture of the Queen
and her family'

The Daily Telegraph

'Like the Countess's previous books, QUEEN
VICTORIA and WELLINGTON, this biography
is informed, thorough and revealing of the human
being behind the public image. Longford creates
a warm feeling in the reader for Queen Elizabeth
II'

Publishers Weekly

'Lady Longford writes a biography of the Queen
which combines tact with literary charm'

The Financial Times

'This is an engrossing book which gives a
balanced picture of the characters and
development of the Princesses Elizabeth and
Margaret'

The Lady

'She brings to this book the perspective she
brought to the monarch's predecessors. Masses of
anecdotes and new information provide a warm,
coherent portrait of a much-loved Royal'

Women's Journal

About the Author

The Countess of Longford CBE is a leading historian and well known as a woman of wide interests. After her degree in *Literae Humaniores* at Oxford, she was a lecturer for the Workers' Educational Association. She has stood twice for Parliament in the Labour interest. Lady Longford was until recently a Trustee of the National Portrait Gallery, a member of the Advisory Council of the Victoria and Albert Museum and of the British Library, and is a Vice-President of the Royal Society of Literature. She is an Hon. D. Litt. of Sussex University. Her previous publications include *Jameson's Raid*, *Victoria R.I.* (which won the James Tait Black Memorial Prize), a celebrated two-volume biography of Wellington (of which *The Years of the Sword* was the *Yorkshire Post* Book of the Year), *The Royal House of Windsor*, *Louisa Lady in Waiting*, *A Pilgrimage of Passion: The Life of Wilfrid Scawen Blunt*, *The Queen Mother* and *Eminent Victorian Women*.

Elizabeth R

A biography

Elizabeth Longford

CORONET BOOKS
Hodder and Stoughton

Copyright © 1983 by Elizabeth Longford

First published in Great Britain 1983 by
Weidenfeld and Nicolson Ltd

Coronet edition 1984

British Library C.I.P.

Longford, Elizabeth
  Elizabeth R.
   1. Elizabeth II, *Queen of Great Britain*
   2. Great Britain – Kings and rulers – Biography
   I. Title
   941.085'092'4   DA590

ISBN 0-340-36374-6

Printed and bound in Great Britain for
Hodder and Stoughton Paperbacks, a
division of Hodder and Stoughton Ltd,
Mill Road, Dunton Green, Sevenoaks,
Kent (Editorial Office: 47 Bedford
Square, London WC1 3DP) by
Richard Clay (The Chaucer Press), Ltd,
Bungay, Suffolk
Photoset by Rowland Phototypesetting Ltd,
Bury St Edmunds, Suffolk.

Contents

Author's Acknowledgments

This book has depended more than any other I have written on oral evidence. While I was gradually discovering the life and character of Queen Victoria from unexplored sources in the Royal Archives, my most intense relationships were with diaries and letters. In writing about Queen Victoria's great-great-granddaughter I have had to learn to do without the written royal records except for those few published by Her Majesty's relatives, such as Princess Alice, Countess of Athlone, and the Earl of Harewood, or included in the official biographies of King George v, Queen Mary and King George vi.

But instead of documents there is a contemporary corpus of memories and ideas to draw upon from people who have known or still know the Queen personally. Since Queen Elizabeth ii has already reigned for over thirty years, these personal impressions have by now built up into something of a recognisable tradition. And because it is a living one, and a fairly long one, it is possible to see the general picture developing from the many detailed changes that mark the course of a human life.

In this personal sphere I must thank first and foremost HRH Princess Margaret, Countess of Snowdon, who, I believe with Her Majesty's benevolent interest, has given me invaluable, most generous and stimulating help. Not only do I owe to Princess Margaret's care and kindness the opportunity to put the record straight in many smaller respects but also the chance to correct some more serious misunderstandings.

For example, neither Princess Margaret nor her sister were conscious of an isolated or joyless girlhood. Moreover Princess Margaret and her mother, HM Queen Elizabeth the Queen Mother, are both convinced that a commonly held view of Queen Elizabeth II is subtly but definitely mistaken. 'The Queen was never shy with people,' they both insist; 'she may have sometimes felt shy inside, but,' points out the Queen Mother, 'other people would be shyer.'

I have tried to reconcile these distinctions; for I have come to see that they are the true measure of Queen Elizabeth II's character. It was only too easy to saddle her with the shyness that did indeed burden her grandmother Queen Mary. But shyness is not the key to Elizabeth II, as I shall hope to show.

If I may speak personally for a moment, I did once experience the formidable shyness of Queen Mary in conversation, and can therefore appreciate the immense difference between that state of inhibition and her granddaughter's approach to any conversation whether formal or informal. I have had the honour to meet the Queen on many occasions over the last thirty years, including one of the first experimental 'dinners' at the Palace and the historic Garter ceremony each June since 1971. On the most recent informal occasion no one could have been more spontaneous and articulate than Queen Elizabeth II. She was looking forward to her first ever visit to California – so far she knew it only as a seemingly endless stream of lights as she flew over it, 'like London only more so' – and she had just enjoyed the magnificent Van Dyck exhibition at the National Portrait Gallery. Although she always deplores the dispersal of Charles I's works of art by the Cromwellians – in fact she made an expressive little face – she revelled in the success of this exhibition. The Russians had lent two Van Dyck portraits bought by Catherine the Great from the Walpole collection and now in the Hermitage. The Queen said jubilantly, 'This is the first time it's happened!'

And if anyone still asks, 'Then did you interview the Queen for your book?' the answer is firmly no. The Queen does not give interviews.

I would like to thank all those who have helped me with my research, beginning with Sir Robert Mackworth-Young, the Royal Librarian, and his Assistant, Miss Jane Langton, for answering nineteenth-century historical questions. I am deeply grateful to those who have served the Queen as her Prime Ministers and have allowed me to consult or talk with them: Harold Macmillan, Lord Home of the Hirsel, Sir Harold Wilson, Edward Heath MP, James Callaghan MP and the present Prime Minister, Mrs Margaret Thatcher; and also to Lord Hailsham of St Marylebone, Lord and Lady Stewart of Fulham, Baroness Phillips, Sir Hugh Fraser MP, Maurice Macmillan MP, the late Lord Butler of Saffron Walden and his widow Mollie who has been most generous in every way.

Lady Pamela Hicks, the Duke and Duchess of Grafton, Lady Rupert Nevill, Lady Gage, Sir John and Lady Margaret Colville, Lord and Lady Cobbold, Mrs William Ladd (formerly the Vicomtesse de Bellaigue), Lord Porchester, Lord Oaksey, Woodrow Wyatt, Dr Alec Vidler, the Right Reverend Dr Edward Carpenter, Dean of Westminster, Sir John Plumb, James Fawcett, Mrs Michael Wall, Sir Martin Gilliat, Lady Abel Smith and Mrs John Woodroffe have all been more than kind. To the many who have contributed off-the-record information or advice I offer my warm appreciation.

Among fellow writers who have given me information I am greatly indebted to Sir Arthur Bryant, Lady Violet Powell, Dr A. L. Rowse, Hugo Vickers, Lady Donaldson, Malcolm and John Muggeridge, Mr and Mrs Joseph Bryan III, Duff Hart-Davis, Mollie Gillen, Philip Ziegler, Christopher Warwick, Theo Aronson, Susan Crosland, Jasper Ridley, Anthony Holden, Robert Lacey; also to Lord

Zuckerman, John Hayes, Director of the National Portrait Gallery, Sir Roy Strong, Director of the Victoria and Albert Museum; General Giles Mills, Governor of the Tower of London, the staff of the British Library, the London Library and the Kensington and Chelsea Library; to Charles Davies of Chipstead Productions, Audrey Russell, Sir Huw Wheldon and the BBC for kindly re-running sections of the *Royal Family* film; to Stephen Parker and W. H. Chapman. For making corrections that I have incorporated in this edition I am most grateful to Kenneth Rose, Alistair Forbes, Anthony Holden, the press secretary at Lambeth Palace, the cultural attaché at the Royal Danish Embassy, London, Margaret Lavender, E. M. Price, Paul H. Gottlieb, Marlene A. Eilers, Rev. Robert Ehrgott, A. J. P. H. van Cruyningen, Wayne Swift, D. Hodgetts, D. E. Slaney, Harold Miller.

I would like to thank my friends and publishers: Lord Weidenfeld, John Curtis, Linda Osband; Lynda Poley and Jenny de Gex for picture research; and Robert Gottlieb of Alfred A. Knopf for his most welcome and perceptive advice. I also thank my agents Graham Watson and now Michael Shaw; I am grateful to Agnes Fenner for undertaking the typing yet again, and also to Maria Ellis.

I thank my daughter Antonia for meticulously reading it chapter by chapter and producing insights on all fronts, my son Michael for extensive reading and important suggestions, my daughters Judith and Rachel and sons Thomas, Paddy and Kevin for sustained enthusiasm; my granddaughter Flora Powell-Jones for research; and Frank as always for keeping the perfect balance between criticism and encouragement.

The Royal House of Windsor

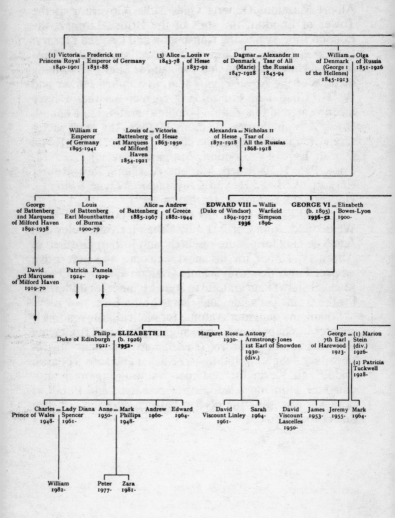

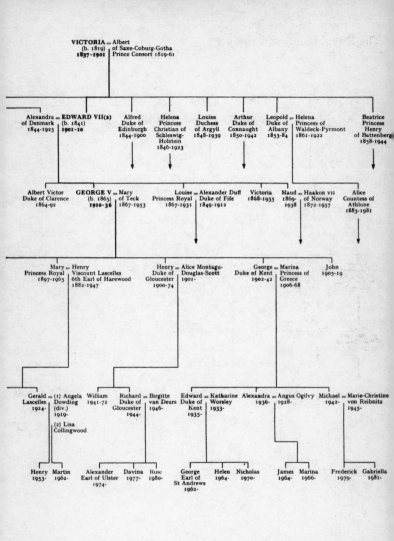

FOR
FRANK AND ANTONIA

I

Today

Some viewers thought she turned a little pale. Others noticed no change of colour. Indeed a general's wife who was watching the event on the television screen at first thought the loud noises came from the clatter of hooves, as a horse out of sight perhaps slipped and fell. It was not until later that the news headlines reported the firing of blanks at the Queen. Then everyone understood. Viewers shouted to non-viewers, 'The Queen's been shot at! . . . shot at! . . . shot at!'

On the Horse Guards approach everything had continued as though nothing had happened. All the people who had ducked stood up again. Her Majesty Queen Elizabeth II gave a pat to Burmese, the black mare presented to her by the Royal Canadian Mounted Police, while Prince Philip and Prince Charles dropped quietly back into their official places in the Trooping the Colour Birthday Parade. The announcer went on announcing.

That Saturday, 13 June 1981, had been the date chosen by an unhappy youth of seventeen to arm himself with six blank cartridges in a replica pistol and perform a sad little mission of self-advertisement. He was jailed for five years under the Treason Act 1842, and was refused leave to appeal. Ironically he was a worker in the Youth Opportunities scheme. Who remembers his name today? But the incident told a good deal about the Queen.

She might have been caught at a disadvantage, for she was riding side-saddle. An expert equestrian, she normally rides astride. But since the earliest days she has always worn a long navy blue riding-skirt with her military tunic for this ceremonial occasion and spent three weeks beforehand practising in the Royal Mews. Even so she would hardly have chosen a side-saddle on which to control a startled, prancing horse. Yet her control was complete. As she passed the window of the Admiralty from which Queen Elizabeth the Queen Mother and Lady Diana Spencer were watching, she smiled and raised her hand as if to wave away this and all other 'incidents'.

Two days later it happened to be the Garter ceremony at Windsor Castle. Every post was bringing in sackfuls of congratulatory letters to the Queen, and her guests at Windsor (of whom the author was one) added their voices to the chorus of praise for her calm and skilful management of the black mare. 'It wasn't the shots that frightened her,' said the Queen in defence of her nineteen-year-old charger, 'but the cavalry!' Two officers of the Household Cavalry had quite correctly spurred their horses forward to take up their positions on each side of their sovereign, so that Burmese began to prance. It was at the sight of these unexpected companions, not lack of courage in the firing-line.

The Queen's own courage is more than an automatic response to danger, however admirable that may be. It is part of her philosophy. No doubt the Year of the Disabled, 1981, helped to concentrate many minds, including the Queen's, on the various faces of courage. In her Christmas message, after being filmed in the gardens of her palace presenting cars to disabled people, she allowed herself to make certain distinctions. There was courage with its bold physical face, the courage of servicemen or firemen. 'But above all,' she said, 'there is moral courage.' In this she included the unshakeable will of the handicapped to endure. 'The golden thread of courage,' she quoted, 'has no end.'

Both physical and moral courage, as her story will show, are an integral part of herself and her inheritance. Her mother has always shown physical fortitude, ignoring an injury to her leg incurred before Prince Charles's wedding, and returning to work only ten days after an operation for removing a fish-bone lodged in her throat, despite the shock caused to a lady of eighty-two by a general anaesthetic. Her father in particular possessed both kinds. But even those among her royal forebears who may have lacked purpose and moral tenacity never failed to show physical bravery. Nor were the testing times as rare as might be expected. Cushioned royalty has its occupational hazards like other businesses. Unlike most others its risk is assassination.

Going back no further than Victoria, the Queen-Empress found herself shot at six times during her sixty-year reign and once was knocked momentarily unconscious with a cane. Her eldest son Edward VII was shot at in Brussels in 1900 by a fifteen-year-old anarchist; but it was in the generation of Victoria's grandchildren that the bullets really began to fly. Her granddaughter, Queen Ena of Spain, had to change out of a wedding-dress splashed with blood before the future George V could propose her 'good health'. Another granddaughter, the Tsarina Alexandra, was murdered with all her family; George V might have given asylum to his cousins but for the political danger to the House of Windsor of sheltering the House of Romanov.* Seventeen years later a loaded revolver skidded under the hooves of King Edward VIII's horse on Constitution Hill.

In our own day the violence of the times has not passed

---

* King George V's generous impulse to help King Manoel, the dethroned King of Portugal, and the Portuguese royal family was snubbed by Sir Edward Grey, the Foreign Secretary. Grey refused to send a gunboat at King George's request to fetch them to England and made a fuss about the King sending the royal yacht *Victoria and Albert*. Nevertheless, the King sent it. This episode may have made him think twice in 1917, with agonising results. And with 1917 most assuredly still in mind, he successfully resorted to 'gunboat diplomacy' in 1922, rescuing Prince and Princess Andrew of Greece from Piraeus and their children, including Prince Philip, from Corfu. See chapter VI, p. 100.

over the Royal Family. There have been politically motivated bombings, letter bombs and an attempt at armed kidnap, as well as the hysterical attack on the Queen at the Trooping. The British Monarch had seemed at first a more promising target, according to Mehemet Ali Agca, the Turk who wounded the Pope – until Agca discovered that the Monarch was a woman. The Queen's advisers would be wise not to bank on such old-world courtesy. Just over six weeks before the Trooping incident, there had been a bomb explosion not far from the Queen as she started the oil flow at Sullom Voe in the Shetlands. If the terrorists had succeeded they might have got King Olav of Norway as well, who was returning with her on *Britannia* from her state visit to his country.

'Something must be done. . . .' One of her ex-prime ministers immediately sent a letter of sympathy after the Trooping in 1981. Questioned by friends, including the author, at luncheon a week later about the possibility of preventive action, Harold Macmillan had this to suggest:

There are two kinds of assassin, the political and the mentally disturbed. The first kind was organized against the Pope by the Russians. Don't tell me that a man [Agca] can wander all over Europe and the East with the necessary passports on his own. It was organized under cover by the KGB. I don't think the Russians have the assassination of the Queen as one of their objects.

The elder statesman then went on to outline a double plan, using metaphors drawn from the glens and the moors.

Two things might be done to counter the kind of attacks like the one made during the Birthday Parade. First, the Queen should move as often as possible in a carriage moving as fast as possible. You know how difficult it is to shoot a moving stag?

Secondly, the Royal Family tend to go about in coveys. You know how a good shot will bring down three birds at once? There is no need, for instance, for the Prince of Wales to ride in the Trooping as well as Prince Philip.[1]

The risks can be diminished but not eliminated. It was the Queen herself who once said: 'I have to be seen to be believed.'

Meanwhile the letter columns of the press were loud with advice, ranging from scornful queries like 'Where were the Lifeguards (so-called) on Saturday, 13 June 1981?' to considered proposals for 'Royal princes (preferably four) riding beside Her Majesty's horse rather than some feet behind, with outriders of the Royal Household Cavalry riding on the outside of the princes for their protection'; or, more redolent of the heavy cavalry at Waterloo, 'a close escort of big men on tall horses'.

Thirteen months after the Trooping incident the Queen faced a new ordeal. On Monday, 12 July 1982, the *Daily Express* scooped a sensation: 'INTRUDER AT THE QUEEN'S BEDSIDE – *She kept him talking for 10 minutes . . . then a footman came to her aid.*' That afternoon the Home Secretary confirmed the news to a shocked House of Commons. A man had entered Her Majesty's bedroom on Friday 9 July and was under arrest. 'The House will admire the calm way in which Her Majesty responded to what occurred.' No one else was calm.

Women imagined themselves in the same predicament and were aghast. A spate of angry letters flooded the papers. Why was the Home Secretary's statement so 'bland'? (But the Prime Minister had cancelled her attendance at the BBC 'Fifty Years' service in the Abbey in order to be available if necessary.) Why did the press publish so many aerial photographs of Buckingham Palace with the Queen's bedroom arrowed 'to avoid any doubt'? Why must the palace's 'low profile' security be also 'low value'? At a Buckingham Palace garden party a guest was overheard saying, 'But what on earth will other countries think?' One journalist saw a silver lining: the Royal Family's obsession with horses, often criticised, was now seen to be justified. 'Riding taught them to be cool in a crisis.'

A general sense of outrage demanded that heads should

roll, starting with Scotland Yard, moving on to the Queen's household and chopping off Home Secretary Willie Whitelaw's *en passant*. When Whitelaw told the House that palace security, despite recent improvements, was still 'not satisfactory', there was hollow laughter. On 22 July the police commission of enquiry under John Dellow, set up on the 12th, reported to the Home Office. Under nineteen headings it revealed something of the Queen's bizarre nightmare.

At 6.45 am on the Friday, Michael Fagan, aged thirty-five and under the delusion at times that his father was Rudolf Hess, was seen climbing the palace railings by an off-duty constable who telephoned the palace police. They made a cursory outside inspection while Fagan was making an inside examination of the door leading from the Queen's Stamp Room into the Palace's interior. It was locked, so he left by the unlocked window through which he had entered and began looking for another way into the Palace. The published report did not include the remark of a sergeant in the Palace's police control room, where the Stamp Room alarm had rung twice: 'There's that bloody bell again!'

After shinning up a drainpipe and removing his sandals and socks, Fagan padded along a corridor leading to the private apartments, picking up and smashing a glass ashtray on the way. Domestic troubles at home involving his wife, four children, two stepchildren and parents had suddenly made him think of slashing his wrists with the jagged edges in front of the Queen. The whole escapade, said a relative in court afterwards, was in no way directed against the Queen, whom he admired. 'It was a cry for help.'

The 'cry for help' might well have come from the Queen, when she was awakened at 7.18 am to see that her bedroom curtains were being drawn, not by the usual maid who brings her tea and papers at 7.45, but by a bare-footed young man in jeans and T-shirt who sat down on her bed and dripped blood from his right thumb on to the bedclothes.

The visitor launched into his unhappy family affairs, the Queen responding with unhurried interest – 'Then Prince

Charles is a year younger than you' – while wondering how she could get help without frightening him. First she pressed her night alarm button connected with the police control room. It was not working. Then she rang her bedside bell into the corridor. No answer. The maid was cleaning in an adjacent room with the door shut and the footman on duty was exercising the posse of eleven corgis. The only armed guard in the corridor had gone off duty according to schedule at 6 am. After the Queen had twice telephoned the palace operator to send police to her bedroom – no one made haste, Her Majesty's voice sounded so 'calm' – she was immensely relieved when her visitor asked for a cigarette. This gave the Queen her chance. 'You see I have none in this room,' she said. 'I will have some fetched for you,' and she went out into the corridor and found the maid. 'Bloody hell, ma'am,' exclaimed the horrified Yorkshire woman, 'he oughtn't to be in there.' At that moment the footman returned with the corgis. He and the maid got Fagan into a pantry, where the footman plied him with cigarettes while the Queen kept off the indignant dogs; for Fagan was showing signs of panic. At last the police arrived – eight minutes after the Queen's first call – and the intruder was led away.

It was the Queen's own view that palace security was entirely a matter for the police. No heads should roll but theirs. Some duly rolled, others were 'transferred'. At the same time the reorganised force were instructed to improve on their task and methods, difficult but necessary, of guarding the Palace from crackpots and criminals without putting the Queen herself behind bars.

In the course of police investigations there was a tragic resignation neither expected nor connected with the Queen's ordeal. Indeed, misfortunes came in battalions during the week of the Dellow Report's publication. One day before publication on 22 July came rumours of the Prime spy scandal in Cheltenham. Two days before, there had been the bombing atrocities in Hyde Park and Regent's Park. Three days before, news had broken of the resignation of Michael Trestrail, the Queen's trusted and efficient bodyguard for nine years. His homosexual affair with a man he had met twelve years earlier had no relevance to his duties. But the fact that his name had got into the papers in connection with the enquiry seemed a chance for the man to try blackmail. The blackmail failed, but not before it had brought further unhappiness to the Queen.

As for Fagan, the law of trespass did not permit him to be prosecuted for his 'intrusion'. Instead he was accused of burglary. It emerged that he had entered the Palace on a previous occasion, 7 June, and drunk half a bottle of wine. The jury acquitted him. But if, as a result of his case, the law of trespass should be changed, there would be a rough parallel between Elizabeth II's experience and that of Queen Victoria. The law of treason was changed in 1842 to deal with any future cases similar to the half-wit Edward Oxford's attack on Victoria two years before. Like Oxford, Fagan was sent to a mental hospital. (He was discharged on 20 January 1983.)

Meanwhile, Elizabeth II's experience produced a rush of historical analogies from journalists and others. Going no further back than 1788, they recalled that Princess Elizabeth, daughter of George III, had twice found an intruder 'in adoration' at her feet; in 1840 the Palace was visited, not for the first or last time, by the 'Boy Jones'; in the 1890s a young woman was allowed by an infatuated footman to watch the old Queen at her solitary meal; shortly before the First World War a foreign intruder entered the gardens with the idea of proposing to Princess Mary; in 1940 a wartime deserter got into Queen Elizabeth's room and poured out his woes while clutching her by the ankles; in 1950 a drunken sailor stole a dispatch box; in 1951 a disturbed youth went in search of Princess Margaret; and three times in 1981 intruders were found in the grounds, beginning with three German tourists who scaled the garden wall thinking it was Hyde Park.

Come fools, come frauds, Queen Elizabeth II will still be on view: 'I must be seen to be believed.' At the end of her first thirty years on the throne, it is time to ask what kind of image the people see.

Elizabeth II is a 'close-up' Queen. The nearer people get to her the more impressed they are by what they see. Hence the uncovenanted boon of walkabouts and television films. There is not much scope for getting to know her except by seeing her at work. The Queen is a private person. Her friends, though close, are relatively few. She gives little away either through the written or spoken word: an occasional forthright remonstrance, usually provoked, to a badly-behaved press; her Christmas messages to the nation and Commonwealth; her speeches on formal occasions such as a jubilee or the opening of a new building. Even here, though, technically her words are always the words of her government.

To look at her is quite another matter. Everyone who sees the Queen for the first time, at whatever period in her life, has the same immediate reaction: this cannot all be real. The complexion to begin with, like porcelain held up to the light. Flawless complexions are not rarities in the Royal Family. Queen Alexandra's became a legendary triumph of artifice. Queen Elizabeth II has kept intact all the charms of complete naturalness. Since nature has been so generous to her, there would be no sense in doing otherwise. Nevertheless, to see her eyebrows in their natural shape does explain something of importance. She is well integrated. She knows who she is and what she is capable of doing. There is no search for identity, no temptation to experiment with a slanting or pencil-thin line that points to the beginning of a new personality. The natural lines round the brilliant blue eyes only add interest and character to the face. They make it a living record rather than a meaningless statement.

The faint attractive mist that now clings to the brown hair above her temples tells the same story. She is in the full beauty of her middle years. Yet the pen-portraits that have come down from thirty years earlier seem still to be re-

levant. Here she is as described by the 7th Duke of Wellington to Harold Nicolson when opening Parliament for the
first time. She was twenty-six:

> *4 November 1952* Gerry [Wellington] told me how struck he was
> by the Queen's astonishing radiance at the opening of Parlia-
> ment this morning – her lovely teeth, hair and eyes, and that
> amazing quality of skin. Then add the wonderful voice and the
> romance, and you have a deeply moving effect.[2]

Both Queen Elizabeth II and her sister Princess Margaret
share the gift of sparkling blue eyes, along with animation,
movement, a glancing look that waits on teasing exchanges
and repartee. It is one of the surprises about Elizabeth II.
Though fundamentally so calm and serene, especially on
state or public occasions when serenity may become blank-
ness, in conversation she possesses an alert and lively
power of giving and evoking responses.

For the rest, the Queen's dignity effortlessly transcends
her stature when measured in mere inches, just as Queen
Victoria's did before her. 'Everybody grows but me,' said
the young Victoria wistfully at eighteen; and though she
was never quite to reach five feet, dignity was always at her
command, enhanced by the solidity of old age. The dignity
of Queen Mary, Elizabeth II's grandmother, was partly a
function of her height. 'Her appearance was formidable,
her manner – well, it was like talking to St Paul's Cathedral,' wrote the diarist Sir Henry ('Chips') Channon after her
death.[3] Queen Elizabeth II makes her unquestionably regal
impression without the aid either of height or weight.

Nor did she have the advantage of being regarded as heir
presumptive from birth, like her great-great-grandmother
Victoria. ('I may call you Jane,' said the little Princess to a
playfellow, 'but you must not call me Victoria.') Lilibet was
ten before she entered upon the dignity of heir to the
throne. It is most improbable that even then she entertained the high opinion of her own position that was innate
in Victoria. Anyone could call her Lilibet. Many children

did. In her thirties some people began calling her names that were not so pretty – 'frumpish', 'priggish'. That too passed. Today she possesses the formidable dignity of one 'born to be Queen' – without having been so born.

Behind the Queen's physical dignity is mental and moral toughness. Her courage, already remarked upon, is one of the tough virtues. Energy and discipline are others. And Elizabeth II is not Victoria's descendant for nothing, sharing with her the toughest of all virtues, truthfulness. No one ever heard either one say – or look – anything she did not mean, simpler though it would sometimes have been to embroider her feelings. Nor has there ever been a pretence on the part of Elizabeth II that she was blithely impervious to adverse criticism or had no 'nerves' over certain public exercises. Neither she nor Victoria smiled when feeling serious. And their seriousness could achieve a formidable downward look. But this look never excluded its opposite.

Personal reminiscences of Victoria frequently included her laughter. It was often thought not always 'silvery'. Elizabeth Robins, an American actress, performed at Balmoral before the Queen in old age. While waiting to go on stage the actress heard 'a curious cackling sound' out in front. She asked someone, 'Is it a foreign bird making that noise?' 'That, Miss Robins, is not a foreign bird. It's the Queen laughing.'[4] The Kaiser, Victoria's grandson, revelled in a nautical story of his grandmother asking the deaf Admiral Foley after the health of his sister. The Admiral, thinking Her Majesty was enquiring about a wrecked frigate, replied, 'Well, ma'am, I am going to turn her over and have her bottom scraped.' His grandmother, concluded William, 'hid her face in her handkerchief and shook and heaved with laughter.'[5] Yet only two photographs have ever been published of this amused old lady smiling.

Traditions in royal portraiture have changed radically since then. Elizabeth II's enjoyment of family, friends and welcoming crowds is reflected in countless photographs of wide smiles. The serious look none the less reflects a serious outlook on life. It is in fact the Queen's tribute to the importance of her royal vocation.

There can be no doubt that her tough virtues will thrust her into any breach which may open, provided she feels she must and can hold it. Though entitled to appoint her prime ministers, up until the 1980s it seemed that this royal prerogative had been whittled away throughout her reign: in 1970 and in 1979 she had no alternative but to send for Edward Heath and Margaret Thatcher. The choice had been taken out of royal hands by reform of the Conservative Party's system of choosing its leader. As for Her Majesty's two Labour governments, there was never any pretence of prerogative, other than the simple right to send for whoever led the majority party in Parliament. Never again, it seemed, would people ask, 'Who will the Queen send for?'

None of this need last. There could be a series of 'hung' parliaments, brought about by a new three-party system, or a pattern of fluid coalitions, following upon the introduction of proportional representation. The Queen might decide that there was not just one man or woman who could, at a given moment, form a government, but two or more. Which should she try first? The old Tory theory of a prime minister 'emerging' could not have stood up to such a situation even if it had survived the 1960s. For it implied that there was only one possible prime minister whose 'emergence' was quasi-supernatural, just as there was only one Messiah and one Dalai Lama.

If the royal prerogative were to be recalled in any sense from the sleep of history, the Palace would have to count on at least two things: the Queen's own stamina, and a reliable corps of advisers. The first certainly would not fail her, even if it meant an end to her carefully planned schedules and the need to fly back from Commonwealth duties once or twice or even three times a year, to deal with lightning resignations.

Her advisers would present a sharper problem. Her secretaries could not be expected to devise instant solutions where her ministers had, in the nature of the case, failed. Some people think Buckingham Palace conferences might again be the order of the day, where elder statesmen would contribute to the crystallisation of the royal choice. Others say this would precipitate the monarchy into party politics, a disaster. When King George v called a palace conference in 1914 over Ireland, the results were not encouraging. Nevertheless, the fact that all her prime ministers like to remember their relations with Elizabeth ii as exceptionally amicable might suggest that she would be admirably fitted to perform this umpirage.

One further introductory thought on this subject. Wisdom and experience will be more than ever the Monarch's crucial requirements. That has surely some bearing upon another favourite question for debate: abdication, as the Queen's way out from a long enough stint and her son's way in. Abdication raises all kinds of other matters connected with the monarchy's natural, organic development. 'It's an idea', as Prince Philip once replied noncommittally to an American television interviewer, giving nothing away. It seems obvious, however, that if an unstable period of quick-change party politics lies ahead, people will value all the more the stability that a constitutional monarchy brings. They will think twice about rocking the royal barge at the same moment.

With the passage of the years she has developed a many-faceted character. Some of her early tastes such as that for the simplest country pleasures have been greatly enriched and diversified. Other qualities have evolved steadily along their original lines: for instance, her intense practicality. One of her friends said that if she happened to be dropped accidentally in the middle of the Sahara Desert she would know just how to initiate survival drill. Another friend says that she would move like a flash to deal with a canine accident and save a precious rug if there were an emergency, though assistance might well arrive before she could act.

Every so often the public are given a glimpse of her

compassionate feelings. When she feels the press are damaging the weak, this gentle Queen can be roused to anger and indignation. Elizabeth II reigns during an era when the unacceptable face of journalism must somehow be masked without at the same time injuring journalism's acceptable, indeed essential features. A queen who speaks out rarely but to the point and from the heart has advantages that other voices lack. If she had been habitually querulous, voluble or loud over what she disliked, no one would have listened.

There is one place where a whole set of quite different royal talents appear. This is in the Queen's stud among her horses, on the race-course, or when she is immersed in her library of technical books and magazines dealing with the arcana of pedigrees and breeding. The animal kingdom can be the perfect antidote to her kingdom of men and women. Horses and dogs never gush (apart from the spaniel breed which this court likes less than the opinionated corgi and dependable labrador). Nor are they burdened with republican consciences. The two kingdoms balance one another; and if the arguments for exercising the prerogative are debatable there is nothing but balm in exercising the dogs.

It might be thought that Queen Elizabeth II would have been adequately 'seen' once people were aware of her appearance and character. But to begin with, today the idea of the Queen includes the whole of her intimate family. This is the Royal Family *per se*.

The Queen has said more than once that she believes in the family. Occasionally she has made her avowal with a smile and flash of wit, for after all it is as hard to disbelieve in the family as to question one's own existence. More often the Queen is serious. In whatever mood she speaks she makes one thing clear: the Royal Family is an extension of herself and she a concentration of that family. Neither can be fully realised without the other. The Queen's majesty *is* the unity, the work, the growth, the interest and contribution of her family, the Royal Family.

There was a time when there were only four of them – King George VI, Queen Elizabeth, Princess Elizabeth and Princess Margaret – and it pleased the present Queen's father to call them the 'Royal Firm'. His phrase was in part a reference to their close partnership, interdependence and joint responsibilities; partly a comment on the fact that his generation worked harder and played less than its predecessors; partly an ironical joke – the irony consisting in the use of a flat commercial word like 'firm' to describe the august and historic Royal House of Windsor. But that, implied King George VI in his dry way, was what the world had brought them to.

Princess Anne seems to believe that the numbers of the 'firm' will drop away as well as increase. Drop away, that is, at the female end. 'Yes, I am the Queen's daughter,' she said on television two days before Christmas 1981, 'and as a daughter I get less involved than the boys. I doubt if the next generation will be involved at all.' By the word 'involved' Princess Anne meant caught up inextricably in the royal system. A release from the wheel she evidently felt would not be a disaster for her children Peter and Zara. Nevertheless, she herself has proved a valiant performer as President of the Save the Children Fund. Witness her brave and memorable tour of East Africa in 1982, which she continued despite threats of violence.

Elizabeth II's 'involvement' rests on something entirely different. Still years from her Golden Jubilee, she is full of energy and enterprise. The two-tier support of the throne will increasingly strengthen both the Queen and her family. The Royal Family itself, together with the wider cousinship, will combine to lighten some aspects of her load. And their participation in the system will give added meaning to their own lives.

One reason for the Royal Family's increasing round of duties has been noted by Princess Alice, Duchess of Gloucester, in her *Memoirs* (1983). 'Before the war,' she writes, 'a fair proportion of the official functions of today's Royal Family was shouldered by local dignitaries. Today such people have far less time and money, and this support no longer exists.'[6]

Elizabeth II's reign has shown a unique interplay of royal tradition and popular trends. She is Queen of a democracy. Her own democratic rights as an individual, such as the right to some privacy, can never be steam-rolled. At the same time she is there only to serve. In Prince Philip's definitive words on the monarchy: 'It exists in the interests of the people.'

Writing near the beginning of last century the historian Henry Hallam detected a remarkable tie-up between the British monarchy's democratic spirit and its vigour; this distinguished it from other European monarchies in the Middle Ages. 'It is, I am firmly persuaded, to this peculiarly democratical character of the English monarchy, that we are indebted for its long permanence, its regular improvement, and its present vigour.'[7]

That was the text for 1818. Is it still the text for 1983? – within the framework of democracy, a combination of continuity and change producing unique vitality.

The World of Her Birth
1900–26

Change has been the keynote of Elizabeth II's reign. Even so, it would be possible to argue that equally great changes marked the reigns of her two immediate predecessors.

The abbreviated decade of Edward VII's reign (1901–10) is apt to seem short on change. His style of monarchy was stockbroker-Tudor (to borrow an architectural metaphor) and was indeed a return to traditional magnificence, compared with the domestic-Victorian of his secluded mother.

King Edward's personal style was to be larger than life, both physically and in the imagination of his people. A girl of seven[1] whose mother was at court caught a glimpse of him in a doorway. She had never seen anything so monstrously broad 'from front to back' as this bearded Majesty, and ever after she was not to feel quite easy with men who wore beards. The King enjoyed everything of the best: fast beautiful women and beautiful fast horses. Yet he managed to preserve the common touch. When he led in his Derby winner Persimmon it was to a popular chorus of 'Good old Teddy!' Even in that splendid Edwardian court, however, or at least in his wife's section of it, there were signs of less opulent times ahead. Queen Alexandra had her coronation robe lined with rabbit instead of ermine to save expense.

In other more significant spheres new voices were already raised, new inventions becoming commonplace. The Labour Party was born in 1900, the same year as Elizabeth II's mother. Suffragettes were screaming in pain and anger. The business world did not listen; it had got its essential quota of women recruits for the typewriters in its offices, and the sound of staccato tapping was all it wanted to hear – that, and the ringing of the new telephone hooked to its tall black pedestal. The telephone was catching up with the telegraph. The car was still enough of an innovation and status symbol for its portrait to be taken with its owner on board. King Edward VII always looked a little too big for his cars. High-speed photography had changed the technique of royal portraiture from blurred effigies of almost medieval gravity to sharp sepia groups with plenty of character.

Queen Elizabeth II admires her grandparents King George V and Queen Mary, and she is completely captivated by the image of her great-great-grandmother Queen Victoria: her sense of duty, the care she bestowed on her dynasty, and the enormous power of her presence – enough to make Bismarck behave, Disraeli worship and Gladstone dream. With Elizabeth II we might substitute names like Nkomo, Macmillan and Churchill.

Queen Mary was to live into her eighties and miss her granddaughter's coronation by two months.

The Royal Family was her guiding star. Every action of hers would be performed to its greater glory. During her impoverished wanderings abroad as a girl she had seen the great art of Italy. But as Queen of England she collected only those treasures that had links with the Royal Family. She would make economies in personal style by abolishing maids-of-honour in order to save on their dowries; but there would be no economies of deference to the monarchical idea. Elizabeth and Margaret Rose would curtsy to her when they first met each day; she would be the first to kiss the hands of Her Majesty Queen Elizabeth II. When Queen Mary stayed away from home in the 1930s two pages took turns sitting outside her bedroom door all night. Their duty was not to one particular old lady but to the King of England's consort. Unwavering dedication to the Royal

Family could not but have its effect on the young, conscientious Princess Elizabeth.

King George v too, like his consort, could claim that all propositions were weighed in his own mind as likely to enhance or damage the idea of monarchy. He saw himself as a trustee for the Royal Family. 'I feel that this splendid old title will be safe in your hands,' he said to his son Bertie on creating him Duke of York, '& that you will never do anything which could in any way tarnish it.'[2] The title was as important as the son who was to hold it.

But the outward signs of monarchy were more important to George v than to his granddaughter. Queen Mary never ventured to come to dinner without a tiara. Indeed a commentary on the changes between the reigns of George v and Elizabeth ii might start with the tiara. When Princess Alice of Athlone's family gave a grand party to celebrate her ninetieth birthday, the invitations read, 'Tiaras if possible'. It was the difference between tiaras *de rigueur* and tiaras preferred. In the same way every male courtier had to appear in his smart Windsor uniform of dark blue with red collar and cuffs, knee-breeches and silk stockings. Knee-breeches, as worn at levées, had been a neuralgic point with radical politicians even in Queen Victoria's day. It was all the more remarkable that George v managed to keep the clock back in the 1920s.

George v is remembered for twice referring his actions back to the long-dead Queen Victoria. 'What would Grandmamma have said?' he remarked anxiously when his young cousin Princess Marie-Louise asked – and received – permission from him to travel by bus. 'I wonder what Grandmamma would have thought?' he repeated when appointing Britain's first Labour prime minister. Elizabeth is never reported as wondering, 'What would Grandpapa say?'*

---

* She never called him 'Grandpapa England' as some writers have said following Marion Crawford's *The Little Princesses*. 'We were much too frightened of him to call him anything but Grandpapa,' says Princess Margaret.

Despite his backward-looking attitudes, the Queen's grandfather had an instinctive feel for the moment when change was the lesser of two evils. At his coronation, an ancient version was updated: the 'colonies' of which his father had been King-Emperor became 'dominions'. This was a whisper of the wind of change that was to roar in his granddaughter's chimneys.

A reactionary in private, in public he knew better than some of his advisers how to be a constitutional monarch. For this he owed a lasting debt to Professor J. R. Tanner of St John's College, Cambridge, who topped up the King's all-too-scanty education with a thorough grounding in Bagehot, the nineteenth-century writer. Not only was George v deeply indebted to Walter Bagehot's *English Constitution* (1867) for a tenacious understanding of his future regal duties, but so were his successors. George vi studied Bagehot under J. R. M. Butler of Trinity College, Cambridge; Princess Elizabeth studied the work under Sir Henry Marten of Eton. You can't catch out Prince Charles on the meditations of St Bagehot, who has become the patron saint of all royal historians, biographers and journalists.

Bagehot began his much-quoted essay on the monarchy with the words: 'The use of the Queen, in a dignified capacity, is incalculable.' By dignified he meant ceremonial or liturgical as opposed to executive. Unlike earlier admirers of constitutional monarchy such as Edmund Burke and T. B. Macaulay, Walter Bagehot wrote in complete detachment from the magic he was describing and eulogising.* There is even a whiff of patronising cynicism in one of his paragraphs:

---

* J. W. Burrow in his *A Liberal Descent* (1981, p. 293) distinguishes the 'two degrees of veneration' which historians have felt for the constitution and monarchy, the one being mere 'approval' and the other full 'participation'.

The best reason why Monarchy is a strong government is, that it is an intelligible government. The mass of mankind understand it, and they hardly anywhere understand any other.[3]

Bagehot proceeds to show that Britain's constitutional monarchy is not really a monarchy at all: 'A Republic has insinuated itself beneath the folds of a Monarchy. . . .'[4] The leaders of government and society all operate, he points out, anywhere but in Buckingham Palace. Even Court balls are less glamorous than private ones.

Nevertheless, the monarchy has its limited uses: 'It is of use so long as it keeps others out of the first place. . . .'[5] Bagehot next asks what the Queen can actually *do*, besides keeping out potential dictators. His answer is sceptical: 'The House of Commons has enquired into most things, but has never had a committee on "the Queen". There is no authentic blue-book to say what she does.'[6] Finally he reduces her scope for action to a bare but now famous trio:

To state the matter shortly, the Sovereign has, under a constitutional Monarchy such as ours, three rights – the right to be consulted, the right to encourage, the right to warn. And a King of great sense and sagacity would want no others.[7]

This was the political bible on which George v was brought up.

Princess Elizabeth of York was a child of not quite ten years when King George v died early in 1936. His direct influence on her was therefore human rather than political. In her late teens, however, when she came to study her future inheritance with her father King George vi, the way her grandfather had tackled the political problems of his reign constituted a lesson in statecraft. There was the raking crisis in 1910 over the House of Lords, when the power of the peers to thwart the will of the people was broken by the Liberal Prime Minister, H. H. Asquith. If the Lords had not given way, the Monarch's ancient prerogative to create peers would have been invoked by his prime minister.

Asquith extracted from the reluctant King a 'guarantee' that he would use his prerogative if required, calculating on the need for some 300 new Liberal peers to swamp the Tories; Winston Churchill (then a rabid Liberal) suggested 500 would be nearer the mark. The Lords caved in before Asquith's weapon had been tested. How would it work? Nobody knew. And the question-mark hangs over the Queen to this day.

Years later Asquith's pungent wife Margot found herself blaming the King's bad advisers for any mistakes in his reign. She may have been thinking originally of Sir Arthur Bigge, one of the Monarch's private secretaries, but after George v's death she added the King's doctor Lord Dawson to her black-list: 'Lord Dawson was not a good doctor,' she told the young Lord David Cecil; 'King George v himself told me that he would never have died had he had another doctor!'[8] Queen Elizabeth ii hears many criticisms in which blame is placed on her advisers rather than on herself; though none of such illogical felicity as Margot Asquith's.

In September 1913, two years after his double showdown with the Monarch and the Lords, Mr Asquith was writing a rather unexpected memorandum on the royal prerogative. This turned out to be Bagehot supplemented by new rights: the right 'to all relevant information' from ministers, 'to point out objections . . . against the course which they advise, to suggest alternative policy.'[9] With his lack of political education, however, the King sometimes found it hard to listen to everything he was told. Harold Nicolson, his official biographer, tells a story of Anthony Eden (later Elizabeth ii's prime minister) being treated to a lengthy royal monologue on his own department, the Foreign Office; when at length the monologue ended and Eden began to 'tell everything' in return, His Majesty rang his little golden hand-bell to start the palace band playing. A golden bell had been used by Queen Victoria as a signal for amateur theatricals to begin – but not during ministerial audiences. Charles ii, however, is said to have brought his barking dogs to the Council.

In due course it will be seen how George v's granddaughter has dealt with the problem of being 'told everything'.

The immediate post-war period saw a growing contrast between the King's authoritarian family life and a public life that was hastening, however slowly, in the necessary direction of change. His children were still suppressed. But the 'children' of his Empire were intuitively felt by him to be on the move. There was a curious parallel between the women of Britain – still treated as children, despite the suffragettes – and the position of India within the Empire. The war-work of both was to win them the beginnings of independence.

The Empire as a whole was changing also. From 1917 onwards – the same year that George v changed his family name to Windsor – the name Commonwealth began to compete with the term Empire: 'The name Commonwealth signified a new adventure in brotherly living,' wrote a Commonwealth historian, calling the name a manifesto and a programme in itself.[10] And the Monarch was even more the father of the Commonwealth than he had been of the Empire. When George v laid the foundation stone of Australia House in London a workman was heard to exclaim above the fanfare of trumpets, 'That's the foundation stone of England laying the foundation stone of Australia!'

'Commonwealth' became the new official designation of Empire in 1921 – but like all weighty changes it took years to establish itself. On her twenty-first birthday, a good quarter-century later, the future Elizabeth ii was still using the two words, Imperial and Commonwealth, in conjunction.

Ireland was another of George v's restless Imperial 'children'. He felt in his bones that the Irish would no longer respond to the old specifics of force and suppression. In the words of a future President of Ireland, Erskine Childers:

George V was torn between the absolutely conservative rigid point of view and a kind of inner sense by which he knew that the policy carried out by the British Government [the Black and Tans] was not going to succeed. He sent Tubby Granard [the King's Gold Stick-in-waiting] to visit . . . the Home Secretary, and at various times he re-iterated that the excesses in Ireland would only increase the number in the IRA and strengthen the extreme Republican Movement. He interceded for some members of the IRA who were to be executed and was successful in some cases but not in others.[11]

'During the reign of my grandfather, King George V,' said the late Prince William of Gloucester in an interview with Audrey Whiting, 'I do not think my father was given the opportunity to make a decision in his life until he was about thirty.' His brother the Duke of York, however, made the happiest decision of his life when, at twenty-five, he resolved against all the odds to marry Lady Elizabeth Bowes-Lyon.

It was a long, dogged pursuit. Elizabeth was twenty when he fell in love, a 'Deb of the Year' before such categories were invented, the youngest but one in a devoted family of ten. Glamis Castle in Angus was their romantic Scottish home, St Paul's Waldenbury in Hertfordshire their elegant English one. Her father, the 14th Earl of Strathmore, traced his descent back through the militant ranks of rampageous Scots to Robert the Bruce. He himself was a dedicated countryman with just the right amount of endearing eccentricity. He would come down to breakfast practising overarm bowling with a cricket ball along the corridors of Glamis. Through her talented mother, Cecilia Cavendish-Bentinck, Elizabeth could boast an ancestral line that led to the Marquess Wellesley, brother of the Duke of Wellington, and on their maternal side to the kings of Ireland. The Bentinck line carried her back to the Netherlands and William of Orange's right-hand man. *The Times* showed goodwill if not strict accuracy in hailing the bride as 'British to the core'.

Elizabeth Bowes-Lyon was a romantic like her castle.

Temperamentally she was too much amused by life to weigh up its every conundrum with painstaking deliberation, or to waste the buoyant hours on analysing problems that could be dealt with more naturally by charm and empathy – head slightly inclined to the side and voice often tentative, never dogmatic.

There was a healthy vein of scepticism in her family as well as grace and humour. Her youngest brother David had no use for the more extravagant legends attaching to Glamis. 'A frightful lot of rot was written about Glamis in Victorian days.'[12] As a girl, Elizabeth would inform gullible visitors that the tick-tock of a grandfather clock was 'the ghost'.

Her education, like that of her class and sex before the end of the First World War, was mainly non-academic. She was educated to sing, to dance, to pray, to please; to speak French; to be hostess to visiting neighbours when necessary and to convalescing soldiers billeted in the castle. Indeed she was guaranteed to restore anyone who might be described as emotionally 'convalescent' to full vitality – including the King's second son.

Prince Albert, Duke of York, or Bertie as he was always called in the family, seemed to have been born under an unlucky star. His birth on 14 December 1895 coincided with Queen Victoria's 'Mausoleum Day', the thirty-fourth anniversary of the Prince Consort's death. As a baby his digestion was not good and this painful weakness dogged him into young manhood. Before he was ten it had been decided that his legs were weak also – surely an exaggeration considering his later athleticism – and he was thrust into night splints to save him from his father's knock knees and seated by day at an invalid table. Here, though left-handed, he was made to write infinitely slowly with his right hand. This, added to the teasing of his siblings, the shyness of his mother and the quarter-deck manner of his father, turned him into a confirmed stammerer.

Yet he bore no grudges. With so many handicaps, nevertheless his was a character of basic friendliness. Whole-hearted admiration, almost worship, for his older brother David (later Edward VIII) made him happy rather than envious. If at any stage life had been easy for him, he would have been easy-going. As it was, he sometimes fell into despairs or flew into rages – as violent as they were short-lived. Notwithstanding these sudden ups and downs Bertie's philosophy was a steady one, emphasising the values of faith, hope – and habit. 'I expect I shall get used to it in time,' he wrote of the horrible invalid table.[13] He was forming the habit of endurance.

'Now that you are five years old,' Prince Bertie's father had written in 1900, 'I hope you will always try & be obedient & do at once what you are told, as you will find it will come much easier to you the sooner you begin.' In other words, make a habit of it. 'I always tried to do this when I was your age,' the King continued, '& found it made me much happier.'[14] Habit, custom: here was the talisman of the old Royal Family.

This was a philosophy which demanded for full success the chance of a regular, predictable life. Such a life was rarely granted to the future George VI. As second son, he was destined for the sea like his father. But his stammer ruined his academic career. He would not answer questions in class for fear of exposing himself to ridicule. To be last out of sixty-eight in his year was the result. But all the time the stammer was secretly working for him. A stammerer must have perseverance to survive at all.

When the war broke out Bertie was still in the Royal Navy but threatened with invalidism. Despite a chronic stomach ulcer he managed to fight in the battle of Jutland. Then came sick leave, an operation, youth work at Cranwell, desk work in the Air Ministry. His career took wings only three times: once, literally, when he won his wings in the RAF and became the first prince to hold a pilot's certificate; again when he won the RAF tennis doubles; and, more lastingly, when he founded the first Duke of York's camp in July 1921. It was his contribution to the cause of social harmony. The camps, where boys from poor and rich homes mingled, were to become a 'habit'.

The years 1920 to 1921 were marked by his falling in love with social work – and with Elizabeth Bowes-Lyon. She was a friend of his sister, and he was a friend of the Strathmores' neighbours, the Airlies, with whom he would go to stay. In spring 1921 he proposed to Elizabeth for the first time and was rejected. The question is sometimes asked, why did she turn down the King's son in 1921 and then accept him two years later? Lady Airlie said emphatically that it was because Elizabeth shrank from a *royal* marriage. But did Lady Airlie know? She was not necessarily in the Strathmores' confidence.

Elizabeth Bowes-Lyon wanted her freedom for a little longer. The war had constricted her youth. Now everyone was in love with her. At twenty-one she was not ready for marriage, any marriage. She was infinitely sympathetic and almost equally indecisive. Meanwhile the most persistent of her many suitors knew his own mind, and the civilised courtship continued. At last on 13 January 1923, the day Elizabeth accepted him, he was able to telegraph his parents: 'All right, Bertie.'[15] It was to be totally right for both of them.

After the engagement, Prince Bertie thanked his parents for giving permission for the marriage. The Prince's extravagantly grateful words today sound strange indeed: 'You & Papa,' he wrote to his mother Queen Mary, 'were both so charming to me yesterday about my engagement, & I can never really thank you properly for giving your consent to it.'[16] But it must be remembered that George v was actually an innovator in this respect: it was he who first permitted the marriages of royal princes to be contracted within the ranks of the nobility, albeit top ranks only. (When his grandson Lord Harewood married Marion Stein, daughter of a Viennese music publisher, in 1949, Queen Mary was 'in a great state and she won't talk about it'.[17]) The press welcomed the Duke of York's engagement to a commoner with enthusiasm, though the *Daily News* saw fit to change

Lady Elizabeth's name. 'Lady Betty's Own Story', it began, continuing with the unlikely statement, 'As the Duke himself said on Tuesday evening: "Lady Betty is already one of ourselves." '

Perhaps the best idea of this royal marriage is to be found by chance in a poem called 'A Prayer for my Daughter', written not by Lord Strathmore in 1923 but by W. B. Yeats four years earlier:

> And may her bridegroom bring her to a house
> Where all's accustomed, ceremonious;
> For arrogance and hatred are the wares
> Peddled in the thoroughfares.
> How but in custom and in ceremony
> Are innocence and beauty born?
> Ceremony's the name for the rich horn,
> And custom for the spreading laurel tree.[18]

The honeymoon began at Polesden Lacey, a mansion in Surrey lent to them by the society hostess Mrs Greville, that benefactor of royal couples (the Mountbattens as well as the Yorks) and of later holiday-makers. Created a Dame by George VI, she bequeathed Polesden Lacey to the National Trust, so that today mementoes can be seen of that distant honeymoon: photographs of the Duke and Duchess playing golf, he in baggy plus-fours and a tweed cap, she in a tweed costume and cloche hat; or the couple standing on the wide stone steps under the portico, looking across the splendid Surrey valley. There is also the little yellow Meissen tea-set with two cups, sugar basin and teapot from which the Duchess poured tea for two. By an odd chance, history was throwing glances backward and forward from Polesden Lacey. The estate had once belonged to Richard Brinsley Sheridan, an ancestor of the Duchess's future Snowdon grandchildren.

If the honeymoon was unostentatious, the couple's next three years were positively inconvenient. The King gave them White Lodge, Richmond Park, to live in. It was too accessible to the public, who could look right into it, and inaccessible from London. There was a momentary hope of change when the Duke's name was put forward to attend a Commonwealth conference in Canada, to be followed perhaps some day by the governor-generalship. His father vetoed the idea because of Bertie's stammer.

Escape by way of a royal tour and safari did indeed take place in 1924. The wildlife the Yorks saw in Kenya was to be watched by their elder daughter in more poignant circumstances many years later.

The Duchess's duties at home, as reported by the press, aptly reflected the changing world of that day. In 1924 she opened the *Daily Mail* Ideal Home Exhibition, spending most of her time on 'the latest inventions in cookers, kitchen cupboards and washing machines'. The reporting of fashion, however, was clumsy and dated. 'She was wearing a frock of black velvet,' said *The Times*, 'printed in horizontal coloured stripes of gold, russet and bronze. It was bordered with fur and with it she had a cowboy hat. . . .'

The King had no fault to find with the new member of his family. She was not a flapper, in the sense that she had put up her hair rather than bobbed it, and did not smoke cigarettes with or without a long holder. Her prettiness made him think up excuses for her unpunctuality. ('You are not late, my dear; we must have sat down two minutes early.') She in return became the first member of his family not to fear him. 'I was never afraid of him. He was so kind. . . .' His insensitivity, as exemplified over White Lodge, she was to call reliability – 'He was so kind and so dependable' – and his quarter-deck chaff was to be re-membered as humour: 'Sometimes he could be very funny. . . .'[19]

But for George v, from 1923 onwards politics were not to develop with the happy omens of the new royal marriage. Post-war unrest declared itself in a year of political stress for the King. As early as 1919 he had ordered his private secretary Lord Stamfordham to express his dissatisfaction with the tepid King's Speech. 'His Majesty thought the allusion to labour troubles ought to be strengthened.'[20] George v wished to show his sympathy with the industrial misery caused by unemployment, low wages and bad housing. In 1923 the King was faced by two crises, one in April and another in December, both types to become familiar in his granddaughter's reign.

The Conservative Prime Minister, Bonar Law, resigned on 27 April, leaving the King to decide between two keen rivals, Lord Curzon and Mr Stanley Baldwin. Lord Stamfordham had to 'go scouting from one person to another in secret trying to find out who should be sent for to succeed'. Thomas Jones of the cabinet secretariat considered this a wrong use of the royal prerogative. 'The King should be guided by a [Conservative] Party meeting or by the meeting of Parliament,'[21] wrote Jones. In the end the King rightly sent for Baldwin; a leader in the Commons was better able to deal with post-war problems than a prime minister in the Lords. (This action appeared to have established a precedent. In order to be prime minister in 1963, Lord Home was to renounce his peerage and sit in the Commons as Sir Alec Douglas-Home.)

Less than eight months later Baldwin was defeated at an election that returned a 'hung' Parliament – a bogey that today hangs over the future of King George's granddaughter. In December 1923 five ways of keeping out a Labour government were suggested to Stamfordham for His Majesty's consideration: by sending for Balfour, or Neville Chamberlain, or Asquith, or Austen Chamberlain, or Reginald McKenna (who was not even in Parliament). Instead the King laid down a general rule – 'I must use my own judgment as each case arises' – and appointed Ramsay MacDonald the first Labour Prime Minister. On 12 February 1924 MacDonald took his seat on the Government front bench.

Next year, 1925, there was a violent hiccup in the Commonwealth. The Governor-General of Canada, the war-hero Viscount Byng of Vimy, refused to grant a dissolution to the Liberal Prime Minister. Byng was no hero to the Liberals, for ten days afterwards he granted a dissolution to the Conservative Prime Minister. This was to have at least two consequences: first, reform of the governor-generalship throughout the Commonwealth; second, an as yet (1984) unanswered query about the sovereign's prerogative. Did the sovereign possess the right to say no, if a prime minister demanded a dissolution? Queen Elizabeth II narrowly avoided having to give the practical answer fifty years later in 1974 – so long can issues lie dormant in an 'unwritten' constitution. She may yet have to give the answer.

Meanwhile, a vital Commonwealth conference was planned for 1926, and the Royal Family had something equally vital, and for them vitalising, to think about. The Duchess of York was expecting her first child.

'Innocence and Beauty Born': 1926–30

The poet Yeats believed that in a home where 'custom and ceremony' reigned there was a good chance that 'innocence and beauty' also would be born. But like innocence the world over, this royal innocent did not appear without some traumas.

George V stubbornly refused to offer his beloved daughter-in-law any other house for her baby's birth but the hated White Lodge. So the Duke began negotiating for a rented house in Grosvenor Square; whereupon the Duchess's mother came to the rescue with an offer to lend her daughter the Strathmores' own town house, 17 Bruton Street.

Queen Elizabeth II's actual birthplace has been obliterated by the blitz and by commercial development. But in 1926 Bruton Street in Mayfair was occupied by prosperous aristocratic families: Tennants, Wyndhams, Montagus, Stonors, Herberts, Pakenhams. Lady Violet Pakenham, then aged nine or ten, saw the street at its most cheerful in the early 1920s.

> Our house in Bruton Street [she wrote as Violet Powell forty years later] faced the Strathmores' and during the craze for the game of Beaver we found ourselves playing it across the street against the daughter of the house and her future husband, later King George VI.[1]

In the mews houses behind Bruton Street less engaging things were to be seen. Violet once saw a naked corpse being washed by a nurse at an open window.

It was a loyal street, though even in those days ladies varied in their response to custom and ceremony. 'Mama did not care for curtsying,' Lady Violet remembers, 'and it was not only because of her arthritic knees, whereas Grandmama [Lady Jersey] did not mind.'

The Duke and Duchess of York moved into Number 17 at the end of January after their Sandringham holiday. The Duchess had performed her last public engagement in December, four months before the birth. Her mother-in-law Queen Mary suggested that Hannah Gubbay, queen of the needle, should be responsible for the layette, while the Duchess's sister Lady Elphinstone released Mrs Knight from her own family to take over the new baby. It seemed fair, since Mrs Knight had also been the nanny of Elizabeth Bowes-Lyon.

Mrs Clara Knight was to be 'Allah' to generations of children. The name, a childish form of Clara and pronounced Ah-la, was spelt with an h, as Princess Margaret firmly states. It had nothing whatever to do with the Muslim religion. Allah was the old-fashioned British nanny *par excellence*, eventually raised to a kind of super-excellence by her long connection with royalty. She was never photographed out of uniform but often wearing her navy-blue belted coat and navy felt hat, pushing a royal pram. Her bearing, wrote Miss Crawford the nursery governess, was 'almost noble-looking', thanks to her height and open, calm face. She was to die in harness (voluntary harness that she could not bear to relinquish) at the end of the Second World War. There is a legend that Allah never took a holiday. It is untrue: she always had one annually.

If Elizabeth II was ever consciously influenced by Allah's devotion to duty, that would not be unusual for those born into the *ancien régime* of the nanny. Winston Churchill introduced old age pensions as an honourable tribute to the dedication of his nanny, Mrs Everest. Until the pensions came, these women had had to make do with an honorary title, 'Mrs'. Mrs Knight never married.

The 20th of April was a day of 'evil April drizzle', recalled one of the Duchess's doctors, probably choosing the word 'evil' because his royal patient was in labour and there were complications. It was a breech baby.

Apart from the doctors, a ceremonial secretary from the Home Office was also present. (Ever since the supposed 'warming-pan' plot of 1688 to place a substitute baby in the bed of James II's wife, the Home Secretary had had to vet every royal birth 'in the Succession'. As Princess Alice of Athlone was to put it, 'to make sure that I wasn't a fake.') The ceremonial secretary on this occasion was a distant cousin of Lady Glamis who had been seconded from the Foreign Office to fulfil the 'waiting about' duties before the birth, in response to the Duchess's forcibly expressed wish: 'If there have to be gentlemen waiting outside my bedroom door I hope it's someone we know!' By the time it had ceased to matter to the Duchess whether she knew the gentlemen waiting outside or not, the Home Secretary himself had arrived, Sir William Joynson-Hicks, the colourful 'Jix'.

As the rainy day wore on and darkness fell, preparations were made to perform the Caesarian section already decided upon; an operation which was later to be described coyly in the first bulletin from 17 Bruton Street as 'a certain line of treatment'. At last the Duchess's long ordeal was over and the baby was safely born. The Home Office announced the birth in language dictated by protocol. (It is said that when the Home Secretary of the day congratulated Queen Victoria on the birth of 'a very fine boy' she corrected him to 'a very fine Prince'.)

Her Royal Highness the Duchess of York was safely delivered of a Princess at 2.40 a.m. this morning, Wednesday, April 21st.

It seemed there were two kinds of female children, girls and princesses. The Court Circular moved in a more normal world announcing the birth to the Duchess of 'a daughter'.

Windsor had been telephoned immediately and at 4 am Captain Reginald Seymour, the equerry, awakened Their Majesties with the good news. 'Such a relief and joy,' wrote Queen Mary in her diary.[2] The Duke's relief and joy were even more overwhelming. He wrote to Queen Mary:

> You don't know what a tremendous joy it is to Elizabeth and me to have our little girl. We always wanted a child to make our happiness complete, and now that it has at last happened, it seems so wonderful and strange. I am so proud of Elizabeth at this moment after all that she has gone through during the last few days, and I am so thankful that everything has happened as it should and so successfully. I do hope you and Papa are as delighted as we are, to have a granddaughter, or would you sooner have had another grandson?

The Princess Royal already had her two Lascelles boys. The Duke of York continued: 'I know Elizabeth wanted a daughter. May I say I hope you won't spoil her when she gets a bit older.'[3]

The new baby would not grow up to be the kind of child grandparents could spoil. Like her grandparents themselves, she was to combine 'official pride with personal humility'.[4]

A child born by Caesarian section can look particularly immaculate – in Queen Mary's words 'a little darling' – and from the first moment this child thrived. Like Queen Victoria she was breast-fed, a courageous act on the part of a mother who had undergone 'a certain line of treatment'. Pink skinned, fair haired, she was an altogether neat and tidy baby, with shapely head and ears and long black lashes. The slate colour of her eyes quickly cleared to a light, bright blue.

Since the Duke of York regarded this treasured daughter as entirely his wife's brilliant achievement, he was determined that she should be called Elizabeth. This could have meant a tussle with George v, who was easily irritated by names. He had considered that the two sets of double names given to his late elder brother, Prince Eddy (Prince Albert Victor followed by Duke of Clarence and Avon-dale), were 'an awful mouthful'. However, Bertie tactfully anticipated all possible objections on the part of his father and answered them in advance: Elizabeth was such a nice name, and there had been no one of that name in 'your family' for so long; 'Elizabeth of York' sounded specially nice; nor would the two Elizabeths get muddled up. George v conceded that the name was 'pretty'. As for the possibility of confusion between mother and daughter, the baby Prin-cess Elizabeth personally swept away this danger by giving herself an easier and more euphonious version of the name: 'Lilibet'.

She was christened on 29 May 1926: Elizabeth Alexandra Mary, after her mother, great-grandmother and grand-mother. But her mother predominated, having the same initials, E. A. M. – Elizabeth Angela Marguerite. 'Of course the poor baby cried,' wrote honest Queen Mary. Her christening ceremony took place in the private chapel of Buckingham Palace and she was baptised with Jordan water from the traditional golden lily-font by Dr Cosmo Lang, Archbishop of Canterbury; the chapel was to be bombed and rebuilt by her as the Queen's Gallery.

The idea of a little princess had its immediate public appeal. At first, however, it was sentimental rather than serious. The press recognised her position as third in succession to the throne, but the *Daily Mail* thought she might 'conceivably' succeed to the throne, no more, while *The Times*, having hinted broadly in 1923 that the marriage of the Prince of Wales was what they really wanted, could hardly go to town about a child of the Yorks. Nevertheless, this coolness must not be exaggerated. In the words of Dermot Morrah, Arundel Herald Extraordinary and an expert on the climate of royal affairs: 'It already seemed more likely that the little Princess would eventually be displaced from the succession by a brother of her own, than by a child of her uncle's.'[5]

Twelve days after the royal birth the General Strike sent the people of Britain reeling to their picket-lines or to their strike-breaking posts, according to their own assessment of personal duty. The strike itself could be seen as a kind of monstrous birth, for Britain had been pregnant with social bitterness ever since the First World War ended. On 12 May 1926 the country was 'safely delivered' of its general strike; 'safely', because in the end it was only the wretched coal miners who suffered, through having their already scandalously low wages cut again.

The Prime Minister Stanley Baldwin had broadcast an address to the nation, a new technique to deal with a new situation. 'Jix' of the Home Office, having duly guaranteed twelve days earlier that the Princess was no 'fake', now decided that the workers' grievances were all faked. On the eve of the strike, 2 May, a message had reached the Cabinet that the *Daily Mail* staff had refused to print an editorial entitled 'For King and Country'. Tom Jones, the humorous Welsh cabinet secretary, was at 11 Downing Street well after midnight, listening to an official named Waterhouse putting through a call to the King's assistant private secretary, Clive Wigram, at Windsor.

> WATERHOUSE: The situation is ambiguous. The *Daily Mail* has ceased to function . . . *ceased to function* . . . *Mail* CEASED TO FUNCTION. . . . Don't be alarmed in the morning. Tell HM that he should not go off the deep end. WIGRAM [a very sleepy person who had at last grasped the message]: We don't take the *Daily Mail* or the *Daily Express*.

Tom Jones summed up this reply as 'in the great tradition of Palace sang-froid'.

In fact His Majesty was more likely to go off the deep end about the sufferings of the miners and their families than the non-delivery of a newspaper. 'Try living on their wages,' he shouted furiously at Lord Durham, a big coal owner who had been cursing his workers. And after reading the first draft of his speech for the opening of Parliament in 1926, George v had insisted on 'a more direct personal appeal to his people on the coal conflict', and less complacency about the Government's 'progress' with housing.[6]

If the nation was divided, the Commonwealth took a significant step during the year of Elizabeth's birth towards that form of unity which she was later to tend and cultivate so assiduously.

During the nineteenth century even the most ardent lovers of the Empire had thought of it purely as a superb English back garden. Joseph Chamberlain, an imperial crusader if ever there was one, liked to call the Empire the British working class's 'undeveloped estates'. An even more obsessive enthusiast, the historian James Anthony Froude, saw the only hope for the English was in the sunlight, the air, the space, the freedom of peasant proprietorship in the colonies.

By 1926 all this was already vastly changed. True, there were still 'colonies', mainly in Asia, Africa and the West Indies, which were generally spoken of as belonging to the 'Empire'. But the white 'colonies' had grown into 'dominions' and the dominions were 'self-governing', if not self-obliterating – for the word dominion was to be dropped altogether. The Commonwealth was to be composed of nation-states enjoying absolute equality with the erstwhile 'mother-country' and with each other.

Where did George v come in? He was to be the agent who would make the co-existence of equality *and unity* within the Commonwealth possible. Without some binding force, what would hold together this assembly of absolute equals? The King stood for patriotism, pride, history, culture, language; and all these common values were the things that held the Commonwealth together.

Such were the end-of-term thoughts of A. J. Balfour (he died soon afterwards), expressed in the famous Balfour

Report of 1926. Balfour also hoped that the Monarch's role would be to heal splits in the Commonwealth caused by the subject of race. When he visited India as a young man in 1906, George, then Prince of Wales, had been astounded to find that Indians could not join British clubs.

The 1926 Imperial Conference embodied the Balfour Report and went on to reaffirm their triple faith: in liberty, equality and unity. They referred to the 'warm vein of friendship' running through this free partnership of nations. And parallel with their friendship for one another ran a 'warm vein' of affection for the crown.

This affirmation of equality further entailed the reform of the governor-generalship in each dominion. The Governor-General was in future to occupy the same position as His Majesty occupied in Great Britain. This certainly did away with the old colonialists' idea of the Governor-General as an agent of the British Colonial Office. But it did not explore exactly what were His Majesty's position and prerogatives in Great Britain.

Vincent Massey, who was representing Canada at the 1926 Conference, found His Majesty less formidable than he had feared, at least ceremonially. Did he really have to 'kiss hands' as the Court Circular said? A lord-in-waiting to whom Massey had nervously put the question gave a loud guffaw. 'By Jove, I don't know – I'll ask Reggie!' (The same Captain Reginald Seymour who had awakened Their Majesties at Windsor with the news of Princess Elizabeth's birth.) Reggie's answer was yes. But when Massey actually seized the royal hand and kissed it George v looked extremely surprised. Clearly the court was moving slower than the King himself. Massey also found that although the King would prefer him to wear a frock-coat at the Palace, it was up to him. 'It was not obligatory but it was customary.'[7] Nineteen twenty-six was indeed a year of change.

South Africa was presenting more serious problems for the Royal Family. Half of white South Africa wished to be a republic. General Hertzog, the Nationalist leader, was fighting tooth and nail with General Smuts, the loyalist, for the soul of South Africa. During the previous year, 1925, the Prince of Wales had been sent out on a South African tour to raise the Smuts flag wherever possible. His gaiety and charm won him and Smuts some success; particularly as the Prince's royal uncle the Earl of Athlone, married to Princess Alice, was Governor-General. But blue eyes, silky yellow hair and a boyish grin were not going to make Hertzog haul down his flag.

Meanwhile, future storms were piling up for the Princess in the Commonwealth, while that same Commonwealth carried away her parents for six out of her first fourteen months. She was left in charge of Allah and her two sets of grandparents.

The King, not having seen fit to launch his stammering son on a Commonwealth tour in 1923 when he had no family, now decided to send the doting parents away for half a year. It was a peculiarly harsh aspect of the royal vocation. 'We are not supposed to be human,' the Duchess once said sadly. They would miss their only child's first birthday.

Nevertheless, the Duchess did find a positive side to this sacrifice of her motherhood, by persuading her husband to make one more attempt at curing his stammer.

Shortly before the long tour culminating in New Zealand and Australia began, they discovered an Australian speech therapist named Lionel Logue, who taught the Duke how to control his stammer through correct breathing. It was one of those events which confirmed the Duchess in the Duke's eyes as 'the most wonderful person in the world.'[8]

Princess Elizabeth's first Christmas was spent at Sandringham House. The King and Queen had moved in only on 14 October 1926, Queen Alexandra having occupied it in solitary state until her death on 20 November 1925. That the Princess's grandparents had lived for so long in constricted York Cottage on the Sandringham estate (now the Sandringham Estate Office) has always amazed biographers. York Cottage was ugly as only a Victorian villa could be and no more convenient. The explanation may be that in King George's youth it looked larger than life, as all objects do to children; that he grew up the slave of habit but entirely free from aesthetic feeling, and that the small rooms reminded him of his beloved cabins at sea.

Biographers have also wondered at the Royal Family's age-long habit of gloating over the Christmas tables at Sandringham, on which their presents were displayed, untouched from Christmas Eve until Christmas Day. This, however, seems entirely understandable. The Royal Family were human; unable to go window-shopping like ordinary people, they set up their own displays at times like Christmas.

After Christmas, the King and Queen and Princess Elizabeth said goodbye to the Duke and Duchess of York on 6 January 1927. 'I felt very much leaving on Thursday, and the baby was so sweet, playing with the buttons on Bertie's uniform,' wrote the departing mother; 'it quite broke me up.'[9] The baby, however, was provided with plenty of playthings after 'Bertie's buttons' had vanished away; notably the deep fur of two chow-chow dogs belonging to her Strathmore grandparents. And her popular parents were to bring back from their tour a tribute of three tons of toys.

King George and Queen Mary were blissfully absorbed by their first granddaughter. To him she was never anything but 'sweet'; to her the child was the cherished *bambino* who came down to the drawing-room after tea floating on a muslin cloud. 'Your sweet little daughter has four teeth now,' the proud grandfather wrote to the Duchess in March, 'which is quite good at eleven months old.' In fact she had always been good at everything she did, including sitting up alone in the middle of a huge sofa before her mother left, looking like 'a white fluff of thistledown'. The visitor who had hit on this pretty simile added the perceptive words: 'The baby is always good, she has the sweetest air of complete serenity.'[10]

Photographs to show the child's development were sent

out regularly to the Duke and Duchess by Queen Mary. One successful double portrait of grandchild and grandmother is a study in royal continuity. Princess Elizabeth sits up on a table-top supported by cushions and her grandmother's hand. The one wears the short lacy confection ordered by Allah, the other the long loose draperies ordered by the King. Each wears a traditional necklace: the baby her mother's first coral beads, the grandmother a multiple rope of pearls. There is something curiously similar in their static, untroubled, aloof pose. Neither looks at the camera. It is said that Queen Mary's first words on seeing her new grandchild had been, 'I wish you were more like your little mother.' Whether or not Princess Elizabeth was to resemble her mother, there was no doubt she possessed from the start a remarkable strain of the old Royal Family, especially of Queen Mary. The photograph was signed, 'Mary R & Baby Elizabeth 1927'.

On 27 June 1927 the Princess made her first appearance on the famous Buckingham Palace balcony. The day was wet. Her parents had returned home at last. But Queen Mary as well as her mother held her up under a spreading umbrella. Was it because the fourteen-month-old baby might be shy with a mother from whom she had been separated since the beginning of her conscious life and could no longer remember?

While the Yorks were away White Lodge had been mercifully forgotten. The family moved into a new London house, 145 Piccadilly. It was to be a real home for nearly nine years: large but not cumbersome, with an elegant glass dome crowning the stair-well, and the nurseries at the top. The Duke allowed his daughter to have a red carpet in her day nursery, although he was not fond of red carpets and all they stood for. As a young man he had agreed to become President of the Boys' (Industrial) Welfare Society as long as no one put down for him a 'damned red carpet'.

The pram could be pushed into the small triangle of Hamilton Gardens behind the house. Directly opposite was

St George's Hospital and, a few doors away, Apsley House, the splendid London home of the Dukes of Wellington.

The next autumn there was a crisis in the family. On 19 November 1928 King George fell seriously ill with an abscess in his lung. A black fog hung over London and black rumours spread that the King was dead. It was indeed touch and go, but the doctors saved him for another seven years, despite Margot Asquith's indictment. In mid-March 1929 his favourite grandchild was sent to cheer him at Bognor, where he had been moping for several chilly weeks. Harold Nicolson, George v's official biographer, gave Princess Elizabeth only two mentions in his 531 pages, one being in a footnote. The other was her visit to Bognor. Nicolson described her as 'an emollient for jaded nerves'. Queen Mary was more specific: 'G. delighted to see her,' she wrote in her diary on 13 March, and next day, 'I played with Lilibet in the garden making sand pies! The Archbishop of Canterbury [who had christened Lilibet nearly three years before] came to see us & was so kind & so sympathetic.'[11] Queen Victoria's earliest memories had been of a yellow carpet and terrifying bishops; those of her great-great-granddaughter may have been of a red carpet and a nice archbishop.

The Archbishop had been presented to the convalescent King at a moment when he was on all fours, playing horses with Lilibet who led him by the beard. 'He used to play,' recalled Lady Airlie, Queen Mary's lady-in-waiting, '– a thing I never saw him do with his own children.' The people of Bognor would see the pair deep in conversation on their outings, he in his bath-chair, she trotting beside him with her bonnet tied firmly under her chin, her spring coat tightly buttoned and her leggings neatly strapped down. His voice boomed like the sea under the March wind; hers was high and clear as his little golden hand-bell at Buckingham Palace.

During that autumn the Princess was left behind when her parents went to Edinburgh for the General Assembly of the Church of Scotland, of which the Duke was Lord High Commissioner. The Duchess wrote regretfully to Queen Mary:

> I fear that it has been a very great disappointment to the people. . . . The Moderator mentioned in his welcoming address 'our dear Princess Elizabeth', which is, I believe, almost unique. It almost frightens me that the people should love her so much. I suppose that it is a good thing, and I hope that she will be worthy of it, poor little darling.

The little darling is said to have made her first quip at a Sandringham Christmas party when she was only two and a half years old. It seems more likely to have been during the next Christmas, 1929, when she was a year older and knew her kind old grandfather better than ever. The story goes that she was listening to the carol 'While Shepherds Watched' and picked out the lines about glad tidings of great joy 'to you and all mankind'. With the sudden perception of an alert child she said, 'I know that old man kind. That's you, Grandpapa. You are old, and you are very very kind.'

The court of King George v has been described as 'luxury without ostentation'. It was also without animation. Part of the small Elizabeth's immense appeal was due to her vivacity and comic fervour in doing what was expected of her. On Easter Monday 1930 she paid a visit to her grandparents at Windsor. She still remembers the reaction of the Bank Holiday crowds to her own performance. They laughed and cheered as the Scots Guards saluted her and the enthusiastic four-year-old took the salute with both arms waving.

So far her upbringing had been sheltered, but not in any ivory tower. She was aware of the outside world, partly through the toys she was given to play with. It was a world in which a colourful part was played by animals. At three and a half Lilibet was presented with her first live pony for Christmas. But long before she was two the capacious glass-fronted toy cupboard in her nursery had been stocked with the most amusing of the small animals brought home by her parents for the Commonwealth's 'Princess Betty'.

Her bigger toys were more utilitarian. She knew that there was such a thing in the real world as work. A dustpan and brush had been Lady Airlie's present to her for her third Christmas; her tidiness was remarkable, and this trait was to remain with her instead of dying away as with most growing children.

She knew that bread had to be delivered, for she was given a baker's van as well as carts and a garden truck called 'Globe Express'; nor was she ever likely to forget that ponies had to be groomed, fed and watered, what with her own zeal and the necessary brushes and pails lined up in the corridor outside her nursery.

At five she was learning to read with her mother, just as the Duchess had learnt from *her* mother at the same age. Indeed we shall see that a great deal of the second Elizabeth's upbringing was based upon the ideas that had borne fruit with the first. No doubt the Duchess had had a little more time than usual to spend with her daughter during that spring and summer of 1930. For soon after Lilibet's fourth birthday her mother had to stop public engagements. She was expecting her second child.

The family went to Glamis for the months before the birth. 'Yes, it is a right good thing that our Duchess is back home,' said a Glamis villager who did not hold with the pace of modern life. 'She will get a wee bit of rest and peace here. Why in London they do nothing but run the poor lady off her feet. There is never a day but she is here, there and everywhere, opening bazaars, visiting hospitals and the like. It is too much for a body.'[13]

This time the Home Secretary in attendance was a Labour working man, Mr J. R. Clynes, who arrived with disconcerting punctuality and definitely was not a gentleman whom his hosts 'knew'. Lady Airlie had him over at Cortachy to help pass the time.

A violent storm burst on the evening of 21 August, when

the signal was at length passed to Mr Clynes. As he sped across to Glamis it is said that the grandeur of the scene inspired him to recite poetry. The lightning playing on the hills was brighter than the beacons soon to be lit.

At 9.22 pm a girl was born. Enough poetic feeling was still bubbling in Mr Clynes to enable him to capture the 'Holy Family' scene with the charm and simplicity of a painter of the Dutch school – except that there were lords and ladies round the crib, instead of shepherds:

> I found crowded round the baby's cot the Duke of York, Lord and Lady Strathmore and Lady Rose Leveson-Gower, the Duchess's sister. They at once made way for me, and I went to the cot and peeping in saw a fine chubby-faced little girl lying wide awake.[14]

This child was always to be wide awake in every sense.

One paper pointed out that she was born under the zodiac sign of Leo and therefore would be clever, dynamic, self-willed. The astrologer attached to the *Sunday Express* went further and foresaw events of 'tremendous import-ance' to the Royal Family and the nation 'near her seventh year'. At least the Abdication would not go unpredicted. Unlike her sister she seems to have drawn from her father no warnings against spoiling. This was understandable, since he was so busy spoiling the child himself.

Mr Clynes added the words, 'It seemed to me that everybody was happy', and Celia Clear, author of *Royal Children*, suggests that perhaps 'Mr Clynes thought it necessary to stress the happiness of all concerned because it was no secret that the parents had hoped for a boy.'[15]

Boys predominated in both the Duke's and Duchess's families. They not only hoped for a boy but expected one. No names were ready for a second girl. There was much family debate, with the result that the baby was not reg-istered by her father until October. The parents wanted Ann Margaret. King George disliked Ann. In the end the Duchess wrote firmly to Queen Mary, but with the King in mind – that King whom she alone did not fear – 'We have decided to call our little daughter Margaret Rose. I hope you like it. I think that it is very pretty together.'[16]

Princess Elizabeth liked it very much, for it gave her the chance to make her second recorded wisecrack. 'I shall call her Bud.'

'Why Bud?' asked Lady Cynthia Asquith, daughter-in-law of the King's first prime minister, to whom 'Bud' probably sounded like American slang.

'Well, she's not a real Rose yet, is she? She's only a Bud.'

There is no evidence that Margaret Rose was ever called Bud. The Rose unfolded far too quickly, especially for Nanny Allah, who liked to keep her babies as long as possible in the pram.

The arrival of a sister was to bring many new experiences into Princess Elizabeth's life. There was one that it did not bring. She was not displaced as third in the line of succession, as she would have been if her parents' second child had been a boy.

Among the most profound changes was the growing presence of a character both like and different from her own. If the Princess had remained an only child her tranquil and responsive temperament might have lacked the stimulus of confrontations, however affectionate, in childhood. For she did not need her 'corners to be rubbed off' in the way that most children are said to require this process. Rather, she needed the diamond to be cut more sharply. And this her sister was to do for her, with a skill that no adult could have achieved.

Except that both sisters were born in the rainswept dark, they seemed at first to have little in common – though neither Elizabeth's drizzle nor Margaret's drenching were symbolic of the two personalities: the one contented and accepting but with a strong interior life; the other witty, sensitive and acute, reacting each moment to the outside world. However, the gap between, say, seventeen and thirteen is much greater than that between fifty-seven and fifty-three. As the sisters entered their middle years the likenesses in their responses were to emerge. They would often find themselves reacting to the same events in exactly the same way, or making the same jokes at the same moment.

Meanwhile the birth of Princess Margaret Rose, the first royal birth in the direct line to take place in Scotland since Charles I's at Dunfermline in 1600, was to emphasise the continuity in the Royal Family. Princess Elizabeth had spent her first summer holiday at Glamis, lying in her pram in the same formal garden into which Allah, then a young nursery maid of eighteen, had pushed her mother's pram at the beginning of the century. Now another daughter was asleep in that garden.

All was peace and unbroken threads at Glamis. They let Princess Elizabeth watch the high beacons glowing in honour of her sister's birth. That was to be the model for their childhood: lights on the hills and customary order in the valleys. No matter what was the political weather in the world outside.

IV

'A Golden Age':
1931–5

The Duke of York never forgot the miseries of a frustrated childhood. Just because of his own grey memories he ardently wished these children of his – so wonderfully, so unbelievably his – to enjoy a lyrical youth. In the words of his official biographer, Sir John Wheeler-Bennett: 'He was determined that, come what might, Princess Elizabeth and Princess Margaret should look back upon their early years as a golden age.'[1]

For opposite reasons the Duchess had exactly the same dream. A rapturous and serene childhood had been hers, and she intended to recreate the same golden age for her daughters.

These children were with their parents as often as possible during the day, not restricted to a starched hour after tea like the children of so many of their neighbours. The day always ended with flying pillows in their bedroom. Shrill cries of "Good-night, Mummy, good-night, Papa,' echoed down the stairwell as their parents eventually retreated from the battlefield. No room in the house was barred to the children, least of all their mother's own room. Here she would read to them the stories her mother had read to her: *Peter Pan*, *Black Beauty*, all the fairy, animal and Bible stories that she could remember.

Margaret's favourite, however, was a contemporary children's book called *The Cock, the Mouse, and the Little Red Hen*. One can see why. When each animal in turn refuses to

help the hen build her new house, she will not give up.
' "Then I'll do it myself," said the Little Red Hen.' Only
Alice offered a wonderland to the sisters that neither could
take. Princess Margaret tried it at five, ten, twenty, thirty
and so on. It was no good. The book contained all the things
that she most disliked: vertigo falling down the rabbit-
hole, claustrophobia underground, animals talking like
dons, an overall disturbing atmosphere. (Prince Philip,
though, was always an addict, knowing much of it by
heart.)

With the arrival of Princess Margaret, the nursery had
become an even more pleasant place than before. There
had always been Allah, with Smith to attend her and
Margaret MacDonald as nursery maid. Now Margaret's
sister Ruby joined them and assisted Allah, who took over
the new baby. Margaret MacDonald, 'Bobo' to her young
charge, devoted herself to Lilibet. They shared a bedroom
and were in time almost to share a life, for Bobo was to be
Queen Elizabeth II's personal maid, dresser and lifelong
friend. She was a Scot, and like many generations of
Scottish royal servants possessed the gift of perfect deference combined with perfect dignity – and outspokenness
to match. Curiously enough Queen Victoria's beloved
wardrobe maid had also been a MacDonald, Annie, and
she was one of the few people whom the old Queen
mentioned by name in her will, hoping to meet her again in
a more equal world.

Those who remember that Bobo was still sleeping in the
Princess's room at the time of her father's coronation are
sometimes surprised. After all she was a girl of eleven. Was
it for reasons of security? Not that alone. All over Mayfair
and Belgravia children were sharing rooms with nannies
and nursemaids. The fact was, there were still so many
servants and often so many children in those pre-war days
that even the stateliest homes could not provide enough
room space without a good deal of doubling-up. Queen
Victoria, of course, had taken the first opportunity to evict
her mother and enjoy a room of her own. But then the

Queen and her mother were as alienated as the Princess and Bobo were devoted.

The creation of a golden age for the children was well under way by 1931. In that year there were two important developments for the family, one adding greatly to their happiness, the other placing it in jeopardy. The bad news came first.

A financial disaster in the United States had begun as the Wall Street crash of 1929. By 1931 the crisis had stalked across the British scene. Ramsay MacDonald's Labour Government came under fire both from the bankers, who wanted 'equal cuts' in a nation where there was no equality, and from the unemployed who were sinking into a slough of hate on the dole. In August the Government resigned. To whom would the King offer the poisoned chalice of the premiership?

One course would have been to send for the leader of the next largest party in Parliament. This was the Conservatives, led by Stanley Baldwin. He was more than willing. Indeed he dashed back from abroad in such a high state of expectancy that he had no time to pack his striped pants but carried them over his arm.

King George, however, with a monarch's traditional dislike of excitable party politics and penchant for equable coalitions, had other ideas. He persuaded MacDonald, Baldwin and the Liberal leader Sir Herbert Samuel to get together under the former Labour Prime Minister and form a 'National' government. The Labour Party split and was virtually wiped out in Parliament at the ensuing election. But the party had a surviving rump which was to nurse itself back to physical health, and also to a chronic state of bitterness: MacDonald, their first ever prime minister, succeeded in making leadership a dirty word.

Some of this criticism was inevitably to rub off on the nation's symbolic leader, George v. It was only fair to the extent that what he got away with in the 1930s would be hazardous for his granddaughter to attempt half a century later. Because Labour's heart momentarily stopped beat-

ing while the patient lay on the royal operating table, it was
felt the surgeon had been partly to blame.

To be sure, a later Lord Chancellor, Lord Hailsham,
argued in his *Dilemma of Democracy* that the King did not
put a foot wrong. Hailsham sees the solution of the 1931
crisis as a shining example of what he calls the 'fail-safe
mechanism' built into the British Constitution. This
mechanism clicks into action in three stages. First, the
Monarch, after taking responsible advice, asks one of the
political leaders to try to form a government. Second, this
leader (or another if the first fails) succeeds in the House of
Commons. Third, he or she may then be endorsed or not by
the will of the people at a subsequent general election. In
1931 the 'fail-safe' mechanism worked perfectly. The King
appealed to MacDonald and Baldwin who successfully
formed the National Government, and through this 'individual co-operation' the coalition government scored a
landslide victory at the polls on 27 October 1931.[2]

In his definitive life of Ramsay MacDonald, Professor
Marquand shows that without question the architect of the
National Government was King George v. MacDonald had
left his colleagues at 10 Downing Street on Sunday 24
August to see the King with the words, 'I'm off to the
Palace to throw in my hand.' MacDonald arrived looking
'scared and unbalanced'. It was the King himself who
restored the balance. That evening he 'impressed upon' the
Prime Minister his indispensability and 'implored' him to
form a national government. Next day the King renewed
his arguments and, writes Marquand, 'The King's appeal
turned the scales.'[3]

What would Princess Elizabeth have made of this *cause
célèbre*, if and when she came to discuss it with her father?
Her grandfather had done nothing unconstitutional. He
had been consulted, had given his advice and had seen his
advice taken. Subsequent attempts by Harold Laski, the
left-wing professor-politician, to indict the King for acting
improperly carry no conviction today.

For King George v, 1931 had been a sad year. It is

unlikely that the passage into law of the Statute of Westminster on 11 December had done anything to cheer him. By this famous statute, the crown's importance as the symbol of Commonwealth unity was spelt out and starred. Hitherto the statute had been nothing more than a token idea in the Balfour Report of five years earlier. The King loved the Empire as he knew it, and any changes had been at best 'a bore' or at worst had 'rather taken HM's breath away'.[4]

No doubt there were some criticisms of the statute. Compton Mackenzie, a novelist rather than a constitutional lawyer, objected to it on human grounds. Those responsible for the statute expected the monarchy to evolve into 'a perfect machine', while human beings – kings and queens – evolved into 'monarchical symbols'. Writing in 1938 and thinking of Edward VIII, Mackenzie found it natural that 'this humanity will occasionally insist on asserting itself'.[5] He could not guess that for thirty years Elizabeth II would work under the aegis of that same statute with complete dedication and growing involvement.

For his family, the King's sad year, 1931, was to produce an uncovenanted gift. The year before he had allowed the Prince of Wales to put in order and then live in a small exotic country house near Windsor, Fort Belvedere.

Now the King was offering an equally derelict country house to the Duke and Duchess of York and their family. This was the Royal Lodge in Windsor Great Park. It had once been used by King George IV as a private retreat. The Duke and Duchess went down to look at it in September. Like a pair of excited 'Capability Browns', they immediately decided it had 'great possibilities'. After the house had been put into temporary order and its unkempt gardens planted, if only with the abundant flora of the flower catalogues, the York family moved in in January 1932.

This marks the beginning of the most tranquil and harmonious years of the Princesses' childhood. Their parents enjoyed the never-ending pleasures of bringing the

Royal Lodge gradually back to the original conceptions of John Nash and Jeffry Wyatville. The subdivided grand saloon, in particular, was restored to its original spacious proportions. A conservatory that had stood between the front door and the main house was demolished. On the top floor were the Princesses' rooms. The drab, peeling outside walls were pink-washed, so that a rosy vision could be glimpsed through real azaleas and rhododendrons. The Princesses were each given a plot of garden to work themselves, on the principle of the miniature Swiss Cottage at Osborne with its row of small patches for Queen Victoria's children. Elizabeth and Margaret Rose, however, preferred working all-out with their parents to bring the main garden under control. Though the girls were photographed beside their wheelbarrow in immaculate jackets and skirts and lace-up shoes, it was possible to get deeply dirty in bushes and bonfire ash, even before the days of jeans and wellingtons for royal children.

Corresponding to the Swiss Cottage itself was 'Y Bwthyn Bach', The Little House, presented to Princess Elizabeth by the people of Wales and now a feature of the Royal Lodge gardens. Its roof was thatched and its decor was chintzy; but everything in it worked, from the vacuum cleaner to the kitchen sink. Queen Mary was later to say that the children ought to learn more history and less arithmetic, since they would never have to add up even their own accounts. (As Elizabeth received only one shilling a week pocket money her personal experience of financial problems was not extensive. Most of her shillings she saved for Christmas and birthday presents.) But if the girls did not understand double-entry, at least they knew how to keep a room clean, and what were the brand names of scouring powders and polishes. Their housework was not too heavy, though, for Y Bwthyn Bach was genuinely little. There was only one place in it where Miss Marion Crawford, their tall nursery governess (5 feet 7 inches), could stand upright.

An upstanding Scots girl of twenty-three, Marion Crawford became nursery governess to the Princesses in 1933. She had recently finished her training at Edinburgh's Moray House and after a short spell with the Leveson-Gower cousins she was passed on to the Yorks. As a nursery governess she was go-ahead and ambitious. The Edinburgh children she had practised on during training were 'not very bright' owing to malnutrition. Her aim was to return to college in due course and become a child psychologist.

Four times at the beginning of her now controversial book, *The Little Princesses*, she goes out of her way to insist that she had considered her private employment as governess to be 'only a temporary post'. This was of course mainly because of psychological interests. It was also due to allegedly off-putting stories she had read in the papers about the royal children. She expected to find a pair of 'very spoiled and difficult little people'. Miss Crawford was later to ridicule such nonsense, especially a report that Princess Margaret was deaf and dumb. (Margaret, of all children, *dumb*? Everyone laughed at the absurdity. The little Princess Victoria had been subjected to similar fabrications in the 1820s.) The true reason for the gossip was probably Miss Crawford's own previous work with deprived children. But Miss Crawford put it down to Allah's incorrigible habit of getting her 'babies' to bed early and keeping Margaret in her pram instead of letting the public see her run about.

This criticism of Mrs Knight was only the tip of the iceberg. She and Miss Crawford, with their very different ideas of upbringing, were to produce many a set-to between nursery and schoolroom. Marion Crawford was slim as well as tall, with an elastic stride (she was engaged by the Duchess of York partly because of her pleasure in walking miles to and from her Scottish jobs), light cropped hair, sharp features, pointed face and a puckish grin.

Nevertheless, whatever their differences, nursery and schoolroom combined to give the children that 'golden age' so much desired for them by their parents. In the next chapter it will be necessary to examine the 'Crawfie episode' in the Queen's life more closely. For Miss Crawford was soon to become 'Crawfie', an important and valued figure in the lives of the two high-spirited children.

'How do you do? Why have you no hair?' was Princess Elizabeth's first greeting to her Eton-cropped governess. Lilibet was nearly six, sitting up in bed and driving an imaginary horse with a pair of toy reins.

'Do you usually drive in bed?' was the governess's question, wisely going on the attack.

'I mostly go once or twice round the park before I go to sleep, you know,' explained the Princess. 'It exercises my horses.'[6]

In imagination Princess Elizabeth had brought the park into her bedroom. Imagination was even more prominent in Margaret. At three and a half she was at the age when exceptionally imaginative children – often the eldest or youngest in a family or an only child – invent a character who becomes an inseparable companion of total credibility in their lives.* The imaginary companion can be either a scapegoat or an instrument for wish-fulfilment or both. Princess Margaret's imaginary 'Cousin Halifax' is remembered by Crawfie as the person who had to be blamed when the Princess did something wrong. 'It wasn't me, it was Cousin Halifax'; or 'I was busy with Cousin Halifax.' When she was a little older Princess Margaret invented the 'Pinkle Ponkle', a creature that hovered over cities. It sounds like the result of hearing Edward Lear's nursery rhymes read aloud. The invention that Princess Margaret herself still remembers with affection was 'Inderbombanks', whom she supposes 'must have been male'.[7]

Curiously enough, the children's quips that have survived seem to show Princess Elizabeth's tongue as no less sharp than her sister's, though the commonly held view is

---

* In *Points for Parents* (reprinted 1969) the present author has devoted a chapter to dealing with instances of this fascinating phenomenon.

that she was always gentle and malleable whereas Princess Margaret showed early wilfulness. As a small child Elizabeth is said to have tartly ordered her grandfather King George v, who had left the room after a difference of opinion, to 'come back and shut the door'. Nor were her compliments sugary; she praised him for being 'not a bad drawer'.

Some people have noticed an apparent contradiction between Princess Elizabeth's affectionate familiarity with her 'very very kind' grandfather and Princess Margaret's recollection that they were 'much too frightened of him' to call him by a nickname like 'Grandpapa England'. The answer may lie in their nurse Allah, who is remembered by Princess Margaret as being nervous of the gruff old King. It is probable that as Princess Elizabeth passed from babyhood to young girlhood her earlier naturalness with her grandfather was affected by the fears of her nurse.

Mr Fitch the royal detective remembered her at about eight going to the Royal Tournament with King George and Queen Mary and being unimpressed by a tableau about the Duke of Wellington at Waterloo. '*Who* is that funny old man with the beaky nose, Grandpapa?' she asked disapprovingly.

'That's the Iron Duke – the Duke of Wellington, you know. You mustn't call him a funny old man. He was a very great general and a fine gentleman.'

'*I* know! He made all those battles in the Peninsular War and I can't ever remember the names of them. Well, he *is* ugly, anyhow!'[8]

The Princess's assenting or acquiescent attitude towards life seems to have gradually developed as a result of conscious self-control – a sign of strength rather than weakness. She was easy to teach, and easy to dress also. She showed little interest in clothes, simply putting on without question whatever she was told to wear.

Princess Margaret's considerable tact and childish finesse are recalled. 'You don't look very angelic, Margaret!' said the Duchess one day to her diverting daughter who was about to set off for a fancy-dress party dressed as an angel. 'That's all right. I'll be a Holy Terror.'

Margaret's tone would change to plaintiveness when she was not noticed. A first memory was of half-falling out of her pram to attract attention. Almost her first quoted (and oft-repeated) sentence was, 'Wait for me, Lilibet. . . . Wait for me.' Lilibet responded by sticking up for her sister's rights and insisting on equal treatment for the two of them. This may explain why they were always dressed alike despite the four years and four months between them. Only once did the elder sister complain, 'Margaret always wants what I want.' Crawfie professed to find in this sentence a hint of sinister jealousies to come. But these are the natural feelings of every younger child; though when you are a princess the situation may seem still more unfair.

While Princess Margaret loved the sounds of words ('Inderbombanks', 'Halifax' and 'Pinkle Ponkle') and the sound of music (she could hum *The Merry Widow* before she was a year old), her sister had a passion for order, system and design. One seemed cut out to be a pianist, singer or comedy actress (Margaret was a 'born comic', wrote Crawfie), but the other seemed cut out to be – a queen. 'Isn't it lucky that Lilibet's the eldest?' said Princess Margaret to her mother in a moment of truth after some act of defiance on her part.

Princess Elizabeth appeared at times almost too self-disciplined, too orderly, too systematic. She would even sort the coffee crystals that her parents gave her as a treat after luncheon into big crystals and little crystals, no doubt eating the little ones first. Yet these orderly qualities in Princess Elizabeth were the very ones needed in a constitutional monarch. She would smooth and fold the wrapping paper off her presents, rolling up the ribbon for future use. (This may have been a family trait. Lord Harewood describes how his mother, Princess Mary the Princess Royal, would save bits of string and wrapping paper.[9]) Her books were always ranged with perfect regularity on shelf or table. When Crawfie said sententiously, 'Nothing is impossible if you try hard enough,' Elizabeth believed her, and went on trying night after night to place her shoes exactly parallel with one another under her chair, with her clothes meticulously folded above, sometimes getting out of bed more than once to try yet again to reach perfection. Margaret demonstrated the impossible simply by saying to Crawfie, 'Have you ever tried putting toothpaste back into its tube?' She made it her business to laugh her sister out of her obsessional tidiness. She took her coffee crystals, like life, at a gulp.

In the schoolroom Princess Elizabeth was conscientious, reasonable and attentive to detail. Of course there were moments when human nature broke through and she brought her written list of French verbs to a close by upsetting the inkpot over her own head. In case her charges should sound inhumanly perfect, Crawfie noted that they sometimes flew into a temper over wearing hats, which they hated, and snapped one another's elastic to cries of 'Brute!' 'Beast!' And Lilibet could not only not do arithmetic but she was bad at knitting as well. Still, she tried hard.

King George v had made only one suggestion when Miss Crawford was first engaged as nursery governess: 'For goodness' sake, teach Margaret and Lilibet to write a decent hand, that's all I ask you. Not one of my children can write properly. . . .'[10] (The King himself, according to Lord Clark, was the slowest writer he had ever seen. Nor could he spell. The word 'business' was always a problem. And Princess Margaret once had the satisfaction of telling her sister there was no such word as 'merang'.) Both the Princesses were to develop good, firm, legible handwriting with plenty of character; not the 'script' that their grand-mother Queen Mary detested. The idea of the Princesses eventually entering a girls' school seems not to have arisen. When it was suggested in 1951 that their father should enter hospital for a serious operation, he refused with the words, 'I've never heard of a king going to a hospital before'; and he would have said the same about princesses going to a school.

Not that the Duchess wanted such a thing for her daughters. She had not enjoyed her own brief schooldays at a London day school and she was always to look on schools as a hardship that her grandchildren unfortunately had to undergo. 'Poor Anne,' she would say when the time came for her granddaughter to leave home for Benenden.

Crawfie was to write lyrically of those carefree, almost study-free days at 145 Piccadilly: 'It has often seemed to me that in those days we lived in an ivory tower, removed from the real world. . . . Looking back on it, it often seems to me as though while we were there the season was always spring.'[11]

Miss Crawford's idea of this perennial springtime was focused on the children's games, walks and general culture, not their lessons. Hamilton Gardens was their first outdoor playground, safely fenced against the outside world, and entered by a postern gate from 'the ivory tower' that was their Piccadilly home. Violet Powell, once the Yorks' neighbour in Bruton Street, remembers Hamilton Gardens in her own youth, with its paths, trees and 'sooty bushes':

> Thackeray mentions Hamilton Gardens as a playground for blue-blooded children, but in my day there was also a sequence of royal babies, beginning with the Lascelles boys and followed by the then Princess Elizabeth. . . . By the time Princess Elizabeth had ceased to be aired on her nurse's lap, in an open carriage, and her pram had come to rest under a weeping willow tree in the centre of the garden, I had passed the age of unselfconsciously making friends with babies and nannies, so I only admired her bonnets from afar.[12]

When Miss Crawford came along, the two Princesses were still at the stage of unselfconsciously making friends with other unknown children – if this had been allowed.

> Other children [wrote Miss Crawford] always had an enormous fascination, like mystic beings from a distant world, and the little girls used to smile shyly at those they liked the look of.

They would so have loved to speak to them and make friends, but this was never encouraged. I have often thought it a pity. The Dutch and Belgian Royal children walked about the streets in their countries as a matter of course.[13]

British walkabouts were to develop many years later in a different way.

Miss Crawford indeed was candid enough to admit that the British democratic monarchy had its own traditions and difficulties attendant on them. It was not possible for a British princess to walk about the streets 'as a matter of course'. On one occasion Miss Crawford herself had to drive off a press photographer with some force.

'I'm sure he thinks now that Crawfies bite!' said Princess Elizabeth, delighted by her governess's savagery. Crawfie knew well that an unauthorised picture of Allah's charges in the papers would have resulted not only in more dis-approval than usual, but in the end of these 'unofficial outings'.

Crawfie's unofficial outings brought their own nemesis the moment the nursery governess ventured beyond Hyde Park and Kensington Gardens. The Princesses had a long-ing to travel by tube in one of those alluring 'caverns measureless to man'. So Miss Crawford took them incog-nito to Tottenham Court Road station and on to a 'jaunt' at the Young Woman's Christian Association in Great Rus-sell Street. From this moment things began to go wrong. The tea-lady bawled at the still unrecognised Princess Elizabeth that she had left her individual teapot behind. 'If you want it you must come and fetch it.' To pay for their tea and bread-and-butter like other children was a treat; but soon someone spotted their identity, a crowd gathered and their detective had to call a royal car to get them home in safety and segregation.

True, there were a few more attempts to see the outside world, from the top of a bus. This amounted to a mutual exchange. For just as Princess Elizabeth could look down into other people's gardens, so did other people gaze into the windows of 145 Piccadilly from the top-deck of buses circling Hyde Park Corner.

A rash of IRA bombs through letterboxes put a stop to even these mild jaunts. Crawfie and her 'little girls' returned to their games around the Byron statue and sooty bushes of Hamilton Gardens where by now they had got used to passers-by staring at them through the railings. The games Crawfie remembered were Red Indians, hop-scotch (in which the expert Duke sometimes joined them), hide-and-seek and 'horse fairs'. It was the horse and everything that he stood for that caused the most golden of all light to play on these years.

Everybody gave Princess Elizabeth toy horses. In the end she and her sister had over thirty, sometimes lined up outside the Piccadilly nursery, sometimes in the Royal Lodge garden. Unsaddling them for the night was as regular a duty for the Princesses as saying their prayers. At five Princess Elizabeth had begun riding lessons with Owen the groom at White Lodge. Owen was her first love. As the pair receded through the trees Miss Crawford would pick up the tail-end of professional talk: 'Burs . . . galls . . . girths. . . .' Elizabeth's father could not be jealous but he made them all laugh one day when he said in answer to her question about some horsey plan, 'Don't ask me, ask Owen. Who am I to make suggestions?'

The Princesses were taken to one pantomime a year. Pantomimes were a chance for Princess Margaret to pick up new tunes. But it was the annual Horse Show at Olympia that Princess Elizabeth could not have borne to miss. She would get hold of Christmas catalogues and mark the books on horses. As a child, her favourite games all involved playing at horses. Either she and her cousin Margaret Elphinstone would prance together as a pair, drawing Princess Margaret in a cart; or Elizabeth would harness up Crawfie and drive her grocer's cart from customer to customer, delivering the goods. For horses could bring her into a workaday world, if only of the imagination. She decided to marry a farmer, because that seemed the one certain way of owning 'lots of cows, horses and dogs'.

Dogs were another essential part of her world, and 1933 was the year of the corgi. The Duke of York brought the first of a long line to 145 Piccadilly.

King George v celebrated his Silver Jubilee in 1935. His serious illness, eight years earlier, had taken the elasticity out of him, along with his quarter-deck manner, loud hoarse voice and thunderous rages. The Duchess, who had always been able to manage him in any mood, was saddened by this change. Now only what he considered exceptionally idiotic behaviour would provoke an outburst. A remark by Sir Stafford Cripps MP for instance. This legal star was one of the three survivors of the 1931 Labour government, the other two being C. R. Attlee and George Lansbury. Cripps was an ultra-montane socialist. He told the Labour students of Nottingham University on 6 January 1934:

> When the Labour Party comes to power we must act rapidly and it will be necessary to deal with the House of Lords and the influence of the City of London. There is no doubt that we shall have to overcome opposition from Buckingham Palace and other places as well.[14]

What other places did he mean? The Inns of Court or Chatsworth or even 145 Piccadilly? When pressed by reporters he said he was 'most certainly not referring to the Crown'. He had used the words Buckingham Palace as 'a well-known expression' to cover 'Court circles' and the officials who advised the Monarch.

In the King's eyes this only made matters worse. 'What does he mean by saying that Buckingham Palace is not me? Who else is there I should like to know. Does he mean the Footman?'[15] A few days later Cripps added, 'I am in favour of a constitutional monarchy . . . in this country we must either have a monarch or a political president and I vastly prefer a constitutional monarch to a political president.'

This episode reflects from afar on the story of Queen Elizabeth II. Cripps was clearly sincere in his disclaimer of any animus against the monarchy. Nevertheless, his original speech and the gloss put upon it are examples of a now familiar ploy: 'Don't blame the sovereign; blame the court.' Elizabeth II was to find this undercover technique still in operation; until in 1982 an extremist named Pat Wall openly nailed his colours to a piratical mast and offered to sink without trace the sovereign, court, peers, generals, judges, Uncle Joe Gormley and all.

Meanwhile the first royal Silver Jubilee of the century was celebrated on Monday, 6 May 1935. There was a Thanksgiving Service at St Paul's Cathedral. On the way there diarist Chips Channon picked out the Yorks' 'two tiny pink children'. They were dressed exactly alike down to their pink strap shoes, except that Princess Margaret wore a flowery pink bonnet and Princess Elizabeth a flowery pink hat. Inside the Cathedral they sat behind their grandparents, their faces buried in their Order of Service – at least that is how they are represented in the contemporary portrait of the ceremony. The words of the anthem were from Cecil Spring-Rice's poem, 'I vow to thee my country'. Elizabeth was to hear it again as a hymn at her mother's eightieth birthday Thanksgiving and her eldest son's wedding.

The crowds in the streets between the Palace and the Cathedral were overwhelming in their loyalty to King George and Queen Mary. How different had been the reactions of the young Vera Brittain – child of a prosperous middle-class family – to a drive by Queen Mary in 1913:

The whole party looked very supercilious. . . . How thankful I am that I don't belong to that class of society; if I am to have any distinction, I want it to be that of intellect & talent – so far, far more worth having than the pomp & circumstance that comes from being the possessor of wealth or the product of generations of intermarriage. Expensive lunatics that are kept in motors & stables by an industrious nation's toil![16]

The youthful genius showed her own share of pomposity and superciliousness.

Two days after the Thanksgiving Service, the King's cousin Princess Marie-Louise asked him how he was going to spend that afternoon. 'I am driving to the little streets,' he replied in a voice full of unexpected emotion, 'the small mean streets, to be among my people and to thank them.' Gradually it dawned on him that all these people, milling in the streets or around the Palace in the sweltering heat, had come to see him personally. 'I am beginning to think', he said to his resident hospital nurse, 'they must really like me for myself.'[17]

There is a world of history in that sentence. During those last years before the Second World War, a modest and diffident sovereign could still feel that the royal office was everything, himself nothing. In his eyes, no one could fail to love and honour the crown, whereas it was a rare moment indeed, and one to be greatly treasured, when the people showed that they not only respected the crown but liked the human being who wore it. Fifty years later the position was to be reversed. No one doubts that Queen Elizabeth II is 'really liked' for herself. It is in fact the respect and affection in which she personally is held that upholds and underwrites the validity of the crown.

Mourning followed quickly on jubilation. King George V was a creature of habit, and on 3 December 1935 one of his favourite habits – a daily talk on the telephone with his sister Princess Victoria – was broken by her death. 'How I shall miss her,' the King wrote in his diary. But he was not to miss her for long. He tried bravely to keep up the Sandringham habit of Christmas festivities, while feeling more and more 'rotten'. On the morning of 20 January 1936 he signed his last state document with a quavering G.R. 'The King's life is moving peacefully to its close,' announced the radio at intervals during the evening. He died at five minutes to twelve.

The first stage of his elder granddaughter's youth (one

decade) had moved to its close at the same moment.

According to 'nursery' and 'schoolroom' opinion at 145 Piccadilly, Princess Elizabeth was too young to attend any of her grandfather's obsequies. She had indeed given some small signs of anxiety by suddenly stopping short in the middle of grooming her toy horse to ask, 'Ought we to play?' No child was ever more conscientious or bent on doing the right thing. Nevertheless, on this occasion the schoolroom advice went unheeded and Princess Elizabeth was taken by her parents to the lying-in-state at Westminster Hall. She showed by her characteristically sensible behaviour that at nine and three-quarters she was as capable as any other child of reacting appropriately to a solemn occasion. Her twelve-year-old cousin George Harewood was taken to the funeral at St George's Chapel, Windsor, and was seized with alarm, as he bowed to the coffin in the vault, that he might overbalance and tumble in.[18]

Dressed in a black coat and beret, Princess Elizabeth held the hand of a lady in a deep black veil whose face she could not see – her mother – and noted how still and silent everyone stood around the catafalque, as if they did not want to wake up her Grandpapa.

Her father had once made a speech at the Guildhall called 'Wake up England'. England must now wake up from the very last of its Edwardian dreams into a time of tempestuous realities.

A telling phrase has been used both by A. J. P. Taylor and Robert Lacey to explain George v's popularity during his last years: he possessed 'the majesty of the ordinary man'. Born more than thirty years before the beginning of a century that was later to be called 'the era of the common man', George v was indeed honoured by these words, with their subtle two-way tribute. For his ordinariness had brought him the majesty inherent in every human being; while at the same time his majesty had conferred honour on ordinariness. Only a monarch who was supremely unassuming and recognised his own ordinariness could dare to claim such praise.

A great deal could be written about ordinariness. To call a person ordinary in certain circumstances may be a compliment, but it is usually double-edged. A strong whiff of irony lurks about it, as in the passage from Rakitin's bitter last speech in Turgenev's *A Month in the Country*, which the Russian censor deleted:

Believe me . . . only the ordinary is natural and healthy; only the utterly commonplace . . . only the commonplace is worthy of respect, and woe unto him who dares break the sacred laws of everyday life.

How far is royalty meant to express those mundane 'laws of everyday life', and how far to transcend them by the delights of pageantry or the inner vision that a sense of vocation gives?

The King's ordinariness did not go beyond a certain point. There was enough of the Victorian left in George v to make him picturesque. We see him out deer-stalking with Dr Cosmo Lang, a triple portrait that Landseer would have loved to paint: the King of England, the Prince of the Church and the Monarch of the Glen. All the virtues of the 'haves' belonged to King George v. He was neither greedy nor grand, but contented and modest. He saw no reason for change in general, which could be disruptive. His rages, that might have seemed extraordinary, were largely a post-naval roar.

On the whole his personal ordinariness could also be astute policy. While it is not necessary for a democratic monarch, who seeks to unite a commonwealth of nations, to represent the lowest common factor, yet it is best not to have too pungent a personal flavour.

His reign was in essence old-fashioned and had little to do with the spirit of a new era. The luxury that Princess Alice noticed in his court was no doubt 'a kind of *staid* luxury',[19] as she said, compared with the flamboyant luxury of his father. But it was still a long way from the *ersatz* luxury that a second world war would soon force on the

Royal Family. Changes there were during George v's reign, vast changes in the symbolism of the Monarch; but change was not the essence of the reign. It was not until George v's 'sweet little Lilibet' had been on the throne for some years that the phrase 'century of the common man' began to have meaning in the court.

Meanwhile the future Queen was to live through a new, brief reign whose essence was expected to be change.

The Year of Three Kings: 1936

Though nothing is unrepeatable, the arresting pattern of 1936 is unlikely to be repeated. For the first twenty days King George v reigned; for the last twenty days, give a few hours, George vi was king; and between this end and this beginning there were the 325 days of Edward viii. Edward's short reign, culminating in his abdication, has accumulated more atmosphere than any other recent royal story, and this is no accident. It has become a folk legend with a twist. For Prince Charming was indeed to marry Cinderella, but instead of his bringing her into his palace she took him into private life. Part of the overwhelming popularity of the Royal Wedding in 1981 was due to the Cinderella story at last being played the right way round.

Perhaps it was the failed-fairy-story aspect of the Abdication that accounts for its many 'psychic' accretions. Mr Baldwin's son recalled that his father had a sudden premonition of Mrs Simpson seven years before she happened. She herself records several *frissons* indicating disaster: one at a court ball, another when an orchid plant given to her by Edward failed at first to bloom. Yet another was the Maltese Cross that fell from the Imperial Crown into the gutter as King George's coffin, with the crown on top, was jolted and jerked to Westminster Hall. 'Christ, what's going to happen next?' exclaimed the new King in Robert Boothby's hearing. The Abdication was going to happen next, as the stars had already foretold! Needless to say,

neither Princess Elizabeth, nor Princess Margaret whose
birth had caused the prediction of something tremendous in
her seventh year, knew anything of these phenomena.

The Princesses were said by Miss Crawford to have
noticed one change in the world outside their ivory tower:
an unaccountable forgetfulness on the part of their
favourite visitor, Uncle David. He still promised them
treats but now often failed to deliver. But this was not so,
for the Princesses saw too little of him to notice any
difference.

Miss Crawford herself, a regular reader of the Court
Circular, did notice a new name at a dinner party in May
1936 given by the King: Mrs Ernest Simpson. The nursery
governess might have thought no more about it had not the
same 'name' turned up to tea at the Royal Lodge, about the
same time. The King brought round his new American
friend in his new American station-wagon, to show them
both off to the York family.

After the visitors had left, Princess Elizabeth was said by
Crawfie to have asked her, 'Who is she?' The question
cannot have been a simple one seeking information, for
introductions would naturally have been made and the
Princess at ten had an excellent memory for names. Miss
Crawford inferred that Princess Elizabeth, sensitive as
always to atmosphere, was suspicious of this 'she' who
monopolised Uncle David's attention. The key question
'Who is she?' was omitted from the British edition of *The
Little Princesses* but published in the American one. Princess Margaret says the question was never asked.

Mrs Simpson commented favourably on the marvellously blonde, brightly scrubbed, beautifully mannered Princesses and their huge jug of orange juice – a superior drink
in American eyes to the usual English milk or sweet
tea – but less favourably, despite her 'justly famous
charm', on their mother. 'I left with a distinct impression,'
wrote Mrs Simpson, 'that while the Duke of York was sold
on the American station-wagon, the Duchess was not sold
on David's other American interest.'[1]

There were no further references to Princess Elizabeth's awareness until she wrote 'Abdication Day' at the top of a sheet of paper. Nevertheless, a significant change in her curriculum was made, with the help of Queen Mary, almost certainly at this time and in the light of coming events.

Queen Mary probably knew as much of what was in the wind as anyone not directly involved. She had shared the apprehensions of her late husband. His most passionate expression of fear had been made to Blanche Lennox, wife of the Duke of Richmond's second son, and passed on to Lady Airlie, Queen Mary's lady-in-waiting: 'I pray to God that my eldest son will never marry and have children, and that nothing will come between Bertie and Lilibet and the throne.'[2] The King had also admitted to Dr Lang, the Archbishop of Canterbury, his 'great concern' over David's future.

After her husband's death Queen Mary became rather more concerned. For the royal stakes had been raised. Mrs Simpson's devoted admirer was now king and could offer her Buckingham Palace as well as Fort Belvedere. Lady Airlie particularly noticed a point made by Queen Mary which was to haunt the Royal Family in years to come: a sovereign could not be allowed the latitude of ordinary individuals. 'He is not responsible to himself alone.'[3] In that sentence, Queen Mary had signposted the most controversial issues of the Abdication. How far can a sovereign claim also to be an individual responsible in conscience to himself alone? And does a sovereign have 'a private life' or not? Each generation of a democratic dynasty may have to pose and answer such questions anew, for itself.

Suppose that King George V's wish were to be granted and nothing were to stand between his 'sweet little Lilibet' and the throne? The intellectual vein in Queen Mary told her that a simple healthy upbringing was inadequate for a princess who, even if she had not been born to be queen, should now be bred up for the crown. Quite apart from

Princess Elizabeth's possible inheritance, there is reason to
think that Queen Mary was not satisfied with the *nursery*
governess's attempts to become a *schoolroom* governess
and discussed the situation with the Duchess. Miss Crawford herself admits that at some point Queen Mary asked to
see the Princess's timetable. Chronology was not Miss
Crawford's strong suit. (She described Balmoral as an
'ancient' Scottish castle, though it was a fabric of Prince
Albert's design begun only in 1853.) But despite the con-
fused chronology it is likely that the educational changes
suggested by Queen Mary dated from 1936, when she
became fully aware of the possible crisis.

The children's grandmother found much room for improvement in their curriculum, particularly in the balance
of subjects. There was too much of the three Rs and too
little Bible-reading, poetry, geography and history. The
present Queen Elizabeth the Queen Mother can still remember her mother-in-law saying, 'How I wish I knew
more history, that I had been taught history properly.'
After consultation with the Duchess, Queen Mary sent a
written list of suggestions to Crawfie, through Lady Cynthia Colville, her talented lady-in-waiting. Learning poetry
by heart, said Queen Mary, was 'wonderful memory-
training', and history would be valuable in relation to
'Princess Elizabeth's future career'. (This 'career' reference provides further evidence that the reformed timetable
was directly related to Princess Elizabeth's likely change in
status.)

'Of course, old-fashioned Geography was hopelessly out
of date,' continued Queen Mary. 'But for them, all the
same, a rather detailed knowledge of physical Geography
might be valuable, and also of the Dominions and India.'[4]

Queen Mary's final thought was for 'genealogies, historical and dynastic', which were very interesting to all children, 'and for these children, really important'. One is
reminded of Baroness Lehzen, Princess Victoria's first
governess, breaking to her the significance of her birth by
laying before her *Howlett's Tables* of the kings and queens

of England. The Princess, who had hitherto not always attended to her lessons, now made her famous resolution, 'I will be good.' Princess Elizabeth, though, did not need to turn over a new leaf.

Queen Mary, considering a princess's education just over a century later, may also have wondered about the actual time spent on intellectual pursuits. But probably she discussed it only with the Duchess, for a shortening of the Princess's 'break', 'rest-time' and 'exercise' would have brought the schoolroom up against the nursery.

Miss Crawford's account implies that Queen Mary was working with the governess against the children's mother. This was quite untrue. The Duchess's daughters both remember their mother saying what an ideal mother-in-law Queen Mary was, never interfering. At the time of her authorship, Miss Crawford bore a grudge against Queen Elizabeth for not appointing her as her own lady-in-waiting, or Princess Elizabeth's, or Princess Margaret's, in that order.

Even in the stepped up schedule, school 'work' occupied only one and a half hours per day (9.30 to 11.00) followed by an hour's break, then lunch, another hour's rest and reading, and afternoons devoted to singing, music, drawing, walks or dancing. Miss Betty Vacani of the celebrated Vacani School of Dancing was invited by the Duchess to teach her daughters. Their French governess, when privileged to watch them, went into loyal ecstasies: 'Margaret Rose may be quick-silver but Elizabeth is pure gold.'[5]

This timetable gave a total of seven and a half hours a week for school lessons, not counting one and a half hours' 'résumé' of the week's work at the Royal Lodge on Saturdays. It was too little for a girl with an active mind and at the age when the ability to learn is most pronounced.

Another of Queen Mary's family contributions may also belong to this period. At a concert, Queen Mary, having noticed that Lilibet was restless, suggested her going home. 'Oh no, Granny, we can't leave before the end. Think of all the people who'll be waiting to see us outside.'[6] Queen

Mary promptly ordered a lady-in-waiting to take her grand-daughter home in a cab. She wanted no film stars in the family, with a film star's concern for 'my public'.

Several years earlier Queen Mary had made another rigorous contribution to her granddaughter's upbringing. 'Good morning, little lady,' the Lord Chamberlain had said on meeting Lilibet in a palace corridor. 'I'm not a little lady,' she corrected him, 'I'm Princess Elizabeth.' Later that morning came a knock on his door and Queen Mary, with Lilibet in tow, announced: 'This is *Princess* Elizabeth, who hopes one day to be a *lady*.'

All the same, it would not have been easy for a girl less conscientious than Lilibet to work out such a fine yet real distinction. When is publicity that of a queen? When that of a film star? By the time she was grown-up she knew.

To do Miss Crawford justice as a nursery governess, she excelled in the teaching of history. Princess Margaret remembers her as 'highly dramatic'; she made everything sound so exciting that one waited breathless for the next instalment. Crawfie's possession of dramatic talent is confirmed by a lady who later came to speak French with the Princesses. 'Crawfie had an excitable manner; often she was quite theatrical.'[7]

In a teacher of history to young children theatricality was undoubtedly a gift, and laid the foundations of a permanent enthusiasm in the Princesses. Elizabeth's elderly cousin Princess Marie-Louise once apologised for boring her with too long an historical disquisition. 'But Cousin Louie,' protested the teenage Princess, '*history* is so thrilling.'[8]

One of the functions of the old royal aunts and cousins was to live out the fascinating continuity of history before the eyes of the younger generations. At Kensington Palace, irreverently known as the 'Aunt Heap', Princess Alice was to spend years in close contact with the Snowdon children. She liked to talk to them whenever she met them outside her apartments. One day after they had said, 'Good-morning, Aunt Alice,' their great-great aunt returned the greeting with an historical anecdote: 'Now, children, I'm going to tell you something I want you to remember. When I was a girl I used to know an old lady who had danced as a girl at the Waterloo Ball. That connects you children,' went on Princess Alice, 'with something that happened in 1815.'

The amount of history that Princess Elizabeth and Princess Margaret would absorb almost unconsciously, living as they did among people and places each with a tale to tell, was considerable. Miss Crawford remembered Lilibet meeting Ramsay MacDonald at 145 Piccadilly. The young Princess, hoping to emulate her mother's social graces, said eagerly, 'I saw you in *Punch* this morning, Mr MacDonald, leading a flock of geese.' 'The Boneless Wonder', as Churchill called MacDonald, returned a wan smile.

Punch and the *Children's Newspaper* were the two journals that Miss Crawford specifically mentions as being consumed in the schoolroom. Thousands of British children were enjoying the same diet during this period. It looked as if the Princesses' education would steadily progress along lines as normal as possible in their special circumstances. Unfortunately the Abdication was to result in disruption of a royal schoolroom which Crawfie described as 'never entirely conventional'.

It is probable that by October the Duchess of York knew as much about the King's infatuation as Queen Mary herself. Indeed she had helped her mother-in-law to move from Buckingham Palace into her new home, Marlborough House, and it is inconceivable that these two devoted women did not discuss the progress of the royal secret. Each piece of news made it seem more likely that someone would sooner or later reveal it to the public, for the King was touchingly indiscreet – such was his love – and, although the British press kept silent, a mail-order newssheet, such as Claud Cockburn's *The Week*, could be relied on to speak out; while the American and continental press were already providing a rich feast of sensations.

In August there had been a notorious cruise along the Dalmatian coast on the yacht *Nahlin*, when the presence of

Mrs Simpson on board caused the King to indulge a holiday mood, strip to his shorts and finally stand on his head. This piece of deck gamesmanship was curiously symbolic. For the King of England, constitutionally bound as he was to focus the unity of his people, was about to become a major source of division.

September brought no better news. The King went to Balmoral, at first to Queen Mary's delight. She hoped it would re-establish 'the habit and customs of the family'.[9] Would 'custom and ceremony' be born again? It was not possible, for Mrs Simpson was to be his guest.

This guest tried to introduce American three-decker toasted sandwiches into a way of life that was as changeless as the seasons themselves: the biscuits served for Queen Victoria's tea, for example, were found by a lady-in-waiting, who had left to get married and returned years later, to be identical in kind, number and arrangement on the plate as they had been before her departure; King George VI was to order grouse every day for dinner in season, while his father-in-law Lord Strathmore never missed plum pudding for lunch.

Whatever pangs the Duchess herself suffered, she let no shadow darken her daughters' holiday. This was still their 'golden age'. It had always been the older Elizabeth's philosophy not to meet misfortune halfway. Moreover, in the last resort neither the Duke nor Duchess could visualise the King actually doing the thing that people more and more hinted at. So the Princesses continued to enjoy their little Scottish paradise at Birkhall – an evocative house, built in 1715, equipped with oil lamps and stoves, no central heating, plenty of Landseers and Spy cartoons of past statesmen. Miss Crawford found these pictures a useful visual aid to history lessons. She noted that Birkhall was the only place at this date where she could teach her pupils their lessons without fear of interruption. Their schoolroom at 145 Piccadilly was a small boudoir next to the Duchess's own room. If the Princesses wanted to go out to tea or lunch, for games or a treasure-hunt, they would go to their neighbours the Hardinges, not to Balmoral.[10]

October ended worse than September. Alec Hardinge, the King's principle private secretary and the Yorks' old friend (Lady Elizabeth Bowes-Lyon had been a bridesmaid to Hardinge's sister Diamond, named after Queen Victoria's Jubilee), called at 145 Piccadilly with the serious news that on the 27th Mrs Simpson had brought successful divorce proceedings against her husband Ernest. He would be the second husband she had divorced. In six months' time, after the decree *nisi* had been made absolute, she would be free to marry a third time.

Just after two weeks later, on 13 November, Hardinge sent a forthright but respectful letter to his royal master drawing his attention to the impasse he had reached – an impasse out of which he, the King, could never escape by his own efforts. Only 'she' could get him out. By going away, Hardinge's letter might as well have been sent direct to the Dead Letter Office. It was never so much as alluded to by the King. Not long afterwards, Walter Monckton replaced Alec Hardinge as King Edward's main adviser.

Meanwhile Edward VIII's utter absorption in his private life was causing his royal prerogative to slip unnoticed from his grasp. It was his right to be informed by his ministers of all that went on, particularly in the foreign field where Hitler had dominated the scene for three years. But Stanley Baldwin, MacDonald's successor as prime minister, had heard stories of royal despatch boxes being left open at The Fort. Gradually top secret documents tended to be omitted from the boxes. A vicious circle developed. As his papers became more boring and his private affairs more pressing, Edward took less and less interest in his documents of state. Years later, in an interview with an American magazine, he was emphatically to deny the old reports that he had not really wanted the crown. 'For a year as king,' he said, 'I worked as hard and selflessly as I knew how.'[11] If that was so, Edward VIII never understood the meaning of 'work' in the same sense as his brother or his niece.

Nevertheless, there was still a sphere where Edward's emotional but undisciplined nature was seen at its warm human best. 'Something ought to be done. . . . Something will be done,' he repeated with deep feeling after a painful visit to the unemployed in South Wales on 25 November. (The press telescoped these two sentences into the more famous, 'Something *must* be done.') This was the compassionate Monarch, the aware, concerned Monarch that his many admirers had been confidently looking for.

Yet even here his *coup* backfired. The miners showed irritation at the royal interference in politics, though it was exerted on their behalf. Thus by the beginning of December this well-meaning but constitutionally uneducated Monarch had managed to tangle the royal prerogative in two opposite senses. One, by not even noticing that his rights were being eroded by Baldwin. The other, by himself marginally exceeding them.

Ironically, it was the King's most solemn and moving prerogative – his right to be crowned in the sight of his people – that indirectly precipitated the disaster. The Coronation, scheduled for 12 May 1937, had caught the imagination of the Church, and Bishop Blunt of Bradford gave an address on 1 December, in which he stressed the King's special need for God's grace at a time like his crowning. When the Bishop wrote his speech he knew nothing of Mrs Simpson, though when he delivered it he knew something. But the editor of the *Yorkshire Post* knew a great deal; so much, indeed, that he assumed Dr Blunt must be referring to the Simpson affair, rather than to the King's slackness over churchgoing, as was the case. Not wishing to be scooped, the editor published Blunt's speech in full next day. This was the first pebble to disturb the still pond of press silence. On 3 December the *Yorkshire Post* followed it up with a lapidary article. Hours later a hail of poster headlines from all over the country were suddenly drumming on the minds of British citizens.

There followed over a week of anguish for the Duke and Duchess of York, of which their daughters officially knew nothing, though with her sensitivity to domestic climate the older Princess felt that something was wrong. The 'something', however, could be put down to her mother being laid up in bed with influenza, while Papa, looking distracted, had to leave her for hours on end while making a round of visits to Marlborough House and The Fort.

Swimming lessons for the Princesses at the Bath Club tided them over this uneasy period. Such an adventure it all was: choosing swimsuits, seeing so many new children at the baths, plunging into the dangerous green water with Miss Daly to instruct and Mummy and Papa to applaud. 'I don't know how they do it,' the Duke would say. 'We were always so terribly shy and selfconscious. These two don't seem to care.'

Of 'these two', it was Lilibet who naturally took the lead. She would consistently act the same part towards her six-year-old sister as she saw her parents performing in relation to herself. One's duty was to be both encouraging and protective. 'Keep steady, Margaret,' she would say as Margaret first practised her strokes on a bench. 'You look like an aeroplane about to conk out.' When Margaret still clung to the steps, 'Don't be a limpet,' her sister called from the water.[12]

A studio portrait of that period by Marcus Adams well illustrated the sisters' closeness. A somewhat wistful Princess Elizabeth sits gracefully with slim legs neatly crossed, while Princess Margaret, with a mischievous expression, sticks her legs out in front of her. A sisterly arm is round her shoulders. The arm may have been placed there by the photographer, but it is nevertheless symbolic. So much concern might be jarring in a ten-year-old, but it has to be remembered, first, that the little Princesses' contemporaries, from Crawfie upwards, have dusted their memories in sugar. Second, that a future queen cannot have too much genuine concern.

The principle actors in the Abdication drama were seen but not heard by the top floor at 145 Piccadilly, as they entered and left the house. Tubby Mr Baldwin was the 'action man' of the affair, but Princess Elizabeth did not converse with him as she had with MacDonald the year before, although he was often featured in *Punch*. This December he was not shown leading Geese like Mac-Donald, but putting 'The Choice' to a king who looked no more than a schoolboy, as he gazed obstinately out of the window. 'All the peoples of your Empire, sir,' says the Prime Minister, hand on heart, 'sympathize with you most deeply; but they all know – as you yourself must – that the Throne is greater than the man.' But not than the woman. The Instrument of Abdication, occupying the centre of the *Punch* cartoon, is laid out on the table between the Prime Minister and King.

Of course all the Prime Minister's pleadings were to fail. Edward would not give up Mrs Simpson, while Britain and the dominions would not give up their preconceived ideas of a suitable queen. These ideas did not preclude a commoner or an American; they did exclude a woman who would soon have been married three times and whose three husbands would all be living. Despite her charm, wit, chic and brains, you only had to think of Wallis Warfield Simpson in certain royal roles to see the absurdity. 'Queen Consort, Empress of India', for instance. It just did not fit. Perhaps the title of 'Queen-Empress' was itself absurd, outdated – indeed within twelve years it was to disappear – but in 1936 the effects which the Second World War would have on the lingering Empire were still unsuspected.

The Bishop of Bradford's address was soon being called mockingly 'a *blunt* instrument', but it was the Instrument of Abdication itself that had the monopoly of bluntness. No method, however subtle, however bold, had been found of parrying its devastating blows.

Subtlety was in the suggestion that a way out for Edward and Mrs Simpson might be found through a morganatic marriage, though it was purely a continental device for preserving the blue blood required by the *Almanac de Gotha*. Under this dispensation Mrs Simpson would have become the King's wife but not his queen; as neat a way as any of putting a slur on her. The dominions turned it down after Baldwin had disregarded the royal prerogative by himself putting the question to the dominion prime ministers. In fact he should have allowed Edward VIII to put it directly to each dominion of which he was separately the King. The Statute of Westminster had given the Monarch this privilege. (On the other hand, without the Statute of Westminster, the dominions need not have been consulted.) In any case, Anthony Eden assures us that Baldwin's question on the morganatic marriage was drafted with such 'scrupulous impartiality' that no one could have told what answer he personally desired.

If subtlety was in the scheme for a morganatic marriage, boldness was in the plan launched by press lords like Beaverbrook and romantics like Churchill: to fight (and 'bugger Baldwin' as Beaverbrook said) with a King's party. This would have been a case of the Monarch entering politics up to the neck, and Edward VIII, seeing the dangers, forbade the campaign. 'Our cock won't fight,' lamented Beaverbrook.[13] He was right about the King. For apart from the special case of Mrs Simpson, Edward VIII agreed with *Punch* that 'The Throne is greater than the man.'

The royal assent was given to the Act of Abdication at 1.52 pm on Thursday 10 December. That afternoon Princess Elizabeth was puzzled by the bustle outside her front door; crowds collecting, noisy cheering crowds. Who were they? What was it all about? At last she went down and asked a footman. From him she learnt for the first time that Uncle David had abdicated and Papa was King. Up the stairs she flew to tell Margaret the news.

'Does that mean that you will have to be the next queen?' asked the younger sister.

'Yes, some day,' replied Lilibet.

'Poor you,' said Margaret.

Princess Margaret thus showed at this early age that the one position she never wanted, even from the beginning, was that of monarch. In later years, however numerous and severe might be the difficulties that beset her, she was not to forget that she had been spared one thing. Many is the gloomy morning when she has woken up with the thankfulness of a younger sister: 'At least I've not got to cope with *that*.'

As for her elder sister, she was the only one of the family quartet who gave no sign of thinking in terms of strain. Her parents were struck down with the sudden misery of their unsought, unwanted eminence. The new King especially suffered from shock: the Queen, hardly recovered from days of influenza, said faintly but bravely, 'We must take what is coming to us, and make the best of it.' The best was coming.

To a more robust Princess Elizabeth, the sight of an envelope lying on the hall table addressed to HM The Queen was not unexciting. She said with emphasis, 'That's *Mummy* now, isn't it?'[14] Then she decided to write up her notes on the last swimming lesson. Picking up a sheet of paper she wrote first at the top of the page in the strong hand her grandfather had insisted upon, 'Abdication Day'.

This striking first response by the Princess happened to reflect the majority mood in the country. Of course there was much individual regret for the loss of a potentially great king. 'I thought we were going to have such a king as never was,' said a railwayman on Abdication Day, '– and now.'[15] But after the nine or ten days of excitement sometimes rising to hysteria, there was an apparently painless return to normal. The surprising follow-up was in fact an act of national will on behalf of the monarchy. It was made possible partly by the steadfastness of the new King and Queen themselves, partly by the welter of confusion and contradiction into which the whole Abdication crisis had finally collapsed.

A band of communists and another of opposing blackshirts, for instance, had both supported a 'King's party'. It was even suggested that Edward VIII might fight and beat Baldwin at an election standing as Sir Edward Windsor;

alternatively, that Queen Mary might become regent for Princess Elizabeth. Politicians of totally opposite allegiances like C. R. Attlee, leader of the Labour Party, and Lord Beaverbrook agreed in believing that the 'prestige of the monarchy' had been so damaged that the whole system 'trembled' on the verge of extinction. Meanwhile the man and the woman in the street, for whom they claimed to speak and write, cheerfully got out the remains of their 1911 bunting and prepared to buy some new; all they wanted was a king and a queen, and now again they had both. It seemed that Anthony Eden, a member of Baldwin's government, was right when he said that the crown had not been 'shaken'. But there was Hugh Dalton, a future Chancellor of the Exchequer, who believed that the 'almost mystic halo' of George v was 'badly cracked'.

There were further disagreements. No one knew precisely what Edward viii had really stood for. Was he a genuine moderniser' or merely a self-indulgent young man who mistakenly believed that a king's private life could be separated from his public duties? He had told Walter Monckton in 1935: 'He would be available for public business but his private life would be his own.'[16] There was not a backbench MP who would dare to claim such a dichotomy and get away with it.

Put another way, was not Edward a mere tinkerer with aspects of the monarchy that happened to irritate him such as court protocol? Sir Samuel Hoare remembered the King's irritation with him on that subject. 'You are out of date,' the King had said, 'you know nothing of the modern world.' Long afterwards in a television interview with Kenneth Harris, the King, now Duke of Windsor, gravely attempted but signally failed to clear up this question: 'Did you want to be a reforming king?' Harris asked. 'No, I wanted to be an up-to-date king.'

Those who had themselves been divorced and happily remarried, like Walter Monckton, tended to take a lenient view of royal divorce in a 'modern' age. Walter Bagehot would have agreed with them. We have no right, Bagehot said, to expect the Monarch to be 'Head of our Morality'; Queen Victoria may have set a good example, but look at George IV.

Yet in Baldwin's masterly speech of 10 December 1936, he recounted to a spellbound House how he had once argued the question of royal divorce with Edward VIII, in a sense contrary to the King and indeed to Bagehot also. The crown, Baldwin had said, might have lost many ancient prerogatives but it had retained something far more important – its 'integrity'.[17] ('Integrity' was a Baldwinesque word for Bagehot's 'morality'.)

Even the King's famous Abdication broadcast about not being able to reign without 'the woman I love' provoked contradictory responses. Some thought it fit only for the 'glossies'; others were deeply moved. Lady Hardinge, herself in tears, noticed that all those around her in St James's Palace were calling it 'very vulgar'.[18]

The confusions in Britain* were strangely paralleled in the United States. Naturally those Americans who had congratulated both the Duke of York and Edward VIII on 'selecting a lady of the people' were insulted when it was the Duke of York's Scots lady, not the American lady, who became queen. On the other hand Lady Londonderry, a passionate supporter of Edward VIII, believed that her hero had been undermined from the start by enemies in the States. 'Personally I cannot but feel the whole thing,' she wrote to Mrs Simpson, 'has been organized from America, with the set purpose of doing "him" harm. . . .'

In New York, the young criticised Edward VIII for 'throwing in his mitt';[19] but the middle-aged, seeing his words of renunciation die away on a teleprinter – 'I take my leave . . . Edward. RI' – had tears in their eyes, as if those last letters had been RIP.

---

* The confusions seem at first to have affected Princess Elizabeth herself. In answer to one of her sister's questions she said: 'I think Uncle David wants to marry Mrs Baldwin, and Mr Baldwin doesn't like it.' (Godfrey Talbot, Radio Programme, 1983.)

Bred to be Queen:
1937–9

The former Princess Elizabeth of York had now become heir presumptive to the throne. Whether she ever thought nostalgically of her York title is not known, but her six-year-old sister exclaimed at the change with comical despair, 'I used to be Margaret Rose of York and now I'm nothing.' The status of heir presumptive rather than heir apparent would remain with Princess Elizabeth for the rest of her father the King's life.

Legally there was always a chance that George VI might become the father of a male heir, and we are told on sentimental authority that Princess Elizabeth used to pray for God to send her 'a little brother' – in much the same spirit that Princess Victoria wished for her aunt Queen Adelaide to produce a living heir to William IV. The legal possibilities of supersession did not bite deep into Victoria's or Elizabeth's childhood.

The full meaning of heir presumptive would come home to Princess Elizabeth at the Coronation, five months later, when 'British phlegm' co-operated in a smooth, almost imperceptible transference of the crown from one head to another. Shakespeare had taught the British that it was possible to serve up funeral meats at a bridal feast. Now they were to transform all the projected coronation festivities – the flags, the loyal mementoes, the inspiration of the coronation service – direct from King Edward VIII to King

George VI. Even the day did not need changing: 'Same date – new king'.

The Princesses were encouraged to look forward not backward. Not a word more was said about the Abdication. It was never so much as mentioned at Buckingham Palace, to which they now moved with their parents. Nor was it ever discussed in front of the Lascelles children. 'My parents never talked about it when I was present,' writes Lord Harewood. Indeed it was to be a two-way silence. For the former Edward VIII, now HRH the Duke of Windsor, was soon saying to his wife apropos of arguments about the Abdication: 'If we keep this up we are never going to agree, so let's drop it for good.'[1]

If the Princesses' thoughts went back at all, it was to a distant past in which irregularities were smoothed over and forgotten. Queen Mary unearthed for them one of the thirty-foot panoramas of state occasions that were popular in the nineteenth century. This one represented the Coronation of King George IV, who had behaved worse on the solemn occasion of his crowning than any monarch within memory, ogling the lady believed to be his mistress.

Preparations were made for the Princesses' parts in the ceremony in an atmosphere of seriousness for Elizabeth and emulation for Margaret, whose one aim was naturally to wear a velvet coronation train if Lilibet did. Her spirited 'me too-ism' was appreciated by her indulgent father, who decreed trains for two. After a brief protest Margaret accepted that her train must be a few inches shorter than Lilibet's since she herself was a few inches shorter.

For Princess Elizabeth there was solid reading to be done. Her father had given her a specially bound volume of the coronation service to study beforehand. This was the beginning of a famous father-daughter relationship in which the mantle of Elijah was gently made ready to fit the young shoulders of Elisha.

The royal diary habit is one that has gone on regularly since Queen Victoria's childhood. In June 1838, the month of her coronation, the nineteen-year-old Victoria was awakened at Buckingham Palace at 4 am by the guns in the park and kept awake by music and cheering until she arose at seven, 'feeling strong & well'. This she recorded on Coronation Day itself, and her diary is preserved at Windsor in the small notebook in which she wrote her journal.

There was even less sleep for the Royal Family at Buckingham Palace on the night before the Coronation of 1937. The wonders of science made it necessary to test the loudspeakers at three in the morning, effectively waking the King and Queen. From then on there was continuous noise. Princess Elizabeth's account is preserved at Windsor like her great-great-grandmother's; but Lilibet's is dedicated to her parents. (Victoria was not on speaking terms with her mother.)

The Coronation, 12 May 1937.

To Mummy and Papa. In Memory of Their Coronation, from Lilibet by Herself.

At 5 o'clock in the morning I was woken up by the band of the Royal Marines striking up just outside my window. I leapt out of bed and so did Bobo. We put on dressing-gowns and shoes and Bobo made me put on an eiderdown as it was so cold and we crouched in the window looking on to a cold, misty morning. There were already some people in the stands and all the time people were coming to them in a stream with occasional pauses in between. Every now and then we were hopping in and out of bed looking at the bands and the soldiers. At six o'clock Bobo got up and instead of getting up at my usual time I jumped out of bed at half past seven. When I was going to the bathroom I passed the lift as usual, and who should walk out but Miss Daly [the swimming teacher]! I was very pleased to see her. When I dressed I went into the nursery.

The most remarkable thing about this passage is surely its energy. Early accounts of Princess Elizabeth dwell so much on her passivity and obedience that it is startling to find that all the verbs here are active – leaping, hopping, jumping.

When they were both dressed the children ran down to their parents' room, where the close-knit family of four, all glittering and glistening, indulged in some mutual admiration. But there were no curtsies from the Princesses.* Curtsies were reserved for Queen Mary.

It was Queen Mary's aim to ease her second son into his new niche. She understood the traumas. As an old friend at the Palace once remarked: 'The King was splendid. Always very unsure of himself.' This was perhaps 'palace paradox' rather than 'palace sang-froid'. It did nevertheless bring out the unusual combination of perseverance and diffidence in George VI that made him so appealing. To bolster his position, his mother arranged for herself to be seen as often as possible with the new Royal Family. By going with them to the Coronation she established a precedent, a solidarity, the significance of which no one could miss. Hitherto a queen-dowager had not attended a young successor's coronation; any more than someone who had once been a sovereign came to the new king's crowning. The Duke of Windsor did indeed stay away.

The old Queen travelled in a glass coach to the Abbey and sat in the royal box next to Princess Elizabeth, with Princess Margaret beyond: 'They looked too sweet,' she wrote, 'in their lace dresses & robes, especially when they put on their coronets.'[2]

Princess Margaret behaved unexpectedly well, indeed so well that Lilibet's main anxiety of the day was allayed. 'I only had to nudge her once or twice, when she played with the Order of Service too loudly,' said Princess Elizabeth afterwards. But Margaret neither fell off her raised seat nor laughed aloud – unlike her father at King Edward VII's coronation. As Prince Bertie, also aged six, he had watched

* Crawfie says that she had taught them how to make sweeping obeisances to the King when he returned home on the first day of his reign; their father was moved but their mother saw at once that it would not do as a regular ritual. None of this was true.

an Order of Service suddenly slip from the fingers of one of 'the aunts', sail over the edge of their box and crash into a large golden vase on the Abbey floor beneath. Bertie and David had laughed and laughed.

The grown-up Bertie may have been thinking of this incident when he said in his coronation broadcast: 'Those of you who are children now will, I hope, retain memories of a day of carefree happiness such as I still have of my Grandfather's coronation.'

Elizabeth, one of the children most in his mind, had been old enough to appreciate the beauty of the pageantry. She thought the lovely white-gloved arms of the peeresses 'looked like swans' as they raised their coronets aloft at the crowning. (At her own coronation, Chips Channon chose the same 'swan' simile as Princess Elizabeth, while Cecil Beaton likened the peeresses' curving arms to 'wish-bones'.) After the long service was over, she allowed her sister to whisper to her as the two of them walked out of the Abbey behind their parents and in front of Queen Mary.

From the angle of Princess Elizabeth's future, the most important things in the coronation ceremony were not those that went wrong and would some day need changing; for instance, the front and back of the crown being almost indistinguishable, so that Archbishop Lang may have put it on the wrong way round; or the Queen's crown being so heavy it gave her a headache. The important things were those that had already been changed.

In Princess Elizabeth's 'special book' of the service given her by her father, he would have pointed out certain facts significant to the future of the Empire and Commonwealth. Whereas he would promise in Westminster Abbey to maintain the 'Protestant Reformed Religion' in Britain, in the dominions he would maintain their 'Gospel', of whatever communion it happened to be. This was to stress the Monarch's individual kingship of each independent country. Not only that, but in his Coronation Oath he was for the first time in the monarchy's history to mention each country separately by name.

Canada in particular was to play a prominent part, through its contribution of Royal Canadian Mounted Police to some of the ceremonies. At first the Lord Chamberlain's department had wondered whether this innovation was quite wise. Horses feared bears. Would not the smell of British bearskins frighten Canadian horses? 'Tell them not to worry,' came an unofficial reassurance from Ottawa: 'We feed the horses bearskins for breakfast every morning.'[3]

Stanley Baldwin resigned as prime minister a fortnight after the Coronation. Tired and discouraged, according to Lady Airlie, he projected his own despondency on to the new reign. George VI would have a great deal to contend with, he told Queen Mary's lady-in-waiting. 'There's a lot of prejudice against him. He's had no chance to capture the popular imagination as his brother did.'[4]

However, the Princesses had already brought as much charm and magnetism into the Royal Family as their Uncle David had taken out of it by going into exile. Their biographers have amused themselves (and us) by collecting lists of whimsical and serious ways in which the Princesses were kept before the public's eyes. There was Princess Elizabeth Land in Antarctica and Princess Elizabeth's face on six cent stamps in Newfoundland; nearer home she had given her name to chocolates, china and hospital wards; her wax effigy sitting on a pony had reached Madame Tussaud's; her portrait had hung in the Royal Academy, and her photograph had appeared on the front of *Time* magazine.

The Princesses themselves continued to enjoy the simple pleasures of an evening at home with their parents, particularly when the King and Queen could escape to Royal Lodge for a weekend. A tradition of do-it-yourself entertainments was already established that continued into the next generation: racing demon, rummy, parlour games that required above all quick-wittedness and no doubt would account for Queen Elizabeth II's pleasure in the naming of her horses; all kinds of acting especially charades and mimicry that were to help carry them through the war; sing-songs that would later shorten the long hours for the four of them, as they steamed in the royal train through South Africa. Princess Elizabeth had her *ITMA* (*It's That Man Again*) on the radio, as Prince Charles was to have his *Goon Show*.

Miss Crawford, though a mine of detailed information, was apt to give a misleading overall picture at times. Generally she erred in the direction of gloom. The change to Buckingham Palace, for instance. She seems to have been over-impressed by the children's first astonished reaction. 'What!' said Lilibet incredulously. 'Do you mean for ever?' asked Margaret. The children clung to their parents at the sight of the huge intimidating crowds gathered outside the Palace for their first entry. Crawfie quotes Lilibet's bright idea of digging an underground passage from the Palace to 145 Piccadilly as an example of her wish to escape from their new surroundings. The passage can just as well have been projected in a spirit of adventure, a wish to keep in touch with both houses. Because the nursery governess herself felt homesick for Scotland in the great house – 'it was going to be too much for me' – she gave the impression that it was too much for the Princesses also. This was not so.

They did not feel cut off from their parents. Racing full tilt down an echoing corridor was just as much fun as running down the spiral stairs of 145 Piccadilly and seemed no longer, since they were that much older and bigger. Princess Elizabeth's remark about the corridors – 'People here need bicycles' – meant that she liked bicycles not that she hated corridors. Indeed, Crawfie herself vividly described Lilibet's fascination with the world of bicycles outside the palace garden. 'One day I shall have a bicycle,'[5] said Lilibet dreamily as through the railings she saw a boy streak past. Princess Margaret has given the Palace high marks. 'Buckingham Palace is a very cosy house,' she said on *Desert Island Discs*. 'We were put into rooms which are nearly always the nursery, and the Queen's children have been brought up in the same apartment.'[6]

Again it was Crawfie herself who admitted that the Princesses had brought nothing but gaiety to their new home. People would say to her, 'It was as though the place had been dead for years, and had suddenly come alive.'[7] The hidden wildlife in the garden came to life too, when Princess Elizabeth fell into the lake while investigating a duck's nest.

Moreover, in Coronation year Queen Mary would conduct her granddaughters on cultural tours of London:* to the Tower, Bank, Royal Mint, and further afield to Hampton Court, Greenwich Palace and Kew. In her sense of urgency on Princess Elizabeth's behalf she would sometimes overdo the good work in respect to the seven-year-old Princess Margaret, who remembers:

> My grandmother would march on ahead, surrounded by whoever accompanied her on these expeditions, while we two would hurry along behind. I was absolutely exhausted by hours on end of walking and standing in museums and galleries.

Probably adding to the strain was the fact that during these years both the Princesses were in considerable awe of Queen Mary.

> When I grew up [continued Princess Margaret] I decided my children should never be allowed to see more than three great pictures at a time, so that they would actually plead for 'just one more', instead of dropping with fatigue and longing to go home.

Buckingham Palace also gave an opportunity for more games with other children. Not only did Miss Vacani continue her dancing classes for the Princesses in more spacious surroundings, but a company of thirty-four Girl Guides, with Brownies attached for the sake of Princess

---

* These tours had begun only in 1936 and not earlier, as Miss Crawford's chronology suggests (James Pope-Hennessy, *Queen Mary*, p. 586).

Margaret, was formed in the Palace. It was a mixed company, some of them being daughters of chauffeurs and other members of the palace staff. Crawfie has her readers' entire sympathy when she describes the first well-intentioned arrival of thirty-four 'little girls' in their party frocks accompanied by the whole paraphernalia of the nursery. The Princesses patiently explained about uniforms.

King George VI needed all the vitality and inspiration he could draw from his family, for the world outside was darkening. Hitler was a force in 1933 and by 1937 his ambitions were advancing inexorably over Europe. Events in England seemed to conspire in his favour. The Abdication crisis had distracted the British Government not only from domestic problems of poverty and unemployment, as Mr Attlee bitterly observed, but also from the foreign dangers of Nazism and Fascism. Eden had told the assistant editor of *The Times* that the 'Simpson case' was 'paralysing foreign policy', while Lady Tweedsmuir, wife of Canada's Governor-General (John Buchan, the novelist), had written to her husband, 'London is seething with excitement about Mrs S. War is never mentioned at all.'[8]

When British MPs said 'Churchill is finished' because of his disastrous espousal of Edward VIII's cause, Hitler overheard and was glad. As early as the evening of George V's death, Duff Cooper, like Churchill a sturdy opponent of the fascist dictators, had noticed how easily Hitler could be deceived about Britain's true intentions. Duff Cooper was dining with two Germans from Hitler's Foreign Office, when the bulletin on the King's approaching exile brought tears to his eyes. 'I fear,' he wrote afterwards, 'that my neighbours were noting them and would make a report to their Führer'[9] – on the softies who ruled Britain.

The Windsors themselves and some of their friends did nothing to ease George VI's political anxieties. Chips Channon, another well-known 'King's man' during Abdication year, visited Nazi Germany in August 1937 and wrote of

Marshal Göring, 'He really is a most disarming man.'[10] In the circumstances, 'disarming' was not quite the right word.

It was the Windsors' own visit to Hitler, however, also in August 1937, that gave rise to the most serious misunderstanding. In fact the Duke and Duchess disliked what they saw of the Nazis; but a published photograph of the pair smiling in the Führer's presence gave a different impression.

The Duke of Windsor's running battle over his wife's withheld title of 'Her Royal Highness' was another source of tension for his brother. The legal position was that the Duchess of Windsor had no automatic right to her husband's title. If she received it, it would have to be deliberately conferred on her by letters patent from the King himself. Her *not* being an HRH, however, was the only card the King held: his brother had vowed he would not return to England with Wallis unless she were created an HRH. But what if the King, together with his wife and his closest advisers, considered it inadvisable for the Windsors to be let loose on England again during those critical months? It was to the Royal Family's advantage that the Duchess's title should be withheld for the very reason that her husband insisted on it: it was the condition of their return from exile. To adapt the saying: *'Ce n'est pas magnifique mais c'est la guerre.'* As always, the unlucky Duke played *his* cards with a sad lack of skill.

Apart from the title, there were other royal matters to keep the King in a state of ferment. Money was the irritant that it so often is in family break-ups; particularly as, in this case, the Duke of Windsor conducted his arguments with the stricken and deeply embarrassed King by long-distance telephone. Eventually Walter Monckton intervened with his master the Duke to stop the calls. The King paid his brother £60,000 a year out of his Privy Purse, as well as buying for £1,000,000 the private royal estates that the Duke, as Edward VIII, had inherited from his father. These estates were Balmoral and Sandringham. They were to be beloved playgrounds for the growing Princesses.

With all these worries it was not surprising that an added untoward incident in 1938 should throw the King into one of his 'gnashes' – an expressive word for his violent rages invented by his household.

Anthony Eden, the Foreign Secretary, resigned because Neville Chamberlain, now Prime Minister, was consistently depriving him of information about negotiations with the dictators. Someone then forgot to tell the King that Eden had resigned. A tremendous 'gnash' resulted. And no doubt the King, after the 'gnash' had quickly subsided, as it always did, instructed his heir on the vital importance of information. Some day it would be her right as monarch 'to be consulted'. Queen Victoria had got Palmerston sacked for failure to enclose Foreign Office despatches in her red boxes.

The sands of peace were running out. It was late spring 1939 and only four more months of peace remained. Hitler had occupied the Rhineland in 1936 and marched with methodical brutality into Austria in 1938 and Czechoslovakia in March 1939, thus breaking his 'Munich Agreement' of 1938 with the unhappy Neville Chamberlain.

The Munich Agreement had not found favour with the twelve-year-old Lilibet. When she heard there would be no war she exclaimed, 'How disappointing!' Allah turned on her. 'Don't say that. You don't know what war is.' She then told the children about the casualties of the Great War.

The policy of appeasing the dictators was in ruins. Now it was time to rally those who might in a short while be joining in the struggle on Britain's side. Who better to send as ambassadors than the young King and Queen? Canada seemed the obvious Commonwealth country to visit. Australia, New Zealand or South Africa in the days before jet flights would have meant too extended a visit at such a time of world unrest. Some royal advisers felt that even a journey to Canada was too risky. But King George and Queen Elizabeth were adamant.

Queen Mary and the two Princesses accompanied them to Southampton to see them off. Margaret said, 'I have my handkerchief', and Lilibet explained, 'To wave not to cry.'[11] They sailed over the Atlantic to a Canadian triumph, followed up by a generous welcome in the United States.

As the first reigning 'King and Queen of Canada' to visit their realm, and also as the first monarchs to visit the lost lands of George III, their tour was unique. Edward VIII, when Prince of Wales, had of course visited Canada, the United States, South Africa and many other parts of the globe; but he was to find 'the programme was my master . . . much of the time I was like a man caught in a revolving door.'[12]

Would Their Majesties bring the children also? asked President Roosevelt. 'If you bring either or both . . . I shall try to have one or two Roosevelts of approximately the same age to play with them!'[13] But to have put all four members of the Royal Family into one ship (a ship which incidentally was for several days trapped by icebergs) would have been tempting Providence. So the Princesses were left behind, comforted by the many letters of sympathy they received from other children with absent parents. Princess Elizabeth, however, had a new source of interest to occupy her mind.

When Queen Elizabeth found she had a spare afternoon, as likely as not she would take her daughters to the National Gallery or somewhere else close by. (Crawfie always kept herself ready dressed for outings at short notice. 'One does not keep the Queen waiting.') It may have been after one of these visits that Queen Elizabeth decided to develop her elder daughter's knowledge of history – constitutional history. After consulting Sir Jasper Ridley,* she arranged that Lilibet should go for twice-weekly coaching to the Vice-

* Sir Jasper Ridley (1887–1951) was a younger son of the first Viscount Ridley, who was given a peerage after he had been Home Secretary in Lord Salisbury's Government. Sir Jasper was a trustee of the Tate Gallery. He also held an office in Queen Mary's Household.

Provost of Eton College, (Sir) Henry Marten. A delightful, balding, learned character with just the requisite degree of eccentricity but neatly turned out, Marten had soon stirred new enthusiasms in the young heir to the throne. It was from him that she learnt to love and respect Queen Victoria, whose vast experience enabled her to influence policy in a perfectly constitutional way; such as bringing her beloved India under the crown, and persuading Disraeli to make her Queen-Empress.

Thousands of schoolchildren, girls and boys, had learnt their history from Warner and Marten's *History of England*. But this was not the same thing as being instructed by the master himself. Marten kept lumps of sugar in his pocket, as though his first ever girl-pupil might turn out to be a pony. He munched them himself, though, between bites at his handkerchief. He never looked directly at the Princess but occasionally addressed her in the way he addressed the Eton boys, as 'Gentlemen'.

If Princess Elizabeth greatly respected the new man in her life, she was soon to meet another new man for whom respect would be a ludicrously weak word.

'How good he is, Crawfie! How high he can jump!' she whispered ecstatically to her governess, as her third cousin Prince Philip of Greece sailed over the tennis net in Admiral Dalrymple-Hamilton's garden at the Royal Naval College, Dartmouth. The King was taking his family aboard *Victoria and Albert* to visit Dartmouth and the scenes of his own youth.

Miss Crawford's distaste for what she regarded as bumptious youth brought the Princess's enthusiasm into even clearer focus. 'He was good looking though rather offhand in his manner,' wrote Miss Crawford, who was used to reverence for royalty rubbing off a little on herself also. 'At the tennis courts I thought he showed off a good deal, but the little girls were much impressed.'[14]

If the eighteen-year-old cadet was indeed showing off, at any rate he had much to show off about. A late entry at Dartmouth, he had been there only one year and in that time had won the King's Dirk for the best all-rounder and the Eardley-Howard-Crockett prize for the best cadet. The year before, he had left Gordonstoun, Kurt Hahn's school in north-west Scotland, where the high-minded refugee headmaster from Germany taught a smallish mixed bag of British boys to become philosopher-kings. A decade after Philip left Gordonstoun, Hahn was proved to have bred up, if not a philosopher-king, a philosopher-consort.

The concept of philosopher-kings – specially selected all-rounders who should be trained to lead their state in war and peace – was originally the idea of the Greek Plato rather than of the German Hahn. But Platonism and German scholarship had always gone well together, and the combination suited Philip of Greece, at least while young. (He was later to reject the idea of philosopher-kings – 'such processed paragons'[15] – because of its threat to individual liberty.) In his last year he had become the 'Guardian' of the school (head boy), captained the cricket team, excelled at the high jump and high dive, and had said of him by the headmaster: 'He has the greatest sense of service of all the boys in the school.'

For a year before Gordonstoun, Philip had been at its distasteful German counterpart where a superabundance of 'ghastly foot-slogging', Nazi-style, cancelled out the pleasure of its being on his sister Theodora's estate, Salem. The distaste he felt was not only the product of an independent and undragoonable spirit, but also of his having been brought up English – at least for long periods. His prep school was Cheam, selected for him by his mother's brother, George, Marquess of Milford Haven. In the holidays he would frequently stay with Uncle George and his family at their home, Lynden Manor, near Maidenhead on the River Thames, where his cousin David Milford Haven was Philip's contemporary and close friend. Philip and

David once hitched by Thames barge from Dover back to Lynden.

But it was the sea not rivers that turned out to be the magnet, perhaps under the direct influence of his Uncle George. Both George Milford Haven and George VI had manned a turret at the battle of Jutland, before either Philip or Elizabeth was born. Uncle George had died in 1938, the year Philip became a Dartmouth cadet. From then on, George's younger brother Lord Louis (Dickie) Mountbatten was responsible for Philip when in England. Uncle Dickie and his wife Aunt Edwina could always put up a bed for him in the sitting-room of their London home, 16 Chester Street, or invite him to Broadlands in Hampshire. In Buckinghamshire, too, there had always been a home for him with his first cousin Princess Marina of Kent.

Not that Philip was by any means orphaned, as this *curriculum vitae* might suggest. But his parents were in different ways victims of Greek revolutionary politics dating from 1922, the year after Philip was born on 10 June 1921.

His birthplace, the nineteenth-century royal palace of Mon Repos on the island of Corfu, today looks rather less attractive than the remains of the medieval castle above the harbour. But in those earlier days it had been considered an enchanting place, with its balconies, terraces and eucalyptus groves.

Prince Philip's father, Prince Andrew of Greece, and his mother, Prince Alice of Battenberg, already had a family of four daughters by the time Philip was born. And by the time Philip was ten all four girls had married into the German nobility. While at Gordonstoun he was given the tragic news that his sister Cécile and her children had been killed in a plane crash. His own life seemed at one moment destined to end in violence and tragedy before it had well begun. His father Prince Andrew, a serving officer in the Greek army, was made one of the scapegoats for his country's military disasters in Turkey. Thanks to the joint action by Princess Andrew, King George V and Captain

Buchanan-Wollaston RN of *Calypso*, Prince Andrew's sentence was commuted to banishment, and he and his wife were whisked off temporarily to England, having picked up the five children from Corfu on the way, Philip in a cot made from a fruit crate.

After Greece was barred to the family, Philip, his parents and sisters lived for a time in Paris, where he attended a boys' school in Saint-Cloud. He spoke English and French, as well as Greek with his parents, for their Greek patriotism was by no means skin-deep. Though Prince Andrew, condemned to perpetual exile, eventually was to settle in Mentone, where he died in 1944, Princess Andrew returned to Athens on later occasions, especially when it seemed possible to help those in distress. She was the granddaughter of Queen Victoria's second daughter Princess Alice of Hesse (Princess Andrew was born at Windsor) and had inherited her grandmother's passionate interest in nursing and mystical religion. She gradually became more interested in religion than marriage. Philip's parents drifted apart and his mother later became the grey-robed foundress of the Mary and Martha order of nuns. She was later to explain to Queen Elizabeth II that in Greece one needed to belong to an order to get charitable work going.

The young Philip was closer to his father's forthright, positive temperament; indeed he modelled his gaiety, sharp wit and quick repartee on the companionable talents of Prince Andrew, just as Prince Charles was to inherit his thrust and parry from Prince Philip.

A favourite introduction to Prince Philip in articles has always been to say that 'he has not a drop of Greek blood', a description that is not particularly helpful. It is not easy to identify 'drops of Greek blood' anywhere, what with centuries of Turks, Franks and other 'barbarians' (in the classical Greek sense) overrunning Plato's country. Nevertheless, go back something over a hundred years, and the first modern king of Greece is found to be a prince of Denmark – William of Denmark who was set up by the European powers as George I of Greece. Prince William himself belonged to the German family of Schleswig-Holstein-Sonderburg-Glucksburg.

That Philip of Greece is a Dane seems to be emphasised by his stalwart height, Norseman's blue eyes and over-adjectived fair hair. His hair in babyhood has been described as 'snow-blond' and 'lint-fair', in childhood 'ash' or 'flaxen', in youth 'golden' with 'red lights', in young manhood 'corn-coloured'. When the thirteen-year-old Princess set eyes on him for the first time, at least to her knowledge, he must have been in the 'corn-coloured' stage. (He may have looked at her with the cool detachment of a thirteen-year-old schoolboy, when she stood in the aisle as a bridesmaid at the wedding of Princess Marina and the Duke of Kent in 1934.) It is not certain, though, that she did fall in love with this 'genial giant' (another popular description) at first sight, for a rival story to Crawfie's records the Princess asking, 'When are we going home?'[16]

According to this account, the Princesses' visit to Dartmouth was a washout. The college was in quarantine for mumps, so that the Princesses could not explore their father's early haunts, but had to be content with the entertainment provided by one cadet – their cousin Philip – in the form of croquet in the garden and trains on the nursery floor. Margaret remembers that she was proud at being invited to join in the croquet.

Why could not Philip give Lilibet a game of tennis instead of just jumping the net himself? Tennis was not her game. Despite King George VI's early prowess, the Royal Family do not seem to have used the excellent tennis court at Buckingham Palace; probably because the strong Strathmore tradition was for open country pursuits such as stalking, fishing and the pleasures of fields and gardens, rather than organised games.

Whether or not Princess Elizabeth wanted to 'go home', it seems that Prince Philip had no such wish. He rowed after the departing royal yacht with the rest of the senior cadets in their flotilla of blue boats. But when the rest turned back, Philip rowed on. Legend relates that it was Dickie Mountbatten's commanding voice which finally made him go back – the last time that Uncle Dickie would send him in that direction.

Seven weeks later the idyll at Dartmouth had been forgotten in the declaration of war. Yet not altogether forgotten.

The Windsor Fortress: 1940–45

With her country locked in a six-year struggle for survival, Princess Elizabeth was to fight a war within a war. The personal war was partly waged against her scrupulous conscience. 'Are we too happy?' she would ask, as the Nazi bomber fleets, sinisterly audible yet invisible, told her that someone – some thousands perhaps – would soon be under attack. But not she, at present. She would plunge with renewed vigour into the Windsor thickets, furiously 'wooding' to save fuel or dragging out rusty tin cans for scrap metal.

Her inner battle was to be extrapolated. It became a friendly duel with her father. How could she persuade him to let her do more – that father who himself, though fully stretched, was never satisfied with his own war effort? It was Queen Elizabeth's task to convince both her husband and her elder daughter, so like him in many ways, that neither was falling short. Indeed it was George VI's unstinted giving of himself to the public cause that set the high standard for the Princess.

On the eve of war, 2 September 1939, the family were at Balmoral, where they traditionally spent their autumn holiday. Immediately the King and Queen returned to London, leaving their daughters behind.

When last at Buckingham Palace the Princesses had gaily watched the cars arriving for court occasions from their nursery window. 'We have a fly's eye view,'[1] said Lilibet.

Her next view of festivities at the Palace would not be that of a fly but of a full participant.

'Who is this Hitler, spoiling everything?' asked the nine-year-old Margaret, as they were swept off to Birkhall for the pleasures of Girl Guides and sewing-bees during the next three months. Elizabeth and Margaret handed round scones to the work force, who eventually included some evacuee mothers from Glasgow. At first Elizabeth had tried to protect her sister from too much battle talk: 'We don't want to upset her.' But soon they were learning from the papers of naval sinkings and hurling cushions at the voice of the traitor Lord Haw-Haw (William Joyce) on the wireless.

Lessons were resumed, though under a handicap; not this time of social interruptions but of the growing disparity in the girls' development. Margaret at nine wanted to be taught seriously but naturally could not keep up with her sister, who in her turn needed more concentrated work. Crawfie found two temporary solutions: she got Mrs Montaudon-Smith to come north and teach one sister French while Crawfie taught English or history to the other; and Henry Marten was invited to continue Princess Elizabeth's constitutional history lessons, though now by post. Even so there were ominous signs that Crawfie was beginning to find it too much for her. 'I had to prepare, the night before, lessons for two children, both of different ages, both extremely bright. It was pretty hard work.' Crawfie was bright herself, but she had been trained to teach only children of nursery school age, certainly not a bright thirteen-year-old.

Yet there seemed no escape from the educational dilemma which had trapped the Princesses for the last three years. The sudden crisis of the Abdication had made Crawfie a solid rock in a sea of change. It had seemed no time to cut the children adrift from her, as they were necessarily torn away from 145 Piccadilly and many other landmarks of their early childhood. How much less did it seem possible to begin the painful process of weaning at the start of a terrible war. The King and Queen telephoned their daughters every evening at six. During the long hours in between they felt absolute trust in the Birkhall set-up. And the Princesses themselves were devoted to their nursery governess, who had now been with them for more than six years. When they received the welcome news on 18 December that they were to go to Sandringham for Christmas, and Crawfie to her home in Dunfermline, Princess Margaret said, 'You will come, won't you, as soon as Mummy wants you?'

There were always visitors even at remote Birkhall, and one of them was to open a door on history. Sir Richard Molyneux, an extra equerry to Queen Mary, had taken part in the British cavalry charge at Omdurman against the Mahdi and his Sudanese followers in 1898. Molyneux took pride in showing the Princesses his battle scars. He had been wounded in the charge and a fellow officer, young Winston Churchill, had given a piece of skin from his thigh to graft on to his friend's hand. Churchill, now aged sixty-nine, was soon to smite Hitler hip and thigh.

Meanwhile King George VI, by nature a man of action, was required to make speeches. 'For the second time in the lives of most of us,' he told the nation on 3 September, 'we are at war.' The first time the royal speaker had himself fought; now he could fight only with words. Nevertheless, the broadcasting he hated had ensured that George VI was king individually of each hearth and home in the land.

Christmas at Sandringham was a joy for the Princesses, once Papa had got over the agony of his broadcast message. This year it had a particularly personal ring, for he quoted a few lines of prose that had struck him because they summed up his own life, as well as the nation's present crisis:

> I said to the man who stood at the Gate of the Year, 'Give me a light that I may tread safely into the unknown.' And he replied, 'Go out into the darkness, and put your hand into the Hand of God. That shall be to you better than light, and safer than a known way.'

The consolation that could lie in an apt quotation may have impressed Lilibet also, for she herself when Queen was to follow her father's example.

It seemed for another few months that the 'Gate of the Year' was not going to open on darkness. Instead of the Princesses being sent back to distant but secure Aberdeenshire they were brought to Royal Lodge in February 1940, where their parents could see more of them. A non-committal news item announced that they were living in 'a house in the country'. Crawfie returned to organise lessons and a weekly dancing class with Miss Vacani. 'We kept it for little girls only,' wrote Crawfie. 'The Princesses did not understand the antics of little boys, and this did not seem to be the moment to teach them.'

It never seemed to be 'the moment' for Princess Elizabeth to break new ground.

Crawfie continued: 'The little girls came with their nannies, wearing their party frocks, and afterwards we gave them tea,' as in the old days at 145 Piccadilly.

One 'little girl', be it noted, was fourteen that April and falling in love with a 'little boy' of eighteen.

Henry Marten renewed Princess Elizabeth's tutorials at Eton College and she was also getting some experience as a personal letter-writer. She had been deeply shocked by the news of *Royal Oak*'s disaster in 1939, springing to her feet and exclaiming, 'It can't be! All those nice sailors.'[2] Another 'nice sailor', fortunately not posted to *Royal Oak*, was Philip Mountbatten. She was able to send him what the King's biographer describes as 'cousinly letters'.[3] Writing in her own hand must have given her pleasure, and even today she does not dictate but prefers to write as well as sign her letters herself. When at the age of sixteen she was given a lady-in-waiting, officially to assist with her correspondence, her parents remarked that most of it was to or from Philip.

Prince Philip was at sea when, on 10 May 1940, the smouldering war in Europe suddenly burst into flame.

The 'war of nerves' showed unmistakable signs of having changed when Hitler invaded Denmark and Norway on 9 April. But the bustle in the Admiralty 'war room', which the King visited that afternoon, only exacerbated his own internal war of nerves. 'Everybody working at fever heat except me,' he wrote.[4] *Except me* was to be precisely the thought of his elder daughter in a similar situation a few years hence.

The King suffered acutely for his unlucky prime minister Neville Chamberlain, and supported him until his resignation. Then the King wanted Lord Halifax as prime minister. But Parliament insisted on Churchill and Churchill it was. This was a classic case of the British system showing itself to be indubitably a 'parliamentary monarchy'. Yet there was no compulsion on the King to be a rubber stamp without political feelings. Firmly he wrote in his diary: 'I met Halifax in the garden & I told him I was sorry not to have him as Prime Minister.'[5]

Two days after the shooting war erupted, Queen Elizabeth was on the telephone to Royal Lodge. The Princesses and their entourage were to go to Windsor Castle for the weekend. They went for the weekend and stayed for five years.

It was now that the greatest decision affecting Princess Elizabeth's future had to be made. Queen Mary had broadcast to the public about the new King George VI in 1936: 'I know you have already taken his children to your hearts. . . .' The question four years later was, would the public have to see these children taken from them?

With one stream of refugees, royal and otherwise, reaching Britain from the continent, and another stream, royal and otherwise, leaving beleaguered Britain for Canada or the United States, there is no doubt that the possibility of the Princesses joining the second stream had to be discussed. Some royal examples seemed to urge go. The Netherlands royal family, for instance.

One day at 5 am Queen Wilhelmina was telephoning King George for more planes to defend Holland; the next day she was entering Britain with the tin hat presented to her by the skipper of her rescue ship. After her grand-daughter Princess Irene had been christened, like Elizabeth and Margaret, in Buckingham Palace chapel, the Netherlands royal family sailed for Canada, where the Earl of Athlone, ably supported by his wife Princess Alice, was still Governor-General. There is a story of Queen Wilhelmina arriving at Ottawa. She had an obsession about 'not giving trouble' and stepped down on to the tarmac carrying her own suitcases, so that she had no free hand to shake with.[6] (She had left Holland in her nightdress with no suitcase.)

It was felt that the life of Princess Juliana, an only child and heir to the throne, must be preserved at all costs for a victorious return to Europe. The same arguments could surely be applied to the heir to the British throne, particularly as another royal family was in Canada also: the Norwegian, quite closely related to Princess Elizabeth. Moreover Princess Alice, Countess of Athlone, the chatelaine of Rideau Hall, Ottawa, was the Princesses' first cousin twice removed.

To the Queen of England all this was one big non-question. The public never dreamt of their King and Queen leaving under any circumstances; and the King and Queen never dreamt of being parted, perhaps indefinitely, from their children. Queen Elizabeth indeed had got the whole non-question reduced to an unassailable syllogism, which as enunciated by her was to become famous: 'The children could not go without me, and I could not possibly leave the King' – who would never go.

Just three concessions were made in the interests of family security. Queen Mary, now seventy-three, was reluctantly convinced that her duty lay in retiring to Badminton in Gloucestershire with a staff of sixty-three – 'Quite a fleet,' wrote Queen Mary[7] – and a limousine available to carry her between Badminton and Windsor on family occasions.

King George and Queen Elizabeth agreed that Madresfield in Worcestershire should be prepared as a secret hideout in case of invasion, from which they would nominally lead the British resistance. (Or not so nominally. The King, Queen and their equerries had been practising with rifles, tommy guns and revolvers on ranges at Buckingham Palace and Windsor since the beginning of the war.)

And the Princesses at Windsor? For five years their baggage was ready packed for an emergency journey to Liverpool. Nor was this the only secret kept by the ancient fortress. In its recesses lay the crown jewels wrapped in newspapers, while on the floor of St George's Chapel were stacked, along with other valuable documents, the archives of the Iron Duke.

To begin with, the Princesses' routine was kept as near 'normal' as possible. Girl Guides were once more resumed, and they were drilled by Sam the Sergeant-Major. He shouted at them even after Princess Elizabeth had become Colonel of the Grenadiers. 'It does one good to be shouted at now and then,' says Princess Margaret. Miss Betty Vacani continued to teach them dancing. It was only the appearance of the Castle that was desolate: one naked light bulb in the Long Corridor and all the vitrines with their faces to the wall.

Henry Marten came up to tutor Princess Elizabeth at the Castle, instead of the Princess going to Eton. He had been in the habit of bringing history to life by showing his Eton boys the college paintings of past statesmen. He could not use this visual aid at the Castle – all the historic treasures had been removed and the heavy gilt frames that had once held royal portraits were now empty. Until, that is to say, a local art student filled them up with posters of fairy-tale figures or characters from their Christmas pantomime. 'How do you like my ancestors?' the King would ask, pointing out to visitors the label 'Pope Pius by Lawrence' beneath a poster of Mother Goose or the Widow Twanky.

The Princesses had to go through some alarming experiences before the summer and autumn of 1940 were over.

(By the end of the war 300 high-explosive bombs would have fallen in Windsor Park, quite apart from incendiaries and buzz bombs.) They heard the gunfire in May and wondered anxiously what was happening to their parents in London. But the guns were at Dunkirk. There were air-raid alarms, though as yet no bombs near. Princess Margaret has described the 'pathetic attempt' to defend the Castle. 'They dug trenches and put up some rather feeble barbed wire, and the feeble barbed wire of course wouldn't have kept anybody out but it kept us in. . . .'[8] Crawfie was at her theatrical best when describing the first air-raid warning at the Castle. The Brunswick Tower, strongly and icily built, was the Princesses' HQ. Lilibet still shared a bedroom with Bobo and Margaret with Allah, which Crawfie now approved of: it would keep the girls calm when the sirens wailed.

But Allah was too calm the first time it happened. Crawfie ran up to the nurseries when no Princesses appeared in the shelter. Allah was putting on her cap and uniform.

'Sir Hill Child [Master of the Household] and everybody else is waiting in the shelter and you must come down. This is not a dress rehearsal. What are you doing?' Crawfie shouted.

Princess Elizabeth called back, 'We're dressing, Crawfie. We must dress.'

'Nonsense! You are not to dress. Put a coat over your night clothes at once.'

When they at last reached the shelter, Sir Hill Child was a nervous wreck. 'You must understand the Princesses must come down at once,' he explained to Allah, of whom he stood in some awe. 'They must come down whatever they are wearing.'

The makeshift shelter was in the basement. Lilibet read a book and Margaret slept on Crawfie's knee. At 2 am the all-clear sounded. Sir Hill Child bowed to Princess Elizabeth. 'You may go to bed, ma'am.'[9]

In time, as the raids worsened, things were better organised. Siren suits were bought for the Princesses. A two-tiered bunk was installed in the shelter, and two small suitcases which had once belonged to the dolls presented by the French to the Princesses, when their parents visited Paris in 1938, were packed with their treasures, including books and their lock-up diaries given them each year by the Queen.

Princess Margaret remembers the first bomb falling in the Home Park close by. She jumped and dropped the ginger biscuit she was eating. Though it was wartime she was not allowed to pick it up off the floor and eat it.

The King and Queen had their own apartments in the basement, paralleled by a similarly equipped shelter at Buckingham Palace. (Their first shelter there had been a housemaid's cupboard.) The improvements to the royal air-raid shelters were preceded on 7 September by the first bombing of London's East End. Two days later the Palace itself was hit by sticks of bombs, the King and Queen being badly shaken. 'I'm glad we've been bombed,' said the Queen in another of her famous comments. 'It makes me feel I can look the East End in the face.'[10] The King was less resilient though no less gallant. For his Christmas Day broadcast he was to take the theme, 'This time we are *all* in the front line.'

Princess Elizabeth had already taken part with 'Uncle Mac' (Derek McCulloch), if not in the front line, at least in *Children's Hour* on 13 October. After being coached in her breathing and timing by her mother, she addressed words of courage to the children of Britain and the Common-wealth. 'We know, every one of us, that in the end all will be well,' she said, perhaps consciously quoting the mystic Mother Julian of Norwich. 'All shall be well. . . .' Eliza-beth's own mother was to choose the same favourite words for her eightieth birthday Thanksgiving. When the broadcast was ending and Queen Elizabeth had finished beating time, the Princess turned to her sister. 'My sister is by my side', she said, 'and we are both going to say goodnight to you. Come on, Margaret'; and Margaret, aged ten, pronounced her first public sentence: 'Goodnight and good luck to you all.'

Everything seemed to be happening in a rush. Midshipman Prince Philip of Greece was suddenly in the thick of it, when Italy attacked his country of birth that October. Up until then he had shared Princess Elizabeth's chronic feeling of not doing enough; for he had been on rather remote convoy service with *Ramillies*, *Kent* and *Shropshire*. Now he was posted to HMS *Valiant*, earning a mention in despatches by Admiral Conyngham after the battle of Matapan in March 1941. His duty had been to assist the British shelling by illuminating two enemy cruisers with his searchlight, one after the other. According to his own terse report, each disappeared in smoke and steam. He then switched off.

With hindsight, it seems just the right part for a prince to have played, who has always been brilliant at spotlighting the evil things, which appropriate agencies can then proceed to destroy.

It is unlikely that Philip was present at the Princesses' first Christmas pantomime, *Cinderella*, in 1941, but he was undoubtedly in the audience during one at least of these annual occasions. Crawfie's account suggests that he first came in 1942, or even later, when the *Sleeping Beauty*, *Aladdin* and lastly *Old Mother Red Riding Boots* were chosen. It will be seen from the last title that the Princesses' aptitude for rollicking satire had developed over the years. The whole series of pantomimes was triggered off by an amazingly successful nativity play in 1940 called *The Christmas Child* – at least the King and Queen were 'absolutely amazed' by what their daughters could do. Margaret as the little girl without a gift, except Christmas roses which she gave away on the road, sang 'Gentle Jesus' clearly and audibly before 600 people; while Lilibet, as one of the Three Kings in crown and tunic, led the schoolboy shepherds through the audience and on to the stage. For once Crawfie's 'little girls' were permitted to share 'the antics of little boys', children of the King's tenants at the Park school. George VI, having made sure beforehand that Lilibet's tunic was not too short, gave himself up to emotion: 'I cried all the way through.' The Princesses, who expected congratulatory smiles from their parents as they walked back through the audience, were astonished to find both of them in tears.

Cinderella was a much more elaborate affair. Written and produced by a schoolmaster from Windsor Great Park, it introduced the Princesses to many more 'little boys', some of them London evacuees; and also to a chorus of tall guardsmen whom King George succeeded in lining up at the back of the stage when they unfurled a Union Jack in the grand finale, instead of obliterating the girls by occupying the front rows. Scenery was professionally painted, programmes printed, tickets sold and powdered wigs hired. Patches were ordered for Margaret as Cinderella and silk stockings, satin breeches and a braided tunic for Lilibet as Prince Charming. Again the King made certain during rehearsal that the tunic was just right: he had something of his father's interest in correct dress. Miss Betty Vacani choreographed all four pantomimes, and in the last one she acted the part of a saucy beach photographer.

Aladdin in 1943 was probably the first pantomime that the other Prince Charming attended. 'Who *do* you think is coming to see us act, Crawfie? Philip.' Lilibet was pink-cheeked with excitement. Philip sat in the front row, noted Crawfie, looking more like a Viking than ever, 'weather-beaten and strained' but with all the bumptiousness vanished from his now perfect manners. A more likely account of the Prince at the pantomime is given by his biographer Basil Boothroyd – 'the young naval gentleman from Greece rolling in the aisles at the appalling jokes.'

'The pantomime went off very well,' continued Crawfie. 'I have never known Lilibet more animated. There was a sparkle about her none of us had ever seen before.'

It was Philip who maintained the 'sparkle' during dinner with the Royal Family. Metaphorically he jumped even higher than at Dartmouth four years before, for Lilibet's delight, when he gave a spirited description of being dive-bombed on his ship *Wallace* at sea. Nearly forty years on, his son Andrew was virtually to repeat the performance.[11]

During the next four years, 1942 to 1945, Princess Elizabeth was to grow to womanhood. The process began with her Confirmation on 1 March 1942. It was performed by the same Archbishop of Canterbury who had christened her, Dr Cosmo Lang. He talked to her on the eve of the ceremony, and afterwards made a revealing report. She was intelligent and understanding, 'though naturally not very communicative'.[12] This report showed that he too was understanding, and aware of her reticence.

She is said to have remarked to a friend afterwards, 'I'll have to try to be good, won't I?' She had no need to try very hard. The story in fact sounds like an apocryphal echo of Princess Victoria.

Queen Mary came from Badminton for the family event, later sending an account to Princess Alice in Ottawa: 'Lilibet much grown, very pretty eyes and complexion, pretty figure. Margaret very short, intelligent face, but not really pretty.'[13] Possibly it was Queen Mary's devotion to the throne that made her see the heir as so much the prettier. To her grandmother, Lilibet 'looked so nice in white with a small veil & was quite composed.' Lady Airlie, present as Queen Mary's lady-in-waiting, was even more laudatory:

I saw a grave little face under a small white net veil and a slender figure in a plain white woollen frock. The carriage of her head was unequalled, and there was about her that indescribable something which Queen Victoria had.[14]

For 'indescribable something' read regality.

Next month the Princess reached another milestone, her sixteenth birthday. The event was doubly celebrated: first, childishly, with a birthday tea; second, more maturely, by her registration under the wartime youth service scheme at the local Labour Exchange. But four months later, on 25 August, something happened to make her father put his own affairs in order – and resolve that his beloved daughters should not be exposed to physical danger. His brother George, Duke of Kent, was killed in a plane crash while on active service. 'It was a great shock,' wrote Crawfie, 'to the two little girls.' The King, with characteristic boldness and sensitivity, immediately sent for Princess Marina's exiled sister, Olga of Yugoslavia, from Kenya to comfort Marina.[15]

The Princesses' uncle was young and amusing and their aunt Marina had always been admired by them when, with their 'fly's-eye view', they used to see her arriving at Buckingham Palace looking beautiful in the most stylish dresses. Their youngest Kent cousin, Michael, was only seven weeks old, while Edward and Alexandra were both younger than themselves.

Meanwhile the elder 'little girl', having been created Colonel of the Grenadier Guards, at first demanded the same perfection of her regiment, when reviewing them, as she herself had shown when folding her clothes as a child. She soon took a tactful hint, however, from the commanding officer to 'temper justice with mercy'. (Lord Harewood heard that his cousin was inspecting the horses' teeth. In his view the essence of all royal inspections was thoroughness. On the way home from Canada the Athlones had insisted on inspecting the ship's engines.[16]) If the small episode had a moral, it could only be that the ardent Princess was underemployed.

Fortunately a new addition was made to both the Princesses' education during this year. A cultured and vivacious Belgian lady, educated in Paris, married to Vicomte Pierre de Bellaigue and whose two sons had been sent to a prep school in England before the war, had escaped with her sons from Belgium ten days before the invasion.

Mme de Bellaigue remembered that in 1914 a cabinet minister had told her father that Belgium would not be overrun. In 1940 the son of this minister told Mme de Bellaigue she would be safe in Belgium. This was enough for her to say, 'I am not going to be caught a second time and suffer occupation once again,' and she left for England.

Her outstanding merits as a French conversationalist were brought to the Queen's notice by the Hardinges with whom she had been staying, and where she was presented to the Queen. In 1942, by royal command, Madame de Bellaigue was asked to come to the Castle as French tutor to the Princesses. As a result, Antoinette de Bellaigue ('Toni' to the Princesses and 'Toinon' to the Household) remained six years with the Royal Family, regularly teaching them literature and history in French. This was a much more advanced enterprise than the elementary though necessary French language and grammar efficiently taught to them earlier by Mrs Montaudon-Smith and other governesses.

Mme de Bellaigue had her own educational aims:

I hoped to bring to the Princesses *une 'formation générale'*. In our general conversations I endeavoured to give the Princesses an awareness of other countries, their way of thought and their customs – sometimes a source of amusement. Sir Henry Marten, a wonderful person, tutored Princess Elizabeth on constitutional history.

Under his auspices, I was asked by him to teach the Princess continental history. He used to set essays on the topics learnt with me by his pupils, which had to be returned in French.

One day Sir Henry told me not to worry if at times the Princess forgot dates or events, but to remember that education broadly speaking was to help a student to learn to appraise both sides of a question, thus using his judgment.

Queen Elizabeth II has always had from the beginning a positive good judgment. She had an instinct for the right thing. She was her simple self, *'tres naturelle'*. And there was always a strong sense of duty mixed with *joie de vivre* in the pattern of her character.[17]

No, the Princesses' education was not academic in the way that better qualified teachers would have made it so, summed up Mme de Bellaigue. All the same, Queen Elizabeth II's education was not neglected, considering the sphere in which she had to live.

There was another significant landmark for Princess Elizabeth in 1942, a pointer to a promised land, though she did not yet know it. Gordon Richards, the King's brilliant jockey, was introduced to Princess Elizabeth at Windsor, after he had won the 2,000 Guineas on Big Game and the 1,000 Guineas on Sun Chariot. The Princesses did not appear at race meetings in public, but fascinating private experiences were already building up for Princess Elizabeth. The children also went with their parents and Mountbatten cousins to see Noël Coward's *In Which We Serve* being shot at the studio. Standing on a simulated deck made the girls feel appropriately seasick.[18] And in 1943 the Princesses attended the Thanksgiving Service in St Paul's for the victory over Rommel, though because they were both dressed alike in blue the diarist Chips Channon thought they seemed 'little girls'. Private activity of this kind throws a rather different light on the Princesses' allegedly dull war.

In that same year, 1943, the Regency Act was amended so that Princess Elizabeth could become a counsellor of state at the age of 18 instead of 21, just as she would be queen if her father died before she was 21. This was a rare case of Princess Elizabeth actually doing something in advance of the normal age. Indeed it was so unexpected as to cause some people to get foolish ideas into their heads. Should she not be created Princess of Wales on her eighteenth birthday? The King made short work of that one. 'Princess of Wales' was a title reserved solely for the Prince of Wales's wife. In any case, the King added revealingly in his diary, 'Her own name is so nice. . . .'[19] – that name sanctified by her childhood, by her youth.

In 1944, when the King flew to Italy to inspect his troops, the Princess sat as one of the four counsellors of state. It fell to her lot to sign the reprieve of a murderer. Her comment was typical of a compassionate teenager: 'What makes people do such terrible things? One ought to know. There should be some way to help them. I have so much to learn about people!'[20]

Terrible things were still happening at home and on the battle fronts, though victory was in sight. The flying bombs, sometimes called 'doodle-bugs' or 'buzzbombs', caused, according to Crawfie, 'signs of strain in the little girls'. One flying bomb caught them on a Guide hike in Windsor Great Park and seemed to race them to their slit trench, where-upon it exploded with a shattering roar on the Great West Road.

According to a story published in America the slit tren-ches were supplemented by a tank that rumbled behind the Princesses wherever they went. When the sirens sounded, the Princesses, their corgis and their attendants popped down the turret, Margaret always aiming to be last in, first out. Princess Margaret calls this story 'nonsense'. But there was an armoured car in attendance.

From the moment of her registration at the Labour Ex-change in 1942, the heir to the throne longed to serve. As more and more of her young relatives and friends disting-uished themselves her own frustration grew. Her first cousins George and Gerald Lascelles, only three and two years older than herself, were both serving. As for Philip, he was now second-in-command of the destroyer *Whelp*. When the Princess protested that 'all my friends' were serving, she was particularly thinking of her cousin Lady Mary Cambridge, who had made a name for herself by nursing in the London blitz. But if Lilibet was too young to nurse she still maintained, 'I ought to do as other girls of my age do.' It was the old feeling become more acute – every-one serves *except me*.

Her eighteenth birthday, in 1944, came and went with only minor advances. There was a family luncheon instead of a tea party. She went to London and made her first public speech on 31 May at the Mansion House, on behalf of the

National Society for the Prevention of Cruelty to Children, of which she was president. Pompous words were put into her mouth: 'I trust that in the days to come we may hope that every child's life may be free and happy.' But at least the word *free* had meaning for her.

It may have been during this excursion that she met the diarist Harold Nicolson with whom she discussed the Grenadiers, a subject in which she was fortunately well informed. 'Princess Elizabeth is a nice clear girl,' he wrote, choosing an adjective that applied to her mind as well as her complexion.

The greatest event of this year, however, was Philip's visit to Balmoral. The Princess had for some years escaped from the nursery and schoolroom into a room of her own. Here she caused friendly interest by setting up a photograph of Philip, first clean-shaven and unmistakable, then in the would-be disguise of a blond naval beard, but still unmistakable.

Queen Mary was to date the love affair from a Balmoral visit; and indeed this was the year when Prince Philip's cousin King George II of Greece wrote to Lilibet's father hoping that Philip would be favourably considered. Lilibet's father replied that, though they all liked Philip, Lilibet was still 'too young for that now'. In fact George VI was 'cool'. In his Christmas broadcast the King addressed a special message to 'the children', in which category he assuredly still included both his daughters. 'To children everywhere we wish all the happiness that Christmas can bring.'

Yet even Princess Margaret, now a precocious fourteen-year-old, was becoming bored with the schoolroom regime, unbroken as it was for her by jaunts to London. When she asked if she could not now begin history tutorials with Sir Henry Marten, the answer was, 'It is not necessary for you.'

Miss Crawford was finding her difficult to teach, never having been trained for this age group and describing Margaret helplessly as 'neither quite a child nor quite grown up'. Discipline was relaxed and she succumbed to

Margaret's blandishments, allowing her to recline during lessons like Mme Récamier on a chaise longue.

Princess Margaret created a modicum of freedom for herself within her own imaginative world of invention, jokes, satirical laughter, leg-pulling. Her grandmother called her *'espiègle'*[21] – an irrepressible *enfant terrible*. There was something essentially mischievous, unstodgy, even Gallic about Margaret's approach to life.

At last, shortly before her nineteenth birthday in 1945, Lilibet could drop her long lament of 'except me'. She got into khaki, causing her envious sister to feel 'madly cross'.

Princess Elizabeth was deliriously happy to become No. 230873 Second Subaltern Elizabeth Alexandra Mary Windsor of the Auxiliary Transport Service (ATS) No. 1 Mechanical Transport Training Centre, aged 18, height 5 feet 3 inches – three inches taller than her mother. Her 'eyes blue hair brown', as baldly specified, did not convey the Celtic contrast in light and shade inherited from her mother. The blue was of a startling intensity, the curling hair dark against a glowing skin. She had been 'long and slender' at thirteen when other children were gawky, and at sixteen had been sturdy, for the only time in her life. Now she had recaptured 'an irresistible delicacy'.

She could soon do a great deal more than 'others girls of my age do': drive a heavy vehicle through rush-hour traffic and service it when necessary. This was the kind of 'service' she really enjoyed, and her parents were not surprised to find her at the Camberley army depot emerging from beneath a lorry with grease all over her hands, or talking sparking-plugs throughout dinner. Still she slept at Windsor, the only concession made to the King's anxieties. Otherwise she was treated like any other girl in this women's organisation. Early every morning she would drive back to Camberley her superior in the ATS, Commandant Wellesley, among whose forebears was Wellington. The Princess was beginning to learn, just as she had wished, 'about people'.

VE-Day was less than three weeks away from Princess Elizabeth's nineteenth birthday. Before reaching that special milestone, it is necessary to wind up the argument about the Princesses' early life particularly in their Windsor fortress. It is generally represented as graduating from a 'secluded' and 'cloistered' existence into 'almost a form of purdah'.[22] All those who have mainly relied on Miss Crawford's *Little Princesses* may be forgiven for the dismal pictures they paint; though to go on to suggest, as Robert Lacey does in his outstanding *Majesty*, to which I owe much, that Princess Elizabeth's upbringing may have stifled her receptiveness to 'ideas coming from outside her circle' is surely adding a new dimension to Crawfie's fancies. To make only one point, if Princess Elizabeth had been unreceptive, she would never have fallen in love with Prince Philip, the supreme 'ideas man' from outside.

During her first months with the Royal Family Crawfie unconsciously resented her loss of a career as child psychologist. When war came she wanted to join the Women's Royal Naval Service: 'I felt I ought not to be shut up in Windsor Castle, but all the Household said I was doing my job of work. . . .' By 1944 she wanted to be married but – 'If I marry now that the war was on I would feel like a soldier who had deserted his post.'[23]

Nevertheless, it would have been better for the soldier and the company she commanded if she had asked for a new posting after long and faithful service. As has been noted already, however, her superiors were not going to get rid of so well-tried a servant until she herself gave notice. All they would do was to supplement her efforts by a number of outside talents.

It was one of these, Mme de Bellaigue, whose memories restore balance to the picture. Secluded?

> The Princesses' lives did not seem secluded to me, partly I suppose because girls in my country, Belgium, did not go to boarding school; but anyway the Princesses at Windsor had plenty of mixed company – all great fun. There were games all

over the Castle involving many amusing 'incidents'. One evening Major Phillips [the Princesses' kindly 'surrogate father']
plonked himself down in Queen Victoria's ivory chair, given
her by some Maharajah, and went through the bottom. The
King, who was there for dinner, said, 'Own up to Mrs Bruce!' –
the very formidable housekeeper.

Queen Victoria herself would have joined heartily in the
laughter. She loved the sound of slips and crashes, especially when her household were involved.

At the beginning of the war, [continued the Princess's former
teacher] there were lots of tea parties given for airmen: some of
the American Eagle Squadron, New Zealanders, Australians
and Canadians. Sometimes they had a very good time. There
were always two young officers at meals, mostly on leave or
convalescent, besides the 'Body Guard' like Hugh Euston [now
Duke of Grafton] and Mark Bonham Carter, whom the Princesses saw every day. There were charades and parlour games.
The earlier tea parties with the Brownies and Guides were also
occasions when Gladys Hanbury-Williams, the organizer, used
to keep everybody amused by her humour and '*repartie*'.
   I joined the Princesses in their walks and played duets with
them. They never forgot there was a war on, and they were
much aware of the sadness brought on by casualties. But there
was no feeling of doom and gloom.[24]

Princess Margaret says stoutly, 'I was brought up among
men.' And Crawfie herself, in between sentimental gush
about 'little girls', would refer to parties for Eton boys,
mixed madrigal classes, treasure hunts and games of sar-
dines, as well as household luncheons at which Princess
Elizabeth would preside with aplomb, sitting opposite the
alert Princess Margaret.
   Mme de Bellaigue adds yet other touches to the friendly
atmosphere in which the Princesses lived:

The Princesses had some friends of their own who came over to
the Castle, such as their cousin, Margaret Elphinstone, Libby
Hardinge, who at one time studied with them, Alethea Fitz-

alan-Howard, Mary Morshead, and on one or two occasions Sir William and Lady Lewthwaite, a young couple – he was stationed in Windsor.

Against the sometimes maudlin atmosphere of Crawfie's story (she went on referring to 'the two little girls' when one was in her nineteenth and the other in her fifteenth year) must be set the nursery governess's lively and well-observed narrative of the fortress years, which would otherwise be virtually unobtainable.

Not that Crawfie's picture of two sugar-babies does not have its human explanation. She knew in her heart that she was no longer competent to teach the Princesses, the elder already a young woman. Therefore by continuing to call them her 'two *little* girls' she seemed to bring them back into her sights. The process was instinctive, an exercise in the preservation of self-respect.

Nor must it be forgotten that King George VI himself, with one throw-away sentence at the end of his VE-day diary, was to do more than anyone else to cast an unreal shadow over his daughters' youthful days. As we shall see, however, there was a touching and totally understandable reason for what the King wrote.

Victory in Europe was celebrated on 8 May 1945. The two Princesses stood with their parents on the famous balcony of Buckingham Palace, a balcony whose cracks from bomb-blast had been repaired, though the french windows behind the Royal Family were still unglazed and barricaded. Eight times the ecstatic crowds called them on to the balcony. Then all the world of London dispersed to enjoy themselves in their own way. The question was, were the young Princesses to enjoy themselves in *their* way – a way that led outside the Palace gates – or must they accept Papa's assumption that they would rejoice indoors?

Both of them besieged their father until in the end his defences fell. He gave permission for them to make up a party including their uncle David Bowes-Lyon and sally forth, though the concession was still slightly against his better judgment, or so it seems. For the last words in his diary on that memorable day were: 'Poor darlings, they have never had any fun yet.'[25]

By exaggerating the 'no fun' element of his daughters' fortress years, he was able to appease his own conscience and feel justified in setting them free on VE-Day.

Mme de Bellaigue was with the exhilarated party on that May evening:

> On VE-Day the Princesses were allowed, chaperoned by Major Phillips, Crawfie and myself and accompanied by young officers, to mix with the crowd. The King drew the line about Piccadilly Circus, which was to be avoided. I shall never forget running wildly down St James's Street, with a puffing Major of the Grenadiers, to keep pace with the Princesses.
>
> When we reached the Palace they shouted like the other people, 'We want the King,' 'We want the Queen.' On the whole we were not recognized. However, a Dutch serviceman, who attached himself to the end of our file of arm-in-arm people (the Princesses being in the centre of the file) realized who the Princesses were. He withdrew discreetly and just said, 'It was a great honour. I shall never forget this evening.'
>
> All our group got back to the Palace through a garden gate. The Queen was anxiously waiting for us. Her Majesty provided us with sandwiches she made herself.[26]

When King George said his daughters had never had any 'fun' he meant freedom as well as the conventional fun of pre-war debutantes. Their future was to be exactly the opposite to Queen Mary's. 'Never since her youth . . . had she enjoyed such freedom as at Badminton.' She left in tears saying: 'Back in London I shall have to begin being Queen Mary all over again.'[27] Princess Elizabeth was to find her first freedom in public life, enhanced by the greater freedom of marriage. In a sense she would begin being Princess Elizabeth for the first time.

VIII

'Us Four' – and Philip:
1945–7

At nineteen, Princess Elizabeth was still prepared to accept her life ready-made, so to speak, from the hands of others. That is, in all respects but one, and he was called Philip. Her pleasures were still the family ones. The King taught an apt pupil how to shoot and stalk red deer, and was rewarded with a silver table-mat inscribed with the story of his daughter's prize bag on 3 September 1945, when the quarry was sighted, stalked and shot in the few hours before lunch.

The father took immense pride in both his daughters, the elder because she seemed an ideal version of himself, the younger because she was so different. For all her dutifulness, Margaret made it her prime business to charm him. Her gifts of mimicry and endlessly varied *tours de force* on the piano became a kind of magic for him. In Elizabeth he saw raised to a degree of perfection his own love of sport, his good eye, his fine seat on a horse, humanity, common sense and 'deep devotion to public service' – to quote Sir John Wheeler-Bennett.

Their mother reintroduced the informal picnics that the Princesses had enjoyed before the war on the moors above Balmoral, with a disused schoolhouse discovered by the Queen as their base. The girls were quite used to washing up plates and dishes and now again they did it in a sparkling burn. Their parents were so close that they often seemed to the girls one person.

Princess Elizabeth had her first grown-up dresses and her first private suite at Buckingham Palace. Again she was content to follow her mother's style and tastes. During the war, the Royal Family's dutiful observance of rationing necessitated much 'make-do and mend' and inter-royal borrowing, especially of hats. The Princess rejoiced like any other teenage girl at being able at last to wear new clothes, but she did not change her style. Her bedroom was furnished in her mother's favourite colours, pink and fawn with white furniture and flowered chintzes. She was given her own footman and housemaid and a second lady-in-waiting (the first was Lady Mary Strachey). The way in which this second appointment was made in March 1945 was characteristic of the Royal Family's touching, almost blind trust in their own inner circle.

The Hon. Mrs Vicary Gibbs was a pretty twenty-one-year-old widow whose husband, a Grenadier officer, had been killed in Holland. Jean Hambro by birth, she was later to become Princess Elizabeth's first cousin by her marriage to Andrew Elphinstone. One day Jean Gibbs received a letter from Sir Arthur Penn, the Queen's private secretary, explaining that an additional lady was needed to serve the Princess, a lady who could talk about the Grenadiers and Officers' Welfare. Mrs Gibbs had never set eyes on the King or Queen. Nor had Princess Elizabeth ever set eyes on her. Yet this extraordinary 'on trust' arrangement was to work perfectly, lasting from 1945 to 1954, and continuing until now on a part-time basis.

Being three years older than the Princess, Mrs Gibbs was considered a suitable chaperone at the 'deb dances' that had now started up again. Fortunately there were not many, for Princess Elizabeth's natural reserve gave some people the impression that she was painfully shy. Though she seemed to put on a brave face it was not always a smiling one, nor was she glib with small talk. She would assure her friends that she was enjoying herself, as indeed she was, but they guessed at other feelings. Some feared that she might turn out as shy as her aunt the Princess Royal. (Lord

Harewood was to write that in his mother's intense shyness people discovered 'gentleness and kindness as well, with in later life a little Hanoverian spleen underneath it all'.)

However, the Queen is not shy. Shyness and reticence or reserve are not the same thing, though it is easy to mistake one for the other. Shyness wants to speak but cannot. Reticence has its own good reasons for silences, connected with the inner citadel.

Cecil Beaton, the sensitive and fastidious photographer who knew the Royal Family well, was to ascribe to the Queen a curious trio of qualities, but shyness was not among them. 'She is meek but not shy,' he wrote; 'assured and even proud.'[1] For 'meek' I prefer to read 'unassertive', but 'assured' and 'proud' are good and entirely compatible with reserve.

There were at least four external factors reinforcing the Princess's reticence during these immediate post-war years.

The continued atmosphere of scarcity and rationing did not encourage a conscientious girl to fling herself into a social 'whirl', that in any case hardly as yet existed. A *cri de cœur* from the King did manage to extract a few extra clothing coupons for his family. But Princess Elizabeth, always acutely aware of the restrictions on others, dressed like a thirty-year-old and without glamour. Perhaps it was as well. 'Food, clothes and fuel are the main topics of conversation with us all,' wrote the King gloomily at the beginning of 1946.[2] The heir had an ample room of her own but only one electric fire to heat it.

Princess Margaret at fifteen was taking the last furlongs of her youth at a fine gallop and rapidly catching up with her devoted sister. Her father had allowed her to stay up to late dinner since she was twelve, so delighted was he with her japes and mischief. It was generally agreed that he disciplined his elder daughter more firmly. On the whole it was good for Princess Elizabeth to have this outgoing, bubbling companion. But at this stage, when she needed to bubble herself, she was sometimes content to leave things to a more liberated spirit.

The male world was already populated in her eyes by one single figure – and he was not around, being still on active service in the Far East. What matter that the 'Madrigal Men', as the Household called them, were invited from the Wellington Barracks to continue mixed concerts? Or that the American press were brightening the Princess's life with fictitious beaux, including Prince George of Denmark the Duke of Rutland and the heir to the Duke of Grafton. True, the Princess had felt a reciprocated admiration for Hugh Euston who had helped to guard her at Windsor when she was fifteen; after he had become Duke of Grafton his outstandingly able wife Fortune became her mistress of the robes. But these solid comforts and enduring friendships were remote from the brittle atmosphere of a 'deb dance' in 1945.

The Princess's reticence was increased by the gaps in her education. As Colonel of the Grenadiers, she impressed her new lady-in-waiting with her 'extraordinary ability to absorb information'. The emphasis was on *absorb*. Up until now her powers of absorption had not been fully exploited. And her high native intelligence told her that the chances of subjects being raised at dinner parties about which she was well-informed were low. 'Believe it or not, I lie in my bath before dinner,' she said to a friend, 'and think, oh, who am I going to sit by and what are they going to talk about? I'm absolutely terrified of sitting next to people in case they talk about things I have never heard of.' It was not surprising that, with her great knowledge of horse-racing and limited acquaintance with the Italian classics, the apocryphal story grew up of her mistaking a remark about Dante the poet for one about Dante the thoroughbred. All this, as we shall see, was to be transformed by her marriage and accession.

Mrs Churchill described the rejoicing at the Thanksgiving Service for victory as 'unclouded'.[3] Unclouded was far from being the immediate outlook of King George VI. 'We have spent a very busy fortnight since VE-day,' he had written in May 1945, '& feel rather jaded from it all.'[4] Yet this tired and highly-strung man would be called upon in less than two months' time to face the greatest upheaval of his political experience. He lost Churchill as his prime minister in the most extreme election swing to the left since the Liberal landslide of 1906, when his grandfather Edward VII was on the throne – and Churchill, incidentally, among the left-wing victors.

Churchill's lack of interest in social reform probably influenced the King and prevented him from realising what a huge backlog of necessary changes had accumulated since the last election of 1935, ten years before. When an item on his agenda about domestic reform had been pointed out to Churchill by his Cabinet secretary, the Prime Minister had said: 'Ah yes, all this stuff about planning and compensation and betterment. Broad vistas and city centres and all that. But give me the eighteenth-century alley, where footpads lurked and the harlot plied her trade, and none of this new-fangled planning doctrine.'[5]

The loss of Churchill meant a loss of confidentiality, a consideration of great moment to any democratic monarch. (Churchill had told George VI about the atom bomb before even Attlee, the Deputy Prime Minister, knew.)

In Churchill's place the King got Clement Attlee, a shy character almost as terse and wordless as himself. Nor was the establishment of the new Labour Cabinet without its constitutional problems for the exhausted King. Whether or not the King's private secretary informed him, there was a move on the part of Herbert Morrison supported by Harold Laski, two Labour leaders, to supersede Attlee as potential prime minister. The King, however, played a straightforward hand, sending for Attlee as leader of the Labour Party and seeing him successful in forming a government.

In the cabinet-making that followed, Attlee at first thought of Ernest Bevin for Chancellor of the Exchequer and Hugh Dalton for Foreign Secretary. According to the

King's diary, he suggested to Attlee a reversal of these two roles, though Attlee in later years 'did not recollect any such intervention on the King's part'. 'I thought of it myself,' Attlee told his colleague Dalton.[6] There followed an attempt, that proved abortive, to convict the King of unconstitutional interference. Even Kingsley Martin, left-wing editor of the weekly *New Statesman*, upheld the King's action: 'The King is not intended to be a rubber stamp,' he wrote; 'there is no ground for suggesting that he brought improper pressure to bear on the Premier.'[7]

If the charge of interference had lain, the prospects for future democratic monarchs would have been dim indeed. After all, as another left-wing writer put it, 'It is perfectly proper for the Monarch to give the Cabinet advice, as indeed it is for anyone else, be it a newspaper or a parson.'[8] Deprived of her right to 'advise', Queen Elizabeth II would have become simply a brake on other people's ambitions. Yet another left-winger, Richard Crossman, was to make the point in 1950 to James Pope-Hennessy, the biographer of Queen Mary. Pope-Hennessy wrote in his diary:

> After dinner I argued (slightly tight, I fancy) with Crossman, who was very amiable. He explained his theory of democratic government – 'to castrate', he said '– to castrate the power-complexes of everyone, bring the level down, have no dominating figures.' He supports the monarchy because it diverts hero-worship into harmless channels.[9]

(Crossman later admitted to Pope-Hennessy that his own aim in politics was to acquire *power*!)

Nineteen forty-six was to be the year of Princess Elizabeth's engagement. Not of the official announcement, for which she had to wait some nine months. But of an unofficial engagement known only to the family and royal House-hold; although already in summer 1946 it was a subject of speculation by the press. Miss Crawford remembered Prince Philip's sports car roaring into the forecourt of the

Palace, and the Prince himself emerging 'hatless' in a wild hurry to be with the Princess.

Crawfie also remembered the occasion when a voice from a crowd of shoppers or factory workers shouted boisterously to Princess Elizabeth, 'Where's Philip?' The Princess was not amused; indeed it seemed to her 'horrible'. Her sister sympathised. 'Poor Lilibet. Nothing of your own. Not even your love affair.'

Again according to Crawfie, what she called 'the older members of the Household' felt there should be an engagement or a break.

Meanwhile a suggestion had come from Jan Smuts, Prime Minister of South Africa, that all four members of the Royal Family should pay a long visit to his country in the spring of next year. The invitation had been promptly accepted. That looked like the 'break'. Except that a counter-suggestion arrived in autumn 1946 – for an engagement.

A conversation between Queen Mary and Lady Airlie provided the first evidence that 1946 was to be the year.

They have been in love for the last eighteen months [said Queen Mary that January]. In fact longer, I think. . . . but the King and Queen feel that she is too young to be engaged yet. They want her to see more of the world before committing herself, and to meet more men. After all, she's only nineteen, and one is very impressionable at that age.

Lady Airlie, large and attractive with piled-up hair, objected that she herself had fallen in love at nineteen and it had lasted for ever.

Yes, it does happen sometimes [agreed Queen Mary] and Elizabeth seems to be that kind of girl. She would always know her own mind. There's something very steadfast and determined in her – like her father.[10]

The Princess's steadfastness and determination were to make themselves felt within that year.

Prince Philip himself was later to confirm 1946 as the date during an interview with Basil Boothroyd, who pointed out that Chips Channon had dated the marriage plan earlier. 'Philip of Greece is extraordinarily handsome. . . . He is to be our prince consort,' Channon had written on 21 January 1941. Prince Philip spoke on Boothroyd's tape recorder:

> I suppose one thing led to another. I suppose I began to think about it seriously, oh, let me think now, when I got back in forty-six and went to Balmoral. It was probably then that we, that it became, you know, that we began to think about it seriously, and even talk about it. . . .[11]

It is assumed by some Americans who have studied Queen Victoria's proposal of marriage to Prince Albert that Princess Elizabeth went back to what was protocol for a queen regnant a hundred years ago, and asked Prince Philip for his hand. A brief consideration of the two people involved shows that this procedure was inconceivable.

Princess Elizabeth's temperament was equable and gentle. She was easily the most unaggressive person in her circle. Her character was strengthening every day, but in early girlhood her happy family life had encouraged passive rather than active attitudes.

Prince Philip's always has been an active mercurial personality, in the sense that he was a messenger of the gods from the tip of his enquiring nose to his winged feet. Boothroyd has called his energy 'numbing'. Sometimes this energy, devoted as it is to getting things done, brushes obstacles aside with a scorn that can appear as arrogance. Albert of Saxe-Coburg and Gotha, Philip's predecessor as prince consort, was called arrogant when he was really diffident. Philip's 'arrogance' is no more than the impatience of a doer with obfuscators – the occasional rough manners of one who has never learnt to suffer fools gladly, or a touch of the royal naval chaff that was so apparent in Edward VII and George V. Real arrogance implies a layer of self-satisfaction, of conceit. Prince Philip is not guilty,

After the marriage of Lady Elizabeth Bowes-Lyon and the Duke of York, with King George V, Queen Mary and the Earl and Countess of Strathmore (left), 26 April 1923. It is a totally serious wedding group, as befitted royal photography in those days. (*Reproduced by gracious permission of Her Majesty The Queen*)

The Duke and Duchess of York with Princess Elizabeth as a baby, 1926. Her father described her birth as 'a tremendous joy'. (*Topham*)

Princess Elizabeth with her nurse Clara Knight, 'Allah', in her open carriage, 17 March 1927. (*BBC Hulton Picture Library*)

Princess Elizabeth sitting barefoot on a windowsill at her mother's old home, St Paul's Waldenbury, June 1927. (*Popperfoto*)

Princess Elizabeth's first appearance on the balcony of Buckingham Palace, 27 June 1927. Queen Mary holds the umbrella, while the Duchess of York holds the baby. (*Popperfoto*)

Princess Elizabeth standing amongst a field of lilies. (*Popperfoto*)

The Royal Family on the lawn at Windsor, 1936: their 'Golden Age'. (*BBC Hulton Picture Library*)

King George VI and Queen Elizabeth with Princess Elizabeth and Princess Margaret in their Coronation robes at Buckingham Palace after the Coronation ceremony, 12 May 1937. (*Popperfoto*)

The romantic Marcus Adams photograph of Queen Elizabeth with Princess Elizabeth and Princess Margaret, 1937.(© *Camera Club*)

Princesses Elizabeth and Margaret at the zoo with Miss Crawford ('Crawfie') (left), Bobo MacDonald and a friend inspecting regal penguins. (*BBC Hulton Picture Library*)

Training to become an ATS officer, Second Subaltern Princess
Elizabeth shows her mother her new skills in car maintenance,
April 1945. 'We had sparking plugs all last night at dinner,'
said the Queen. (*Popperfoto*)

Broadcasting her twenty-first birthday speech, 21 April 1947. 'I
declare before you all that my whole life . . . shall be devoted to
your service.' (*The Times*)

VE Day: The King and the Queen on the balcony of
Buckingham Palace with Prime Minister Winston Churchill,
Princess Elizabeth and Princess Margaret. (*Illustrated London
News*)

The first engagement picture of Princess Elizabeth and Lieutenant Philip Mountbatten, RN, at Buckingham Palace, 10 July 1947. The Princess is wearing her ring for the first time. (*BBC Hulton Picture Library*)

After the marriage of Princess Elizabeth and Lieutenant Philip Mountbatten on 10 November 1947, the Royal Family pose for a formal wedding photograph. In the back row, fourth from left, is Lord Mountbatten; on the extreme right are Princess Itelena Victoria and Princess Marie Louise; on Princess Margaret's right, in the front row, stands Princess Alice, mother of Prince Philip; the Marquis of Milford Haven is best man; the pages are Prince William of Gloucester and Prince Michael of Kent. Princess Elizabeth cannot help smiling broadly. (*Photo by Bassano, Camera Press*)

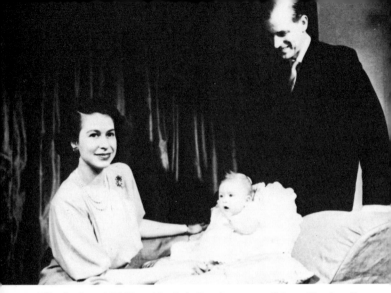

Elizabeth and Philip with their first-born son, Prince Charles. 'I still can't believe he is really mine.' (*Photo by Baron, Camera Press*)

Relaxing at the Villa Guardmangia in Malta as an ordinary wife, 26 November 1949. (*Topham*)

Square-dancing at Government House, Ottawa, 1951; Bobo was sent to buy the skirt. (*Popperfoto*)

partly because he is as little introspective or concerned with himself as he is intensely focused on external achievement.

He has wanted to bring the monarchy into the twentieth century. He was an agent of change, on the side of the innovators, the initiators. The Duke of Windsor got him right when he brought Prince Philip into the interview already mentioned.

> KENNETH HARRIS: You once said you . . . 'collided with the Establishment'. What did you mean by the Establishment?
> DUKE OF WINDSOR: Authority. Prince Philip is not a member, nor was I.
> KENNETH HARRIS: Why?
> DUKE OF WINDSOR: Independent. . . .

Of course the Duke of Windsor exaggerated, for a highly successful naval commander, as Prince Philip was, can never despise authority. Nevertheless, Philip shared with the Duke a certain unconventionality, a tendency to say, at moments inconvenient to the Establishment, 'Something must be done.'

His proposal to Princess Elizabeth was a case of getting something done in a situation which might become dead-locked. It was also inconvenient to authority, parental authority. Nevertheless, the Princess said yes. This was the first time she had acted on her own initiative over a major issue without consulting her mother and father. Perhaps Balmoral seemed the right place in which to say yes. It was on one of those much-loved hills that Crown Prince Frederick of Prussia had presented Queen Victoria's eldest daughter Vicky with a symbolic sprig of white heather.

The engagement was unwelcome to the King. Not that he objected to anything personal about Philip. On the contrary. 'I like Philip,' he had earlier written to King George of Greece. 'He is intelligent, has a good sense of humour & thinks about things in the right way.'[12] It was just Philip's existence. Without him, the 'Royal Firm' of four, as the King liked to call his family, were poised to capture South

Africa as a single compact unit, and by this operation the King set much store. With Philip present as his future son-in-law, the King would not have his elder daughter's undivided attention.

There was something like an argument between the King and Princess Elizabeth, the Queen supporting her husband, about whether the engagement should be announced before or after the South African tour. But the story that Princess Margaret joined in on her sister's side is untrue. 'I knew nothing of the engagement,' she says. The parents won; though not without scruples on the King's part at causing his daughter unhappiness. However, Princess Elizabeth had been crossed before, over her wish to join the ATS the minute she reached the normal age of eighteen, and the 'Firm' would emerge from this difference also as strong as ever.

The 'Royal Firm' sailed from Portsmouth aboard HMS *Vanguard* on 1 February 1947 in the manner that the King had set his heart on – all four together. 'I took a sad farewell,' wrote Queen Mary in her diary, though her collector's instinct was able to draw comfort from noting how many fittings from the old *Victoria & Albert* had been adapted to *Vanguard*.[13] Princess Elizabeth had attended *Vanguard*'s commissioning service and launched the ship.

There was a shadow over the King's pleasure also: the worst winter of the century held Britain in its grip. Had he shared his people's struggles against General Guderian or General Rommel only to run away from General Winter? The King needed South African sunshine, but he needed a clear conscience even more. While Mr Attlee tried to reassure him, the King constantly told himself how valuable the 'Firm's' mission would be. For he intended not only to thank the Union of South Africa for its part in the war, but also to make sure that the Union continued to play a part in the Commonwealth.

Princess Elizabeth had her own sorrow: many weeks' parting from the man she loved. She showed her disapprov-

al of the situation by commenting sharply on their programme: 'Well, I hope we shall survive, that's all.'

Nevertheless, a photograph was published of the family
on board which showed them relaxed in deck chairs lined
up under *Vanguard*'s vast jutting guns, the King in shorts
and the Princesses actually hatless. They rubbed up on
South African history and the Afrikaans phrases they had
begun to learn the year before[14] and they played deck
tennis with the midshipmen, a new sort of people it was
good for them to get to know. More than thirty years later,
in 1981 and 1982, they were to hold *Vanguard* reunions.
The selection of their personal staff formed an interesting
pattern in the light of coming events. Queen Elizabeth II's
future influential private secretary was there in the person
of Michael Adeane, now serving the King under Sir Alan
('Tommy') Lascelles; the Princesses' shared lady-in-
waiting was Lady Margaret Egerton, who was to marry
'Jock' Colville, Princess Elizabeth's first private secretary;
and there was Group-Captain Peter Townsend, the equerry whom the King had chosen from a non-court circle for his
bravery in the war. Townsend's squadron had shot down
the first Nazi bomber, over Yorkshire. On this tour, Townsend told the Household he was going to give up the royal
job and farm in the Transvaal.

Another royal anxiety was whether the Nationalists in
the Union, still marshalled by Hertzog against Smuts,
would give the Royal Family a cool reception. The ecstatic
welcome at Table Bay on 17 February seemed to quell all
doubts. The people had not perceived that the whole Royal
Family would turn out at 8.30 in the morning, prepared to
face the sweltering heat of summer. But there they all were,
standing on a lofty platform beneath the loftier guns, and
when Queen Elizabeth gave her well-recognised wave the
huge crowd burst into wild cheers. It was the first time that a
British monarch had sailed to them and they sang 'God
Save the King' with a will – not forgetting to follow it up by
'*Die Stem van Suid Afrika*'.

One South African family, the Aronsons, loyally followed the royal party round on many of their engagements, ending with a glimpse of them taking walking exercise by the new gold and ivory royal train. The train seemed a miracle of inventiveness. It was a third of a mile long, with a pilot train and 'ghost train' for repairs and, more important to Princess Elizabeth, a post office and telephone exchange which could be connected up with the main exchanges at stops. The Queen would walk off the train in one of her 'towering, flowery, sumptuous' hats on her head – but 'sensible' shoes on her feet. Theo Aronson, a friend and later the biographer of Princess Alice of Athlone, believed that the tour had been 'made' by the Queen. Her spontaneous graciousness to all, though already well known, nevertheless came as a delicious surprise; nor was she lacking in wit. One riposte to a disgruntled Boer has often been quoted but bears repeating: 'Pleased to have met you, ma'am,' he said, 'but we still feel sometimes that we can't forgive the English for having conquered us.'

'I understand that perfectly,' replied the Queen with her disarming smile. 'We feel very much the same in Scotland.'[15]

Princess Elizabeth, however, was able to steal the picture when she climbed one of the Matopo hills in stockinged feet, to see Cecil Rhodes's lonely grave at the top. She had lent her sandals to her mother, whose high-heeled shoes on this occasion were not 'sensible'. 'So like Mummy,' said Lilibet with daughterly amusement at her mother's high heels, 'to set out in those shoes.'

She also occupied the stage's centre when she opened the new East London graving-dock. It was vast, alarming and dominated by a fiercely windswept dais. But the Princess was successful, as always, when on her own. Later the King listened to her broadcast speech. Just as in the far-off days of the nativity play at Windsor, tears came into his eyes.

As always, there were plenty of family jokes. When wearing their finery they would ask one another, 'Is this a

special occasion?' During his Canadian tour in 1939 the
King had noticed a mayor without his mayoral chain. He
offered to present a chain if the mayor did not possess
one.

'Oh yes, sir, I have one.'

'But you are not wearing it.'

'Oh, but I only wear it on *special occasions*.'[16]

It was probably Theo Aronson's all-absorbing admiration for the Queen that made him occasionally assess the
rest of the family with a critical eye. (And certainly the
Queen never failed in circumstances however unattractive.
In the Snake Park at Port Elizabeth, three snakes were
tangled in the keeper's hand, two more on the ground at his
feet. The Queen managed to look interested, the Princesses were horrified, Elizabeth clutching herself, while the
King looked firmly in the opposite direction.) At times the
heat and the worries irritated the King almost beyond
endurance and he would have one of his 'gnashes'. It was
embarrassing for the young Princesses, especially when he
'gnashed' at the Household. But the Queen coped. A
spectator noticed her stroking his arm to calm him during a
tediously slow parade. He was justifiably infuriated by the
Nationalists' hostility to Smuts, once bursting out to the
Queen, 'I'd like to shoot them all!' To which she replied
soothingly, 'But Bertie, you can't shoot them *all*. . . .'[17]

Princess Margaret had a different method for breaking
the tension. She would make her father laugh, even when
he was angry with her. There was the occasion when she
brought a dinner-table 'gnash' to an end by suddenly
throwing a spoon over her shoulder. As it clattered on to
the floor everybody burst out laughing, and there was
nothing for Papa to do but laugh too.

Princess Margaret was said to have made a more 'pi-
quant' impression than her sister despite the occasional
'gaucheries' of youth, while the heir looked sometimes
'grave', sometimes 'rather stolid'. The fact was that neither
of the Princesses was very good at following behind her
parents. They tended to look bored or distracted. And no

one yet knew – though they speculated – that Princess
Elizabeth's heart was elsewhere; nor that the King was
already suffering from the cramps in his legs that were to
become so serious the next year. All told, though, the
verdict was not unenthusiastic:

> If the two Princesses did not wear clothes with their mother's
> assurance – they were in simple, girlish dresses – they, too,
> were more attractive than had been supposed. Both had clear,
> peaches-and-cream complexions and dazzling smiles . . . all in
> all they made an engaging family group, fresh, well groomed
> and with a lustre that was not entirely due to their rank.[18]

The praise was well deserved, for the tour had been a killer,
with only two or three days' rest.

Before they returned home they learnt something of the
shadow-side of a country they all thought 'wonderful'.
Children lining the streets between Government House
and Cape Town were sharply segregated like a chequer-
board into black and white, whereas in Rhodesia the Girl
Guides were mixed. In nationalist Stellenbosch the crowds
maintained a significant silence. H. F. Verwoerd, nationalist editor of *Die Transvaaler*, referred to the royal visitors
only as the cause of more burglaries in Johannesburg than
usual, because the police were out on the royal route. The
King was tactfully to touch on all this at a Guildhall speech
after his return home. He spoke of South Africa's unique
task:

> Nothing less than that of adjusting from day to day, the progress
> of a white population of well over two million, with that of a far
> greater number of other peoples, very different in race and
> background – coloured, Indian and above all African. There is
> no easy formula for the wise discharge of that formidable task.

The Union's formula was to be apartheid.
Meanwhile Princess Elizabeth had flown for the first
time, on an internal flight in the Union. And she broke a
record in being the first heir to the British throne to

celebrate her twenty-first birthday in the Commonwealth. Her broadcast speech on 21 April in Cape Town impressed the South Africans with how much she had come on during the tour, and inspired 'Boy' Browning, a distinguished soldier in England, to enter her service when she came home. 'It is my vocation to serve that young woman,' he said. (He became her Comptroller of the Household.)

Her coming-of-age at Cape Town she saw as a coming of self-dedication.

> I should like to make that dedication now [she said]. It is very simple. I declare before you that my whole life, whether it be long or short, shall be devoted to your service and the service of our great Imperial Commonwealth to which we all belong. But I shall not have strength to carry out this resolution unless you join in it with me, as I now invite you to do; I know that your support will be unfailingly given. God bless all of you who are willing to share it.

Despite the Princess's moving sincerity, the two points that stand out today are both somewhat ironical. There was no such thing as an 'Imperial Commonwealth' even in 1947; and South Africa, the very country in which she was speaking, was to 'support' her and 'share' her 'resolution' only for a limited number of years.

She took the salute of the South African troops wearing her favourite pale fawn, but at the city balls she glittered in a cloud of silver tulle and twenty-one diamonds.

Her father had set up two records also: he was the first British monarch to take his whole family with him on his travels, and the first to open a Commonwealth parliament. All these precedents were linked by deeply felt but unspoken thoughts. The Royal Family were aware that the Commonwealth was likely to go through a process that in any other international grouping might have been regarded as revolutionary. It would include the independence of India. In Britain, however, it was simply to be known as the New Commonwealth.

But first the King had to sanction his daughter's official

engagement, in many ways a harder fact for him to face than India's official independence.

As the great grey battleship sailed out of Table Bay the small receding figures were photographed again, waving under the guns. All but the heir presumptive. She stood with her hands clasped behind her back.

It is often said that Princess Elizabeth had a possessive father but an open-minded mother. This is a simplification as far as the King was concerned. His emotional feeling for his heir often brought him near to tears and sometimes, as we have seen, they overflowed. Yet his personal devotion was enhanced by a wider dedication to the Royal Family, inherited from Queen Mary. With his dry sense of humour he preferred the more quizzical term 'Firm' to 'Family'. Indeed an American had already described George v as 'Head of the greatest business organization the world has ever known.'

Princess Elizabeth's ordeal was almost over. She had told Lady Airlie before leaving for South Africa that they would have a celebration when they got home – 'perhaps two'. On 8 June the Princess said to another friend, 'Something is going to happen at last. He is coming tonight.'

He had also been through some frustrating experiences. Whether he wanted to remain in the Royal Navy or marry Princess Elizabeth, or both, he had to become a British subject. But his naturalisation had been held up by various vicissitudes connected with Greek and British politics, but not with him. In any case, Prince Philip had been a British subject from birth. This was not known, however, until a contemporary German prince named Ernest Augustus of Hanover established by law in 1972 that all descendants of the Electress Sophia were *ipso facto* British subjects, by the Act of 1705. There were several hundreds of the Electress's descendants alive in 1947, of whom Philip of Greece was one. Earl Mountbatten of Burma, Philip's uncle, argued that owing to this discovery Philip had all along been 'Prince Philip of Great Britain and Northern

Ireland'. The Lord Chancellor, Lord Dilhorne, however, could not agree. 'That would indeed be a novel title,' he wrote to the author in 1973. Today one view is that the Act applies only to the male line.

Philip was unnecessarily 'naturalised' on 7 February 1947, taking the surname of his mother's family, Mountbatten; a felicitous suggestion made by the Labour Home Secretary, Mr Chuter Ede.* With his naturalisation papers to hand, Philip's title went out of the window. The engagement was announced from the Palace at midnight on 10 July 1947 of a young naval lieutenant to the heir to the throne.

> It is with the greatest pleasure that the King and Queen announce the betrothal of their dearly beloved daughter the Princess Elizabeth to Lieutenant Philip Mountbatten, RN . . . to which union the King has gladly given his consent.

On the whole the press gave the match a warm reception. The Communist *Daily Worker* of course found it 'not to our liking'; but the Liberal *News Chronicle* approved of the marriage as 'a love match' and not 'arranged', though they exaggerated the element of 'childhood' romance: 'The Princess and the lieutenant have known each other since childhood, and have always been friends.' Warnings about 'an austerity wedding' and 'a housing problem' for the young couple were also issued by the *News Chronicle*. Though the *Sunday Pictorial* announced that forty per cent of its readers were against the Princess marrying a foreigner, this was nothing compared with what Philip's great-great-grandfather had had to put up with. Even the then Poet Laureate himself, Lord Tennyson, must have had some curious feelings about Prince Albert's foreign birth, for he dreamt that the Prince kissed him, on which Tennyson commented, 'Very kind but very German.'[19]

---

* Basil Boothroyd seems to imply that Chuter Ede was in turn 'advised' by Uncle Dickie Mountbatten (Boothroyd, *Philip: An Informal Biography*, p. 39).

Princess Elizabeth's life was suddenly transformed from patient endurance to limpid happiness. 'They both came to see me after luncheon,' wrote Queen Mary, 'looking radiant.'[20] The old Queen amused herself with working out the tables of their relationship: third cousins through Queen Victoria, second cousins once removed through King Christian IX of Denmark, fourth cousins once removed through collateral descendants of George III.

There were to be other changes in the Princess's way of life even before her marriage. Her staff was enlarged, notably through the addition of John ('Jock') Colville, her first official private secretary.

His appointment was well in line with previous examples of royal trustfulness, especially that of his future wife Lady Margaret Egerton. And the appointment of 'Meg' Egerton was no less informal in manner than that of other ladies-in-waiting. Princess Elizabeth happened to have stayed with Meg's family in March 1946 for a race meeting. The Princess was a somewhat withdrawn guest and hardly sat down, so that everyone had to remain standing. Meg's family tried to break the ice with party games. Three weeks later Meg received a request to call at Buckingham Palace with a view to serving Princess Elizabeth in her Household in June. In a panic, Meg put on a black hat and coat, rushed to London, arrived half an hour early for the appointment and walked up and down outside the gilded railings feeling like a prostitute on her beat. Once in the Princess's presence her excuses tumbled out: 'I can't write speeches. I can't spell. I get hay fever. I don't like racing. And in June I'm going to Skye.'

The Princess ignored the first four excuses but took Skye seriously. 'Come in May, then,' she said calmly, 'so you'll be free for Skye by June.'[21]

Jock Colville, an up-and-coming young man in the Foreign Office, was telephoned one day by 'Tommy' Lascelles, the King's private secretary. 'Look, I talked to the King,' Lascelles began. 'And the King remembers that as a young

man he was never told anything. So he thinks Princess
Elizabeth ought to have somebody who could write her
speeches for her and who knows how the machinery of
government works. Anyhow your family have long connec-
tions' – Jock's mother Lady Cynthia Colville was a lady-in-
waiting and both his grandfathers had been lords-in-
waiting – 'so would you do it?'

'May I think about it?' said Colville on the telephone.

Colville had been working as acting assistant head of the
Southern Department of the Foreign Office. He was bored
with dealing with 'tiresome Balkan countries', the endless
problems of Yugoslavia, Greece, Bulgaria. He had been
wondering whether he would not leave the Foreign Office
as it was so tedious and depressing in that hideous winter of
1946–7. But he remembered that his mother, despite being
a lady-in-waiting herself, had warned him against what she
called 'the gilded cage' of royal service. He should not get
enmeshed in the gilded cage because those who went into
the Household ceased to have contact with the outside
world and reality. He felt this would indeed happen after a
time, as one tended to become divorced from real life. Most
courtiers did not feel this divorce, he reflected, since they
were probably young aristocrats who had led a pleasant
life – shooting and so on (very agreeable entertainment) –
meeting pleasant people.

Remembering his mother's words, Colville went to see
Churchill and told him that he had been invited to become
the Princess's private secretary. What did he advise? Churchill said, 'If you have been invited it is your duty to accept.'

So Colville went back to Lascelles and said, 'I don't want
to throw up my life in the Diplomatic Service. So could I be
seconded for two years?'

Lascelles said he would talk to the King about it and the
King agreed.

Later Colville broke the news to Lord Rosebery. 'Yes,
she is a most charming young lady,' said Rosebery.

'I've never met her, except when she was in her bath aged
six months.'

'Don't tell me you've been made her private secretary without knowing her?'

'Yes.'

'Well, what about the King and Queen?'

'No, I don't know them either.'

'This is madness. I've never heard of such a thing.'

Just before the Derby, Lord Rosebery led Jock Colville into the paddock and presented him to the King and Queen and to his 'future boss' Princess Elizabeth. The Queen said charmingly, 'You must get to know us. You must come and stay for Ascot.' So Colville got permission to go to Windsor and remembers being received by Peter Townsend.[22]

There are two comments to be made on this extraordinary story. First, the debonair, highly intelligent young man was not appointed quite 'unseen', as he himself realised. Apart from the posts of his forebears at court, already mentioned, his maternal grandfather was the Liberal statesman Lord Crewe, and his paternal grandfather had been Lord Chamberlain to Queen Alexandra, Lord Derby's Chief Whip and Queen Victoria's Master of the Foxhounds. Jock Colville belonged to the magic circle all right; but, of course, he had already been private secretary to three prime ministers, and this in itself was considered a powerful recommendation.

Second, appointments by magic circle or 'old boy' network have changed in the royal system, just as they have disappeared from the Conservative Party in their selection of the leader. Today no one 'emerges' or is taken on as Jock Colville was thirty-five years ago, without even an interview.

During the rest of that summer things continued to happen, some on a gigantic scale, some minuscule, some only of great importance to those involved. Earl Mountbatten, Viceroy of India, brought India to full independence within the Commonwealth on 15 August 1947. This was only five weeks after Princess Elizabeth's engagement and was another big change for the King to accept. Queen Mary felt that the loss of the capital letter 'ɪ' from her son's title was 'very sad': GR instead of GRI (George Rex Imperator).[23] India was never to be an 'imperial' jewel in Elizabeth ɪɪ's crown; and there were more changes to come.

Marion Crawford married George Buthlay the next month in Dunfermline Abbey. He worked in Drummond's Bank. She scanned the Birthday and New Year Honours' lists in 1947, 1948 and 1949 hoping for a DCVO (Dame Commander of the Victorian Order) which she felt would have topped up the pension, the grace-and-favour cottage, the dinner service from Queen Mary, the coffee set from Princess Elizabeth and the table lamps from Princess Margaret. When this honour did not come her way ('a bit above her station,' said a courtier who nevertheless felt she had 'a nice side'), she launched into *The Little Princesses* in 1950 ('Book of the Month' in the United States), followed by magazine articles in Britain and across the Atlantic.* A publishing firm, Heinemann, who had been offered the book the year before, 'hinted darkly' to their adviser, Malcolm Muggeridge, that Crawfie had been assisted by a distinguished literary figure. Muggeridge and his friends guessed it was either Harold Nicolson or Osbert Sitwell.[24] Royal control on memoirs has been decidedly tightened since the 'Crawford' best-seller, and any breaches of the rules are known as 'doing a Crawfie'.

The Royal Family feel that they had relied on Crawfie completely and she broke faith, irretrievably damaging the old system of trust. Their friends agree. 'Crawfie had not just taught the Princesses,' says one; 'she had grown up alongside them. . . . The Queen's closest associate was Crawfie and now I wouldn't dare mention her.' There is a story of Peter Fleming the writer and sportsman once mishearing a remark of the Queen's at a luncheon party in Scotland. Thinking Her Majesty had said something about

---

* Crawfie's literary career came to an abrupt end when she published a gushing article in *Woman's Own* on the Queen at Trooping the Colour and Royal Ascot. Unfortunately the Trooping was cancelled and Ascot postponed owing to a rail strike! (Lacey, *Majesty*, pp. 180–1.)

'Crawfie', he replied, 'Oh, ma'am, how is she?' The Queen looked surprised and repeated 'Porchy', the name of her stud manager Lord Porchester. Peter Fleming waded on, 'I thought you said Crawfie.' Silence ensued.[25] The Royal Family may sound unforgiving, but they feel themselves to be in a special position where silence is their best defence. Other families might bring libel actions and clear up such cases in the courts. The Royal Family occasionally takes action, but more often freezes out the offender.

Meanwhile Philip Mountbatten accepted the things that had to be accepted. He was received into the Anglican Church in September by the Archbishop of Canterbury. The *News Chronicle* had announced authoritatively that Lieutenant Mountbatten would not change his faith, as the Greek Orthodox Church and Church of England were in communion. The *News Chronicle* was wrong on both counts, for though the Greek Church recognised Anglican orders, there was no inter-communion. The change would not distress his pious mother because of the traditionally warm relationship between the two churches.

On his wedding morning it was announced that the King had created him Baron Greenwich, Earl of Merioneth and Duke of Edinburgh. He was given a new armorial bearing, including hearts, lions, a cross and a turreted castle, his supporters being a golden lion with a ducal coronet on its head and a naval coronet round its neck, and the hero Hercules complete with bulging muscles, bushy blond beard, lion-skin round his waist, and cudgel. But as the Marriage Service was already in print, the bridegroom's name appeared on the day without a title.

On 9 November he had also been created a Knight of the Garter, Princess Elizabeth having been similarly honoured by her father, though a full week before Philip. This was protocol. Though the new name, Duke of Edinburgh, was adopted by the court, the old name of Prince Philip was still often used by press and people. Within ten years Queen Elizabeth II was to create the nation's prince a prince of the

United Kingdom and Northern Ireland. But not until the need was demonstrated.

At St James's Palace the royal wedding presents were laid out. There were said to be 1,500 on display, compared with 3,000 for Prince Charles and Lady Diana in a more lavish age. But the proportion of silver objects to be cleaned and polished was higher in 1947 than in 1981. And there were many gifts of clothing coupons, all of which had to be returned to donors. Two of the Princess's presents were magnificent and a third unintentionally controversial. The Aga Khan gave her a filly which she cleverly named Astrakhan; the people of Kenya gave her Sagana Lodge, a hunting lodge in the Nyeri country; and Gandhi wove the thread for a crocheted tray-cloth. Unfortunately Queen Mary, who was not usually strait-laced, mistook the tray-cloth for a loin-cloth. Philip had to drown her hisses of 'indelicate' in loud testimonies to Gandhi's greatness. 'Queen Mary moved on in silence,'[26] noted Lady Airlie – royalty's time-honoured method of dealing with an awkward situation. The next time round, Princess Margaret hid the object from Granny's view.

On the grey morning of the wedding, 20 November 1947, the 'custom and ceremony' of past events held Princess Elizabeth in its reassuring clasp. Bobo brought her early morning tea. She went down to her parents' room, she looked through her bedroom curtains at the gathering crowds in the Mall; all just as she had done before her parents' Coronation. She was silent while her wedding dress was being fitted, though at the end she said to Norman Hartnell's leading assistant, 'Mademoiselle, it is really lovely.' The white satin shimmered with garlands of stars embroidered in crystals and pearls. Then Jock Colville had to make a dash for her pearl necklace, still on display at St James's Palace with the other wedding presents (Colville argued his way through cordons of police), while everyone else hunted high and low for her bouquet until they found it cooling in a cupboard.

She set off for Westminster Abbey at 11.16, swaying beside her father in the Irish State Coach. Following royal custom she wore her veil off her face. The streets had been only moderately decorated in deference to 'austerity'. Indeed the Labour Government were warned by their trade union supporters not to exacerbate the timber shortage by using it up on scaffolding for stands. A cross-section of the immediate post-war age was provided by the guests in the Abbey. In the front pews and around the altar was gathered a concourse of still active European royalties, to support the couple with pageantry and consanguinity; flanking the aisle up which the Princess walked on her father's arm stood the Labour Cabinet and Government, half of whom were 'working men'.

Mr Attlee could not allow a public holiday while even potatoes were still rationed. The bride had been allotted 100 extra coupons for her trousseau and her bridesmaids twenty-three each.

There were perhaps a few regrets among feminists that the bride promised to 'obey' her husband as well as loving and honouring him – as indeed her daughter was to do also, although not her daughter-in-law. But then, Princess Elizabeth, like Princess Anne after her, was what her daughter would describe as 'an old-fashioned girl'.

Clementine Churchill walked up the aisle with her husband, the Leader of the Opposition. She had not thought much of life at Windsor for the young Princess – 'educated at Eton and all those dogs (horrid corgis) and poneys [sic]' – but to her as to everyone else the wedding was 'a shining miracle'.[27]

Outside in the Mall was a young reporter of eighteen, Anne Sharpley. She had been given a glimpse of the wedding cake a few days before and was in a mood to enjoy everything on the day, after seeing the cake's little temples of love and garlanded pillars, all made of sugar (rationed) icing. Yet even at eighteen she knew it was a hungry world that they lived in, cold, 'spiv-ridden', on strike at the Savoy, Smithfield and (*absit omen*) on the two *Queens*. But all that

sort of thing only made the day more glorious. The Household Cavalry, the plumes, the breast-plates, the singing of
'Land of Hope and Glory' and 'Oklahoma', the bands, the
cheers:

> The sight of so much glitter and finery [she remembered
> thirty-four years later], our first post-war experience of these
> things, was a hunger allayed. . . . White satin especially seemed
> the most exquisite pleasure, we'd looked at drab things for so
> long! All along the procession route people had brought out
> their old bits of ribbon and trailed and waved these in a kind of
> acknowledgment to the need of the day for smooth, beautiful,
> joyful, luxurious things.[28]

After the heather-decked wedding breakfast the bridal
couple set out for Waterloo Station, attended by the Princess's corgi Susan (a stowaway) and a pair of hot water
bottles. The honeymoon was to be spent at Broadlands in
Hampshire, home of the Mountbattens and years before
that of Edwina Mountbatten's forebear, Lady Palmerston.
The Palmerstons had not been above scuffles with Victoria
and Albert; but it was not the ghosts of ancient gunboats
that drove the honeymooners out of Broadlands and up to
Birkhall.

Peeping Toms ruthlessly invaded their privacy, even
rigging up the gravestones of Romsey Abbey as grand-
stands on which to watch them at prayer. Philip was not yet
soured, however, by years of prying and he devised a
good-tempered exercise in irony to be delivered as a
farewell message:

> Before we leave for Scotland tonight we want to say the
> reception given us on our wedding day and the loving interest
> shown by our fellow countrymen and wellwishers . . . have left
> an impression which will never grow faint. We can find no
> words to express what we feel.

There was someone else who could scarcely express what
he felt: the Princess's father. Unlike his own less sensitive

father, he did not write after the wedding, 'I know you will miss your old home.' But he did put into touching words how much he would miss her:

> . . . I was so proud of you & thrilled at having you so close to me on our long walk in Westminster Abbey, but when I handed your hand to the Archbishop I felt that I had lost something very precious. You were so calm and composed during the Service & said your words with such conviction, that I knew it was all right.

'All right' had been his own words telegraphed by him to his parents on his engagement.

Then his conscience stirred again over the long wait in South Africa and after:

> I am so glad you wrote & told Mummy that you think the long wait before your engagement & the long time before the wedding was for the best. I was rather afraid that you had thought I was being hard hearted about it. I was so anxious for you to come to South Africa as you knew.

Last came the famous heartfelt paean for the King's concept of the Royal Family – 'Us Four', the 'Firm', the company named 'Royalty and Son-in-Law'. This was to be the King's philosophy, worked out over the past ten years and in which his heir had been brought up:

> Our family, us four, the 'Royal Family' must remain together with additions of course at suitable moments!! I have watched you grow up all these years with pride under the skilful direction of Mummy, who as you know is the most marvellous person in the world in my eyes, & I can, I know, always count on you, & now Philip, to help us in our work. . . . I can see that you are sublimely happy with Philip which is right but don't forget us is the wish of

> Your ever loving & devoted

> PAPA.[29]

There were to be four more years in which Princess Elizabeth would have a father standing at the apex of the family. Beneath this protective figure she would have time to create her own independent patterns.

Interlude for Living:
1948–51

Three months after her wedding the happy Princess was pregnant, an achievement that was to be paralleled many years later by her own daughter-in-law. At Whitsun 1948 she was off to Paris on her first visit abroad with her husband. She had explained the situation to her private secretary and he wondered how she would stand up to it: the enormous crowds, the exhausting schedule, the hottest Whitsun ever recorded in Paris. There were to be four days on end with no rest days and five speeches, written by Colville and afterwards put into French. The Princess's accent was excellent.

When we arrived at the Gare du Nord [remembers Colville] it was all protocol – Princess Elizabeth met by the Chef de Protocol, procession, ambassador. By the time she left four days later – Versailles, luncheon at the Trianon, Fontainebleau, the races, the crowds thick in the streets cheering and shouting 'Vive la Princesse' – by the time she left Paris, feeling at times extremely ill, the French were absolutely at her feet.

It started as if it were going to be all rather cold, thought Colville, but at the end of the few days many hundreds of thousands had come out to see her.

I remember she read one speech at the top of an enormous flight of steps – at the Trocadero – followed by a special thing at the Town Hall. De Gaulle's brother was the Prefet of Paris at the time – the walls all papered in leather – terribly crowded – far too many people asked to every single function.

The pay-off, however, came not in a crowded room but in an empty one. The Princess was not feeling very well and Colville was deeply distressed at what went wrong.

One evening was to be arranged as a private one. We went to a most select three-star restaurant; the French had been turned out, so we found a table, just a party of us all alone in this vast restaurant. Prince Philip spotted a round hole in a table just opposite us, through which the lens of a camera was poking. He was naturally in a frightful rage. We went on to a night club, again the French all turned out. One of the most appalling evenings I have ever spent. Everybody dressed up to the nines – nobody in either place – except the lens.[1]

But no provocation ever made Elizabeth, whether as princess or queen, lose her temper. She could be highly critical of people if a task were not performed properly, but never malicious. Nor was she, or is she, in the least amused by jokes about officials, however laughable they may seem. On this same occasion at Whitsun 1948 there were some well-meant attempts to rescue her from protocol. But about things like that she was enduringly, immovably correct.

Prince Charles Philip Arthur George was born at Buckingham Palace six days before his parents' first wedding anniversary, at 9.14 pm on 14 November 1948. Apart from the portentous string of names (tongue-twisters for the lady becoming his wife thirty-one years later) the atmosphere of this child's birth had a refreshing informality.

His father had a workout in the palace squash court and pool while Charles was on the way, and was ready to bound in to the Princess with a huge bunch of red roses and carnations as soon as she came round.

'It's a boy,' shouted the policeman at the gates to the gathering crowds. Lustily they sang and for two hours called for 'Dad' and 'Grandad', until they were persuaded to go home and let the baby and mother sleep. Malcolm Muggeridge's diary read:

> Wrote leader [for the *Daily Telegraph*] on Canada, but it was mercifully scrapped after the first edition because of the royal baby, newly born. Everyone very pleased. How very much more satisfactory is the institution of monarchy than, for instance, the American presidency, with all the dangers and vulgarities inherent in the process of election.[2]

Next day the rejoicing all started again, with almost medieval abandon. Guns saluted, bells pealed, bonfires blazed and fountains ran with blue for a boy for a week. A suite was soon to be written by Sir Michael Tippett in honour of Prince Charles's birth, in which one can hear the bells.

But the part of one historical character had not been scripted this time. For the first time since the seventeenth century there was no Home Secretary present at a royal birth. Mr Chuter Ede had agreed with King George VI that a warming-pan was no longer likely to be smuggled into the Palace containing a spurious baby boy, nor was the Home Secretary's presence a statutory necessity.

The christening of Prince Charles was equally informal. It was conducted in the Music Room at the Palace (the bombed chapel was not yet restored) and attended among others by Bobo MacDonald and her sister Ruby. The Princess admired her son's hands, lying like perfect miniature wax models on the lace and satin christening robe, first used for Queen Victoria's children. 'Fine, with long fingers,' she noticed, '– quite unlike mine and certainly unlike his father's. It will be interesting to see what they become.'[3] They were to become the hands of a skilful amateur cellist.

Queen Mary wrote, 'I am delighted at being a great-grandmother! I gave the baby a silver cup & cover which George III had given to a godson in 1780 – so I gave a present from my gt. grandfather, to my great grandson 168 years later.'[4] The continuity of history could hardly go further. And what great changes had happened in those years. George III seemed as far away from Elizabeth of Windsor as he did from Elizabeth I.

'Don't you think he is quite adorable?' wrote the Princess to a friend, in a human spirit of baby worship which she half mocked. 'I still can't believe he is really mine, but perhaps that happens to new parents. Anyway this particular boy's parents couldn't be more proud of him.' But she gave herself only a moment for personal pride. Then her well-trained thoughts flew back to the public weal. 'It's wonderful to think, isn't it, that his arrival could give a bit of happiness to so many people, beside ourselves, at this time?'[5]

Her father was one to whom happiness was particularly necessary 'at this time'. True, the observant Chips Channon had noticed nothing untoward about the King's state opening of Parliament on 26 October; only its magnificence and His Majesty's charming smile for the Queen as he led her out at the end. 'It was like a Grand Slam in hearts.'[6] Channon, in his exalted mood, was disgusted to observe Mrs Leah Manning, a Labour MP, still dictating at her office desk in Whitehall as the National Anthem was played and the royal cavalcade 'passed under her nose' on its way home. Four days later the King's painful legs were examined by specialists and on 12 November tests revealed that he was suffering from early arterio-sclerosis. It might mean amputation of the right leg. Princess Elizabeth was not told until after the birth of her son. A royal tour of Australia and New Zealand was temporarily abandoned, and in March of the next year, though the King's leg was saved, a right lumbar sympathectomy was performed at Buckingham Palace.

On 18 June, Waterloo Day 1949, the King was well enough to give a splendid ball at Windsor with the Queen. Queen Elizabeth in a dazzling white crinoline showed her guests round the Waterloo Chamber, with its restored royal portraits, and the Canalettos and Zoffanys and French furniture in the passages and the amazing 550 feet of the Long Corridor.

> The Edinburghs [wrote the ubiquitous Chips Channon] made a somewhat late appearance (he had been to the Channel Islands or somewhere) and they looked divine. She wore a very high tiara and the Garter. . . . They looked characters out of a fairy tale. . . . At a quarter to five the Queen told the band to stop; everyone bowed and curtsied to the remaining Royalties and we left, and drove back in the dawn – looking back, the Castle rose romantic in the pink morning light.[7]

For the King it was becoming evening light. His incessant anxieties over the home front and Commonwealth during a turbulent period gave him no rest. At the end of this year, his fifty-fourth, it was a change to welcome his grandson for Christmas, while Charles's parents were in Malta. The King added a few words of his own to the text of his Christmas broadcast, in order to bring in Queen Mary and Prince Charles to his message: 'Here at Sandringham the Queen and I are very glad to have with us both the oldest member and youngest member of our family. . . .'

Queen Mary was eighty-two, Prince Charles thirteen months. Perhaps old age and babyhood seemed the only tranquil oases in a world where even 'our Commonwealth' was having acute growing pains.

For his earlier Christmas broadcast of 1948, King George VI had made some brave remarks about the Commonwealth. After reflecting on the new 'human relationship' involved in modern monarchy, he looked at the broader changes in his own work. 'Our Commonwealth – the British Commonwealth – has been subject to the laws of evolution,' he said on the radio. 'We would not have it otherwise. . . .'

That last sentence was the only doubtful one in a sincere fireside talk, for already 'evolution' had carried Burma away from the Commonwealth and Ireland was about to leave. The freedoms offered to Ireland within the partnership of which the King was to talk next had been too little and too late.

The King went on in regard to the existent Commonwealth:

> . . .it is stronger, not weaker, as it fulfils its ancient mission of widening the bounds of freedom wherever our people live; and for myself, I am proud to fulfil my own appointed share in that mission.

Princess Elizabeth probably knew little or nothing of what her father's next Commonwealth 'mission' would be. During this short four-year interlude in her life her mind was on other things. Nevertheless, on 21 April 1949, her twenty-third birthday, the second vast change within the Commonwealth was to be set rolling. It would radically reconstruct the Commonwealth within a generation.

The first great change has already been mentioned. This was India's independence, together with that of Pakistan and Ceylon as self-governing dominions, on 15 August 1947. The question to answer then had been: 'How the Commonwealth would fare if and when it lost its existing character as a fraternity of white peoples in a white-dominated world.'[8]

One way of answering was to look at the population figures. In 1911, when George V was crowned, the future 'Commonwealth' was ninety-nine per cent white and European. Thirty-seven years later, when George VI broadcast about Commonwealth 'evolution', the white population was only eleven per cent. That was the effect of independent India, Pakistan and Ceylon joining the Commonwealth.

Now in 1949 India took another step. With the assent of the Commonwealth Conference assembled in London, India became a republic. On 26 April, under the chairmanship of Clement Attlee, the seven Prime Ministers conveyed to His Majesty at Buckingham Palace the news of his own new status. India was to become a republic *within the Commonwealth*. India would no longer owe *allegiance* to His Majesty, but would acknowledge His Majesty as 'Head of the Commonwealth'. In future only the United Kingdom and the old dominions would owe *allegiance* to George VI, and these countries would henceforth be called his 'realms'. Therefore, as a concomitant change, the Monarch would no longer be the actual 'link' binding together the members of the Commonwealth. Instead the Monarch would have become a 'symbol': the symbol of Commonwealth unity.

And if any foreigner cared to ask how a republic could belong to a club of which a monarch was head, he only had to be informed that laws were made for men, as in the Bible, or that words must mean what they were told to mean, as in *Alice*. Or as the Quebec *Le Soleil* put it: 'The solution of the problem is in the good British tradition; it is both efficient and devoid of logic.'

Soon after this revolution by consensus, the Royal Family glided smoothly into its summer stream of 'custom and ceremony'. But for the first time an equestrian Princess Elizabeth took a prominent part in the June 1949 Birthday Parade and Trooping the Colour. Her father was well enough to take the Parade, but from his carriage, while his daughter rode beside it. His Christmas broadcast for 1949, listened to by Princess Elizabeth in Malta, was intended to be a review of the country's economy. Yet no daughter, especially a totally devoted one, could have failed to see how pathetically it described her father himself. Having spoken of 'the progress that has already been made', he went on to look at the future. 'But none of us can be satisfied till we are again standing upright and supporting our own weight, and we have a long way to go before we do that.'

The King none the less had made a good enough recovery to release his son-in-law once more for active service. (During the crisis of George VI's illness Prince Philip had studied at the Royal Naval Staff College, Greenwich, in

order to be at hand.) In autumn 1949 Philip joined the First
Cruiser Squadron in the Mediterranean of which Earl
Mountbatten was Flag Officer. Uncle Dickie too had
climbed back on to the naval ladder, but from the hard
golden seat of a vice-regal throne. Philip was First Lieutenant (second-in-command) of HMS *Chequers*, leading ship
of the flotilla. He was one step away from his heart's
desire – full command. Then came a crash – and Philip,
paradoxically, emerged from it at his unqualified best. The
somewhat broken studies at Greenwich had evidently left
him below par in one paper ('Torpedo and Asdic') of the
Command Examination. He had failed it. Admiral Power,
the Commander-in-Chief, sent for Michael Parker, Philip's
ADC, and ordered him to give Lieutenant Mountbatten the
bad news. In Power's own bluff opinion, however, the
examiner had been 'bloody' and Mountbatten's Torpedo
paper was 'a damned good pass'.

As it happened, Lieutenant Mountbatten was particularly prickly on the subject of princely treatment. He always
insisted on being judged on his own merits – or demerits.
Though Parker kept his lips sealed about the Admiral's
outburst, Philip knew enough of royal magic to suspect the
worst. 'If they try to fix it,' he exploded, 'I quit the Navy for
good!'[9] Sadly he had to quit the Navy for good within
eighteen months, for other reasons, but meanwhile he
passed the exam second time round and in July got his own
ship at last, the frigate *Magpie*.

Princess Elizabeth left Charles with his grandparents for
Christmas, as we have seen. 'He is too sweet stumping
around the room,'[10] wrote his doting grandpapa. (For all
George V's love of baby Lilibet at the same age, her
grandpapa had never got beyond one word to describe
her – 'sweet'. George VI saw things more vividly.) The
Princess joined her husband in Malta where their Uncle
Dickie handed over to his niece and nephew his own
delectable villa Guardamangia.

Clarence House in the Mall had been occupied by the
young couple only since 1949 and the paint of its Adam-

green grandeur and white nursery simplicity was hardly dry. Before that they had hoped to rent Sunninghill Park (it was burnt down) and did rent Windlesham Moor in Berkshire, while using a suite at the Palace as their London home. Now they were in their first rare Mediterranean paradise together, and at the beginning of a fairy-tale existence, fairy-tale because it was ordinary.

Ordinary everyday life is of course not limited to one particular mode. Elizabeth, princess and queen, has found it again and again wherever her family is and she with them. It may be behind closed doors, but there she undoubtedly lives one kind of ordinary everyday life.

Another kind was at Malta from Christmas 1949 to summer 1951, with gaps. It was the time from which some things were rigorously excluded and forgotten: ceremonial receptions, official functions, openings, plantings, layings, cuttings, unveilings. And it included shopping around, swimming, going to the hairdresser, making up parties with other officers' wives, picnicking, visiting restaurants, laughing, joking, suntanning, enjoying.

On one occasion one of the ladies-in-waiting was called at a few hours' notice to accompany the Princess, the lady on duty having suddenly fallen ill. The substitute parked her children on her mother, called for brandy and a laundress, and at the end of it all, after a dash to the ship, was awarded by the Princess the 'Order of the Pier-head Jump'. Princess Elizabeth lent her the only item she had forgotten, dark glasses. 'Even today,' this lady says, 'the Queen rather likes things to go a bit wrong. Then she copes.' The Maltese shopkeepers noticed that she was slow in handling money, but the wonder was that she handled it at all. None of 'the aunts' had ever held a purse. That was what a lady-in-waiting was for.

A few things naturally still marked out the Princess. Her detective; her royal conscience (she could not forbear visiting the odd school and hospital, and the sight of the very poor living in caves was an eye-opener); and her title of 'Ma'am', used by everyone except her relations. But there were several of these around, especially Dickie Mountbatten's family.

Mountbatten's wife Edwina was still the intrepid world traveller and worker for the oppressed, and the two Mountbatten girls were particular friends. Patricia had organised the Kingfisher patrol of Girl Guides for the Princesses at Buckingham Palace in the old days, and her two royal cousins Elizabeth and Margaret, together with her sister Pamela, were her bridesmaids when she married John Brabourne in 1946. Pamela was to marry David Hicks in 1961. She was one of the Princess's ladies-in-waiting.

Among the sites that the commander of *Magpie* took his wife to see was 'the birthplace' – Greece. *Magpie* was not equipped to carry a princess, so Admiral Power sent her from Malta to the Gulf of Corinth in his own despatch vessel, HMS *Surprise*, escorted by her husband's frigate and a destroyer. We are indebted to Boothroyd's *Informal Biography* of Prince Philip for recording the equally 'informal' messages that passed between *Magpie* and *Surprise* after a rough crossing.

SURPRISE TO MAGPIE: 'Princess full of beans.'
MAGPIE TO SURPRISE: 'Is that the best you can give her for breakfast?'[11]

This exchange happened to be *en clair*; but the Princess developed a nimble wit for coded signals also, some of them picked from the Old Testament. A warning about 'tacklings' being 'loose' from Isaiah 33:23, for instance, could be repudiated with a reference from Samuel 1.15:14, to 'this bleating of sheep'.

In Athens they saw the sights, including the floodlit Parthenon, the King and Queen (Philip's cousins) and the British ambassador in his pyjamas (seen by Prince Philip). His wife had given Philip the key to the ambassador's beach-house for a late-night cook-up, but forgotten to tell her husband. As the merry party, cutlasses in teeth, scaled the cliffs to the house, an upper window opened and a voice roared, 'Who's there?' Later the ambassador joined the invaders for sausages.[12]

If Greece was wildly exhilarating, Rome, visited by the Princess at about the same time, was somewhat daunting. Roman society was above everything smart and critical. And British ultra-Protestants at home raised the usual clamour about a royal visit to the Vatican.

The Princess flew home in spring 1950. She found her father deeply worried about the political situation. The second Labour Government under Mr Attlee (there had been a cliff-hanging election result in February) was barely clinging on, and the question kept arising in the columns of *The Times* – what was the King's prerogative in regard to a dissolution? Must the Monarch grant it if his prime minister wished to go to the country again, even after only two or three months? The King's private secretary, Lascelles, brought the argument temporarily to a close with an anonymous letter to *The Times* signed 'Senex' – Old Man.[13] He argued conclusively that the Monarch had the right to refuse a dissolution provided he could find another prime minister to carry on. Mr Attlee in fact carried on until October 1951.

At Royal Ascot in June, Chips Channon mistook the King's perennially youthful looks for good health. 'Ascot this year was highly enjoyable,' Channon wrote, 'and obviously the King, who now dotes on society and parties, adored it. He looks much younger than the Duke of Windsor.'[14] The Duke, too, looked young though pathetically lined, and the King never 'doted' on anything except his family – the miraculous three who with himself made up 'Us Four'.

On 15 August Lilibet presented him with the wonder of a second grandchild. Princess Anne Elizabeth Alice Louise was born at Clarence House at 11.50 am. The name Anne was a family choice, once ruled out by George v, and now reinstated as favourite; Elizabeth was for the baby's mother and grandmother; Alice for Philip's mother; Louise for their common relative, the Queen of Sweden. Truly a 'family' baby.

Queen Elizabeth, always the public's idea of a perfect queen consort, had won added sympathy over the King's illness. When she went from Buckingham Palace to see her daughter soon after the birth, the *Daily Mail* plotted – or plodded – the visit:

Princess Elizabeth and her daughter are continuing to do well. . . . The new Princess has blue eyes and weighs 6 lbs. The Queen drove to Clarence House from Buckingham Palace at 5.0 p.m. and stayed for two hours. Although she was at the birth, she did not see the baby then. On her second visit the Queen went straight to Princess Elizabeth's room.

She sat at the bedside and talked for a few minutes. As soon as she was content that the Princess was comfortable the Queen asked Sister Helen Rowe if she could see her granddaughter.

Sister Rowe handed the Queen a fine-meshed cotton mask. The Queen placed it over the lower part of her face before bending over the cot.

The baby was sleeping.

'Isn't she lovely,' remarked the Queen. She tiptoed away from the cot before removing the mask.

Downstairs she joined the Duke of Edinburgh for tea. For an hour and a half they sat talking. Then with her lady-in-waiting, Lady Spencer, at 7.7 p.m. she left to return to Buckingham Palace.[15]

Queen Victoria had publicised chloroform, Queen Elizabeth publicised face masks. Gynaecology moves on but royal family relationships seem to be as fixed as the stars. Lady Spencer, the Queen's lady-in-waiting, was the grandmother of Prince Charles's future wife.

Princess Elizabeth's ideas about her children's early days were derived from her mother's ideas about her own. Like her mother she began by nursing them herself; she provided them with a 'Mrs' Lightbody to correspond with 'Mrs' Clara Knight. (The former was ex-nanny of the Gloucesters, the latter of the Elphinstones.) There was no need for a pram to be bought, for her own was refurbished for

Charles and Anne. Charles can still remember looking out like a tiny Jonah from the inside of this whale of a pram.

There were two innovations however: Mrs Lightbody's assistant, Miss Mabel Anderson, was engaged through an advertisement, not family recommendation; and the Princess had to ration the time with her children more severely than her mother had found necessary. Clarence House was not the tranquil oasis that 145 Piccadilly had been. She played with them for half an hour after breakfast, not before breakfast as well; and though she always romped with them after tea, bathed them and put them to bed herself, her mornings and afternoons were often full. This pressure was to grow, not lessen, during 1951.

On 3 May 1951 an obviously ailing King opened the Festival of Britain on the South Bank of the Thames. It was a Labour brain-child, inspired by the Paris Exhibition of 1889 that had shown the world a French nation proudly recovered from the Franco-Prussian war. George VI doubted Britain's comparable recovery, but appreciated the added tribute to Prince Albert's Great Exhibition of 1851. Before making his opening speech on the steps of St Paul's, the King turned with a wry smile to the heralds and pointed out that the Skylon, centre point of the Festival, was not the perfect symbol for the British economy, since 'it had no visible means of support'.[16]

By the end of May a resistant attack of bronchitis made the King's doctors suspect that he had cancer. Even the early autumn at Balmoral failed to restore him, and on 23 September 1951 his left lung was removed. Eight doctors signed the bulletin, which told the public that 'His Majesty's immediate post-operative condition is satisfactory.' But the press were given to understand that there must be at least three or four weeks of 'healing' followed by 'convalescence'. That would bring the King's recovery to the end of November. Nevertheless on 7 October his daughter and her husband flew off to Canada and the United States on a long-arranged state visit. The Princess carried with her a sealed envelope in case the worst happened while she was away. It contained her Accession documents.

There was one advantage in the harassed visit. Prince Philip insisted that they could not go at all unless they were allowed to save time by flying, so for the first time the heir to the throne flew the Atlantic.

She left London Airport (not yet Heathrow) in the British Overseas Airways Corporation stratocruiser *Canopus*, captained by a pilot of unrivalled experience, Captain O. P. Jones. The journey was 3,400 miles, taking an unbroken sixteen and a quarter hours. After landing at Montreal, the royal party began their tour on 9 October at Quebec.

Racial problems that were later to beset Canada, such as 'bilingualism' (two official languages, French and English), had not yet reached their later proportions. A royal visitor had none the less to tread carefully in the post-war Commonwealth. After all, one reason why India had become a republic was because it disapproved of Canada's and Australias 'white' policy towards immigrants – though of course India objected above all to South Africa's anti-colour laws.

Prince Philip's instinct has never been to tread delicately. He has always written his own speeches and when feathers are ruffleable he sometimes ruffles them – as when he called Canada 'a good investment'. It was true and it was well meant, but some papers did not like a phrase that seemed to hark back to the days of Britain's colonial 'estates'. Even the Princess's young motherhood could give a handle for criticism. 'How could she leave those children?' asked one carper. It was a relief in Ottawa to have no worse problem than the need for a flared cotton skirt. The Princess sent out Bobo to buy one so that she and Prince Philip might join in the square dancing.

All told, however, the journalists and officials who criticised Philip for sharp remarks also admired him for making the tour 'go' and for piloting his wife with manifest love, concern and success. If his humour could sometimes make journalists frown, it could raise a smile in her at moments when she was looking unnecessarily grave. Something of the growing interest felt in this young couple overseas was conveyed by the crowds that welcomed them: 25,000 at the airport and 500,000 in the streets of Quebec.

On a brief visit to President Truman in Washington, the Princess and her husband struck him with the same kind of enthusiasm that her parents had raised in the Roosevelts twelve years before. 'They have a way of making friends, these young people,' Mrs Roosevelt had said. 'As one father to another,' wrote President Truman to King George, 'we can be very proud of our daughters.'

The Princess arrived home with her husband in mid-November, just too late for Charles's third birthday on the fourteenth. A photograph of him sitting beside his grandfather and earnestly holding forth was taken on the day. It never leaves Queen Elizabeth II's writing-table.

She found that her father had struck one more blow for his – and her – rights as a constitutional monarch. He was well enough to resume his instruction to her in 'the art of statecraft',[17] so it may be assumed that the latest development in Parliament formed part of his re-newed training. The object lesson was again the royal prerogative.

At the General Election of 25 October, Churchill had gained a narrow majority of seventeen seats over Attlee's Labour Party, the Liberals and three 'others' combined. The King sent for Churchill who, in presenting his cabinet list, had named Anthony Eden not only Foreign Secretary but also 'Deputy Prime Minister'. At once objecting that there was no such thing as the latter, the King had it deleted; his argument being that the existence of a 'deputy' would circumscribe his royal prerogative to appoint the next prime minister.

No doubt he explained to his daughter that, according to constitutional 'usage', Mr Attlee had been 'deputy' to Churchill during the war, and Herbert Morrison 'deputy' to Attlee from 1945 onwards. But the constitution, itself 'unwritten', would allow certain usages to exist which nevertheless could not be *written* into a cabinet list. Elizabeth II would find her Prime Minister Harold Macmillan in 1957 refusing to appoint R. A. Butler as his 'deputy'; but eventually agreeing that Rab should '*act* as deputy'.[18] Such is the subtlety of the British constitution.

George VI honoured Clement Attlee's long, selfless years of public service by bestowing on him the exalted personal Order of Merit. Though the mutual shyness of the King and his Labour prime minister had prevented them from unbending together, their terseness matched up to one another's high standards. On greeting for the first time a member of Attlee's government who happened to be an aristocrat by birth as well as a socialist, the King simply said, 'Why did you join them?' On hearing from Earl Mountbatten that the wrong man had been told he would be Chief of the General Staff, Attlee simply said, 'Untell him.'[19]

There was nothing laconic about the King's thanks to Elizabeth and Philip for their work in Canada. He created them both privy councillors on the same day. More work was ahead of them. An often-postponed tour of Australia and New Zealand by the King and Queen had finally been handed over that October to Princess Elizabeth and Prince Philip. The few weeks between their return and second departure were weeks of celebration: on 2 December a Thanksgiving Service for the King's recovery, his fifty-sixth birthday at Buckingham Palace exactly a month after Charles's, a gay Christmas at Sandringham unspoilt by the dreaded broadcast. The King was able to listen to his own voice thanking his peoples for their prayers for 'my recovery', the speech having been pre-recorded in short instalments as his strength allowed.

His new Governor-General of Canada visited him at Sandringham on 25 January and was anxiously asked by the King how he looked. 'I told him,' remembered Vincent Massey, 'that he seemed much better than he had in the early spring, which was true.' Massey carried away a picture of unbreakable courage, sense of duty, honesty of mind – all in 'a very endearing person'.[20]

The King's doctors visited him at the Palace on the 29th and after an examination congratulated him and themselves. Next evening the celebrations continued with a visit to *South Pacific* at Drury Lane theatre: the King, Queen, Princess Elizabeth, Prince Philip and Princess Margaret all in the royal box together.

On the morning of 31 January Princess Elizabeth saw her father for the last time. He stood on the tarmac of London Airport, hatless, watching and waving as his daughter and Philip rose into the windy skies on the first lap of their long journey.

The King was never told of the cancer, though he may have guessed. They warned him, however, that another thrombosis might make his life a short one. This knowledge seems to have brought him serenity rather than distress.

The King's religious faith was that of a simple believer, and in this Princess Elizabeth resembled him. Princess Margaret's interests were more like her mother's. They would both discuss theological problems, as they arose, with the Canons of Windsor. One of the former Canons, Dr Alex Vidler, remembers the Queen's questions about the famous theologian Reinhold Niebuhr. Niebuhr was the greatest American Christian thinker of the age and his British rival was C. H. Dodd. A saying among theology students went, 'Thou shalt love the Lord thy Dodd, and thy Niebuhr as thyself.'

The King had not a shred of the usual embarrassment felt by Englishmen over the word religion; indeed, after listening to an early morning religious programme called *Lift Up Your Hearts*, he lifted up his luncheon partner's spirits by suddenly asking her, 'What do you think of the Ten Commandments?'[21]

Whereas Queen Victoria had had a lofty pulpit placed in her private chapel at Windsor to remove the preacher as far as possible from the presence, the preacher now sat on a

level, fixed attentively and at close quarters by five pairs of
royal eyes.

The Canons of Windsor were an intimate part of the
family and allowed much latitude. Dr Vidler's corgi would
later sometimes get entangled both with Elizabeth II's
corgis and her baby's pram in the park. He would apologise
profusely and she would say with a charming smile, 'My
corgis have become pram-minded. They pay more attention to the pram than to me. They know it means a walk.'

Dr Vidler's thoughts might also get entangled, at least in
the King's eyes. He once published in the journal *Theology*
an article arguing that Christians should not participate in
Freemasonry. This caused a stir. It was taken up by the
Archbishop of Canterbury and the Dean. 'He must think
the Archbishop and I are heretics,' said the King – but
lightly, not in anger. Dr Vidler extricated himself by main-
taining that the Freemasons did not take all their rites
seriously, nor what they had to say. He was luckier than one
of the parochial clergy in the park. An eccentric but
popular preacher, this gentleman chose to celebrate Princess Elizabeth's wedding with a sermon on 'The Mating of
the Greenfly'. The King had to have him moved – to
Coventry.

Altogether King George VI was a deeply sincere son of
the Church, as he was also its head. This did not prevent
him from having 'ecumenical' perceptions before that word
was popular. It was against his better judgment that he was
prevented from sending a representative to Cardinal Hins-
ley's funeral. He would have rejoiced to know that a
cardinal and a moderator were to join in prayers with the
Archbishop of Canterbury for his wife's eightieth birthday.

In all these ways his heir was to tread in his footsteps.

As the shadows lengthened, it became clear that the King
had trained his heir in more than 'statecraft'. She had been
born with good judgment and had learnt to apply it from
watching her father. Jock Colville, her private secretary,
was impressed by the instinctive rightness of her decisions.

One difficult decision had to be made when she was still only twenty-one.

Shortly after her wedding Colville received a letter from Sir Stafford Cripps, President of the Board of Trade, begging that in the New Year Princess Elizabeth's wedding dress should go on tour to advertise British materials and workmanship. Colville took the letter to the Princess and showed it to her, with the recommendation that it was a good idea. After reading it the Princess said forcibly and without hesitation, 'I can think of at least five reasons against.'

At this distance of time Colville can no longer remember the five points separately, but the root of her objection is still clear. 'She thought that to do these things would be rather vulgarising the monarchy. It was her wedding dress. She didn't wish to part with it. Or show it more openly than in St James's Palace, where it was displayed. It might seem to be advertising the expense that must have gone into such a dress. I think she felt there was something vulgar. . . .'

After her refusal an astonishing reply came back from Cripps – handwritten in red ink. The gist of his remarks was as follows:

This country is very fortunate to have a young lady who one day will be queen with such judgment. I entirely agree with all her points. I signed the letter which had been prepared by the appropriate department without giving the matter proper consideration.[22]

And Cripps was the man who had once said when Labour got into power they would have trouble from the Palace!

But with all her good natural judgment, the Princess did not yet have much political knowledge or even curiosity about politics. In holding the position of her private secretary for two years, Colville felt it was his duty to awaken her interest. She could not see the cabinet papers, but he thought she might get the Foreign Office telegrams, or at least the more interesting ones. At first the King was unwilling and Colville spent several months of persuasion, through Tommy Lascelles – to the annoyance of everyone, including the Princess. At last Tommy agreed and the telegrams started coming. They were of course the dull ones. So Colville made a scene with the Foreign Office. Gradually the selection improved and he removed any dull ones that remained.

Colville's final impression was of a very human person who was not really involved in politics at that date, apart from the conversations with her father. 'Seeing some of the telegrams was in a sense preparatory,' he says; 'she wasn't interested in foreign affairs. She was young, just married, and all those kind of things. She wasn't interested until she was personally involved.'

That moment was to come all too soon.

After the departure of Princess Elizabeth and Prince Philip, the King and Queen with Princess Margaret returned to Sandringham, where Charles and Anne were again dependent on their grandparents and aunt for entertainment.

Sandringham was at its wintry best on 5 February. Only a few hours of daylight but all of them sunny. The King went out shooting, accompanied among others by Lord Fermoy, maternal grandfather of the as yet unborn Lady Diana Spencer. It was 'Keeper's Day', end of season. Everyone joined in clearing the fields of left-overs. In a sense it was 'King's Day', too, for he had never shot better. After dinner Margaret played the piano to him. When the footman took up his cocoa to his room he was reading quietly in bed. About midnight a watchman saw him come to the window and fasten the catch. With 'custom and ceremony' his last day had finished.

By 5 February the Princess and her husband had reached the Treetops Hotel in Kenya.[23] It was hardly a hotel; more a resthouse with three bedrooms, a dining-room, a small room for the hunter behind, and in front a specially constructed platform for watching wildlife. In a way it was a piece of wildlife itself, for it had been built into the branches of a giant *mgumu* or wild fig tree. In high spirits, they had arrived about three that afternoon from Sagana Lodge, their exciting wedding present from the Kenyan people. Built of cedarwood it stood on the bank of the Sagana River in the Aberdare Forest Game Reserve, near Nyeri.

Beneath the Treetops' platform was a salt-lick and large pool, which could be floodlit to represent moonlight and which was visited nightly by rhino, warthogs, deer and other wild animals of East Africa. There were wild men, too, in the forest, though the Princess did not know it. Jim Corbett, a famous hunter, had been stationed at the foot of the Treetops' ladder. He was on guard all night with a heavy calibre rifle. Princess Elizabeth had been told it was to protect her from wild elephants. If she had known it was to protect her also from the beginnings of Mau-Mau she would still have gone ahead.[24]

At first all looked tranquil: Colobus monkeys swinging in the Cape chestnut trees whose purple flowers were reflected in the still pool. But in fact the Princess's party were entering the oval clearing – 200 yards by 100 yards – an hour after forty-seven elephants, including five cows with calves and three trumpeting bulls, had crashed out of the forest. A white pillowcase was fluttering on the roof of Treetops to warn the party of danger. When they saw a huge old cow elephant with two calves standing beside Treetops flapping her ears, a whispered consultation took place. There was fifty yards of open ground to cover in front, and behind them a narrow forest path, with safety ladders hanging from some of the trees. Should they advance or retreat? They were ten minutes away from their cars. The cow had not scented them and there were three guns in their party including Prince Philip's. 'Go ahead!' he said.

It was decided to divide the party in two, Lady Pamela Mountbatten and Mike Parker (lady-in-waiting and equerry) waiting for five minutes or so beside a ladder each. (They were told next day that 'those ladders were absolutely useless – if an elephant wants to get you out of a tree it just shakes the tree and down comes the ladder.') The Princess would run less risk by going steadily forward than going back. Steadily and silently she went, not treading on a twig; up the Treetops ladder into the thirty-foot tree, from which she would descend the Queen of Kenya.

Before sunset they had a hilarious time watching the elephants blowing dust over pigeons and over themselves, with plenty of trumpeting. Treetops had been decorated with white bunting as if in their honour, some baboons having reached through a window and stolen the toilet rolls out of the little house, and draped the branches of the fig tree.

In the pause after sunset the Princess spoke of her father: the cold day he had faced at London Airport – 'He's like that, never thinks of himself.' But she felt he had turned the corner when he raised his walking stick to his shoulder recently, saying, 'I believe I could shoot now!'"

All night in shirt and slacks the Princess worked with her cine camera; then an hour or two's sleep, ready to be photographing again at dawn. This time it was an old rhino at the salt-lick. Kenya time was three hours in advance of British time; it is therefore more than likely that it was at a moment when the King and his successor were both asleep that the crown passed. King George VI died peacefully in his sleep during the very early hours of 6 February 1952. *

At Mombasa the staff of Queen Elizabeth II, as she now was, were busy packing up, ready for the long passage from East Africa to New Zealand and Australia. There was a lot of cheerful noise. Stands were being erected, poles hammered into place, to welcome the royal couple; bunting and flags unfurled to give them a joyous send-off. Lady Abel Smith, a lady-in-waiting, was in charge of the typewriters, getting them stowed. Suddenly she noticed that the hammering had stopped. There was a dead silence. The Comptroller of the Household, General 'Boy' Browning, dashed up, his face ashen. 'The King has died!'

* The Queen was to visit Kenya in 1983, the thirtieth anniversary of her Coronation.

The 'New Elizabethans': 1952–3

Another day of quiet pleasures seemed to be unfolding as the lady they still called Princess left Treetops before ten o'clock on the morning of 6 February 1952. She and her husband were off to fish for trout in the Sagana stream, twenty miles away. Jim Corbett, the hunter, had spoken of Her Royal Highness's 'cool courage' and now Eric Sherbrook Walker and his wife Hazel, the hotel managers, on receiving the Princess's thanks as the party said goodbye, had the same thought. 'It's been my most thrilling experience yet,' she said.

He replied, 'Ma'am, if you have the same courage in facing whatever the future sends you as you have in facing an elephant at eight paces, we are going to be very fortunate.'[1] Prince Philip laughed, his usual reaction to compliments. No one in the group guessed that the next demonstration of courage required of her would not be physical.

The news of the King's death was received first by Martin Charteris, Princess Elizabeth's private secretary who had succeeded Jock Colville in 1949. (When Colville returned to his Foreign Office career, the Princess had said, 'You must find someone to take your place.' Martin Charteris was his 'find': a professional soldier and member of the talented Wemyss family.)

While lunching at the Outspan Hotel across the valley from Sagana, Charteris was summoned urgently to the telephone. A reporter was in the booth. There had been an unconfirmed newsflash to Nairobi from Reuters. 'The King is dead,' the reporter repeated. 'It seems he died in his sleep.' Some difficulty arose about confirming the message, since the Governor of Kenya and his staff were already entrained for Mombasa, expecting to welcome and see off the royal party on *Gothic*. But within an hour Charteris was able to call a press conference, having informed Commander Mike Parker, who told Prince Philip. The Prince looked as if the whole world had dropped on him, said Parker afterwards. 'The lady we must now call Queen,' were the words Charteris used to the press. He felt stimulated by the challenge to get his lady home as smoothly and speedily as possible.[2]

Nevertheless, the first twenty-four hours of the Queen's reign were not only grief-stricken but also entirely unlike the usual well-oiled royal procedures, being a series of hurried makeshifts. Prince Philip broke the news to his wife, as she stood in a white summer dress under an overclouding tropical sky. They had both taken a brief siesta and she had gone out to ask Bobo to order the riding horses early next morning. Now there were quite other orders to be given. Messages to be drafted by her and despatched to her hosts in East Africa thanking them; to those in New Zealand and Australia who should have been the Princess's hosts but now would be the Queen's subjects; above all to her mother and sister. After the letters and telegrams were finished, her husband took her back to the peaceful Sagana stream where they walked together up and down, up and down, along the bank. She felt utterly overwhelmed but knew she must not show it.

After her husband, her cousin Pamela came to her.[3] She still remembers vividly the contrast between the 'wonderful, marvellous night' they had all spent at Treetops and the morning's news – almost impossible to believe'.

One couldn't think what to say, and I suppose one's only reaction was that it was her father who was dead – it didn't sink in that it was the King. And it was such a shock. We would never have left England if there had been an inkling that there was any danger, as it seemed so certain he was recovering marvellously.

In her usual extraordinary way, when I went in she was thinking about what everybody else was having to do. Typically she said, 'Oh – thank you. But I am so sorry that it means we've got to go back to England and it's upsetting everybody's plans.'

Then the questions and answers began again. Charteris had to open and prepare for use the sealed Accession documents she had been carrying around with her since the Canadian tour last autumn. Her name was needed on them. But what name? Her father had changed his name on accession from the presumed Albert I to the chosen George VI. She might choose to be Queen Mary III (her second name) rather than risk confusion with Queen Elizabeth her mother. When Charteris put the question she answered with characteristic directness: 'My own name, of course – what else?'

In fact there was no confusion, even at court. Henceforth Elizabeth II was to be known as The Queen and her mother as Queen Elizabeth.

Still the questions went on.

'Have I any mourning here?' No, it was all packed on board *Gothic*, and would have to be flown from Mombasa to join her plane. So the Queen would start her sad journey still in her white dress, hat and gloves. (Not that mourning was ever a fetish with Elizabeth II – one respect in which she differed radically from her revered great-great-grandmother Queen Victoria. Though she always wore mourning in public for as long as was correct, she would not necessarily darken her own rooms at home, for herself and her children, with months of black.) When the party's black clothes arrived, Pamela Mountbatten remembers thinking, 'I must get into mine.' But there was no way the Queen would put hers on. 'I know she wore her ordinary clothes,' says her cousin, 'till literally the plane doors were open and we were in London. The sort of feeling, "If I put my black on now, that's admitting he's dead. . . ."'

It was five in the afternoon when the royal party began their drive to the nearest airfield, Nanyuki, whence they would fly by Dakota the 500 miles to Entebbe in Uganda, changing at Entebbe on to the same plane, *Atlanta*, that had brought them out only a week before. Before leaving Sagana the Queen was seen to look back at Mount Kenya, glittering like a 'vast diamond' beneath the fast disappearing sun and oncoming stormclouds. The next 'vast diamonds' that the Queen would see would be in the regalia.

All along the road were scattered groups of Africans, there to salute the Queen of Kenya, and then the Queen of Uganda, in heartfelt silence. The press were persuaded not to photograph her in her gay summer clothes when she arrived at Nanyuki. The weather was not so considerate. After a bucking flight from Nanyuki, tropical thunder and lightning burst over Entebbe, holding up the tense travellers for three frustrating hours.

They were over London when the February dusk was beginning to fall on the afternoon of the 7th. As she looked down the Queen saw the black cars that had come to fetch her. 'Oh, they've sent those hearses,' she said, using the name that she and Princess Margaret always used for the royal cars – but using it now with a difference.[4] The words were a lament not only for her father's death but for the death of her own youth. If only they hadn't sent the hearses; if only for another half hour she could have had her own personal life. But at twenty-five her personal carefree life was over. 'Her return was terrible,' said Pamela Mountbatten; 'it was a double grief. She was stunned.'

Beneath the Queen's circling plane was also drawn up on the dark tarmac a group of politicians in black overcoats: Winston Churchill her Prime Minister; Clement Attlee, Leader of Her Majesty's Opposition; Lord Woolton, Leader of the House of Lords; Harry Crookshank, Leader of the House of Commons; and Anthony Eden, Foreign Secretary.'

'Shall I go down alone?' she asked her nearest relative

who had boarded the plane to greet her – her uncle the Duke of Gloucester.

The eighteen-year-old Victoria had met her Archbishop, Lord Chamberlain and the late King's physician for the first time '*alone*', having deliberately freed herself from her mother's hand in order to do so. Now Prince Philip stepped back of his own accord. The slight black figure of the young Queen, strong in her loneliness and the chivalry it aroused, walked slowly down the gangway into her new life.

Anthony Eden was to remember vividly the Queen's arrival. 'The sight of that young figure in black,' he wrote in 1960, 'coming through the door of the aircraft, standing there poised for a second before descending . . . is a poignant memory.'[5]

The impression was to be repeated with variations next morning, 8 February, at the Accession Council of Queen Elizabeth II, held in St James's Palace. Again the young Queen in black appeared before a gathering of elders quite alone, after pausing for a moment in the doorway. This time it was Vincent Massey, the Canadian privy councillor, who remembered how 'a slight figure dressed in deep mourning, entered the great room alone, and, with strong but perfectly controlled emotion, went through the exacting task the Constitution prescribed'.[6]

She had walked across the courtyard from Clarence House to St James's Palace, picking up a few flakes of snow on her shoes. If there was an icicle inside her it was a mixture of grief and fright. Yet she read her Declaration of Sovereignty to the assembled privy councillors in a clear steady voice. The need to mention the King's much-loved name twice over was a test of control – 'the death of my dear father. . . . I shall always work as my father did. . . .' – and it was more than a mere relief when Prince Philip stepped forward at the end and silently led her out. They drove down to Sandringham that afternoon, where her father was to lie by nightfall in a coffin of Sandringham oak.

St James's Palace had been the sovereign's palace long before the former Buckingham House was bought by George III; and indeed ambassadors are still accredited to the Court of St James, not of Buckingham Palace. But if historic custom had been maintained at one point it was changed at another. Queen Victoria, the last Queen Regnant, had received the homage of her privy councillors individually, each one kissing her hand; whereas the privy councillors had bowed in unison to Elizabeth II as she entered the chamber.

Queen Mary, who was beginning to be very old, had insisted on the ancient form of homage when her granddaughter had arrived at Clarence House the evening before. 'Her old Grannie and subject,' said Queen Mary, 'must be the first to kiss Her hand.'[7] She was to be the first by many months, since formal homage was not made until the Coronation, a year and four months later. Nor had the Queen's husband, mother or sister paid this kind of antiquated respect.

After the Declaration, Her Majesty Queen Elizabeth II was proclaimed by heralds from the ramparts of St James's Palace and elsewhere in London. James Pope-Hennessy and Clarissa Churchill, the Prime Minister's beautiful niece, were present at 'the scarlet and gold proclamation of Queen Elizabeth II at Temple Bar'.[8] And for the first time a sovereign was able to watch her own proclamation on television, though only in black and white not scarlet and gold.

Though Pope-Hennessy had reacted warmly to the pageantry at Temple Bar, he was one of those who felt shocked by the flood of emotion that the King's death and Queen's Accession let loose. He described the eulogies of George VI as 'press hysteria . . . this national obsession'.[9] Some years later, as the official biographer of Queen Mary, he was to understand and interpret better than anyone the impact of royal events on the human heart. But in 1952 and the years that immediately followed, the 'hysteria' which already distressed a few fastidious spirits was to get ever more out of hand, until it toppled over in equally excessive criticism.

Calm in joy, calm in grief. This was to be the impression made on those nearest to her by the new Queen. Her emotional father had observed the first, as she walked up the aisle beside him on her wedding day. Now it was the other kind of calm that struck everyone. Both were aspects of the same powerful, inherent reticence that seemed to spring from remoter genes than those of either her father or mother. Perhaps from that 'old Grannie' of hers? Queen Mary had once lamented that some quality labelled 'finesse' had vanished from the modern world, where all was surface, brash, obvious. Finesse and reticence have an element of secrecy in common.

Or perhaps the Queen's reticence came from even further back? 'Little mysterious Victoria' was how Thomas Carlyle had described a young sovereign more than a century before. Change the name to Elizabeth, and you had a hint of the new young Queen.

Her mother had always been different; taking the breath away with her confidentiality and outgoing, not secret, smiles. On 17 February, ostensibly to make it known that henceforth she wished to be called Queen Elizabeth the Queen Mother, she issued a long, intimate message to the nation that staggered and delighted the radical *News Chronicle*. 'It is a statement without parallel in the history of kingship,' its editor declared. Towards the end of her statement the Queen Mother passed significantly from the late King's pledge of service, taken 'at the sacred moment of his Coronation fifteen years ago', to the future of his successor.

> I commend to you our dear daughter: give her your loyalty and devotion: in the great and lonely station to which she has been called she will need your protection and your love.

People were already thinking about the Coronation, and what it would and should mean. The proclamation had emphasised matters of high constitutional import. For the first time a sovereign had been proclaimed 'Head of the Commonwealth', London leading the way, on 8 February, in this novel and down-to-earth phrase that stuck out so forcibly from the traditional language surrounding it. And as Head of the Commonwealth, the Queen now at last presided over 'realms' not 'dominions' – in formal language as well as in fact. Moreover the crown was no longer referred to as 'imperial'.

London had led the way and was followed in the new formula by three of the other 'realms', Australia, New Zealand and Ceylon. It was only because of the vagaries of the clock that the ultra-independent Canadians and South Africans paradoxically proclaimed their own queen in the old-fashioned terms: 'Our only lawful and rightful Liege Lady Elizabeth the Second by the grace of God, of Great Britain, Ireland and the British Dominions beyond the Seas.' London's new lead had run as follows:

> Queen Elizabeth the Second, by the grace of God Queen of this Realm and of all Her other Realms and Territories, Head of the Commonwealth, Defender of the Faith, to whom Her lieges do acknowledge all of the Faith and constant Obedience, with hearty and humble Affection. . . .

India, as we have seen, was no longer a 'realm'. She sent Elizabeth II a message of 'hearty' if not 'humble' affection on the same date through her prime minister, Pandit Nehru:

> May I also welcome Your Majesty as the new Head of the Commonwealth and earnestly trust that this great fellowship will continue to work for the cause of human understanding and peace throughout the world.

The Queen was soon to be carrying her own message into the 'great fellowship' of the Commonwealth. But first there were a thousand duties to perform in the United Kingdom before the Coronation: state papers to sign, addresses to receive, people to meet, cities to visit. Above all and first of all, the sorrowful farewell to her father.

There were three queens and no king round the catafalque in Westminster Hall, a solemn preview of the new age which women would claim for their own. Yet the three queens, in their dense black clothes and long veils, also carried the imagination back to Tennyson and Malory. At the burial in St George's Chapel, the medieval banners resplendent with towers, suns and phoenixes, hung above the royal coffin, seeming to hold promise of new life. The Chamberlain broke his white staff, Elizabeth II threw in her handful of Windsor earth, and the most poignant moment of her reign was over.

But for the silent congregation it was the new Queen's own solitary figure that gathered all the pathos of the ceremony into itself. One venerable Labour peer, Lord Pethick-Lawrence who was sitting next to me, spoke aloud his very human thought: 'Charming little creature! I only hope they don't work her too hard.'[10] (His wife had been a militant suffragette.)

Expressions of solicitous anxiety were soon to be heard from the Queen's grandmother and her doctors. Queen Mary was particularly pleased to report on her granddaughter's visit to Edinburgh in July 1952: 'It was a wonderful success. The Queen captured all hearts. She is certainly a real *Sovereign*, always doing the right thing instinctively. I only hope they will not kill the poor little girl with overwork,' she ended.[11] And *The Lancet* stated, 'As doctors we should have special reason to welcome an assurance that . . . Her Majesty's health and vitality will be protected from her hereditary sense of duty.'

There was one matter over which the Queen was not going to tire herself, and that was by dreaming up ways of doing things differently from her predecessors. She read what she had to read 'like lightning', said her private secretary, twice as fast as her father, and remembered all that she read with the same accurate retentiveness that he had shown. But the Queen was not 'steamed up on reforms; she was *utterly* constitutional'. That was her guideline, almost her lifeline.

Most appropriately, her first public duty was to dispense the 'Maundy' gifts in St Paul's Cathedral. The ritual went back to the twelfth century, and the recipients in 1952 were pensioners who had rendered Christian service to the community. They all looked good, unpretentious people, the women in thick gloves clutching large handbags. The Queen presented a red and a white purse to each pensioner, the red containing an allowance for clothes and food, the white containing the Maundy silver pence – the only silver coins still minted. Two other groups, whose roots went far back into history, played a part in the service. The Chapel Royal Choir had sung at the victory of Agincourt, and the Queen's Bodyguard of the Yeomen of the Guard were the oldest English military corps in existence, having been created by the victor of the Wars of the Roses, Henry VII, in 1485.

For the moment the Queen's active, energetic mother could not help her much. Few realised how desolated and drained the Queen Mother had been by the death of her husband. During his last illness she had seemed to talk to ordinary people she met quite happily and optimistically, as if she and they together were going to get him well. 'We must look after him. We mustn't let him do too much.' Her gallant message sent out only ten days after his death hinted at deep resources of faith and hope. Her intimate friends and ladies-in-waiting, however, realised that the wound went so deep she might retire altogether to her native Scotland and let the world go by. But a recently published letter from the Queen Mother to the poet Edith Sitwell shows that her vein of mysticism possessed a saving power.

Dame Edith had sent her friend Queen Elizabeth a copy of her new literary anthology, *A Book of Flowers*. In thanking her, Queen Elizabeth wrote on 15 September 1952:

. . . I started to read it, sitting by the river, and it was a day when one felt engulfed by great black clouds of unhappiness and misery, and I found a sort of peace stealing round my heart as I read such lovely poems and heavenly words.

I found a hope in George Herbert's poem, 'Who could have thought my shrivel'd heart, could have recovered greennesse. It was gone quite underground' and I thought how small and selfish is sorrow. But it bangs one about until one is senseless, and I can never thank you enough for giving me such a delicious book wherein I found so much beauty and hope, quite suddenly one day by the river.[12]

The other member of the Queen Mother's household, Princess Margaret, was in a scarcely better position to share the royal burdens in 1952. She was under a double strain. First, there were her own poignant feelings for a father who could never see anything but enchantment in his gay, entertaining, provocative, altogether delightful younger child. Now the contrast was dark indeed. In a house of mourning, she turned more and more to another male figure, Peter Townsend.

Those who had been with the Royal Family in South Africa five years before noticed that everyone was 'in love' with Peter Townsend – everyone except Princess Margaret. The Queen, the ladies-in-waiting, even Princess Elizabeth when she was not telegraphing or telephoning to Prince Philip. Certainly to most women he was irresistible, with his appealing kind of good looks, excellent mind, and interest in spiritual problems and values not always to be discovered in every group-captain, however heroic. Unhappily tied to a hasty wartime marriage, he would occasionally irritate and overburden his men friends with too many confidences. 'He was inward looking and one of the world's egocentrics,' remembers one such confidant; '"I want to have a talk with you," he would say, and then talk for three-quarters of an hour entirely about himself – all the internal problems. If I had been a psycho-analyst and been paid for doing it!'[13]

Margaret at sixteen-plus had found him easy to talk to and easier to tease.

Then things changed. By the next year, 1948, a few people close to the Princess are said to have noticed something new in her feelings for the equerry. The first occasion was at the investiture of Juliana as Queen of Holland. Townsend escorted Princess Margaret and was seen dancing with a young woman so radiant that several of those present guessed at the implications. Another year passed and Chips Channon, after the Windsor ball, entered in his diary the strangely tragic impression made by Princess Margaret's beauty. She had a 'Marie-Antoinette aroma' – the sparkle not of diamonds but of tears. 'What will the future hold for her?'

The writer Paul Johnson was the first to point out that Channon, however observant, did not observe the slight figure in RAF uniform standing near the Princess.[14] Scarcely surprising, since not even members of the Royal Family had 'observed' Peter Townsend in this sense. When his wife Rosemary left him and he obtained a divorce in December 1951 with custody of his two sons, there were still no 'observations'. Indeed the Queen Mother appointed him her major-domo at Clarence House. (There had been another change around of houses, the Queen and her family occupying Buckingham Palace while Queen Elizabeth and Princess Margaret retired to Clarence House.)

Then in the summer of 1953, shortly before the Coronation, the head of the Queen Mother's Household declared his love to the Princess.

The first thing for the couple to do in this new and dramatic situation was to tell the Queen, her family and advisers.

If the young Queen still had anything to learn – and who has not, at every stage of life? – it was about people. Her unusual maturity in her work was not matched by the same mature perception of how people were thinking and feeling. A member of her staff in those early days said that she 'never fussed if a speech was mislaid nor faltered when on the job, whether it was talking to a mayor, town clerk or hospital nurse; but she did not get on nearly so well with the young of her own class'. At her desk she was a marvel of concentration and accuracy. Serving Her Majesty was like working with a man who had run an office successfully for twenty years. She was never late, never impatient. 'There was no one – there could be no one – better to work for. You knew where you were, you really did.'

No time was ever wasted on trivia; she would stand over a pile of documents and suddenly place a finger on one paragraph with the words, 'I think *this* is the important bit. We must go into this.' Her training in the ATS no doubt partly accounted for her methodical manner of going about things. It had not given and could not give an equal training of the imagination.

Both the Queen and Prince Philip, with their phenomenally good health, had little concept of how often most people have moments of 'not feeling very well'. A secretary with a cold was anathema to Prince Philip, for if he caught it himself a vital engagement might be missed. The young Queen seemed to suffer from no physical frailties whatever: she never got hot and bothered or needed to dab at her nose; the pearly complexion remained cool and smooth. There was no such thing as backache. Those elegant small feet and ankles did not swell like other people's so that she could stand for hours on end without complaint. Even today it is usually Prince Philip who says, 'Why are we standing?'

The Queen's eagerness to get on with the job sometimes made her seem insensitive. With her wide, radiant smile she would accept a present from a friend – and then forget to open it until after the donor had left, taking with him a sense of disappointment. It is not easy for royalty to enter into the day-to-day feelings of ordinary people, unless like the Queen Mother they are born with a sixth sense.

In a way it was unfair to demand more of any human being than the young Queen was already giving. Goodness allied to efficiency is a rare combination indeed. During the early Victorian age the public expected little else of what they called 'a female sovereign' beside tenderness and compassion. In the case of Elizabeth II, a delightful 'female sovereign' offered the public, in addition to the 'female' virtues, an array of talents that no male sovereign could have bettered. If she had been a consort instead of a queen regnant, she would not have had to peform a dual role as sovereign and woman. There would have been more time to watch the human dramas going on around her, even to listen to the gossip, both home-brewed and foreign. As it was, she was taken almost unawares by the vagaries and intensities of the human heart.

Princess Margaret broke the news herself. The Queen was torn between personal pleasure at her sister's happiness with a man whom the whole family liked, and dismay at the public issues involved. As Head of the Church of England, it could scarcely be her duty to condone the breaking of its canon law against divorce by giving her consent to her sister's marriage with a divorced man; even though that man was the innocent party. Unless of course she were to be advised not to withhold consent by her head of government, the prime minister. But such advice was to be far from forthcoming – despite one astonishing hiccup – as events were soon to demonstrate.

Meanwhile, she went on to see her sister and Townsend together, giving the latter a strong impression of her own continuing ambivalence, following the first surprise. She was 'movingly simple and sympathetic' in her acceptance of her sister's love for Townsend; but none the less found it 'a disturbing fact', such as to cause her 'not a little anxiety'.[15] For the moment she made only one request of the couple: 'Under the circumstances, it isn't unreasonable for me to ask you to wait a year.'[16] These words were to be taken as a warning, but one delivered with the most tender concern.

Very different was Peter Townsend's reception by the Queen's private secretary Sir Alan ('Tommy') Lascelles, to whom, as a friend, Townsend personally told his story. 'You must be either mad or bad,' exclaimed the indignant Lascelles to a soon equally indignant Townsend. (Lascelles might have added the third of Lady Caroline Lamb's strictures on Lord Byron – 'Mad, bad *and dangerous to know*.') But despite his initial outburst, Lascelles was never to give the anxious lovers that clear-cut if bleak picture of their position, legal and otherwise, which they needed. There were no precise instructions to them, for instance, about the working of the Royal Marriages Act 1772.

This piece of by now outmoded legislation had once proved a neat way of preventing George III's sons from making unsuitable marriages. Permission had to be obtained from the sovereign and Parliament before any member of the Royal Family in line of succession could be legally married. At the age of twenty-five, it is true, the royal person could marry without the sovereign's or Parliament's consent, having given a further twelve months' notice to the Privy Council; but this concession was granted only on the condition of surrendering all royal rights, not to mention financial benefits from the Civil List. None of this was brought home to the Princess and Townsend. Instead, Lascelles said, 'It's not impossible.'

Today Princess Margaret feels that if they had understood from the start the hopelessness of the situation, Peter would have departed and no major tragedy ensued.

It may be asked, why did not Lascelles speak out, considering his powerful personal feelings on the subject? The answer is a curious one, throwing some light on the royal 'system' as worked by a man of the old school who was to live to be ninety, and who, having once served Edward VIII, was determined above all to avoid another royal scandal. Lascelles's complete and undivided devotion was to the throne, mediated by its present personal occupant, Elizabeth II. Rather than upset the Queen by blighting her early hopes of some solution to the marriage problem, he would allow Princess Margaret to entertain unreal dreams. His duty, as he saw it, was solely and absolutely to the Royal Family as such, to the Queen; *her* happiness, not her sister's. To Princess Margaret this code was to seem heartless. She never spoke to him again.*[17]

Lascelles's next move was to send for Jock Colville, now Churchill's private secretary. 'The Queen Mother wept when I talked to her,' said Lascelles in great concern. 'I have never seen her shed tears before.' Then he went on to put Colville in the picture: the Royal Marriages Act, Parliament's final decision in two years' time, the need to end the affair before it reached that climax. Colville went down to Chequers, the prime minister's home in Buckinghamshire. At luncheon he delivered to Churchill the message from Lascelles. To his amazement Churchill's romantic spirit took fire and he exclaimed, 'What a delightful match! A lovely young royal lady married to a gallant young airman, safe from the perils and horrors of war!'

Colville broke in – 'But Winston, this isn't at all what Tommy was trying to say. . . .'

Clementine Churchill overheard the conversation and added her cold douche: 'Winston, if you are going to begin the Abdication all over again, I'm going to leave! I shall take a flat and go and live in Brighton.'[18]

Churchill retreated and called a Cabinet meeting. Unanimously the Cabinet decided that the Prime Minister must advise the Queen against such a royal marriage.

Some writers have expressed surprise that the Queen should have tolerated Townsend, as she did, at Clarence House after she knew of the love affair. Such a reaction was quite natural, however, especially in a 'female sovereign'. If the King had lived longer it is safe to say that the romance would have been shorter.

* In gratitude for past kindnesses, I must add that when there was no conflict of duties, Tommy Lascelles could be the most charming informant and correspondent, in my case about Queen Victoria or Winston Churchill.

The Queen was grateful for Townsend's service to her father. She also realised how wretched her sister had been made by their father's death. If Margaret's love for this much older man, Townsend, could change with time into devotion to a new father-figure, this would be the happiest result.

Whatever the feelings of Princess Margaret's family – and they were deeply sympathetic – it was obvious that the unfortunate Princess had enough problems of her own at this stage. The new Queen must look elsewhere for support. She had no distance to look.

To say that Prince Philip's chivalrous and positive ideal for himself was to be husband of the Queen would today be a platitude. This admirable eventuality, however, was far from clear in 1952, even to Philip himself. When questioned about his position during the year in which he reached his fiftieth birthday, Prince Philip at first seemed to be sure of one point only. Before the Queen's Accession he had been head of the family. 'Within the house, and whatever we did, it was together,' he said. 'I suppose I naturally filled the principal position. People used to come to me and ask me what to do.'[19] He would have been thinking of that everyday life in Malta, or in Clarence House.

Then came the Accession and with it the handing over to Elizabeth II of the whole of George VI's court to serve her: the offices of the Lord Chamberlain, the Privy Purse and Treasurer, the Lord Steward; the Master of the Horse and Crown equerry who looked after the royal mews; the Keeper of her pictures and the Surveyor of her works of art; a private secretary and assistant private secretary, a press secretary and many more. The Queen's tasks had been vastly multiplied, but so had the number of her servants. And they were *her* servants and *she* had to settle their problems.

Because she's the Sovereign [explained Prince Philip to Basil Boothroyd] everyone turns to her. If you have a King and a Queen, there are certain things people automatically go to the Queen about. But if the Queen is also the *Queen*, they go to her about everything. She's asked to do much more than she would normally do. . . . Many of the Household . . . the fact that they report to the Queen is important to them, and it's frightfully difficult to persuade them not to go to the Queen, but to come to me.[20]

He did persuade 'many of the Household' to bring him some of the problems that a woman, even when she was queen, would normally be excused from. His criterion has always been, What would save the time and energies of this queen who was his wife? He is not primarily a prince consort planning for a queen regnant, but a man planning for a woman, a husband for a wife. It is possible to see how he reached this vocation by following up a process of elimination that also occurred to him.

To begin with, he has never wished actually to be created 'Prince Consort', a title which would emphasise his official status without correspondingly underlining his human vocation. Far less was Prince Philip tempted to request the status of 'King Consort', as Lord Guildford Dudley had asked of his wife Lady Jane Grey, the 'nine days' queen'. (Jane refused; but this did not save her young husband from being executed along with her.)

Comparisons between Prince Philip and his great-great-grandfather Albert tended merely to irritate. This was because the differences between the two consorts were far greater than any resemblances. They had some things in common: the same interest in science and industry; and both believed in the modernisation of things like palaces and royal estates – though Philip alone aimed at updating the monarchy itself. (Albert's endeavour had been to make the Sovereign more strict socially and more like a continental ruler in regard to power.)

The differences were radical ones. Queen Victoria was so lacking in any real secretariat that her methodical young husband had to play many secretarial roles on her behalf. In his own words he was both her private secretary and permanent minister. Elizabeth II, on the contrary, became immediately the centre of a complex and actively functioning office in which there seemed little need for a freelance husband. And whereas Albert, having arrived on the scene when Victoria was mistress of her own house, had to work for his place as 'master', Philip had already been head of his family for four and a half years, before his wife became queen. Thus Prince Philip's position as husband and father was from the beginning his immeasurably strongest suit.

His own instincts were to distance himself from the 'mystique of monarchy' and to assert his rights and duties as a man. On the question of 'mystique', he not only pointed out that the constitution forbade him to participate, but he also absented himself from purely formal and traditional occasions like meetings of the Privy Council. That he was a man rather than a symbol, however exalted, was something that he always insisted upon. No doubt his attitude was partly due to the King's early death and his own consequent premature loss of his career at sea, a career where each serving officer was stripped down to his essentials as a man. Philip guarded these essentials as far as possible in his new sphere. There is a story of his rebuking an obsequious woman – 'I don't like to be "Highnessed". Just call me "Sir". This is the 20th century. You're not at King Arthur's court, you know!'[21] – and another story of his snubbing a footman for jumping to open a door for his young son – 'He's not helpless. He's got hands, hasn't he?'[22] A man has hands, and a tongue too.

Boothroyd wrote perceptively in *The Times* of 10 June 1981 that while 'it is not "advisable" to drop the reasonable observances, Prince Philip is not mad about bows and scrapes; sees himself as a man first, a prince second'.

One remembers Wellington's repeated, unexpected humility, 'I am but a man.' Every true man of action, knowing his own limited strength against the elements or the enemy, guards more closely than most the precious consciousness of being only human.

It was thus as a man that Prince Philip could best serve the Queen. The chivalrous sense of vocation felt by 'Boy' Browning for the young woman at Cape Town was Philip's also, intensified and heightened by incomparably stronger ties.

Hardly had two months of the new reign passed before the partnership of man and wife was put to a test that was as unnecessary as it was ludicrous. In any case it was to be a rough passage for the young Queen; but it could have been far rougher but for her husband's dedication.

The consort's throne had already been removed from under the 'Cloth of Estate' (canopy) in the House of Lords and stored, according to custom, in Lord Cholmondeley's country house. It was believed – mistakenly as was later proved – that only a queen consort could occupy a throne and share the sovereign's canopy at the State Opening of Parliament; a prince consort must apparently sit outside the magic ground on a mere chair of state. This was in fact an unnecessary slight on the prince consort's position, even under a mysteriously vague constitution, as will be shown in due course. A royal ukase of 9 April 1952 was an even more unnecessary blow at the Prince's status as husband.

The contretemps did not arise through any disagreement within the inner circle of the Royal Family. It was Queen Mary who happened to hear that Lord Mountbatten had been pointing out, quite correctly, the change in the family name since the Accession – from Windsor to Mountbatten. Since 6 February 1952, said Uncle Dickie, a Mountbatten had sat on the throne. The old Queen took umbrage, retorting that *her husband* had founded the House of Windsor *in aeterno*, and no 'Battenberg' marriage, however solemn and effective in English law, could change it. In other words it was a clash in the family pride of 'Granny' and 'Uncle', a state of affairs not unknown, with adjustments for circumstances, in many other families in the land.

However, Queen Mary sent a messenger to apprise Churchill of what she regarded as an outrage. According to the
messenger, Churchill, egged on by Beaverbrook, 'went
through the roof'. He summoned the Cabinet there and
then, and the Cabinet with one accord authorised the Prime
Minister to advise the Queen that the name of the royal
house was the House of Windsor. 'They were absolutely
resolute and firm behind Queen Mary, who was the real
mover.'

Thus the unfortunate wife was forced to expunge her
husband's name from the family tree. In vain Prince Philip
waxed indignant against a process that made him 'an
amoeba – a bloody amoeba'. Elizabeth II had to obey her
Cabinet's will, and the wording of her declaration was not
without irony:

> The Queen today [9 April] declared in Council her Will and
> Pleasure that She and Her Children shall be styled and known
> as the House and Family of Windsor, and that Her descendants
> other than female descendants who marry and their descend-
> ants shall bear the name of Windsor.

This curious and anomalous situation was to last for eight
years, after which the misunderstanding was cleared up and
a necessary distinction drawn, as will be shown, between
the House and Family of Windsor and the surname of
Mountbatten-Windsor.[23]

The Queen was able none the less to make some restitu-
tion to her husband as early as 18 September 1952. Before
the State Opening of her first Parliament she was 'graciously pleased to declare and ordain that HRH the Duke of
Edinburgh should henceforth have, hold and enjoy the
Place, Pre-eminence and Precedence next to Her Majesty'.

As the Coronation drew near, outstanding problems were
solved. The Queen's 'title' was finally agreed by the Commonwealth prime ministers at a conference in London on
12 December 1952. She would be crowned in six months'

time in accordance with her proclamation, as 'Elizabeth the Second, by the grace of God of the United Kingdom of Great Britain and Northern Ireland and of Her other Realms and Territories Queen, Head of the Commonwealth, Defender of the Faith'. No sovereign had ever been crowned before in words such as these. The reference to Northern Ireland was left out by Canada, South Africa and Ceylon, while the two latter also omitted 'the grace of God'. Thus was the sovereign's title shown in this new age to be no longer 'indivisible'.

Queen Mary, who had fought and won her last battle that April, was failing fast. But before her death on 24 March 1953 she was able to perform one more selfless act for the throne she had served so long. She asked that if she died before June, court mourning should not interfere with the date or splendours of the Coronation. Her devotion to the crown was indeed entire and exclusive. She left the whole of her possessions to the reigning monarch. 'Poor Cynthia Colville!' said a courtier. 'Thirty years of devotion, and not even a toque to show for it!'

James Pope-Hennessy's magnificent biography, *Queen Mary*, has done much to reserve history's early judgment of the Queen's grandmother. Hitherto she had appeared as a monument of inhuman grandeur – either the noble grandeur of St Paul's, to which Chips Channon likened her, or the rigidity of an obelisk. In fact she was delightfully sympathetic to the young, and not only to her own granddaughters. One of the Queen's young ladies-in-waiting was put up at Marlborough House while moving homes; another was sent for by Queen Mary a few months after her appointment. Nervously she wondered what fault the severe old lady would have to find with her. Instead Queen Mary said, 'Come and talk to me, my dear. I feel I don't know you.'[24] A story from long ago showed that left to herself she lacked neither humour nor interest in human nature. To his surprise, one of her courtiers, the father of Sir Arthur Bryant the historian, was asked to read aloud to her and her lady-in-waiting his son's far from mealy-mouthed volume on Samuel Pepys. Noticing Bryant senior's startled look, Queen Mary explained: 'I want to watch Lady Ampthill's face.'[25]

Towards the end of her life she was to confide in Queen Elizabeth the Queen Mother some of her unfulfilled desires: 'Do you know there is one thing I never did and wish I had done: climb over a fence!'

In the year before the Coronation a subtle change had come over Queen Elizabeth II herself. It was a change away from diffidence and towards a new relaxed confidence. She put it into words in a conversation with a friend soon after her Accession:

> Extraordinary thing, I no longer feel anxious or worried. I don't know what it is – but I have lost all my timidity and somehow becoming the Sovereign and having to receive the Prime Minister, for instance . . .

— well, instead of unnerving her it had helped her to become much more self-assured and uninhibited.

Coronation fever was mounting apace in spring 1953. More than one writer has described the popular mood as 'hysteria'. And many more than one theory has been advanced to explain it. Could it be due to a loss of national balance after the horrors of war? – a kind of 'mad anti-climax'? Or was it a sign that people had suddenly found in this young queen, known to them since childhood, a sense of their own 'rootedness'? – or *thought* they had found their longed-for roots in her? The war and its after-effects were common to most of these ingenious theories. Professor Nicholas Mansergh, however, an expert on the monarchy and Commonwealth, simply pointed out that the reaction to the Coronation was 'unrealistic'. Writers who had hitherto shown no interest in the future of the Commonwealth and Empire were suddenly 'inspired by a steady resolve to press, beyond the limits of sense and endurance, analogies with sixteenth-century Tudor England'.[26]

Those last two words – Tudor England – were a dignified academic reference to the popular shibboleth of 'The New Elizabethans'. The historian A. L. Rowse has been a good deal more pungent. In a lecture entitled *Queen Elizabeth I and Today* he began:

> When Queen Elizabeth II came to the throne I well remember being asked by a lot of ladies in luncheon clubs, did this portend a second Elizabethan Age? What a silly question! – a mere matter of nomenclature. . . .[27]

Chips Channon was among the first to promulgate the order – for order it was in all but name: an order to the people to pull up their socks and become reincarnations of Drake, Raleigh and Elizabeth I. King George VI's lying-in-state might not seem the most appropriate place for dreams of glory. But this was where Channon had his vision. 'I rejoice in the new reign and welcome it,' he wrote in his diary. 'We shall be the new Elizabethans. . . .'[28]

The phrase was already being repeated like an advertisement for a new commodity. Even a classy children's magazine sprang up with that name and enjoyed a short if respectable run. Rather than seek for a single deep cause of the phenomenon, it is simpler to note the several 'Elizabethan' coincidences that did indeed occur. These in turn were to give an iridescent validity to the natural hope for better times.

The new Queen bore the same name as her great predecessor Elizabeth I, and came to the throne at the same age, twenty-five. A few erudite people indeed noticed that while Elizabeth I had heard of her accession while 'under a tree' at Hatfield, Elizabeth II had come to the throne while 'in a tree'. Churchill, with his romantic buccaneering spirit, was back at the helm and created a Knight of the Garter in coronation year; his government were 'making a bonfire' of wartime controls; freedom, enterprise, merchant adventuring were the new slogans. And the news that three living young men had really and truly performed an act of 'Elizabethan' daring was made public on Coronation Day itself, though it was actually on 29 May that John Hunt, Edmund Hillary and Sherpa Tenzing climbed Everest. Twenty years after that first triumph, the highest mountain in the world had been scaled five times, and in the next decade even its hitherto unconquerable south-west face was to be conquered. Such things were indeed symbolic of the stupendous changes during the Queen's reign. But they did not imply a new Elizabethan age.

Needless to say, the temperament of Elizabeth II was not such as to absorb and give back other people's hysteria; far less a wave of hysteria focused on herself. She had inherited all her parents' boundless pride in the office they held along with their personal modesty as holders. While the hysteria was mounting, the Queen was busying herself with practical preparations for the day.

In the ivory and gold ballroom of Buckingham Palace, beneath the six great chandeliers, she had white sheets fastened together in order that she and her attendants might rehearse the movements of her very long coronation train. An atmosphere of charades was not allowed to develop, and the Chester Herald who was present professed to have heard the Queen say, 'Don't be silly,' to her husband; 'Come back here and do it again properly.'[29] Two silver stars were fixed to the front of her crown, so that the Archbishop should not be tempted to put it on back to front. Meanwhile the bishops were being rehearsed by the Earl Marshal. 'If the bishops don't learn to walk in step,' he thundered, 'we'll be here all night.'

That this was a post-war coronation was proved by the number of missing items. Dray horses had to be borrowed for the Queen's carriages. Even the wooden box containing the formula and samples of holy oil used for previous anointings, such as Queen Victoria's, was rumoured to have been bombed; but it was intact, and the new oil was compounded by John Jameson, head dispenser of Savory & Moore, New Bond Street. This was fortunate, for the only original items of the regalia that had escaped the attentions of Cromwell were the spoon and ampulla, in the form of an eagle, for the holy oil.

The correct length of pile for the Abbey carpet was insisted on by the Queen. (At George vi's coronation the pile had been so deep that some of the old peers could hardly drag their robes across it; while at Edward vii's the heels of Queen Alexandra and her ladies became embedded.) Even so the pile was laid the wrong way, so that the metal fringe of her golden mantle clawed her back; she had to signal the Archbishop, 'Get me started!' The orb and sceptre were too heavy for a woman to hold comfortably; Elizabeth ii had brackets fixed inside the state coach for her return journey from the Abbey.

Anxious thoughts for her welfare flowed in from all quarters, beginning with Churchill. 'I fear they may ask her to do too much,' he said. Concern was expressed by women's institutes and a bowling association among others. The Queen's comment was always the same: 'Did my father do it? Then I will too.' When they suggested she take a brief rest halfway through the ceremony, she said quickly, 'I'll be all right. I'm as strong as a horse.' Only the Communist *Daily Worker* did not think Queen Elizabeth ii would suffer any prolonged strain. There had been such a 'slump in monarchs' since 1917, it pointed out, that her tenure would be short and the British system would surely be overthrown in due course by the same 'trend against monarchy'.[30]

Coronation Day arrived on 2 June 1953 in a thin drizzle, but it was not worse than the one which had accompanied the Queen's birth. The festive routine that has since become so familiar struck many writers with amazement: 30,000 people waiting under blankets with spirit-lamps beside them throughout the cold night; the wild cheers when the Royal Family appeared, with an astonishing 'slump' in thefts instead of monarchs as the *Worker* expected. One writer has put the slump in thefts down to the mystique of the

Coronation. But the same benign influences were at work during the Royal Wedding in 1981; which suggests that the common source of grace was royalty itself.

A third generation of princely youth sat in the royal box watching a parent (or parents) crowned: first it had been Prince Bertie entranced by the programme falling into the vase; followed by Princess Elizabeth keeping an eye on her sister as well as her parents, and now it was Prince Charles. He was brought in by a back entrance in time to see the crowning. The Queen smiled at the small apparition with satin suit and silky hair, sitting alert and attentive between his grandmother and his aunt. Princess Anne, though not quite three on Coronation Day, can still remember her sense of outrage at being left behind. (She was allowed on the palace balcony afterwards, from which she slipped and vanished for a few moments.)

All in the Abbey on the day found that the three hours passed like a flash, despite the peeresses in their satin gowns feeling too cool, and the peers in their velvet and ermine up to the throat being too warm. The power and build-up of the service had lost nothing of its impact over the centuries, though this was the twenty-eighth coronation to take place at Westminster. She was crowned with St Edward's crown, made for Charles II. The Imperial State Crown, worn on the return journey and designed for Victoria, contained Edward the Confessor's sapphire, the Stuart sapphire and the Black Prince's balas ruby. The Stars of Africa, cut from the huge Cullinan diamond (a present to Edward VII) adorned the sceptre, Imperial Crown and two pieces of jewellery belonging to Queen Mary and known to Elizabeth II as 'Granny's chips'. At the moment of her mother's crowning sixteen years before, Winston Churchill had turned to his wife Clementine with tears in his eyes and said: 'You were right; I see now the "other one" wouldn't have done.'[31] With the daughter's crowning as queen regnant the vital sense of continuity had been fully restored.

The parts of the ceremony – the Anointing, Crowning,

Communion and Homage – had all grown out of the nation's history and for that reason were moving. But if the ceremony's roots were in an undeniably Christian past, could it be that there had also been pagan accretions which now, in a pagan age, were feeding on the ancient Christian tree like a beautiful parasite? Robert Lacey sees something of this sort developing between the crowned Queen and her people.

> She did not find it demeaning [he wrote] to be a doll dressed for her subjects' pleasure. She saw it as the essence of her job. The holy puppet clothed in magic robes for the peoples' comfort went back to the very roots of primeval monarchy.[32]

It may be true that the idea of the priest-king goes back beyond Christianity. But once the Christian *muthos* captured the old pagan rites, they have never reverted. The description of the 'holy puppet' in 'magic robes', however beguiling, makes the coronation ceremony by implication into a fertility rite and the Queen into a corn dolly. This view might be more defensible were 'magic robes', so called, to vanish from everywhere in the country except the chest holding the sovereign's *supertunica* and *colobium Sidonis*. But this is not so, as the historian and don A. J. P. Taylor points out: 'All those who dress up to perform their functions,' he writes, '– mayors and judges and liverymen, perhaps even university dons – have a common interest with "royals" who dress up most dazzlingly of all.'[33]

If there were any undertones to the coronation service of Christian dedication – Queen to people and people to Queen – they came from the story of the Cross not of the Golden Bough. Christ gave himself as a sacrifice and the Queen showed by her exaltation that she was prepared to do the same. Dermot Morrah, Arundel Herald Extraordinary, was to write: 'Certainly the sense of spiritual exaltation that radiated from her was almost tangible to those of us who stood near her in the Abbey'; while Robert Graves the poet and writer was to say after an audience: 'The holy oil has taken for that girl. It worked for her alright.'[34]

The many expressions of fear lest the Queen should sacrifice herself too generously sprang from unconscious associations of this kind. As one who was in the Abbey wrote for the *Manchester Guardian* afterwards:

> The inarticulate hopes of the multitude are centred on her person, but what should one expect of this girl? One feels that she must on no account be 'victimized'. There will be a temptation for all of us to place too heavy a burden on her for our own purposes, but no human being should be used in this way.[35]

A curious incident concerned with television in the Abbey confirms the Queen's total involvement.

When the Cabinet Papers of 1952 were opened under the 'thirty year' rule on 1 January 1983, it was revealed that there had been an unsuspected controversy over coronation television. After a first swift inspection of the papers, journalists reported on 2 January that the Queen had wanted no television cameras in the Abbey. She had been overborne by public opinion. Headlines in the *Sunday Telegraph* ran: 'The Queen wanted to ban TV at Coronation'; in the *Sunday Express*: 'When the Queen said No, but the Nation said Yes.'

A week passed, and this hasty – and false – impression was corrected by Sir John Colville in a *Sunday Telegraph* article. Colville, as the prime minister's representative, had attended the first meeting of the Coronation Joint Executive Committee on 19 May 1952. To his dismay he heard a chorus of weighty voices arguing that Her Majesty should be officially advised to spare herself the strain of the cameras' heat, glare and publicity by refusing to submit herself to ordeal by television. The Earl Marshal (Duke of Norfolk) and Archbishop of Canterbury (Dr Fisher) had informed the Committee – on what authority Colville still does not know – that this was Her Majesty's own wish. Only Garter King of Arms (Sir George Bellew) and Colville himself disagreed with the overwhelming majority.

Churchill accordingly strongly urged the Cabinet to let the Queen know they were utterly against her being televised; which they unanimously did.

What was Churchill's surprise when the Queen received this paternalistic message without enthusiasm. In fact she favoured television at her coronation, believing that all her subjects should have the chance to see it. Churchill at once complied. 'After all it was the Queen who was to be crowned,' he told Colville, 'and not the Cabinet. She alone must decide.' A second cabinet meeting was summoned to reverse their earlier decision. 'Thus it was,' wrote Colville, 'that the new 26-year-old Sovereign personally routed the Earl Marshal, the Archbishop of Canterbury, Sir Winston Churchill and the Cabinet, all of whom submitted to her decision with astonishment, but with a good grace.' No one guessed that this reserved young woman would be the first to propel her reign into the heat and glare of the television age. Yet her motivation was clear. Nothing must stand between her crowning and the nation's right to participate. Only the most sacred moments, such as the Communion, were to be for herself alone.

The great moments of the Coronation evoked nothing but awe and admiration: the presentation of the Queen to the people – 'Sirs, I here present unto you Queen Elizabeth your undoubted Queen. . . .' – followed by the shouted acclamations 'Vivat! Vivat!'; the homage of Prince Philip – 'I, Philip, Duke of Edinburgh, do become your liegeman of life and limb and of earthly worship; and faith and truth I will bear unto you, to live and die, against all manner of folks.'

Within three or four years Philip was defending his wife and sovereign against all manner of folks, including some who thought themselves loyal – until the press blew up their 'constructive criticism' into a full-scale assault on the monarchy.

Nor did this fourth coronation of the twentieth century

itself escape all criticism. Some felt there was an overdose of medievalism for a modern ceremony, however historic in origins. Others said it was altogether too British and lacking in Commonwealth emphasis. (Dr George Borg Olivier, Prime Minister of Malta, would have agreed; he almost cancelled his attendance owing to a supposed slight on Malta in the arrangements. Nor was Dr Malan of South Africa happy; as an extreme nationalist and republican he had refused to address one word to his partner, Princess Elizabeth's lady-in-waiting, at the Cape Town dinner in 1946.) According to one view, there was too much snobbery in the *placements*, a cabinet minister who was a mere baron sitting behind a non-cabinet minister who was an earl, while the faithful Commons were relegated to an upper balcony. According to another view, however, there was too little snobbery. Chips Channon regretted that Aneurin Bevan, the left-wing Labour MP, was permitted to come in a blue lounge-suit; though Channon was somewhat mollified by the sight of Jennie Lee, Bevan's pretty wife, in 'a little veil'.

And the sight of another beautiful lady, vivaciously flicking a speck of fluff from the uniform of Group-Captain Peter Townsend as they stood together after the ceremony, sent a thrill of speculation through the whole press.

'Uphill All the Way?':
1954–7

Twelve days after the Coronation a sensational Sunday paper, the *People*, decided that the decencies had been adequately observed and they need wait no longer before spilling the beans. A paragraph therefore appeared on 14 June:

> It is high time for the British public to be made aware of the fact that newspapers in Europe and America are openly asserting that the Princess [Margaret] is in love with a divorced man and that she wishes to marry him. The story is of course utterly untrue. It is quite unthinkable that a royal princess, third in line of succession to the throne, should even contemplate marriage with a man who has been through the divorce courts.

The ploy was to speed the gossip by forcing an official denial of the story.

If the Queen and Queen Mother had ever entertained any hopes that the love affair would fade out or be quietly transmuted into friendship without any blaze of publicity, those hopes were now doomed. Only two possibilities were open to Princess Margaret (not yet twenty-three): either to renounce Peter Townsend at once or to wait until 1955 when she would be twenty-five, and then try again. Townsend agreed to take the post of air attaché at Brussels. The lovers were not to see one another for two long years. But there was the telephone and the post. And 'Tommy' Lascelles had said, 'It's not impossible.'

For those who did not forget the episode during the two years that were now to pass, it seemed that a first awkward question mark already hung over the 'New Elizabethans'.

By contrast, the Queen's first grand tour of her reign did much to keep the Elizabethan image fresh and shining. It was indeed a royal progress in the old and new terms. In the old sense, loyal subjects became addicted to writing up its glories mile by mile and decibel by decibel, though the statistics did not always agree. The official distance she covered was 43,618 miles; 41,674 according to an American source. Her dates of departure and return were officially 24 November 1953 to 10 May 1954.

The first brief refuelling stop was in Canada, followed by a full day in Bermuda, two days in Jamaica, one in Panama, two in Fiji, one in Tonga, five weeks in New Zealand, a month in Australia, a day in the Cocos Islands, eleven days in Ceylon, a day in Aden, two days in Uganda, one day in Libya, four days in Malta and the last day in Gibraltar.

It was reckoned that she had visited two 'dominions', six crown colonies, four territories described respectively as a commonwealth, a protectorate, a protected state and a 'territory', and had called at two foreign countries. The Queen and Prince Philip had listened, it was said, to 276 speeches and to the singing of 'God Save the Queen' 508 times, while the Queen had made 102 speeches. (Queen Mary confessed to her grandson Lord Harewood that she had made only two speeches in her whole life: one during the First World War and the other at her Silver Jubilee.) Curtsies to the number of 6,770 were miraculously totted up, followed by 13,213 handshakes. (According to a different calculation, the Queen was curtsied to 2,500 times and shook hands 4,800 times.) She received 190 substantial presents including a cattle-whip twice as long as Philip and a model of the Rock of Gibraltar. Among gifts to her hosts and staff were listed cuff-links, wallets and picture frames – exactly the same items as those noted by a lady-in-waiting on Queen Alexandra's gift list after a Mediterranean cruise.

In the modern sense, this 'new Elizabethan' progress made a profound impression; indeed the Queen's whole record of spectacular travels continues to do so. A change in the habits of present-receiving was instituted in 1965, however, after an official letter from the Queen's then private secretary, Sir Michael Adeane: she would accept fruit and flowers from individuals as well as 'very small presents of purely sentimental value offered by children, veterans, etc.', where refusal would lead to 'hurt feelings' – but no expensive presents from commercial concerns which bore the taint of advertising.

The three advantages of a royal Head of the Commonwealth emerged more clearly during the 1953 to 1954 tour than ever before. The Queen's position, because inherited rather than elected as a president's would be, was not disputed. Her office was to be continuous not changed every five years or so. She was outside political life and therefore not subject to political pressures. No president of the 'mother-country', not even a posse of presidents travelling between one another's countries, could ever have performed or been invited to perform the prodigies of the Queen's first tour. It was an exercise in bonding, in holding together a Commonwealth that was a supremely worthwhile experiment in international co-operation.

The Commonwealth is unique in its manner of change from empire, and in its subsequent growth, for the end of the British Empire signalled gradual devolution instead of the chaos and ruin into which all past empires fell.

By something almost like magic, or at least sleight of hand, it has turned itself into a different body. Today there are forty-seven nations wishing to remain in it: seventeen realms recognise Her Majesty, others are republics, a few have their own monarchs. Only four who might have been inside are not. Burma failed to enter; South Africa was not acceptable on her terms; Ireland and Pakistan left. The Queen is particularly devoted to her work for this Com-

monwealth: 'The Commonwealth to which *I personally*
attach great importance . . .' she said emphatically to visiting Nigerians on 18 March 1981.

Professor Nicholas Mansergh has summed up the 'great
importance' of the Commonwealth in moving language:

> At a time when the liberal democratic world appeared so often
> on the defensive the Commonwealth, it seemed, had embarked
> on an experiment which had about it a quality of greatness.[1]

Mansergh has called his own attitude that of 'tempered
optimism' appropriate to the second half of the twentieth
century. It was in the same spirit that Queen Elizabeth II
had launched herself across the world on 24 November
1953.

'The structure and framework of monarchy could easily
stand as an archaic and meaningless survival. We have
received visible and audible proof that it is living in the
hearts of the people.' So said the Queen at the traditional
Guildhall luncheon immediately after her return. She had
given it life by what she had said from her own heart, first in
Jamaica and later in New Zealand and Australia. 'The
strongest bonds of all,' she said in Jamaica, 'are those which
are not recorded in documents but in the hearts of the
people who share the same beliefs and the same aims.' In
other words, the Commonwealth could afford to have a
virtually unwritten constitution, precisely because it was
written in the people's hearts.

On Christmas Day in New Zealand she was to broadcast
her own aspirations: 'I want to show that the Crown is not
merely an abstract symbol of our unity but a personal and
living bond between you and me.' The Maoris in fact had
never dreamt of seeing her as an abstract symbol; they
called her 'The Rare White Heron of the Single Flight'.

In opening the Australian Parliament in February 1954
she repeated her two major themes: personal commitment
and the sense of something new. 'It is my resolve,' she told

the Australians, 'that under God I shall not only rule but serve. This describes, I believe, the modern character of the British Crown.' (Today she would probably use the word 'reign' rather than 'rule'.)

Australia compared in importance for Elizabeth II with South Africa's significance for George VI. In each country there was a republican party, and some Australians had been turning towards the United States since the early Far Eastern débâcle of the Second World War.

The Queen gave pleasure by wearing her coronation dress at the opening of their parliament. (The only time when the dress failed to give *her* pleasure was in Colombo where the metal paillettes got red hot in the burning sun.) Outside Parliament there was little ceremony. Lord Home was to speak in 1956 of Australia's 'unbounded youthful energy'. The young would shout from trees and rooftops, 'Good on yer, Phil! Good on yer, Liz!'; a Sydney newspaper syndicated the personal memoirs of Prince Philip's former valet, John Dean. Prince Philip's high spirits were no less 'unbounded' than those of the Australians. On one occasion when the press bus arrived very late to meet the royal train, the Prince hailed the journalists from his observation platform, 'Ah, I see that the pubs have just closed!'[2]

But his popularity also was unbounded, for in the new Australia it was better to say anything to the press, however astringent, rather than nothing. As the Queen's cousin Lord Harewood was to find when he visited Australia in 1972 and gave a 'no comment' reply to a journalist, there were dangers in saying nothing to the press. The journalist promptly invented a 'quote' from Lord Harewood, excusing himself with the words, 'Well, he didn't say anything and I felt I had to put in something!'

Prince Philip was always 'putting in something' not only to amuse himself and his wife; though there is no need to put absolute faith in the story that before one public speech, when he thought the microphone was not yet switched on, he had said to her encouragingly, 'Don't look so sad, Sausage.' When asked by the press afterwards whether it was true that he called the Queen 'Little Sausage', he replied with a bland smile, 'I don't, but I well may.'

The Queen had to learn to lift up her pearl necklace when no one was looking so that there would not be a white mark on her neck in the evening; and to duck when the stick of a little Union Jack suddenly flew towards her out of an excited child's hand. At every siding, especially in New Zealand, there would be people waiting for them to stop, if only for a moment. 'If I were Mummy,' said the Queen once, 'I would be out there and they would adore it' – but she knew she had not that easy way of doing it. Lady Pamela Hicks (then Mountbatten) her lady-in-waiting recalls the first problem of smiles:

> What the Queen did find a strain was that as she was passing somebody it was the one moment in their life when they could see the Queen, and therefore she must be smiling; but she couldn't maintain that smile for a motorcade which was lasting perhaps 45 minutes. You get a twitch. So there is a moment when you have to relax your muscles, and of course that one moment when you are not smiling – it's the despair of some people who then think you are looking frightfully cross.[3]

Lady Pamela also remembers the Queen's 'ordeal by race-glasses', which again she had to get used to:

> She went through some awful ordeals – the Queen would be in her box looking at the race-course and the entire crowd between the box and the course would have their backs to the course and would gaze at her with their racing-glasses. There is a strain after, say, the first 20 minutes. And the same at all civil balls and so on. People were so fascinated to see what they might have thought of as a waxwork, actually moving and speaking.

On their ship *Gothic*, which they had joined at Bermuda (the same ship that had carried Princess Elizabeth's mourning outfit to Mombasa in February 1952), Prince Philip boosted the morale of the ship's company by insisting on partial democracy in the swimming pool. Two sergeants of Marines with whom he had played deck hockey were at first banned – then admitted.

A short visit to Tonga was at Elizabeth II's own insistence. The towering Queen of Tonga had won all hearts by sitting through the coronation downpour that June under a small umbrella in an open carriage. Queen Salote welcomed Queen Elizabeth II again in December under an umbrella for two, for it was raining in Tonga also. Slightly less welcome to the Queen was the feast of lobsters as well as sucking pig (she never eats shellfish) and the night-long chirp of crickets and Tonga guards, and dawn serenade of nose-flutes; not to mention the admiring throng of Commonwealth brothers and sisters who from the garden, through open shutters, watched the Queen of England, after a sleepless night, wandering up and down looking for the brand-new shower. None the less history spoke to her, past and present. A descendant of Fletcher Christian of the mutinous *Bounty* was introduced to her, after she had walked under an arch inscribed 'I LOVE YOU'; and she met Tuimalila, 'King of the Palace', the giant turtle who in turn had met Captain Cook. Though he was somewhat dented, having been kicked by a horse and run over by a lorry, he was greatly venerated by the people of Tonga and so was among the first distinguished inhabitants to be presented to the Head of the Commonwealth.

She was yet again under an umbrella in Uganda, towards the end of her tour, to keep off the tropical sun. 'I feel like an African Queen,' she said to Prince Philip. 'You *are* an African Queen,' he replied, pointing the moral of the new Commonwealth. But in Uganda itself the second lesson of the new Commonwealth – thou shalt love thy neighbour as thyself – had not yet been learnt. An arch stretching right across the road in Kampala read, 'God Save the Queen from the Goan Community'.[4]

It had often been noticed that the Commonwealth countries though on warm terms with the erstwhile 'mother-country', were less than sensitive to one another's problems. Not that the relationship between the African and Asian partners and the United Kingdom was perfect either. There was some complacency during 1956 when the Queen installed a Nigerian equerry at the Palace for a few weeks before her official visit to Nigeria; he was said to be the first non-white to hold an official post since Queen Victoria's Indians. Many years later people are still hoping that a post might be found for someone from her black Commonwealth, high up on her permanent staff.

The Queen had sailed away from New Zealand with a cargo of frozen meat in the *Gothic*'s hold, the yacht *Britannia* having been accepted by the Labour Government for fitting out (if necessary as a hospital ship) but not yet completed. In Tobruk the Queen and Prince Philip stood on King Idris of Libya's balcony to watch *Britannia* bringing in Prince Charles and Princess Anne from England – a joyful family scene following upon months of deprivation that has been re-enacted so many times by the House of Windsor. Charles had learnt to read while his mother was away and she first heard him perform on the telephone.

The few days with their children in Malta were a reminder to the royal couple that only two years before they had lived there as 'ordinary' people. Such was their uninhibited freedom that the English community today claims Malta to have been the scene of the first royal 'walkabouts'. Officialdom, however, sticks to New Zealand in 1970 as the earliest date.

It was said that Prince Philip baited the press on Gibraltar when he saw a group of journalists photographing him from an empty ape's cage. He threw them some peanuts.

On 4 May they sailed up the Thames estuary, the Queen waving to the crowds for four and a half hours on end, until her arm was exhausted. Winston Churchill had joined *Britannia* off the Needles on the 3rd and sailed up the river with the Queen the following day. He was about to begin with her the last full year of their working life together.

Winston Churchill's first reaction to the new reign had been ambivalent. 'Now the accession of the young Queen Elizabeth II,' records his daughter Mary Soames, 'aroused in him every instinct of chivalry.'[5] In private he nevertheless confided to Jock Colville, who had become his private secretary once again, how much he dreaded the change from George VI to Elizabeth II. He had served her experienced if highly strung father for seven years all told, and had a deep affection for him. How could he, in his eightieth year, adapt to this youthful sovereign? 'I don't know her. She's a mere child. I knew the King so well. . . .' Colville did his best to put him right about the 'child'. But events were to accomplish Churchill's enlightenment better than any argument. If it was a question of shirking one's homework, Churchill was now more of a child than the Queen.

An occasion is described by Colville when a telegram of considerable importance arrived from the British ambassador in Baghdad.

I put it on the top of Winston's box [Colville remembers] with a little note (because he was always bored with the Foreign Office) saying, 'This is really something you should read, it is very interesting and somebody is bound to mention it in Cabinet – J.R.C.' But he shoved it aside and said, 'Bring it up at the weekend – it's a long telegram.'

So I tried to get him to read it at the weekend, but he had something else in mind. Anyhow, when he went to his audience on Tuesday with the Queen she said to him, 'What did you think about that most interesting telegram from Baghdad?' He had to admit he hadn't read it.

He came back in a frightful fury and asked, 'Why wasn't I shown it?' So I said, 'This is going too far. I've been trying to get you to read it for the last four days.' 'Well, let me see it at once.' He read it and found it interesting – but the Queen had caught him out.

This story throws light on what must now be regarded as a secret royal game – 'Catching out the minister'. For Herbert Morrison has told a similar story of himself and

George VI – 'On occasion he enjoyed trying to trip up his ministers. . . . I got into the habit of checking up details . . . of this friendly contest of knowledge.' And Sir Harold Wilson later played the game with Elizabeth II: discussing her voracious appetite for all state documents he said that if she quoted one he hadn't yet read, he felt like an 'unprepared' schoolboy.[6]

The game was perhaps one of the things taught to Princess Elizabeth by her father.

If Churchill began by being nervous of the new Queen, the new Queen was every bit as nervous of Churchill. On his first visit to Balmoral, the young people present were 'petrified', said a friend, at the prospect of having to entertain the magisterial old hero. But the visit was a mutual delight. Indeed, the romance between the young Sovereign and her venerable Prime Minister well illustrates her advance during these five years from timidity towards self-confidence. It is tempting to compare their relationship to that of Queen Victoria and Lord Melbourne. Elizabeth II, however, was a great deal more sophisticated than Victoria, as well as having a vigorous and supportive husband.

She was eventually to admit her special feeling for Churchill when someone asked her, 'Which of your prime ministers, ma'am, did you enjoy your audiences with most?'

'Winston, of course, because it was always such fun.' (This was before the premierships of James Callaghan or Margaret Thatcher, but the Queen's verdict is unlikely to change.) Winston was fun when she invited him and Clementine to Doncaster for the St Leger, on the day of their forty-fifth wedding anniversary in 1954; fun when he and Clementine invited her and Prince Philip to a farewell dinner at 10 Downing Street on 4 April 1955, on the eve of the Prime Minister's resignation. Churchill had at first intended to regale the Queen with a relatively small party of twelve, but it grew into fifty, including almost all his own

family, his private secretaries and their wives and Mrs
Neville Chamberlain.

Sir Robert Menzies, Prime Minister of Australia at this
date, was to record a telling story about the Queen's
enjoyment of Churchill's impish humour.

After a dinner at Buckingham Palace, Churchill engaged the Muslim Prime Minister of Pakistan in conversation. 'Will you have a whisky and soda, Mr Prime Minister
of Pakistan?'

'No, thank you!'

'What's that?'

'No, thank you!'

'What, why?'

'I'm a teetotaller, Mr Prime Minister.'

'What's that?'

'I'm a teetotaller.'

'A teetotaller. Christ! I mean God! I mean Allah!'

Menzies went on to relate that there was at once a
general rush to tell the story to the Queen. Menzies thought
he had got there first but the Queen interrupted him.
'You're too late,' she said; 'Tommy Lascelles has told me
about it and Tommy says that as the footman, in his
astonishment, dropped the tray and caught it before it
reached the carpet, without spilling a drop, he ought to be
put into the English cricket team, where the slip-fielding
needs improving!'[7]

There have been suggestions – endorsed mischievously
by Churchill himself – that the 'fun' he had with his
sovereign consisted entirely of racing talk. It was true that
his Tuesday audiences, for which he dressed up in frock
coat and top hat, got longer and longer (6 pm to 7.45 pm so
that he was often late for his dinner); and that when Colville
once asked him what he and the Queen talked about
Churchill replied, 'Racing. . . .' But the story of the Baghdad telegram shows that racing was in fact not their only
subject of discussion.

It is probable (though no more than a guess) that on the
day Churchill resigned he talked to his Queen in his weighty

yet whimsical manner about yet another matter close to both their hearts – her royal prerogative. At any rate, he returned from the Palace after his last interview as prime minister to read Colville a lecture on this important question. His words to his secretary sound like a repeat performance of what he might have said to an august personage an hour earlier.

Colville began it by saying, 'Did the Queen mention your successor?' Churchill said, 'She didn't mention his name or mention the question of my successor at all, and it would have been totally improper for me to mention the matter unless I was asked. Before you leave this building,' added Churchill portentously, 'make a note to the effect that an outgoing prime minister has no right whatever to advise upon his successor unless he is specifically asked to do so. That is a very important constitutional point. The theory that an outgoing prime minister can just say, "Oh, by the way, I think the person you ought to send for is so-and-so", is rubbish. Once the Prime Minister resigns he can't advise.'[8]

Not everyone would accept Winston Churchill's argument, as expressed so forcibly in 1955. But no one could doubt one thing: he cared profoundly for preserving the royal prerogative.

Next day the Queen, unadvised by Churchill, sent for Anthony Eden. He had been 'deputy prime minister' for several years. And though the constitution knew nothing of such a post, it had the force of something called 'usage'. Guided by a new prime minister, the Queen now had to cope afresh with that thorny confrontation: the Princess and Parliament.

During her two years of waiting, Princess Margaret's chic, wit and alternating moods of gaiety and pensiveness made her a favourite. In July 1953, immediately after her temporary separation from Peter Townsend began, she toured Rhodesia and a sympathetic Labour paper, the *Daily Herald*, noted, 'Our little Princess has hardly smiled. . . .'

Both the *Mirror* and *Express* announced that their readers wished her to please herself about marriage, a *Mirror* poll showing ninety-six per cent for Townsend and the *Express* reporting that 'ordinary folk' left the choice entirely to her. Her beauty and taste were winning sophisticated praise. At twenty-six she would be on the list of 'Best Dressed Women', tied with the Duchess of Windsor and just below Grace Kelly. Her long cigarette holders were famous in places where elegant people dined and danced. Among her so-called 'escorts' were interesting names like Colin Tennant, a scion of the family that had reared the incomparable Margot, and the distinguished Lady (Kay) Elliott; Mark Bonham Carter, son of Lady (Violet) Asquith; and Billy Wallace, grandson of the celebrated architect Sir Edwin Lutyens and stepson of Herbert Agar the scholarly American writer. There was no longer anything to prevent men of this impeccable background but without the blood royal from aspiring to a princess's hand. Nevertheless, Princess Margaret waited with exemplary patience and fidelity for the two years to go by, fully convinced that she and Peter Townsend would receive permission to marry.

On 12 August 1955 Princess Margaret was photographed at the remote Castle of Mey, which her mother was having floodlit in honour of Princess Anne's fifth birthday on the 15th. Six days later came Margaret's own birthday, her fateful twenty-fifth. She spent it as remotely as ever, rowing on Loch Muick with friends at Balmoral. But the public and press were already whipping each other up. She was two days short of twenty-five when the *Mirror* shouted at her, 'Come on Margaret! Please make up your mind!'

Throughout September, though the Royal Family and Townsend were still in Scotland and Brussels respectively, the clash and clamour in the papers grew. 'An apostasy', 'an illicit union' was how one clergyman described the proposed marriage, while another declared that the voice of God in the guise of *vox populi* had given the lovers the 'All Clear'; yet a third pointed out that if anything happened to Prince Charles and Princess Anne so that Princess

Margaret's children by Townsend came to the throne, the royal line would have become illegitimate in an ecclesiastical sense. But this would never come about, said rumours of a different brand. The Princess's love affair was over and she intended to enter a convent.

Princess Margaret's sharp remarks about the press, when acclaimed as 'Castaway of the Year' on the radio programme *Desert Island Discs* in 1981, were clearly a release of long pent-up feelings. She had suffered from press misrepresentations and misreporting since she was seventeen, she said. 'I find them extremely aggravating. Of course if they're absolutely invented, as they sometimes are, one can laugh at them with one's friends.'[9] There was nothing to laugh about between 12 and 31 October 1955.

On Wednesday the 12th, Townsend flew into Lydd Airport in Kent, drove to London and stayed with the Abergavennys in Lowndes Square. Next day Princess Margaret arrived at Clarence House from Balmoral where she and the Queen Mother received Townsend. The Queen had shaken hands affectionately in public when he left for Brussels two years before. Now the Queen Mother treated him with every kindness.

It had been in the Queen's mind to make her own part in the drama as calm and unhurried as possible. While still in Balmoral she quietly informed the new Prime Minister (he had been in office five months) of her sister's desire for Parliament's consent to her marriage. After the Cabinet's verdict, whatever it was, the Queen hoped that her sister and Townsend would take up to six months, seeing each other in friends' houses, before gradually reaching a decision.

The Queen had reckoned without the press – not only the world press, but her own press officer in the Palace, Commander Richard Colville. In an attempt to damp down speculation, Commander Colville issued a statement from Clarence House that drove the world press into an excited spin: 'No announcement concerning Princess Margaret's future,' he said, 'is at present contemplated.' What could '*at present*' mean?

In order to find out, a cavalcade of cars swept down on Allanbay Park in Berkshire, where Princess Margaret and Townsend had been invited to spend their first weekend with the Hon. Mrs John Lycett Wills, the Queen's first cousin. The couple may together have 'strolled gaily through the wooded parkland of the Wills's lovely country estate', as the *Daily Mirror* insisted, during the 'idyllic weekend', but their every smallest movement was being charted (10.35 Princess leaves for church in Rolls Royce . . . 10.50 enters royal chapel for service of one hour . . . forty minutes' private talk with Queen Mother . . . forty-year-old Group-Captain waits on mansion steps . . .); and even then the long lenses were only kept out of the house by a defence force of police armed with walkie-talkies organised by the chief constable of Berkshire.

And so it went on. Afterwards the press were found to have recorded five visits by Townsend to Clarence House, four dinner parties, two country weekends and many comings and goings at Lowndes Square.

Suddenly at 7.21 pm on the last day of October it was all over.

Holding to her principle of keeping down the temperature, the Queen had chosen Balmoral as the place to receive Eden on Tuesday the 18th. The news he brought was bad as well as being personally awkward for him. Amid a confusion of cabinet voices, Lord Salisbury, the Royal Family's oldest political friend after Churchill, had firmly put the religious objection to the marriage. If the Cabinet gave consent to it he would resign. The Cabinet withheld their consent. Eden was in no position to fight for the Princess. Like Townsend himself, Eden had been the innocent party in a divorce and was now remarried, to Clarissa Churchill. On whichever side Eden argued he would have been open to misinterpretation. He therefore simply accepted the Cabinet's decision and passed it on to the Queen.

The religious ground had thus been lost. Six days later, on 24 October, the 'Thunderer', as *The Times* was called in its heyday, let out a long rumble and captured the moral, social and ethical ground for itself. Princess Margaret, it declared, had only two options. One was to maintain her 'high place' in the Commonwealth's love and respect; but that would mean renouncing her happiness. The other was to renounce her royal status and marry Townsend; but this would mean letting down the Queen as the symbol of people's 'better selves', particularly in family life. Sir William Haley, the editor, had written this crucial piece himself. The country was not to hear such words and such a tone again until the Profumo case eight years later, when Haley again wrote the leader, 'It *is* a moral question.'

Though the *Mirror* tried to keep the struggle going – Is the Princess 'to live her life in devoted spinsterhood', it asked, 'fortified by the knowledge that she has done right by Sir William Haley?' – Princess Margaret had already made up her mind. When she and Townsend met at Clarence House they had said in the same breath, 'It's not possible. It won't do.' They did not even think about the Civil List. It was an overwhelming sense of 'no deal'. Then they sat down together and devised her statement for the press. But before it was published she went alone to Lambeth Palace to tell Dr Fisher, Archbishop of Canterbury, her decision.

After she and Dr Fisher had exchanged greetings, he put on his spectacles, went over to the bookcase and began to haul out a large reference book. 'Put it back,' said Princess Margaret. 'I have come to give you information, not to ask for it.' So he sat down again and she told him she had decided not to marry Peter Townsend. The Archbishop's comment was made with a beaming smile: 'What a wonderful person the Holy Spirit is!'

The above is Princess Margaret's own account, told to the author. Randolph Churchill published an account in the *Spectator* of 23 May 1958 which up until 1983 held the field. (Christopher Warwick, author of *Princess Margaret*, like the present author consulted the Princess.)

The Archbishop [wrote Churchill], supposing that she was coming to consult him, had all his books of reference spread around him, carefully marked and cross-referenced. When Princess Margaret entered, she said, and the words are worthy of Queen Elizabeth I, 'Archbishop, you may put your books away: I have made up my mind already.'

Churchill's 'Elizabethan' simile was felicitous; but Dr Fisher was later to tell his biographer that there were no books whatever on his table, however 'carefully marked'. Dr Fisher was also to tell James Pope-Hennessy in 1957 that Princess Margaret 'is a *thoroughly good churchwoman*' and '*really understands doctrine*'; the rest of her family, he added, were intensely religious but did not have this doctrinal interest.[10]

It is probable that Princess Margaret had been 'fortified', to use the *Mirror*'s word, by the Rev. Andrew Elphinstone and the Rev. Simon Phipps, the one a cousin, the other a close friend, when she issued her actual statement of renunciation on 31 October 1955. The *Mirror* gave it powerful headlines: 'DUTY BEFORE LOVE'.

I would like it to be known [the Princess announced] that I have decided not to marry Group-Captain Peter Townsend. I have been aware that, subject to my renouncing my rights of succession, it might have been possible for me to contract a civil marriage. But, mindful of the Church's teaching that Christian marriage is indissoluble, and conscious of my duty to the Commonwealth, I have resolved to put these considerations before any others. . . .

Princess Margaret had thus publicly laid her sacrifice on the altar of Church and Commonwealth: the Church in so far as it did not recognise divorce; the Commonwealth because opinion had not really changed over the past eighteen years, since Mrs Simpson's two divorces had made her an unacceptable queen. Princess Margaret still meant what she said twenty-five years later, when she took part in *Desert Island Discs*. Among her choices were the hymn

'Guide Me O Thou Great Redeemer' to express her religion, and 'Rule Britannia' to express her patriotism. These were the two altars. But the Royal Family knew, none better, that the most intimate altar of all had been the Queen's welfare and happiness.

Peter Townsend went out of Princess Margaret's life. He married a young Belgian girl named Marie-Luce Jamagne and they had three children. He says in his memoirs, 'I have outflown the storm.'

There are two more points to be made on the subject of divorce as it affected the Royal Family. First, the social rules had been gradually relaxed even by George V when 'innocent parties' were no longer prohibited from the enclosure at Royal Ascot. Under Elizabeth II 'guilty parties' were admitted to the enclosure but not to the Queen's Lawn. Nor were they invited into her palaces nor on to *Britannia*; though in so far as they held 'public office' the rules were waived. The whole movement towards relaxation but away from condonation could be seen as keeping up with the times but not with the Joneses – who were more and more getting divorced.

Second, despite the relaxations, divorce still gave members of the Royal Family acute feelings of *angst*. This was partly an after-effect of the Abdication; partly a concern for example-setting. Lord Harewood, the Queen's divorced first cousin who was remarried in 1969 with Her Majesty's consent, had to go to an analyst beforehand; yet even the analyst could not entirely exorcise, he wrote, 'the horror with which I initially looked upon the idea of divorce. . . .'[11]

Lord Harewood also reveals that Harold Wilson, perhaps aided by Arnold (Lord) Goodman, found a formula which would minimally involve the Queen. The formula ran: 'The Cabinet have advised the Queen to give her consent . . .' to the remarriage. Why could not some such formula have assisted Princess Margaret? The answer on a non-religious plane was twofold: because she was third in line to the throne in 1955 and Lord Harewood was seventeenth in 1967; and because public opinion had moved in the twelve years between 1955 and 1967.

The tragic drama within the Royal Family was prologue to a far deeper and more violent national schism a year later. What is now known as the 'Suez adventure' had no direct public effect on Elizabeth II. But it further tarnished the gilt of the new reign. When Egypt led by Colonel Nasser nationalised the Suez Canal; when Britain, France and Israel invaded the Canal Zone; when the United Nations Security Council called a halt to the invaders; when the United States threatened to let the pound collapse unless a halt were made forthwith; when a double collapse did indeed ensue, of the Suez adventure and of the British Prime Minister's health; when all these humiliations were strung one after another on the same thread, then it seemed indeed that the 'New Elizabethans' had bitten the dust.

Those who were pro-Suez did not like to read that Her Majesty had signed the national call-up in the Duke of Richmond's HQ on Goodwood racecourse. (In fact it was signed at Arundel Castle.) Did Suez not merit even a royal trip to London? (This was absurd carping. The unquestionably constitutional George V also held a council at Goodwood.)

Those who had been 'against Suez' wondered whether their Queen, as well as Sir Anthony Eden, was 'in it'. An ingenious dilemma was later propounded, by which she either knew all, and so deceived the foreign ambassadors she saw at the Palace during the five months of plotting; or she knew nothing, and so was humiliated and herself deceived.

This 'all-or-nothing' dichotomy is not the scenario of real life, even of real political life. The public will never know exactly how much Eden told the Queen; nor would it be right that they should. No secretary is ever present during the Tuesday prime ministerial audiences – they are strictly between the minister and the sovereign. Queen Elizabeth II keeps a diary, but those who know her feel certain that it is as brief and non-committal as possible.

All one can say is that the Tuesday audiences of half an hour to an hour gave Eden time enough to 'consult' Her Majesty about his general plan – his concerted international effort, shall we say, to prevent Nasser from reaping the full benefits of his *fait accompli*. Lord Avon (Anthony Eden) told Robert Lacey some twenty years later that the Queen 'understood what we were doing very well' and was not anti-Suez, 'nor would I claim that she was pro-Suez.'[12]

At this stage of the Queen's story it is not appropriate to go into further detail about the state of her prerogative in 1956; nor is it necessary at this stage to consider the Queen's appointment of Macmillan as prime minister in place of Eden, who had resigned through acute ill-health. Her procedures were not criticised at the time, though they have been since.

Another most vexatious boulder, however, had suddenly been rolled into the Queen's uphill path.

The naval career of the Duke of Edinburgh had been abruptly cut short by the death of George VI. Had the Duke continued in the Royal Navy he would assuredly have attained to the eminence of his uncle Lord Mountbatten and become First Sea Lord. But if the career was closed, the sea was still open. And Philip was a man first – a seaman – and a prince second.

In the autumn of 1956 the Queen and Duke together decided that he should put in four months' active service in their common sphere of devotion, the Commonwealth. The Duke chose to visit Malaya, New Zealand, Ceylon and the Gambia, besides some of the most outlying parts of the Commonwealth, including Antarctica, Darwin's Galapagos Islands and the Falklands. These latter were interesting because generally unvisited and yet rich in the Duke's favourite problems: wild life and conservation.

But Prince Philip's thoughts were never far from home, even in the course of his 39,000-mile tour. He sent his wife white roses on the ninth anniversary of their wedding and took a photograph of two iguanas with their arms round each other, spoke to her and the children continually on the radio telephone, especially at Christmas from the Falkland Islands, and arrived back on the dot to meet her on *Britannia* for the Portuguese state visit from 16 to 21 February 1957.

Nevertheless, there was tetchiness at home. *Britannia*, on which he travelled, was labelled 'Philip's Folly'. It was noted that he had not been home to enliven his wife's Christmas broadcast – which indeed was somewhat 'solid', as the awkward repetition of that word suggested: 'We are the solid facts beneath the words and phrases,' she said of the Royal Family, 'we are the solid flesh-and-blood links which draw the Commonwealth under the Crown.'

More awkward still, the Duke had been absent for the Suez débâcle in 1956 and for the change of ministry in 1957. Not that he would have handled either crisis had he been there. The Queen has always strictly adhered to her unique, independent role as monarch. But in a welter of other irritations, the Duke's absence was another neuralgic point for the press. A rift was rumoured.

'It is quite untrue that there is any rift between the Queen and the Duke of Edinburgh,' announced Sir Michael Adeane from the Palace. The very fact, however, that he had had to deny a rift added to the sense of unease.* The Duke, remembering the press on his honeymoon, in Paris, and later around his sister-in-law, lashed out at the journalists who seemed guilty. 'Those bloody lies that you people print to make money. These lies about how I'm never with my wife.' 'If photographers poke a long lens through a

* Towards the end of the year 1957 a 'rift' between the Queen and Princess Margaret was also falsely rumoured, and another in 1963; on both cases Nigel Dempster, a writer and journalist, was to comment, ' "Royal rifts" are a favourite theme of the Press whose members are never privy to first-hand personal glimpses of Royal Family life. . . .' Princess Margaret's own comment to me was, 'In our family we do not have "rifts" – a very occasional row but never a rift.'

keyhole into my private life,' he was to say two years later, 'then I'm bloody nasty.'[13]

Fortunately, as it turned out, the Duke was still only a royal duke not a prince. The Queen was able to signal her feelings by giving him a new title in 1957 for his services to the Commonwealth and herself: Prince of the United Kingdom.

During the young Queen's first years as monarch, her husband made frequent speeches on subjects that stimulated him, especially youth and disadvantaged people. In view of the criticisms launched against his wife, some of his thoughts had a curious, unconscious relevance. The young, he said, must be shown how to 'find' themselves, to become aware of their own 'possibilities'. Again, all of us, even social scientists, must strive to think as 'whole men'. Yet again, 'people have the maddening habit of behaving like people, and not like rational electronic computers and, what is more, they never will.'

Putting together these extracts from three of Prince Philip's speeches delivered between 1956 and 1959, one could say that the moral was clear: Elizabeth II was never going to be a blueprint for something called modern monarchy, nor an electronic machine, however well programmed by her articulate critics. On the other hand, as a young woman of only thirty-one, there was room for an awareness of new 'possibilities'.

Prince Philip's sage and generalised thoughts, however, were not immediately applicable to a situation where incandescent heat had been generated by two press bombs.

The first took the form of an editorial written for the August 1957 number of the *National & English Review*, an obscure monthly edited and owned by Lord Altrincham. This whole number was devoted to discussion of 'The Monarchy Today'. Altrincham wrote off the Queen's entourage as stuffy and 'tweedy'. While blaming the Queen's alleged shortcomings on the 'tight little enclave of English ladies and gentlemen' who formed her court, he also mocked the way in which she personally appeared in public. He called her style of speaking a 'pain in the neck'. 'The personality conveyed by the utterances which are put into her mouth is that of a priggish schoolgirl, captain of the hockey team, a prefect and a recent candidate for Confirmation.'

The Queen's mentor continued with what he intended as his 'loyal and constructive' criticism:

> When she has lost the bloom of youth, the Queen's reputation will depend, far more than it does now, upon her personality . . . she will have to say things which people can remember and do things which will make people sit up and take notice.[14]

Altrincham's editorial at least did precisely that. It made people sit up and spit. But not Malcolm Muggeridge. He described Altrincham as 'a youthful, amiable and earnest peer' who had aroused a furore by saying much that was true.

Muggeridge, though his father had been a respected Labour MP, had never had a good word to say for politicians of any brand. Indeed he distrusted the display of all human 'authority', whether political, academic or royal. He was editor of *Punch* and a provocative voice on television. In 1956, he had written an article on the monarchy for the *New Statesman*, entitled 'The Royal Soap Opera'.

Nothing much more was heard of Muggeridge's soap opera until two events the next year: Altrincham's piece that August, and a state visit to Canada and the United States by the Queen and Prince Philip in October. The New York *Saturday Evening Post* promptly commissioned its own 'Royal Soap Opera', publishing it on 19 October to coincide with the Queen's visit. Its title had now become. 'Does England really need a Queen?', words which inspired a few Americans to ask whether England really needed Mr Muggeridge. A network interview with Muggeridge was blacked out in Washington in case the Queen were there. Many years later, on 26 March 1981, the *Post* article was republished, this time by the BBC's *Listener* under the new headline, 'The Monarchy Provides a Sort of Ersatz Religion'. Those who were sensible enough to reread it must have been surprised by its lack of ferocity. Peter Brookes, the cartoonist, drew for the cover illustration a large cat with no claws but 'St Mugg's' benign smile, looking at the breeches, stockings, buckled shoes, sceptre, orb and hands of a king.

The target for Muggeridge's satire was not in fact the Queen but the materialistic age in which she and all of us lived. It was only because the people had no real religion that they had perforce discovered a substitute or ersatz religion in the monarchy. Muggeridge spent several columns of his article on past history, arguing that the idea of 'popular monarchy' began only with George v. The first four Georges had been freely criticised, since people did not need to regard their kings as deities; they possessed a genuine deity in those days.

No doubt Muggeridge accused the courtiers, press and media of being 'unctuous' and 'luscious' in their presentation of royalty. But the Queen herself, he added, with her 'charming personality', played a necessary role in the nation.

> History shows that institutions survive only to the degree that they fulfil an authentic purpose. The British monarchy does fulfil a purpose. It provides a symbolic head of state transcending the politicians who go in and out of office. . . .

Nor was he, Muggeridge, anything but favourable to the Queen's simple style. Her clothes might not always be 'elegant' but she dressed 'pleasingly' enough.

> It is duchesses not shop assistants who find the Queen dowdy, frumpish and banal. The appeal of the monarchy is to the gallery rather than to the stalls. Those whose wealth or birth brings them into its orbit are inclined to turn up their noses at a show so obviously designed to bring in the masses. Their attitude is rather like that of a cultivated Anglican divine toward Billy Graham.

Provided the Monarch realised she no longer ruled but reigned – and reigned in the purely ceremonial sphere of processions, honours and other 'baubles' – one must not underestimate the 'great symbolic utility the institution embodies'.[15]

A tornado of anger was none the less whipped up against Muggeridge as it had been against Altrincham, only more vicious. The *People* described the article it had not yet seen as 'ruthless, shocking, patronizing, gruesome, a diatribe'. Both Altrincham and Muggeridge were greatly out of pocket through cancellations of contracts or television programmes; each was slapped by a member of the public, and Muggeridge's wall was defaced by the League of Empire Loyalists. (The League at first defaced an innocent neighbour's wall but returned to Muggeridge's later.) Razors and excrement were put through his letterbox, together with one incredible letter. The writer, hearing that Muggeridge's youngest son Charles had been killed by an avalanche when skiing, wrote, 'It means one Muggeridge less.'

Years later, as we shall see, Altrincham and Muggeridge were to come back to the subject, the former in 1972 and both in 1982. Muggeridge stands by his first comment: that no one had ever read his article. 'No one reads today.'

For the Queen 1957 might have seemed a bad year, a year to forget. If Muggeridge, according to a *New York Times* profile, was 'Britain's angry middle-aged man', there was an angry *young* man to attack her too. Playwright John Osborne, in that same October 1957, described royalty as 'a gold filling in a mouth full of decay'.[16]

The royal gold tooth had worked hard throughout the year. Four state visits: Portugal in February, France in April, Denmark in May, Canada and the USA in October. Nevertheless, some people criticised the number and expense, overlooking the fact that the Queen was Britain's best ambassador. All the countries wanted her to visit them and there was a big backlog to make up since her father's illnesses.

Not altogether a bad year, though. Already the stallion Aureole had carried the Queen to the top of the world – a different world. From this angle 1957 was a miracle year, the year of the fillies.

XII

The Sport of Queens

Love of horses and dogs is generally accepted to be 'normal'
among royal personages. George Harewood, the music-
lover royal, tells a story that well illustrates the point.
'It's very odd about George and music,' said the Duke of
Windsor one day to Topazia Markevich, wife of the great
composer Igor Stravinsky. 'You know, his parents were
quite normal – liked horses and dogs and the country!'[1]

Queen Elizabeth II was born with a love of 'horses and
dogs and the country', but by no means the humdrum
conventional kind of love that the remark quoted above
implies. It was to become a deep love, which fully extended
her; it required both reason and active thought. In the old
territorial dispute between the arts and sciences, the Queen
treated horse-racing and breeding as an art and science
combined, with moral virtues like courage and patience
thrown in. If there were any gaps, physical or mental, in her
full life, this first love helped to fill them.

For first love it was. We have seen her sitting up in bed
driving an imaginary team round the Park; grooming a
string of toy horses; owning her first real pony in 1931. She
decided that hired horses in the Row needed a rest-day on
Sunday. So far it might have been almost any child – except
for the total absorption. When her grandfather died she
showed she was aware of the intensity of pleasure in merely
grooming a toy horse by asking, 'Ought we to play?' You
couldn't feel properly sad with a brush in one hand and the
other on a horse's neck.

At Balmoral ponies meant freedom. The Princesses were allowed to ride over the moors by themselves. This was again like other children – except for the single policeman pedalling in the distance.

Then came the war at Windsor; shortages in the stables as everywhere else, so that now the Princesses groomed their own horses of necessity and learnt stable management. Princess Elizabeth knew a good deal by 1942, when she had her first unforgettable experience of the racing world: she was sixteen, and her father took her to Beckhampton on the Wiltshire downs, to see Big Game and Sun Chariot, the latter ridden by Gordon Richards, do their final gallops before the wartime Derby and Oaks. Fred Darling, their trainer, had his stables there and trained those horses, among them Big Game and Sun Chariot, that the King leased from the National Stud. Next year, 1943, Captain Cecil Boyd Rochfort, 'The Captain' (who died as Sir Cecil aged ninety-three), was to train the King's home-bred horses at Newmarket, with Darling ('The Guv'nor') training those leased from the National Stud. All these names – Beckhampton, Darling, Richards, Boyd Rochfort – were significant not only in the training of racehorses but in the training of the Princess.

Beckhampton was the scene of two important 'firsts' in her life. Here she met her first jockey, the champion Gordon Richards. Sun Chariot had gone through the 1941 season unbeaten and was to win the Oaks and St Leger for Richards. Nevertheless, she was a bit of a 'lady'. John Oaksey, the former steeplechase rider and expert on racing, has since written:

> As a student of breeding and equine heredity, the Queen now no doubt recalls Sun Chariot's antics without surprise. Captain Boyd Rochfort always said that Hyperion's best offspring were those with a bit of temperament. . . . [2]

And Sun Chariot was among the many offspring of Hyperion, that great stallion who in the 1930s had won the Derby for Lord Derby himself.

It was also at Beckhampton that the Princess first got to know Lord Porchester, her present racing manager who at that time trained with Fred Darling and was to share with her a passion for new ideas. Beckhampton is thirty miles from the more famous village of Highclere, where 'Porchy's' enterprising grandfather, the 5th Earl of Carnarvon, operating on the home front, founded the Highclere Stud; on another front, he was responsible for the discovery and opening of Tutankhamen's tomb. (Lord Porchester's great-grandfather, no less original, had been both Viceroy of India and negotiator with Charles Stewart Parnell over Irish Home Rule. If the 4th Lord Carnarvon's advice had been taken by Lord Salisbury's government, Anglo-Irish history might not be the chaotic thing it is.)

The Queen would not like to remember Sun Chariot in 1942 without recalling the exploits of Big Game also. He too had been unbeaten in 1941, his first win occurring on the eve of her fifteenth birthday. Next year Big Game, ridden by Gordon Richards, won the 2,000 Guineas for George VI. Awed and exhilarated at her first Beckhampton visit, the young Princess was allowed to run her hands over Big Game's silken coat. For several hours afterwards she refused to wash them. 'Great horses certainly have an aura about them,' wrote Bill Curling of the *Daily Telegraph*, versatile biographer of Cecil Boyd Rochfort and author of *All the Queen's Horses*.[3]

Boyd Rochfort and Fred Darling were the next two names on the Princess's wartime list. The former had his 'yard' at Freemason's Lodge, a rambling Victorian house at Newmarket where the Princesses were taken in 1944 to see the horses 'working' on the Heath. Princess Elizabeth and Boyd Rochfort were to share many triumphs during the next decade. And from her first sight of Freemason's Lodge she learnt the routine of a really big racing-stable. Discipline must be strict – a law that was by no means uncongenial to the King's daughter.

As for 'The Guv'nor', he believed in discipline even more firmly than 'The Captain', adding a rigidity of perfection that was all his own. Whatever the situation, Darling's 'yard' must always be kept spotless by his stable boys, his horses gleaming. He could be compared to an old-fashioned matron, the terror of her nurses, the pride of her hospital. It was 'The Guv'nor' who noticed Princess Elizabeth taking the lead with her family on that first day at Beckhampton. As the horses circled in front of the King, Queen and two Princesses, Elizabeth made a quick mental picture of each. When they began 'working', the King found himself constantly turning to his elder daughter to ask her which was which. 'Princess Elizabeth must have a natural eye for a horse,' Darling remarked to Gordon Richards.[4]

In the same year as her experiences at Beckhampton, 1942, the Princess visited the mares, foals and yearlings at Hampton Court, then the Royal Stud. (It is now a stud for the royal carriage-horses only, the Queen's racing studs being divided between Norfolk and Hampshire.) As a child of the 1930s and 1940s she was never without her camera, and at Hampton Court she picked out and photographed the foal Rising Light. The 'natural eye' was unblinking, for this filly was to win the Burghfield Stakes at Ascot in 1945 – the first royal horse that the Princess actually saw win a race.

The 1930s had not been a period of royal racing successes such as to tempt King George VI to take his two young children to race-meetings. Breeding and racing did not greatly interest him, and indeed there seemed little reason during the first two years of his reign why they should. The Royal Stud's lowest ebb was reached in 1937 and 1938.

At this point another 'name' rises from the Queen's racing past. King George V had appointed as his racing manager a tall, handsome, grey-haired Irishman named

Charles Moore. It was Captain Moore's policy to lease promising yearlings from the National Stud and on these he mainly relied to carry the King's colours to victory. Already in his late fifties on his appointment, Moore ran a small stud of his own in Tipperary. He would send the royal foals to Ireland after they were weaned, for rich grass and a change of scene. This was good psychology. But it meant that the foals' royal owners – George V, George VI and Elizabeth II – hardly saw them until they were grown up.

Captain Moore had other policies which can only be called prejudices: he would not use horses like Fair Trial with any trace of American blood in their pedigrees, and equally turned down Nearco because he was owned by a bookmaker. Lord Porchester remembers him as being like an old cook guarding her recipes. He would withhold information from the young Porchester saying, 'Ah, well, I'm not going to tell you. You would use that information yourself – you would not use it for the Queen.'[5] Nevertheless, Moore's eye for a thoroughbred was infallible and he knew more than most of his contemporaries about breeding. For a mere 100 guineas he bought Malapert, whose son Pall Mall was to give the Queen her first home-bred classic win, the 2,000 Guineas in 1958. His Irish wit added a special charm to the Queen's 'horsey' talk with her first racing manager. And because Moore and Boyd Rochfort, her first manager and trainer respectively, were both over six feet tall, the small figure of the girl-queen walking between two giants attained a dignified poignancy not known since Queen Victoria.

Princess Elizabeth's knowledge of horses grew apace during the few but rewarding years between the end of the war and the death of her father. Despite the pre-war doldrums, there had been one mare in the royal stables since the early 1930s who was to run well herself – second in the 1,000 Guineas and third in the Oaks in 1936 – and to become a brood mare of outstanding qualities; in stud language a 'prepotent' mare. This was Feola. By the next decade she was what her stable lads called affectionately an 'old lady'. But her daughters, among them Hypericum who won the 1,000 Guineas in 1946, were already laying the foundations for the Queen's triumphs in the 1950s and indeed up to the present day.

Princess Elizabeth, at twenty, welcomed Hypericum in the unsaddling enclosure as the first royal horse she had seen win a major race; but the filly's character and breeding interested her almost as much as her victory. She was a curious collection of paradoxes: wonderful in her box where other excitable horses could be difficult, and a good 'doer', that is, eater, an essential quality in a racehorse and one not always found among highly strung animals. At the same time she was so awkward in training that even the phrase 'a bit scatty' was not too bad for her. She would misbehave abominably when being shoed, and was in fact 'the devil to plate'. Here indeed was a problem to engage the imagination of an ardent twenty-year-old, already trained to appreciate human genealogical tables. Put succinctly it amounted to an eugenic knife-edge: achieving enough breeding and temperament to win, and not so much that the mental instability undid the physical prowess.

With Angelola, another of Feola's daughters, the story is again of breeding and its mysteries. Though not destined to be a big winner herself, Angelola was to prove capable of producing among her descendants the very best. After being mated to Hyperion, her first foal was Aureole – a name for the Queen to conjure with. But before following in the wake of Aureole's unpredictable majesty, a note on the Queen's naming of her horses is appropriate here. Her interest and skill in this eclectic field throws as much light on her own character as on the horses she names.

Choosing a foal's name is not a task she ever delegates. This is in part because a certain mystique will attach to the name of a successful horse. In Lord Oaksey's words, 'Historically there have been very few good horses with unattractive names. . . .' In part also the Queen's concentration on this task derives from an interest in playing about with words and their meanings – this in turn springing from a mind that enjoys crossword puzzles, choosing, manipulating, contriving associations and even making puns. Thus Angelola, being a filly by Donatello out of Feola, had been associated through the second half of her name with her dam, while the 'Angel' prefix linked her to Donatello, the sculptor of saints and angels. And when Angelola's first son arrived, the name Aureole linked him again to Angelola's sire, the sculptor of haloes or aureoles round his saints. A bay colt by Queen's Hussar out of Christchurch emerged as Church Parade; and a filly by High Top out of Circlet became Round Tower. A colt by Halo out of Joking Apart owed his name to a conversation between the Queen and the Bishop of Winchester, who suggested St Boniface, patron saint of clowns; while a filly by Bustino out of Strip the Willow was called drily Bare Minimum. The need for the Queen's ingenuity and wit increases as the most obvious or euphonious names become exhausted.

Meanwhile there had been some other pleasant additions to Princess Elizabeth's experience in those last years of George vi's reign. In 1947 the Aga Khan gave her a filly as a wedding present, which she aptly named Astrakhan, as we have seen, grateful and thrilled to own her first thoroughbred. She also chose her personal colours – scarlet, purple-hooped sleeves, black cap – as near to the royal colours as possible without causing confusion. Astrakhan won at Hurst Park in 1949, the only flat-race winner ever to run under the Princess's own colours. That same year a steeplechaser, the delightful Monaveen, also carried the Princess's colours to victory.

In the story of Monaveen is summed up Princess Elizabeth's brief love affair with steeplechasing. At a now-famous dinner party at Windsor Castle in 1949, Lord Mildmay tempted and prevailed upon Queen Elizabeth and her daughter to own a jumper between them. Monaveen's gallant career – and his young part-owner's patronage of steeplechasing – were cut short by the horse's death at the Hurst Park water-jump. The stricken Princess decided to concentrate on flat-racing in future, leaving the 'winter game' to her mother. The Queen Mother's totally involved and indispensable contribution to that sport shows how right was the decision.

When in February 1952 Queen Elizabeth lost her husband, she had already gained a new interest for the future. To her daughter came the vastly expanded interest of owing the Royal Stud.

In Aureole, Queen Elizabeth II had inherited the hope of the decade. As a two-year-old colt he won easily at the York summer meeting, which took place after Goodwood. A chestnut described variously as 'bright', 'rich' and 'flashy', Aureole had a great deal of white about him and, as Hyperion's son, a great deal of 'hyper' in his temperament. Nevertheless, he was confidently expected to shine in Coronation year.

The first season proceeded pleasantly enough as a curtain-raiser. At the Queen's first Royal Ascot of her reign she had a win; but with a 'hireling' from the National Stud, Gay Time. She had to wait a year for her first home-bred Ascot winner when Choir Boy, ridden by Doug Smith, won the Royal Hunt Cup. Far from starting as favourite, Choir Boy was a surprise triumph for his trainer's patience – another most acceptable lesson to the Queen. It showed what could be done when firm human character imposed itself on equine moods.

Goodwood was the Queen's next new experience, the first Goodwood to be attended by the sovereign for twenty-five years; and the first ever race-meeting where a running radio commentary was used. The enchanting Sussex racecourse had been founded by the 3rd Duke of Richmond in 1802, where the Prince Regent's Rebel defeated Richmond's Cedar; while in 1830 the sailor king William IV, just enthroned, showed an unsurpassed enthusiasm for his newly acquired stud. When asked which of his three royal horses should run in the Goodwood Cup he replied like the Lord High Admiral he had once been, 'Start the whole fleet!' His orders were obeyed and the royal flotilla took the first three places.

A story of coronation morning dramatically shows the extent of the young Queen's self-identity with her favourite Aureole.

'Is all well, ma'am?' asked a lady-in-waiting shortly before the Queen left the Palace for the Abbey.

'Oh yes,' replied the Queen fervently, 'the Captain has just rung up to say that Aureole went really well.'

The three-year-old chestnut with the 'explosive and exhibitionist tendencies' was all set to win the Epsom Derby for Queen Elizabeth II four days after her coronation. He was up against the gigantic Pinza, however, ridden by the diminutive Gordon Richards, a giant in spirit and determined to pull off the Derby at last – on his twenty-ninth attempt. The Queen had knighted him in her coronation honours and when he won his Derby victory by four lengths from Aureole she was not the one to stint her congratulations. Sending for Gordon Richards and Norman Bertie, Pinza's trainer, to come to the royal box, she said, 'Congratulations, Mr Bertie, on winning the Derby.'

'May I congratulate you, Your Majesty,' he replied, 'on winning the world.'[6] All around were stunned into silence by such a burst of untutored eloquence from someone who was usually a doer not a talker. Richards afterwards called the Queen 'a marvellous sport' in defeat. And Fred Darling, breeder of Pinza, died happy three days after his win.

There was no further coronation year success for Aureole. He went on to be beaten again by Pinza in the King George VI and Queen Elizabeth Stakes and to be beaten in the St Leger by the distance; in all to be beaten by his own character defects. Having been hot favourite for the St Leger, he had shown less and less 'co-operation' during his training at Newmarket, more and more tension. Reform of this disturbed genius was urgently called for.

It was at this point that the Queen showed her emphatic reliance on new ideas. Knowing that some of the over-excitable horses used at her coronation procession had been successfully calmed by a London neurologist (not a vet), she called a meeting with both the Captains, Moore and Boyd Rochfort, to discuss the application of the new method to Aureole.

The neurologist in question was Dr Charles Brook, his treatment known as 'the laying on of hands'. With the consent of her trainer and manager, the Queen called Dr Brook in. Soon Brook had Aureole tranquilly eating from the hay-net in his stall (hitherto something of a lion's den) while Brook for twenty minutes laid his calming left hand on the horse's withers, his right hand on his back or stomach, and his head on Aureole's shoulder. Bruce Hobbs, assistant trainer to the Captain, said, 'He taught the horse to relax'; and Oaksey writes: 'Without any doubt the treatment played an important part in Aureole's brilliant four-year-old career.'[7]

One more new idea occurred to the Queen's manager, Moore, before Aureole's test the next year. This was to change jockeys: from the dedicated Harry Carr to the more congenial (to Aureole) Eph Smith. It involved a disagreement between Boyd Rochfort (Carr's employer) and Moore, which could be settled only by Aureole's owner, the Queen. She showed appreciation of Carr's devotion yet ultimately was overridingly decisive in choosing the jockey for whom Aureole went most happily.

It is possible that the young Queen's handling of delicate psychological problems in her racing stables was also of assistance in her councils of state. And far from being unresponsive to new ideas, the Queen was becoming an instigator of change.

Nineteen fifty-four was to be Aureole's year, an integral part of the Queen's great racing decade, though it began with two misfortunes for the horse. While the Queen was still on her Commonwealth tour, a horse ran across Aureole at Sandown depriving him of his win. 'The Queen is a very good race-leader,' wrote Curling, 'and would undoubtedly have seen the incident if she had been present. The Stewards were apparently unsighted and took no action.'[8]

The day before Aureole ran in the Hardwicke Stakes at Royal Ascot with his owner present, he was near to becoming 'unsighted' himself. He damaged his left eye in his stall. In breaking the news to the Queen, Eph Smith added, 'So we are both handicapped, ma'am. Aureole's half blind and I'm stone deaf.' (Eph wore a hearing aid.) None the less, victory attended the handicapped pair, to the Queen's delight, both at the win and the wit. Not only that, but her colt Landau won his race also, giving the Queen her first double at Royal Ascot.

Aureole's greatest triumph of all, preceded by high drama, was in the King George VI and Queen Elizabeth Stakes. The dashing four-year-old was favourite in an international field that included the French horse Vamos. On the way to the start someone suddenly put up an umbrella. It was enough for Aureole. He got rid of his jockey and started off riderless round the course. In the teeth of disaster, Eph Smith seized a bunch of grass and called, 'Come here, old boy.' Aureole returned, to finish three-quarters of a length in front of Vamos. It was the signal for the Queen to 'almost run' to greet her favourite, outstripping the old Guv'nor a good deal more easily than Aureole had outstripped the French horse.[9] Aureole's performance in 1954 made Elizabeth II leading British owner in terms of stake money, and Hyperion champion sire yet again. This was the glorious end of Aureole's racing days. Retired to Wolferton stud, he was to become a champion sire himself, producing among other famous progeny the Derby winner St Paddy.

Nor was the Captain forgotten. At the end of the year the Queen presented him with an engraved cigarette box, 'To Cecil Boyd Rochfort, leading trainer, from Elizabeth R, leading winner owner, 1954.'

Despite the departure of Aureole, the Queen's racing career rose to an even more impressive peak in 1957. Again new ideas were involved. Two years earlier the Queen had seventeen new yearlings in her stables, nine of them home-bred; and the next year Boyd Rochfort was among the first to introduce stable girls, mostly to look after the fillies. Nineteen fifty-seven was to be the year of the fillies.

Meanwhile in 1956 the Queen herself had fallen in love with a little filly called Stroma at the Doncaster yearling sales, which she attended with Lord Porchester and Captain Moore. Stroma proved to be the bargain of the sale. At only 1,150 guineas she produced, when mated with Doutelle, a son Canisbay who won the Eclipse Stakes for the Queen in the sinking 1960s. Stroma was also to become second dam (grandmother) of Dunfermline, star of Silver Jubilee year.

The Queen's favourite, Doutelle, died as a result of biting his rack-chain. For the first time since she was a child the Queen wept over a horse. When Magna Carta died nine years later through biting his hay-net, the Queen banished hay-nets from her stables.

The three top-class fillies of 1957 were more fortunate. Mulberry Harbour, bred at Sandringham, was by a French Derby winner; a tribute to the Queen's enterprise in ranging further afield. Mulberry Harbour won the Cheshire Oaks and Newmarket Oaks, becoming the third best filly trained in England. Next came Carrozza (leased from the National Stud and niece of Sun Chariot), 'a fat little lady and a bit lazy but full of guts', according to Lester Piggott, who forcefully won the Epsom Oaks on her by nine inches; the first royal victory in the Epsom Oaks since the race was founded in the eighteenth century.

But it was Almeria, the third of the Queen's star fillies, who had the superstar quality. She won the first position as best three-year-old filly trained in England. Another of Hyperion's close progeny, Almeria suffered from – and also gained by – the hypertension of his outstanding offspring. No handicap seemed to daunt her. She won the

Ribblesdale Stakes at Royal Ascot, despite the hard ground being unkind to such a big animal; she won at Goodwood and in the Yorkshire Oaks, and again at Doncaster even though she was in season. (Did she experience PMT?) Three weeks later, in October 1957, she found herself at Hampton Court Stud, having pulled a muscle, but was sent back for further training at Freemason's Lodge in February 1958, her manners at Hampton Court having been intolerable. She had developed into 'a real madam'.

Some of the things said about Almeria by her doting stable girl Valerie Frost are worth quoting, not only for the light they throw on equine temperament but on the Queen herself. If Elizabeth II was never likely to wear her heart on her sleeve, it is legitimate to infer from another young woman's outpouring something of what this royal young woman felt also.

Almeria stood out amongst the Queen's fillies [Valerie Frost told Bill Curling]. She walked with a tremendous superiority, swinging her hips and with an air of nonchalance and from the start she would like to do things in her own time. If you were too familiar with her she would take advantage of you. She could be very aloof. I adored her.[10]

Here in truth was a young 'madam' for that disagreeable year 1957, when 'an air of nonchalance' was as necessary at the Palace as in the Lodge. But Almeria had the advantage over Elizabeth II. She could indeed do new things 'in her own time'; and once when a stable lad at Freemason's Lodge annoyed her she picked him up by the seat of his pants and dropped him in the manger.

The Queen's personal talents had by now clearly declared themselves. She had unusual powers of observation and accurate memorising, as witness her pointing out to Boyd Rochfort that two yearling colts, Doutelle and Agreement, had been mixed up when they returned from Ireland and given each other's names. She had seen them together as foals and was the only one to know them apart.

Again, she had developed confidence in her own judgment, real enterprise and openness to experiment. It was her own idea to gamble on the French inbreeding (through Prince Chevalier) that produced Canisbay, and even more her own idea to run Canisbay, a twenty to one outsider, in the 1965 Eclipse Stakes, against all the pundits' advice. The desperately exciting finish made a much-needed highlight for the 1960s. Elizabeth II was in fact the first reigning monarch to win this important race since it was founded in 1886; with the help of Aureole and Doutelle (second and third stallions) she was again, for this one year of the 1960s, high on the list of winning owners and breeders.

Her personal stamina was becoming proverbial. While still in her thirties herself, she nimbly outran her ageing trainer and manager and never seemed tired when others were completely exhausted. She would cram into one day at Newmarket a visit to the earliest string of 'working' horses, an inspection of mares and foals, a second outing on the Heath, racing all afternoon, 'evening stables' and a drive home to Sandringham.

As the royal graph subsided during the 1960s it became clear that radical changes were due. Captain Moore, to whom the Queen owed so much in the past, was still a fanatical devotee of 'the laws of nature' and against all 'artificial' aids. But the Queen decided to try Norah Wilmot's special training at Binfield and the 'Faradic electrical treatment' developed by Sir Charles Strong. Much against his will, Captain Moore was persuaded to retire in 1963 at the age of eighty-one, to the grace-and-favour Hampton Court 'Pavilion'. When the Queen and Queen Mother called on him, the old man came downstairs in his dressing-gown.

'How are you feeling?' asked the Queen.

'Well, ma'am, I feel like a rabbit who has been bolted by a ferret.'

The Queen burst out laughing. 'I may have been called many things behind my back, but I have never been called a ferret to my face before!'[11]

A year later the National Stud converted itself into a stallion station, so that the royal leasing of young stock abruptly ended. This in turn meant new breeding policies for the Queen. In 1969 the Captain, now Sir Cecil Boyd Rochfort, retired to Ireland, his 'yard' (Freemason's Lodge) being sold and demolished. By the 1970s the Queen's horses were in the hands of an entirely new team. The aims and even the geography had changed; and the toll of defeats once more fell sharply. (It is reasonable to put the graph in this negative form, since only one foal in four wins, on average, any races at all.)

The first outstanding name of the 1970s was Highclere. A shining outcome of the Queen's and Lord Porchester's new attempt at introducing 'hybrid vigour', Highclere was called after her racing manager's stud. In Bill Curling's words, the Queen decided to achieve 'hybrid vigour' by mating Highlight, a mare 'inbred to the prepotent stallion Hyperion', with the stallion Queen's Hussar, who was himself 'inbred to the prepotent stallion Fair Trial'. Queen's Hussar stood at stud at the paltry fee of 250 guineas! But these two stallions, Hyperion and Fair Trial, 'had no common ancestors close up in their pedigrees'.[12]

In pursuit of this more imaginative breeding, the Queen sent some of her mares to leading American or French sires. The French understood how to respect the Queen's privacy; during the year in which Lord Porchester took over, 1967, he escorted her together with his wife and Michael Adeane on her first private visit to the French *haras* (studs) in Normandy.

As the Queen went about Normandy, some of the older men would raise their berets and shout, '*Vive la Duchesse!*' remembering the English royal descent from the dukes of Normandy. The *prefet* who accompanied them was surprised and turned to her escort for an explanation. 'Why do they call Her Majesty "duchesse"?' They left it to the Queen to answer. 'Well,' she said with a smile, 'I suppose in a sense I am!'[13] A French lady remembers the only 'gag' of this royal visit. Charles de Gaulle had sent roses to Elizabeth II. When the local telegraph operator was asked to transmit a thank-you message from the Queen of England to the President of France, the operator, thinking it a hoax, added, 'And I am Joan of Arc.'

From the 1970s onward, all the Queen's foals born in the Sandringham studs were moved as yearlings to Polhampton, where the grass of the chalk downs is good for the horses' bones. Her new stud manager was Michael Oswald and her trainers were Major Dick Hern cvo at West Ilsley in Berkshire, Ian Balding in Hampshire and William Hastings-Bass at Newmarket.

In 1974 came the testing of Highclere and 'hybrid vigour'. Having won the 1,000 Guineas in a photo-finish, Highclere was flown to Chantilly for the Prix de Diane, the French Oaks. The Queen had decided to run her there rather than in the English Oaks, as she felt the downhill of Epsom would not suit her filly's action. She won by two lengths from the French Comtesse de Loir. It seemed a miracle. As the jubilant Queen led her in, the ecstatic French crowds surrounded '*la Reine*'. Her entourage had to link arms until the French police took over. In Jubilee year an album of Highclere's triumph was presented to the Queen.

By the happiest of chances Dunfermline, the second great name of the decade, won her victories for the Queen in Jubilee year itself. Prince Philip had marked his wife's hopes for 1977 by commissioning from Barrie Linklater a painting of her favourite mares with foals at foot in the Wolferton fields. Dunfermline was by Royal Palace out of Strathcona, a strong, placid mare whom the Queen and her manager had fortunately decided not to cull, despite her apparent lack of brilliance. Dunfermline herself had seemed perhaps to lack the will to win as a two-year-old, having been placed third at Sandown and second at Doncaster and Ascot. But she had a great future, which was about to unfold.

There were few occasions in Jubilee year when the Queen was free to watch her horses. Dunfermline won the

Pretty Polly Stakes at the Guineas meeting, but the Queen arrived back from her first long tour of the year only just in time for the unsaddling. The Epsom Oaks was Dunfermline's next great race. This time the Queen had to watch it all on television as Prince Andrew was arriving home from Canada. Would it be a disaster? Dunfermline's jockey Willie Carson was in a car crash on the morning of the race – but made it. Dunfermline hated the starting stalls, and always had to be blindfolded before entering. Then she was 'stopped' during the race, and, having got ahead again, wanted to hang towards the leader instead of passing. Despite everything she won by three-quarters of a length, the first Oaks victory for the Royal Stud since 1892.

The St Leger was Dunfermline's third Jubilee year win and the most thrilling; though again the Queen could watch it only on television, since the Prime Minister James Callaghan was her guest at Balmoral. The Queen had decided to run a pacemaker for her filly, to ensure a good gallop from the start. He did the job exceptionally well. Over the whole of the last two furlongs a duel developed between Willie Carson on Dunfermline and Lester Piggott on Alleged, a duel so close that it needed the patrol film to assure the vast, cheering crowd that Dunfermline had not touched her rival, Carson having straightened her in the nick of time. The Queen had never before won the St Leger. It was a triumph for Dunfermline's stamina and will to win, for the Queen's trainer and all concerned, and above all for the Queen's choice of mating. She was the leading English breeder of Jubilee year.

Queen Elizabeth II has won every classic except the Derby. Naturally this is now her supreme ambition. In 1982 she bought from the Sobell family the racing stables at West Ilsley, where many of her horses were already being trained. She hopes that the greatly demanding up-and-down Epsom course, with its premium on tough horses without nerves, will be conquered in the 1980s by some prodigy of her own breeding and training. Her purchase may have brought that hope 'a hoof-beat nearer', particularly as her trainer Dick Hern has already achieved two Derby winners with Troy and Henbit.

But whatever the Queen's ambitions, they will always take second place to her duty. The racing world sometimes finds her attitude quixotic. One journalist hoped James Callaghan had 'appreciated' her magnanimity in not deserting him for the St Leger in 1977; another wrote, 'It was the decision of a courteous and unselfish person.'[14] A not altogether dissimilar decision was to face her on 6 June 1982, when Height of Fashion (who had won all her three races in 1981) and St Boniface were both to run at Newmarket. If the Queen watched, the police could not guarantee to get her back to London through the traffic in time for her next engagement. So yet again she had to miss the direct thrill – this time of a double. 'But I saw it on television,' she said to the author the next day without the trace of a moan in her voice.

Lord Porchester was recently asked, after giving a lecture to the Eton Equestrian Society, why Prince Charles was not more involved in the royal sport including breeding. 'Hands up how many of you are keen gardeners,' asked the lecturer in reply. Two hands went up. 'How many of your parents are keen gardeners?' A forest of hands. 'That is the nearest simile I can think of,' said the lecturer. 'When you own horses you become interested. You're not a keen gardener until you own a garden.'[15]

I asked Lord Porchester what were the Queen's top qualities as an owner-breeder. (She is in touch with him all through the year, mostly on the telephone, though there are no formal committee meetings.) He nominated three things as paramount:

She's been in it so long, delving into it, that she really understands pedigree and knows what she wants. Mention, say, Busted, and she immediately thinks, 'likely to stay a mile and a half'. Mention Gold Bridge and she thinks, 'speed'. She never has to ask people what they mean.

Next, she is a good judge of conformation – as good as a show-ring judge – and would see at once if a horse had a good shoulder, short cannon bones, good feet, flat feet, bent or straight hocks, good quarters, a nice eye or quality head. Her knowledge and judgment are backed by a photographic memory.

Thirdly, she is an extremely good reader of a race. She would say, 'I don't think that horse stayed. Did you see it swerve? I didn't like the way its ears went back. I liked the way it accelerated,' or 'I think it will be better on a left-handed than a right-handed course.' She also quickly spots whether an animal has gone back in condition or is improving. All these things make her very knowledgeable about racing and breeding.[16]

Woodrow Wyatt, Chairman of the Tote, believes that the Queen's knowledge is today unsurpassed.[17] Returning to what was a somewhat dismal racing period for the Queen, in 1960 she had twelve horses in the Captain's stables but not one winner among them. There was a triumph, however, in another stable. Prince Andrew was born in that same year. And the human scene that had become so discouraging for the young Queen in the later years of the 1950s picked up marvellously in the 1960s, just when her racing was going into decline. A pattern of ups and downs, roundabouts and swings, seems to have been woven into the Queen's reign, leaving her never without joy and hope.

XIII

A Family in the 1960s

The 1960s came in like a lion for the Royal Family – an heraldic lion – with a change in the family's name, the birth of a lion-hearted prince, and the pageantry of a royal marriage in Westminster Abbey; they were also to go out like a lion with the investiture of Prince Charles at Caernarvon.

Prince Andrew's birth on 19 February 1960 had brought back his father's name into the family tree. The Queen saw no good reason why she should give birth to a third child who was permitted to carry on only his mother's name, contrary to British law. At least Prince Charles and Princess Anne had possessed Mountbatten for a few years as a 'secret' or 'latent' surname – or so the lawyers said.[1] The Queen, therefore, in Council made an authoritative statement eleven days before the birth:

> Now therefore I declare my Will and Pleasure . . . while I and my children will continue to be styled and known as the House and Family of Windsor my descendants, other than descendants enjoying the style, title or attributes of Royal Highness and the titular dignity of Prince or Princess, and female descendants who marry and their descendants, shall bear the name Mountbatten-Windsor.

After this announcement the Queen was to confirm with the Home Secretary (acting for the Prime Minister) that 'all the children of Your Majesty who may at any time need a surname have the name of Mountbatten-Windsor.' Meanwhile the Queen had concluded her original statement with the words:

> The Queen has always wanted, without changing the name of the Royal House established by her grandfather, to associate the name of her husband with her own and his descendants. The Queen has had this in mind for a long time and it is close to her heart.

In fact the Queen had had this change in mind even before Churchill and Eden retired. Within a few years she had persuaded her newest prime minister, Harold Macmillan, to fall in with her wish – a family wish if ever there was one. To be sure, some traditionalists continued to argue that the new surname would not come into force until the third generation; namely with the Queen's grandchildren. They were proved wrong.

On the marriage of Princess Anne to Captain Mark Phillips, though the register was signed by 'Anne', the Princess's names were filled in by the registrar as 'Anne Elizabeth Alice Louise Mountbatten-Windsor'. Thus the 'latent' surname had broken cover in the second not the third generation.

Buckingham Palace was to comment on this fact in October 1975:

> This was the first time that the surname 'Mountbatten-Windsor' was used on an official document by any of the Queen's descendants. It was the Queen's decision that this should be done as Her Majesty wished her husband's name to appear on the Marriage Register of their daughter.

The Palace added a sentence to the statement, which, though placed in brackets, had considerable significance: '(The Queen did not seek the advice of her Ministers in this matter.)'

However, there were some 'latent' consolations for the traditionalists. When Prince Charles married Lady Diana Spencer, he signed himself 'Charles P.', while his name was entered on the marriage register as 'His Royal Highness Prince Charles Philip Arthur George The Prince of Wales', despite many stout convictions that it would be 'Charles Mountbatten-Windsor'.*

Their last child, Prince Edward, was born to the Queen and Prince Philip on 10 March 1964. The Queen's completed family thus divided neatly into two: Charles and Anne separated from one another by under two years, Andrew and Edward by just over four; but a gap of nearly ten years cutting the family in half.

There has been some speculation as to why Elizabeth II and Prince Philip waited so long for their 'second family'. In a sense that question is unanswerable; many couples wait, expectantly. The years 1955 to 1958, as we have seen, were strenuous ones for her, with the public honeymoon over and rumbles of criticism perhaps heralding a storm. For every reason there must be rejoicing that the two young Princes, Andrew and Edward, arrived when they did.

There was to be one further development from the Queen's successful activities on behalf of her husband. It concerned the Prince Consort's seat at the State Opening of Parliament. By a law of 1539, the sovereign's children sat on chairs of state *outside the canopy*, so that the sovereign and consort might sit side by side *under* the canopy. An anomalous procedure had grown up, however, according to which only *queen* consorts (like Queen Mary and Queen Elizabeth) sat on a throne under the canopy; *prince* consorts (like Prince Albert and Prince Philip) were relegated to a chair outside.

But what was to happen on 31 October 1967, when for the first time Prince Charles and Princess Anne were to attend the State Opening and take their correct seats

* The present author wrote in *The Royal House of Windsor* (1974): 'There can be no doubt that when the time comes, the signature of "Charles Mountbatten-Windsor" will bring intense satisfaction to all concerned.' Robert Lacey took the same view in *Majesty* (1977). The whole matter, up to 1965, was discussed by the distinguished lawyer Edward F. Iwi in *The Law Journal*, March 1960, and in an article entitled 'The Heir Apparent' in the 1965 edition of *Debrett's Peerage*.

outside the canopy, to their mother's right and left? Was their father to be removed altogether from the dais and dumped among the dukes?

Of course not. The consort's throne was sent for from the country where it was kept in store by the Lord Great Chamberlain, and Prince Philip at last occupied his rightful position beside the Queen, under the canopy.* 'Custom and ceremony' had been restored.

Princess Margaret's engagement a week after her nephew Andrew's birth completed the royal hat-trick of February 1960. 'You've never had it so good,' the Prime Minister, Harold Macmillan, had told the people three years earlier, and everything about the wedding of the decade seemed 'good'. The bridegroom, Antony Armstrong-Jones, created the Earl of Snowdon, was born two years before the Princess and was a commoner; but this fact raised no difficulties. The wedding was the first great royal event since the Coronation seven years before, and in that seven years the nation had changed its skin. It was about to enter a period of brittle animation and, if this was only to paper over its growing economic cracks, nobody yet knew. There were no more ersatz pleasures. Street decorations were lavish, particularly, it seemed, the silken banners and entwined initials of M and A on the handsome masts in the Mall. The Abbey was full of flowers, among which glimmered twenty-six closed-circuit television screens. Those who were not near enough to see anything but the two sleek heads of the bridal pair could turn round and watch them full length on the pillars.

There was an air of youthful informality as well as exuberance. Eight bridesmaids – but boy scouts instead of morning-coated ushers, and eight Queen's scholars of Westminster School to lead the bride's procession. As the

* The ancient name for the canopy was the 'Cloth of Estate'. In researching the meaning of this term, Randolph Churchill found it described as a 'carpet' – despite the fact that 'people don't generally sit under the carpet'. (Randolph Churchill, *They Serve The Queen*, 1953.)

married couple set off for their Caribbean honeymoon, the *Daily Telegraph* reported: 'The Queen and her mother, with Prince Philip, ran alongside the car as it was moving along the inner quadrangle.' The day had been all 'sunshine', 'sparkle', the 'warmest day of the year'. Three million people watched the pageantry on television.

The marriage was happy until the mid-1960s. The Princess had been introduced into a completely new world by her photographer husband, who could design an aviary or wheelchair as soon as say 'take!' Tony Snowdon brought a new zest into her public duties also, and excitement into the lives of Charles and Anne with friends such as Peter Sellers and Harry Secombe.

The painting they bought from John Piper symbolised the time when the Snowdons literally saw eye to eye. After their marriage Piper invited them to choose any painting from his studio. They fell with one accord upon the same picture, a splendid painting of Santa Croce in Venice, with marble like water and water like marble. John Piper congratulated them on having chosen, together, the best picture of all.

But if this painting symbolised their closeness, their two holiday houses signified their later falling apart. Tony rebuilt a cottage in the woods at Nymans, the former home of his Messel relations and then National Trust property, where his mother, Anne Countess of Rosse, now lives. The Queen Mother came down to cut the tape and declare Old House open in an impish skit on her own regal style. But Princess Margaret found Old House 'too clinical'; while her husband disliked houses on islands, especially when sun-drenched. That ruled out the house on Mustique, named by Princess Margaret Les Jolies Eaux after the breathtaking view of sparkling waters.

The difference went deeper. Tony turned out to be a streamlined, dedicated, integrated artist. As a commoner, he could work with the media or the press in a totally natural, uninhibited way that was inconceivable for royalty. His forebears on his mother's side were distinguished and always of an artistic bent: the playwright Sheridan who ran off with one of the beautiful Linley sisters; the Kensington *Punch* illustrator, Linley Sambourne. His maternal uncle was Oliver Messel the theatre designer who incidentally designed Les Jolies Eaux for Princess Margaret.

Princess Margaret shares the artistic, even bohemian vein; but it is firmly embedded in Windsor rock. On Mustique she may be tempted to be a sybarite, never a rebel. The Clock Court at Kensington Palace where she now lives is perhaps most typical of her dual nature: on one side of the Court her drawing-room and dining-room, her exquisite Fabergé ornaments, her triple photograph of herself, her mother and sister with its subtle hint of Van Dyck's Charles i, her John Piper; on the other side of the Court her office block. Both buildings suit her. Neither is the least like a studio, certainly not a studio in Pimlico, the London of Tony's first youthful choice.

The two children of the marriage, David Viscount Linley and Lady Sarah Armstrong-Jones, were born in 1961 and 1964, thus forming a quartet of first cousins with Prince Andrew and Prince Edward. A quartet of second cousins were also to be born in these family years: George, Earl of St Andrews (1962) and Lady Helen Windsor (1964) to the Kents; James Ogilvy (1964) and Marina Ogilvy (1966) to Princess Alexandra and Angus Ogilvy. An essential factor for a flourishing Royal Family – plenty of blood relations, but all fanning out and connecting with different walks of life – was in the making.

It was Charles who produced a vein of responsibility for his younger brothers, not unlike his mother's feelings as a child for her young sister Margaret. The only girl in the family, Princess Anne, was a bit of a tomboy. The many dolls Anne was given interested her less than the first pony her mother taught her to ride at the age of two and a half.

The publication in 1980 of Prince Charles's youthful fairy story, *The Old Man of Lochnagar* ('My idiotic book', he now calls it), brings us uncannily close to the ethos of the family in the 1960s. The fact that Charles told this tale to Andrew and Edward while cruising on the *Britannia* is interesting in itself; few young men of twenty-one have the patience to become bards and minstrels to their siblings. Even more interesting is what Prince Charles told them.

The second and third sentences of the story etch in the theme with unmistakable precision. The author is describing the Old Man's cave on the side of Mount Lochnagar:

> The door was made of deer skin and the doorknob consisted of a stag's antler which, when pressed, prodded a tame grouse and made it cry out 'Go back, go back!' That way the Old Man succeeded in remaining totally alone for years and years.[2]

That desperate cry of 'Go back, go back!' Who can it be addressed to but a milling throng of press photographers?

After exploring the world immediately round him – the capercaillies of Loch Muick and the little Gorm people in their cairns – the Old Man decides to visit London. That he fails to reach the great city does not unduly depress him. 'Secretly he was rather pleased. . . . He couldn't think of anywhere more special to be, than to be living at the foot of Lochnagar.'[3]

The word 'special', used here with such childlike effect, has also its totally adult meaning. To the Queen, as to her children, it was 'special' to be at Balmoral, to be together, to be in a blizzard, out on a limb, off beat. It was 'unspecial' for her to grin at a faceless crowd or to read twenty words of typescript when a plaque was unveiled, a bottle thrown, a tape cut. These things, however, were to become a little more congenial in the 1960s.

Elizabeth II was planning certain changes in her style of monarchy long before the articles of Altrincham and Muggeridge saw light. It was annoying for her, but that is the way of the world. A system where self-reform is slow but sure – the monarchical system – is often overtaken by a wave of criticism while in the very act of change.

As early as 1955 Elizabeth II had decided to abolish the traditional 'presentation parties' for debutantes. But the mills ground exceeding slow. By November 1957 (after both Altrincham and Muggeridge had written but obviously not because of them) the debs' demise was officially announced: the season of 1958 would be positively the last.

There were many good reasons for this minor social revolution. It was felt that since the war, the ritual of presentations represented money rather than birth or glamour. An aspiring mama had to do no more than pay a lady who had been herself presented at court to sponsor her daughter and perform the presentation; her daughter was thereupon on the list and inside the Palace. There was not much harm in it. But it was not what kings and queens had intended.

The performance itself was static to a degree. First of all the debs in their hired limousines got into the queue and were pinned in the Mall for hours, crawling round and round Queen Victoria's statue until at last the gilded gates were flung open. Meanwhile they would pass the time playing backgammon or being looked over by the often caustic crowds. Before the throne, their curtsies varied in technique from the small cautious jerk of a pouter pigeon to the billowing of a voluminous galleon in a gale, though most had taken lessons. Girls who were presented after their marriage sometimes became pregnant before the day. Then their curtsy was more like the collapse of a bell-tent.

Even so there were groups who regretted the end of presentation parties. James Frere, sometime Chester Herald, wrote that without them the Royal Family would be 'stranded' between the 'meritocracy' and factory workers.[4] It was sad for journalists too. An enterprising photographer decided to take shots of one of the last of the debs. He seated her on the floor surrounded by a pile of shoes; as if Cinderella had dropped not just one glass slipper in her flight but fifty.

It must be admitted that at any rate in the old days a presentation was a personal affair, unlike the royal garden parties of today. A warm or cool reception by the female monarch could make the difference between a loyal and a critical female subject. Miss Agnes Strickland, biographer of *The Queens of England*, wrote a letter about her presentation to Victoria and Albert in 1840:

> When my name was announced to Her Majesty, she smiled and looked most kindly. Nothing could be more gracious than her reception of my homage. Prince Albert returned my curtsey with a very courteous bow, and I passed from the presence with feelings of increased interest for the royal pair. . . .

Then, being an historian, Miss Strickland had to paint also the gloomy side of the picture:

> . . . but [I] heard the most cruel and bitter remarks uttered by some of the ladies who had preceded me through the ante-room on what they style the ungracious and repulsive behaviour of the Queen to themselves and others.[5]

Two years before Elizabeth II's presentation parties vanished, a novel form of royal favour had appeared. In 1956 the first informal Buckingham Palace luncheon was held, causing quite an emulous stir in readers of *The Times* and *Daily Telegraph*. Who were these captains of industry, the stage, the universities, the sporting world, the church, the police, whom Her Majesty was set to entertain at intervals apparently for the rest of her reign? In truth they were the 'meritocracy' against whom ex-Chester Herald Frere had inveighed. At first there were informal dinners also, but the Queen prefers daytime sessions and the dinners have been dropped.

Today the luncheons have become a notable fixture of palace life. They take place about five times a year, say in March, May, June, October, December, according to the Queen's engagements abroad and at home. All begin at 1 pm and are generally held on a Tuesday or Thursday in the 1844 Drawing Room, though occasionally in the Chinese Dining Room. Twelve people are present, including the Queen herself and Prince Philip, and seven guests organised by the Master of the Household, his deputy and a lady-in-waiting.

One looks in vain to find any preferences, far less prejudices shown by the Queen for or against any particular categories of guests. True, there have been show-jumpers, and vets such as James Herriot, but then there have also been Margaret Drabble and other highbrows or the doyen of novelists, Graham Greene. Sometimes music crops up more often, sometimes less. Young people such as Susannah York and Simon Gray are likely to be present, as well as mature persons from the top of the churches, rabbis jostling with the Church of England.

Nor does this meritocratic mixture leave the royal hosts 'stranded'. On one of the earlier occasions Prince Philip had much to say not only about tower blocks but also about the splendid edifice one of his guests was wearing on her head. When she confessed it had been sent in separate parts from Paris to be reassembled in London he said, 'I see, a form of prefabricated do-it-yourself architecture.'

The Queen had recently delivered her first Christmas television message in 1958 and regaled the company at one of these luncheons with a poignant peep behind the scenes. First the electricians had drilled holes through the walls at Sandringham to get the cables in, and incidentally had let in so much icy air that she trembled even more from cold than fright. 'The family looked absolutely horrified and thought I was going to break down with nerves.' The theme of her message – 'I welcome you to the peace of my own home' – began to look ironic. Next the make-up girls dabbed bright yellow spots of paint on her forehead, cheekbones, nose and chin, which at least made her laugh.

Everyone at the luncheon knew the happy ending. She had delivered her message live (as it had to be in those days) and with considerable tension; then, thinking the infernal machines had been switched off, she flashed her husband the most bewitching of smiles. If Her Majesty could feel such a wave of deliverance at the end of the day, she must after all be human.

What have these luncheons done for the nation as a whole? Over 1,200 'meritocrats' have probably met their Sovereign in her palace since this idea was launched in 1956. Its value can perhaps be expressed in terms of representation – a mutual exchange of that art. The Sovereign as hostess represents the people as they would most like to see themselves. She is charming, well-groomed, gracious and entertaining in a setting of great beauty and interest. The clock, for instance, in the 1844 Drawing Room that ticks away the time all too swiftly (at least for the guests) is an object of perennial admiration. Bought by George IV, it is the famous Negress's Head whose rolling eyeballs mark the hours and minutes, while an ear-ring controls a sixteen-pipe organ that can play eight different tunes.

The Queen can be grave, but is more often light-hearted. To the great conductor Barbirolli she said, 'Tell me, Sir John, you have been in the public eye for many years. You must have received some adverse criticism from time to time. How do you react to it?'

'I do nothing about it, ma'am. I made up my mind long ago not even to notice it. It has no effect whatever.'

Her Majesty looked thoughtful. 'I wonder if that can really be possible?'

If Sir John had offered her an unattainable ideal others gave her moments of pure relaxation. Hugh Scanlon of the TUC was to see a piece of his roast potato fly off his plate on to the carpet. He hoped that Her Majesty had not noticed – until one of the corgis approached the morsel, sniffed it, turned up its nose and stalked away.

'It's not your day, Mr Scanlon, is it?' said the Queen.

Asparagus was another source of fun. A guest sitting immediately on her left realised that Her Majesty would be served first and himself last. He was eager to see how she would deal with the stout, buttery, home-grown stems.

Prince Charles instructs his grandfather. (*Popperfoto*)

The King instructing Princess Elizabeth in statecraft. (*BBC Hulton Picture Library*)

A family photograph taken in the grounds of Clarence House. Princess Anne is approaching her first birthday and Prince Charles is nearly three. (*Keystone*)

The Royal Family at Sandringham, 1951. Back row: The Duke of Kent, Princess Margaret, Princess Alexandra, Princess Marina, the Duke of Gloucester, Princess Elizabeth, Prince Philip, the Duchess of Gloucester; seated: Queen Mary, King George VI, Princess Anne, Prince Charles, Queen Elizabeth; front row: Prince Richard of Gloucester, Prince Michael of Kent, Prince William of Gloucester. (*Reproduced by gracious permission of Her Majesty The Queen*)

Wearing a black taffeta dress strikingly similar to that worn by her future daughter-in-law, 1952. (*Photo by Dorothy Wilding, Camera Press*)

The Coronation, 2 June 1953. After the Crown is placed on the Sovereign's head, the peers and peeresses put on their own coronets. One of the heralds who stood near the Queen at the Crowning felt the 'spiritual exaltation that radiated from her'. (*Topham*)

The Queen smiles to acknowledge the cheers of the crowd as her coach makes the return journey from Westminster Abbey (*Popperfoto*)

Photographed by Cecil Beaton on the day of the Coronation, Queen Elizabeth II holds the Sceptre and Orb and wears the Imperial State Crown, which has the Black Prince's ruby in the centre. (*Camera Press*)

In Brisbane during the 1953 Commonwealth tour of Australia, the Queen and the Duke of Edinburgh inspect a Guard of Honour of the 1st Battalion Royal Australian Infantry. Their mascot, a tiny Shetland pony, attracts the young Queen's attention. (*Topham*)

With Queen Salote of Tonga, the Queen and the Duke of Edinburgh look at the tortoise supposed to have been presented by Captain Cook to the King of Tonga, 29 December 1953. (*BBC Hulton Picture Library*)

Pietro Annigoni's first portrait of the Queen, 1954. (*Camera Press*)

The Queen and Princess Anne place the harness on the pony Greensleeves in the grounds of Balmoral, August 1955. (*Photo by James Reid, Camera Press*)

The Queen driving Prince Charles and Princess Anne in her Daimler, *c.* 1956. We were to see more of this in the Royal Family film of 1969. (*BBC Hulton Picture Library*)

A formal portrait by Antony Armstrong-Jones of the Queen and Prince Philip in the Music Room at Buckingham Palace, 12 October 1957. This was the most 'uphill' year of the reign. (*Camera Press*)

The State Opening of Parliament, 28 October 1958. The Sword of State is carried by Viscount Montgomery of Alamein (right) and the Cap of Maintenance by Lord Home, who was to be the Queen's fourth Prime Minister. (*News Chronicle*)

The Queen's Prime Ministers.

Winston Churchill. (*Universal Pictoral Press*)
Anthony Eden. (*Universal Pictoral Press*)
Harold Macmillan. (*Universal Pictoral Press*)
Alec Douglas-Home. (*Universal Pictoral Press*)
Harold Wilson. (*Universal Pictoral Press*)
Edward Heath. (*Universal Pictoral Press*)
James Callaghan. (*Universal Pictoral Press*)
Margaret Thatcher. (*Universal Pictoral Press*)

With baby Prince Edward and Prince Andrew in the Blue Drawing-Room of Buckingham Palace, 14 June 1964. The Queen, like many mothers, was more relaxed with her younger children. (*Photo by Cecil Beaton, Camera Press*)

The Investiture Ceremony of Prince Charles as Prince of Wales at Caernarvon Castle, 1 July 1969. The 'set' was designed by Lord Snowdon to look good on television – which it did. (*Popperfoto*)

After he was served, the Queen turned to him with a sweet smile: 'Now it's my turn to see you make a pig of yourself!'

A tribute to this allegedly shy Queen for dissolving the shyness of others was paid to Bill Beaumont, captain of the English rugby Lions.

We swept up to the Palace, through the main gates [he wrote of his royal luncheon in February 1981] and moments later there I was – Bill Beaumont from Chorley – having lunch with the Queen of England. I was immediately put at my ease when the Queen began to talk about her visit to watch the Welsh Centenary match. . . . She remarked how much she had enjoyed the game, and although I was absolutely petrified, a quivering bundle of nerves, I managed to relax a little after that and really enjoyed the next couple of hours.

At one stage the subject turned to the question of management in industry. At once the Queen brought me into the conversation by saying that I must know something about that as captain of the England rugby team. I was very impressed at the way she was able to involve every one in the discussions and make each of us feel completely at ease.[6]

Homeward bound, it is hoped that her guests have represented their own segment of the nation's life to the Queen, and will in due course represent to their friends what they have learnt from her. The chances are that she has proved better informed, in the round, than any of them.

There is a postscript to add, however. These luncheons can obviously be only a limited move in the direction of royal accessibility. Though the first such item to appear in the Queen's campaign to communicate, they have been overtaken by other stratagems.

Two quite spectacular changes were focused on Buckingham Palace. Away went the traditional garden parties, which had been as much a part of the old 'season' as the presentations. They had managed to seem as static outdoors as the presentations had been indoors. No one could forget Edward VIII's attempt to receive the obeisances of ladies from a throne in the garden, when the sky and his face darkened together and he finally called it all off.

Today the royal garden parties, whether in Buckingham Palace or Holyroodhouse, represent that most desirable aspect of any people in any country – a cross-section. Something like 35,000 different individuals have a chance to see the Queen really close year by year; that is, if they succeed in getting inside the vast bee-like swarms that gather around members of the Royal Family, as they progress from the honey-coloured Palace to the green and white striped tea tents facing one another across a sweep of rich green grass, strengthened in places with camomile. In fact the lawn is full of little holes, as if thousands of starlings had been at work, but actually made by the sharp points of umbrellas. The royal and diplomatic tea tents are distinguished from the ones opposite in having Moorish lattice-work as well as scalloped edges. An improbable family of salmon-pink flamingoes, first seen on an island through the trees, makes visitors catch their breath and wonder if the Royal Family have fallen for plastics.

The ex-Chester Herald would of course have complained that no one knows anyone else at these new-style garden parties. And indeed you are lucky if you can say hallo to twelve couples between 4 and 6 pm. Nevertheless, thousands of the Queen's subjects – what Philip Howard calls 'the garden party classes'[7] – have enjoyed her presence year by year under the new regime, taking the opportunity if they are wise to enjoy enchanting lakeside scenes, herbaceous plants grown to gigantic proportions, miniature pavilions and temples, renderings of Gilbert and Sullivan, the classical frieze on the Nash façade and, as they pass in and out from front to back of the Palace, showcases of porcelain between portraits of Queen Victoria's more distant relations. On an even more generous scale, Queen Elizabeth II has permanently opened a small part of the Palace itself to the British public and visitors from all over the world.

On 13 September 1940 one of Hitler's bombs destroyed

the Private Chapel at the south-west corner of Buckingham Palace. Originally a conservatory designed by John Nash about 1831, it had been converted in 1843 by the prolific royal architect Edward Blore into a chapel for Queen Victoria. The bomb left only the four walls standing. (Hence the many subsequent royal christenings in the Music Room.) But on 22 March 1960 it was announced that the Chapel was to be 'rebuilt and part of it used as a small Art Gallery, to which later the public will be admitted'. (The Gallery could be incorporated with the Chapel when a large service required it.) It was a typically restrained way of describing an imaginative idea originating with the late Patrick Plunket, the Queen's delightful Master of the Household, and with the Queen and Duke of Edinburgh themselves – though George VI had contemplated something like it before his death.

Two years later, on 18 July 1962, the Lord Chamberlain announced that the Queen's Gallery would be opened in a week, showing 'Treasures from the Royal Collection'. Adults would be charged two and sixpence each to pay for the upkeep (one pound today) and 'NO OTHER PART OF THE INSIDE OF THE PALACE WILL BE SEEN'. There was added as background information:

Her Majesty had always wished to make it possible for the works of art which belong to her family, and which have in the main already been shown on a considerable scale, to be even more widely seen by the public. The Queen therefore hopes that this exhibition will make a serious contribution to the appreciation of the arts.

The Queen's hopes were not disappointed. Over 200,000 people flocked to this first exhibition; 'Royal Children' the next year attracted 100,000, followed later by 240,000 to see the 'Dutch Pictures' in the year of the Queen's silver wedding and 457,000 for 'The Queen's Pictures' at the Silver Jubilee exhibition. February 1982 marked the end of a truly sumptuous display of George III's paintings by

Canaletto – then the finest collection of the artist's work ever assembled and now seen together for the first time. The most recent exhibition, called 'Kings and Queens', gave many insights into the Royal Family's own preferences. There was the Queen's purchase of a poignant youthful sketch of the Duke of Windsor; Prince Charles's choice of a three-quarter length portrait of his mother in her Silver Wedding year, looking wistful, quizzical and serious (is that how he saw her?); and an imaginative group which goes far to explain the Queen's feeling for the Stuarts – two romantic Stuart princes hung on either side of George III, the King full-blooded and florid, the princely brothers with their exquisitely soft features and sharp, winkle-picker gloves.

By the mid-1960s, the article by Lord Altrincham must have seemed to the Queen not unlike her prime minister's troubles of 1958. Criticism by his cabinet Macmillan described as 'a little local difficulty'. Even the Queen's voice had won praise; that of Harold Nicolson who wrote in his diary at Christmas 1957: 'She came across quite clear and with a vigour unknown in pre-Altrincham days.'[8]

In 1961 the United States voted her the 'Third Most Admired Woman in the World', after Eleanor Roosevelt and Jackie Kennedy; while Prince Philip next year, having installed his team of efficiency experts in Buckingham Palace to develop its potential as a modern office block, was acclaimed Britain's 'Best Dictator' – the sort who would make the trains run on time – in the event of Britain's needing a dictator.

Nevertheless, there was still a long way for the Royal Family to go. The most far-reaching change of all was not to be in full swing until the next decade – the cult of the 'walkabout'.

Meanwhile, how was the Queen expected to cope with the 'Swinging Sixties'? She had indeed sent out Bobo to shop for her in Ottawa, while still Princess Elizabeth, so that she might enjoy the new square dancing in a properly swinging cotton skirt. The mini-skirt, however, ushered in a swing with a difference. 'Hem lines: a neat 4 inches above the knee,' exulted the *Daily Telegraph* on 9 March 1967, describing six eye-catching British show-girls at the International Motor Show. Three years earlier the newspaper had reported the first bottle-battle on the beach at Margate: mods and rockers burning corporation deckchairs, smashing shop windows, scaring villagers as they swept down from London, black-jacketed, on their black motorcycles, like Jean Cocteau's death-corps in his film *Orphée*. The mods and rockers also were part of the 1960s.

'Minis, symbol of the Swinging Sixties', were already fading from favour, the *Telegraph* corrected itself in July 1967, since Associated Fashion Designers had expressed the hope that Britain's young clothes were getting less 'kooky'. Would the leather jackets and the mini-skirts go away together? Hems were dropping down like the safety curtain at the theatre.

In any case, no one wanted Elizabeth II to promote the mini. If the Swinging Sixties were to be shared in any subtle sense by the Queen, it would be through her growing family.

Two guiding words might have been pinned over the royal nursery door. 'Ordinary' and 'Normal'. It was the settled aim of the Queen and Prince Philip to bring up Charles, Anne, Andrew and Edward in the ways that were known to be best for all children irrespective of birth or status. To be singled out, to be given special treatment could be the best thing only if the child was already a special case, say handicapped. The royal parents were lucky to have four above average children; and they rightly brought them up as if they were strictly average.

No doubt their nursery ran more smoothly than most, though this was not always so. General 'Boy' Browning used to say: 'It's more difficult to get Prince Charles's cot from Windsor to Buckingham Palace than to move an army across the Rhine!' Prince Philip's reforms (dictographs and amplifiers to link all the operational rooms) eased the nursery situation as they did all others.

Again, these children had the advantage of a placable royal temperament. The descendants of King George vi do not tend to rebellion. (Princess Margaret confirms this with her children.) If Princess Anne had been kept at home with a governess, as her mother and aunt were, she might have rebelled; but, as we shall see, she was not. Nor was the nursery regime of a kind to encourage eccentricities such as greed or fads. It was bread and butter before cake, clean plates before the next course, clothes handed down before thrown away. ('Handing down' has always been a feature of the thrifty Royal Family. Queen Victoria made her boys pass down their kilts. Princess Margaret remembers wearing Princess Elizabeth's pre-war crêpe-de-Chine dresses during the war, and being proud that people would come up to feel that rare thing, pure silk.) A favourite story is of Prince Charles dropping a dog-lead in the grounds and being sent back by the Queen to find it. 'Dog-leads cost money.'

Other favourite 'Prince Charles' stories with an austerity ring concerned the school beds, the tummy upset and the boats. 'You won't be able to jump up and down on *these* beds,' said the Queen to her son as he gazed for the first time at the hard pallets in his school dormitory. An early tummy upset he put down to the 'rich' food at school; he was not used to it at home. And when there was a school craze for toy boats, the one they sent Charles from home turned out to be the smallest on the pond.[9] He himself knew what it was to be a small fish in a big pond.

To return to the nursery. There was a moment when it looked as if the old nursery film was being rerun with new names. 'Mrs' Helen Lightbody and Mabel Anderson, both Scottish-born, played the parts of Allah and Bobo, Miss Catherine Peebles ('Mispy') of Miss Marion Crawford. (Helen Lightbody had been recommended by the Gloucesters, and Mabel Anderson was later to care for Peter and Zara Phillips.) But when Charles was only eight the reel ended. Prince Charles was sent to a London day school.

Hill House Preparatory School for Boys formed a comfortable triangle with Harrods and the Palace. Its stated aim was a dual one: to promote healthy individual rivalry and the will to win. This did not sound on the face of it very suitable for constitutional royalty. But the winning spirit was learnt through a team, and this Prince Philip wanted for his son. There was no corporal punishment.

Would the press punish Charles for his parents' temerity? Anticipating a scourge of photographers, the royal parents had already issued a dignified and convincing appeal to editors eighteen months before:

> . . . Her Majesty and the Duke of Edinburgh have decided that their son has reached the stage when he should take more part in more grown-up educational pursuits with other children.

The pursuits referred to were visits to museums and other places of interest 'outside the home'. Then came the nub:

> The Queen trusts, therefore, that His Royal Highness will be able to enjoy this in the same way as other children without the embarrassment of constant publicity.

The appeal had some effect in the sense that the publicity became epidemic rather than 'constant'. And the same process was repeated for Hill House.

By the time Charles was nearly nine, the cocoon of 'custom and ceremony' was clearly going to wrap him round with the same blandishments as it had enfolded his mother. He passionately loved his home, as she did. But his father's version of 'custom and ceremony' laid its cloak around him too. He was sent to his father's prep boarding school, Cheam in Hampshire, and in choosing to go on to Gordonstoun like his father he sent himself on a tough assignment. His mother had felt that the more civilized and homelike pilgrimage to Eton might be more congenial to her sensitive son.

Not that Gordonstoun was all that spartan compared

with, say, Balmoral. Queen Victoria's taste for cool rooms had not altogether deserted her descendants. When the Greek cousins visited Balmoral after attending Princess Marina's funeral, they had come equipped only for the London service and needed woollies. 'So they had to be outfitted by us,' says Princess Margaret. 'Everything fitted!'

To send a prince to school at all was already custom-breaking on the part of the Queen, and indeed Charles was the first heir to the British throne to be educated by schoolmasters – and by other boys – away from home, instead of by tutors at the Palace. Even so the Queen's decision did not give total satisfaction. Lord Altrincham for one hoped that Prince Charles would be sent to an ordinary school to be educated with the sons of bus drivers. The present author was commissioned by the old *Daily Herald* to write an article on this subject, the argument being that if Prince Charles was to meet ordinary children at any period in his schooldays, the early years would be the best.

Every change of course brings its own neuroses. The press of the world made sure that a more accessible monarchy should occasionally regret the cushioned, if static system of upbringing they had abandoned in all good faith. It would be an exaggeration to say that Charles's schooldays were made a misery by the press. But they were not ideally happy.

The press activity with which the Queen had to grapple was awesome. There were sixty-eight 'Charles' stories during the eighty-eight days of his first term at Cheam. This despite an appeal from the Palace to fellow-parents before the term began:

> It is the wish of the Queen and Prince Philip that there shall be no alteration in the way the school is run and that Prince Charles shall be treated the same as other boys. . . . His parents' wishes are that he should be given exactly the same education and upbringing as the other boys at the school.

But how could it be 'exactly the same' when Charles was prayed for – as part of the Royal Family – at Matins? Charles thought: 'I wish they prayed for the other boys too.'

It may have been about now that Charles's destiny began to dawn on him, later to be described so graphically to Jack de Manio.

> I think it's something that dawns on you with the most ghastly inexorable sense. I didn't wake up in my pram one day and say 'Yippee . . .' you know. But I think it just dawns on you, you know, slowly, that people are interested in one and slowly you get the idea that you have a certain duty and responsibility.[10]

At Gordonstoun two incidents of allegedly world-shaking proportions centred on a glass of cherry brandy and an exercise book. The first was the sad story of how the press drove the heir apparent to drink. While on a school cruise at Stornoway, Charles was hounded from the saloon of the hotel by a crowd outside flattening their noses on the windows. He fled into the bar, where he panicked and ordered a cherry brandy. 'Having never been into a bar before,' he recalled, 'the first thing I thought of was having a drink, of course.' Immediately, in his own words, 'the whole world exploded round my ears.' Fourteen-year-olds are forbidden by law to sip liquor and there was a journalist present to tell the world that the heir apparent had broken the law. Such a storm in a liqueur glass. It was made to seem as if the future monarch would be the first heavy drinker since George IV. There were two nice points of irony: the young Prince was if anything puritanical; and the hotel in which he was humiliated was called The Crown.

When, two years later, the continental magazine *Stern* published an extract from Prince Charles's exercise book that had been stolen from his desk, the laugh was against the magazine. For it printed as Charles's original essay his précis of a piece from William Lecky, the great nineteenth-century historian of morals.

If it wasn't the press it was the Lord's Day Observance Society or the Anti-Blood Sports people. His skiing on the Sabbath; his shooting a stag. From her own experience the Queen gradually taught her son to laugh at these things. Had she not been chided for visiting the race-course at Longchamps on a Sunday with the President of the French Republic? But Charles could not forgive the Sabbatarians for forcing him and his friends at Cambridge to cancel their last performance of a student revue because it was on a Sunday. As the 'Singing Dustman', he must clamber into his bin only on a weekday. 'Very silly. It made me very angry.'[11]

Thanks to his parents' earnest wish to cover all possible eventualities, Prince Charles's education turned out to be something of a patchwork, though every patch had its point. Timbertop, the country branch of Geelong Grammar School, Australia, cut into his time at Gordonstoun. It was to make sure he got to know the Commonwealth, and they him, at an impressionable age – namely seventeen. Away in the great gum forests 200 miles from Melbourne, Timbertop was regarded as abnormally tough for a prince. He had hated leaving home – 'a pretty sad moment,' he said afterwards, 'leaving England and seeing one's father and sister on the tarmac waving one goodbye.' In fact it gave him the first normal experience that royalty can have: he was liked for himself. 'I absolutely adored it,' he said. 'In Australia there is no such thing as aristocracy or anything like it.' And later, 'You are judged there on how people feel about you.' They felt about him as a 'pommy bastard', the highest possible endearment.

Then back to Gordonstoun, to add two Advanced Levels (with a distinction in his special subject) to the five Ordinary Levels he already possessed towards a looming university career. In the end he gave Gordonstoun a general 'A' Level mark, for its teaching of self-control and self-discipline – 'giving shape and form and tidiness to your life.'[12]

It was all so like his mother. The acceptance of what fate

sent. The resolve of a conscientious person to learn self-discipline. The passion for 'tidiness'.

At Trinity College, Cambridge, he added two new father-figures and two new studies to his repertoire. His own father and his great-uncle Dickie Mountbatten were to be his lifelong guides. But Charles now also acquired as his gurus R. A. (Lord) Butler, the Master of Trinity,* and the Rev. Harry Williams (now a member of the Community of the Resurrection), its chaplain. Thanks to Williams, Charles would go regularly to early service in the college chapel. It made him seem 'square' in the increasingly materialistic society of the 1960s, but why should he mind? 'If people think me square,' he said, 'then I am happy to be square.' Again it might have been his mother speaking.

As for 'Rab' Butler, if he was the best prime minister we never had, no one could be a better mentor for a monarch he would never see enthroned. There was something beautifully apt about the situation: the Queen being called on weekly by the actual Prime Minister, and her heir calling weekly on the mighty might-have-been. On one of these visits Charles asked, 'May I join the Labour Party?' 'No,' said the Master, realising this unconstitutionalism was the result of a marxist living on Charles's staircase.

As Elizabeth II had patched Gordonstoun with Timber-top, so now she patched Cambridge with Aberystwyth. Prince Charles broke off from Cambridge to spend a term at this university college of Wales, much to the disgust of Rab Butler. He wanted his favourite pupil to get the highest honours in the two disciplines of his choice, archeology and anthropology, instead of learning Welsh and then turning on to British constitutional history, as he did. The Royal Family were adamant.

Elizabeth II had created her eldest son Prince of Wales at the age of nine, in the face of certain obstacles; one being an acute attack of sinusitis, so that she had to record her

* 'Rab' Butler was formerly a Tory Chancellor, Foreign Secretary and Home Secretary.

announcement on the radio. In his twenty-first year, her son was ready to be solemnly invested by his mother as Prince of Wales at Caernarvon Castle. The obstacles had meanwhile become more serious, comprising most of the Nationalist Party of Wales. Bomb threats, bomb hoaxes and even real bombs formed part of the 1969 scenario. The Prince must know something of the Welsh language and some of the Welsh people must know him, if he were to appear with any credibility at historic Caernarvon, dressed imaginatively in thirteenth-century fashion, as befitted twentieth-century television.

So he spent his term profitably at Aberystwyth and went on to win an honours degree at Cambridge, the first future monarch to do so. His parents' plan had worked.

Meanwhile the Queen's daughter had reached the beginning of a royal road that led to a very different destination. In 1968 Princess Anne left school and was presented with her first horse, coming in seventh in the Novice Class of the Windsor Horse Trials. By 1969 she was dedicated to the world of eventing, besides being patron of Riding for the Disabled. It was the horse that would carry her into the triumphs of the next decade. For the first time a princess was competing with ordinary people in a line that happened to be exceptionally tough. Her natural skill and determination were assisted by her parents' encouragement.

Elizabeth II, having first put the reins into the hands of two-year-old Anne, got vicarious pleasure from her daughter's aptitude. Prince Philip also had the satisfaction of seeing one of his theories confirmed in Anne. 'I've always tried to help them master at least one thing,' he said, 'because as soon as a child feels self-confidence in one area, it spills over into all the others.'

At thirteen Anne began a five-year stint at Benenden, a girls' boarding school in Kent; but there was no break in her riding lessons. (She was not the first princess to attend Benenden. The Queen was reassured to know that the scholarly Princess Benedikte of Denmark had been a pupil.) Anne picked up six 'O' Levels and two 'A' Levels, with merit in geography, between gymkhanas on High Jinks.

But one thing above all she learnt from Benenden which was to affect her whole lifestyle. The school had a system of 'house-mothers' among the girls, who provided a ready-made group of friends. At first Anne confessed to being overwhelmed by 'the amount of people and noise'. Her group, however, gave her confidence, since they were '*a caustic lot who knew exactly what they thought about other people* and saved one a lot of embarrassment [author's italics].'

That, surely, is the key to Princess Anne's own later proficiency in the caustic *mot* – that, and two other factors. The world of horses and trainers was no less outspoken than the 'group' at Benenden; while her admirable father was becoming famous for what he called 'dontopedalogy', opening your mouth and putting your foot in it. But Prince Philip had another saying also. 'You must sometimes stretch out your neck,' he would advise, 'but not actually give them the axe.' His adventurous daughter would occasionally find herself doing just that.

For the rest, Princess Anne had grown up with a full complement of youthful dreams and idealism. For her seventeenth birthday present she chose a cruise on her father's yacht *Bloodhound* off the Scottish coast. One of her school essays explained why: 'It gives me an utterly detached sensation that I have only otherwise experienced on a galloping horse . . . testing your skill against Nature, your ideals and the person you would like to be.'[13] It was a moving tribute to freedom, paid by a girl born a British princess who had none the less savoured freedom's evanescent delights.

By the mid-1960s, we are now well into Elizabeth II's family journey through the media. The Queen had no need to bolt down a magic rabbit-hole to find herself in medialand. All she had to do was to open a selection of her palaces to the

BBC and ITV. But, like Alice, she was not at first sold on living in this new dimension. Things were apt to get 'curiouser and curiouser'. The normal Windsor face could look cross in repose, but there had to be a new face for the media. Always smiling.

Nor did St Bagehot say anything about allowing the public to see right into the royal homes. On the contrary, he wanted the monarchy to be kept in mysterious half-light. 'We must not let in daylight upon magic.'[14] Daylight? If that were all. . . . But it was to be arc lights, or whatever more powerful, more penetrating radiance the television cameras required.

Prince Philip, however, had no doubts. A television film called *The Royal Palaces of Britain*, based on six of the most magnificent palaces, would do more for the relationship between Queen and people in one hour than all the Bagehots in a hundred years.

To be sure, this first essay in royal communication must be in impeccable taste. No pop music echoing from the children's floors as yet. The beauties of Buckingham Palace, Windsor Castle, Kensington Palace, St James's Palace, Hampton Court and Holyroodhouse were put into the enthusiastic but reverential hands of Sir Kenneth Clark (later Lord Clark – of *Civilization* fame). He referred to the kings and queens 'who had built these palaces and filled them with the greatest private collection of art in the world.' They were the 'heroes' of the story, even George IV. (It was not often that the 'First Gentleman of Europe' was called a hero – except when he himself fancifully recalled that he had led the charge at Waterloo.) Yet heroes they all were for this hour. Had not George IV succumbed to the 'mania for magnificence', unlike his three Hanoverian predecessors, and thus given us the fairy-tale castle of Windsor? 'Taste is to some extent a reflection of character,' added Clark, 'and by looking at successive monarchs as patrons of art it has been possible to give our film some of the contrast and drama of history.'

And also to give the public some of the influences that

have formed the tastes of their present Queen. She once asked, 'Could our portrait of Henry v really have been taken from life?' It looked to her too gentle for the hero of Agincourt. The answer was: 'It may be a little later – but it must have borne some relation to the subject.' And so it was no surprise when the Mayor of Caernarvon said of her sensitive eldest son after his Eistedfodd speech at the time of his investiture, 'That wasn't just a boy. That was a Prince. You could have put a suit of armour on him and sent him off to Agincourt.' Heroes did not all have to look tough.

The pink flamingoes at Buckingham Palace, which had hitherto been seen only by the new garden party intake, were suddenly dazzling the eyes of millions of ordinary viewers. What kind of flowers did the Queen like in Windsor drawing-rooms? Pots of lilies and bunches of carnations and irises; nothing very elaborately arranged. But in Buckingham Palace ballroom, when prepared for a state banquet, the Queen would have spectacular displays of red and yellow carnations, all home-grown to match the gold plate, crimson damask chair seats and scarlet and gilt baldaquin above the two royal chairs.

One light-hearted fact may have escaped notice. In the making of this film, Her Majesty fulfilled one of her most vital roles, at least symbolically – the role of uniting the nation. *The Royal Palaces of Britain* was a joint BBC/ITV production, announced the official brochure. 'By kind permission of the Queen cameras were allowed to enter into the private apartments of Britain's Royal Palaces for the first time.' A photograph was published at the end of their labours showing the two rival television groups working together at the Palace in beautiful accord. Lord Windlesham, the executive producer, rubbed in the 'joint' idea. 'With the decision of Her Majesty the Queen to open the palaces to cameras, the BBC and Independent Television formed a consortium to produce an hour long film of the six palaces.'

This film, first shown in Britain on Christmas Day 1966,

was to pave the way for the *Royal Family* film of three years later. After the six palaces, the six people.

The Royal Family worked hard to make their film story, which was shown in the week before Prince Charles's investiture: bread and butter before cake, according to royal rule. It was worth it. For the first time the Queen was seen at work in her 'office' with her secretary (Michael Adeane) ushering in visitors. People noticed how full her room was compared with Philip's shipshape office – piles of papers and magazines, flowers, the odd toy, all the clutter of a working wife and mother. You might almost call it untidy, except that the word was not in the royal vocabulary. The whole thing carried conviction and set up vibrations. Why were there not more women executives in the world?

We saw the Queen driving her own car in the Home Park, organising barbecues, ponies, corgis, labradors. For the first time we saw a good deal of the two young Princes, Andrew and Edward. Their mother sat between them on the sofa, showing them a family album and occasionally asking them who was who. For small boys they showed a creditable knowledge of their distinguished elders. The Queen's manner was gentle, quiet and encouraging. She would have got high marks in a teacher training college.

Royal Family involved seventy-five days of filming, and was seen by a larger world public than any other documentary. By the time it was finished the Queen, said Richard Cawston who made it, knew all about lighting set-ups, how to avoid shadows and how to help the sound recordist.

A feature of the 1960s had been the unpublicised lives of the Queen's 'second family'. Since the last royal prince to be kept out of the limelight had been Prince John, epileptic youngest son of George v and Queen Mary who died at fifteen, it was assumed by shrewd observers that Andrew and Edward had something wrong with them – and perhaps the Queen too. She was reported in the foreign press to be exhausted, unhappy, on the verge of abdication after Edward's birth; the investiture of Prince Charles would herald her own withdrawal. The diarist Harold Nicolson, however, had had a satisfactory glimpse of Andrew as a baby, finding him 'nice' and not like a poached egg as most babies were.

Now both boys were seen to be intelligent and handsome – and Edward stoical. When Charles's cello string snapped in Edward's face he did not scream, though only five. (Prince Charles kept a cello in his rooms at Trinity rather as his predecessor Lord Byron had kept a bear. He was later to sell it in aid of Covent Garden opera.) As for Prince Andrew's courage, that was to be amply tested thirteen years later during the Falklands crisis.

The ultimate importance of the *Royal Family* film could be seen in terms of 'Lochnagar', the fairy-tale that Charles was busy spinning. You could say that the Old Man of Lochnagar had at last been enticed out of his cave, to come south. The adventure with the media had begun.

The preparations for the investiture were shrouded in considerable anxieties. For Prince Charles the anxieties included vocal Welsh Nationalist opposition, sometimes rising to the roar of a bomb. The date of the ceremony at Caernarvon was fixed for 1 July 1969. On that day at dawn two terrorists blew themselves up while fixing a bomb under a bridge; on the 5th a bomb on a football ground blew off the leg of an eleven-year-old boy.

For the Queen there was the added anxiety that she might have inadvertently brought on all this violence by promising, in 1957, on the radio to present her son in person some day to the Welsh. Would she be sending him to his executioners? Could the dais at Caernarvon prepared for the future Charles III turn out to bear a gruesome family likeness to the platform of Charles I at Whitehall?

If Elizabeth II ever suffered such nightmares – and she certainly had deep qualms – the brilliance of the Caernarvon scene belied them.

The pageantry was fit for a prince. And a prince in the framework not only of one rugged castle and its walls, but also of millions of uncompromising oblong boxes. Lord Snowdon, as Constable of Caernarvon Castle, had designed the setting with television in mind. There was no canvas opaque tent such as Prince Edward of Wales had disappeared into in 1911.

But the future Edward VIII did, like Prince Charles, speak fluently in Welsh at his investiture, as Mr Fitch the King's detective testified: 'In picturesque robes, with an ermine cape over his shoulders, the Prince paid homage to the King, assumed the ancient crown of Wales, and addressed the gathering in Welsh, with a wealth of Welsh idiom and proverb. It was the first occasion on which a Prince of Wales had used the national tongue, and the crowds who heard him went wild with enthusiasm.' The difference was that while Edward could only read Welsh (as coached by Lloyd George for the occasion), Charles could speak it.

Lord Snowdon created a mammoth perspex canopy above the dais, surrounded by wide green grass. No red carpet. To Charles it would have looked a 'damned red carpet', to use the expression of his grandfather when Duke of York; not to mention the expression of the Duke of Edinburgh, 'The man who invented the red carpet ought to have his head examined.' The spectators were kept out of the way so that the viewers might be in on the scene.

Not everyone admired the traditional Welsh crown designed for Charles (not by Lord Snowdon) with its whiff of a princely Gruffydd living at the College of Arms in Queen Victoria Street. But the Queen's silk coat of the colour of Welsh gold dug from the mountains, and her hat with its medieval lilt, captured the spirit of history, of simple grandeur. As Prince Charles swore fealty, she found herself listening again to some of the words her husband had pronounced at the Coronation:

I Charles, Prince of Wales, do become your liegeman of life and limb and of earthly worship; and faith and truth I will bear unto you to live and die against all manner of folks.

The reference to 'all manner of folks' was the same, though the critical 'folks' themselves may have spoken with varying accents during the intervening sixteen years: Chips Channon – American, Altrincham – Eton, Muggeridge – South London, and now Plaid Cymru – Welsh. Nevertheless, something had changed. Not a Welsh Nationalist – not even the ones who shouted most vociferously 'Go home!' – could find anything to say against their Prince personally. And nothing whatever was said against the Queen. One need not count the banana skin thrown under her horse's hooves on the way up to the castle.

Three weeks later, on 21 July, Neil Armstrong the thirty-eight year-old American astronaut climbed down the Eagle's ladder on to the powdery ashen-grey surface of the moon. 'That's one small step for man,' he said, 'but one giant leap for mankind.'

The investiture had been a real step for the Queen and her son. One of her children had stepped into public life.

On his mother's twenty-ninth birthday, celebrated at Windsor, the seven-year-old Prince Charles had said encouragingly to her: 'You're getting quite old!'[15] Now that she was forty they could no longer say that. There were no grey hairs, no lines, and she was slimmer than she had been at twenty. Asked how he had learnt his royal trade, Prince Charles would reply, 'I learnt the way a monkey learns – by watching its parents.' But for that method to succeed – as succeed it did – the monkey needed to have the very best of parents.

The Queen and the Magic Circle: 1952–64

'She has already seen off more prime ministers in her first twenty-five years,' said Sir Harold Wilson to me in 1981, 'than Queen Victoria did in the same period.'

The eight 'New Elizabethan' premiers are as unlike one another as possible; yet the majority have tended to pick out the same outstanding quality in their experience of the Queen. They feel that they are received by a woman who shows them quite exceptional favour and cordiality. One of them observed that she probably gives the same impression to all: namely, that each is 'special'.

The Queen's team of eight falls naturally into two consecutive groups, the first being all Conservatives and all associated, either loosely or closely, with what afterwards came to be called the 'Magic Circle'.

Winston Churchill, as we have seen, was the first of her team. When his resignation was accepted on 5 April 1955, she was twenty-eight and he eighty – and as much in love as an ageing prime minister could be. If he was not an over-indulgent Lord Melbourne to her Queen Victoria – 'on the contrary, I sometimes find him very obstinate,' she said[1] – he was certainly a devoted guide and father-figure. One problem, therefore, immediately arises. How could she be expected to exert her three royal rights: to be consulted by him, to encourage him and to warn him – this infinitely experienced prime minister? At first sight it looks as if her prerogative must have been stood on its head by Churchill. Surely it would be for her to consult him and for him to encourage her? (The royal right to 'warn', as we shall see later, has slipped into a different key during this reign and with this particular lady.)

Yet the fact is that the young Queen did without question 'encourage' the venerable Prime Minister. That actual word is used of the Queen's effect on Churchill during his last active year. Shaken by a stroke, he accepted with some trepidation an invitation from the Queen to himself and his wife which would culminate in a weekend at Balmoral. 'It was a target and a test,' wrote his daughter Mary Soames. He came out of this ordeal by Majesty with revived spirits. 'Everyone from the Queen and her family downwards made much of them. . . . The two days at Balmoral were most agreeable, and when they returned Winston was refreshed and encouraged.'[2]

As for the Queen's consulting Churchill or being consulted by him, this aspect of the royal prerogative is like a constitutional iceberg. A tip of the iceberg occasionally surfaces; its main bulk is hidden in the Royal Archives. 'It is the unalterable rule of the Queen's private secretaries,' says one of them, 'not to discuss anything that occurs during an audience.' Nevertheless rumours about the iceberg's general shape float around. At the time of the Silver Jubilee, for instance, the *Daily Telegraph* wrote of the Queen's 'spirit of self-sufficiency' which throughout twenty-five years had made her 'the match of any Prime Minister'.[3]

When Winston and Clementine Churchill gave their farewell dinner party to the Queen at 10 Downing Street the Prime Minister was not thinking in combative terms. In proposing the toast to Her Majesty the Queen he said, 'I used to enjoy drinking it during the days when I was a cavalry subaltern in the reign of Your Majesty's great-great-grandmother, Queen Victoria. . . .' It was fitting that the sweep of his nostalgic emotion should link his long personal service to the crown's own continuity. There had been eleven prime ministers since Churchill flourished his sabre at Omdurman and only one Royal Family.

Not only that, but he spoke of 'the wise and kindly way of life of which Your Majesty is the young and gleaming champion.'[4] (She was literally gleaming with jewels and a tiara worn in his honour.) The old wizard had managed to get into his speech the twin seminal ideas of the crown's symbolism and continuity without mentioning either banal word.

Outside in Downing Street the crowd was not large, because of a month-long newspaper strike. After the strike was over, Donald McLachlan of the *Daily Telegraph* described the 'intimate and miniature' ceremony that had taken place that evening:

> We were waiting to see the Queen and Duke of Edinburgh leaving the party of distinguished guests which we knew to be assembled for dinner behind the blinds of the first floor.
>
> Would it or would it not be a poignant scene? When the front door opened and the floodlights came on in the Foreign Office opposite, no doubt remained. The picture was too brilliant to be sad.[5]

The Queen's 'wise and kindly' nature was to be expressed in her consideration for the ex-Prime Minister and his family. She had given Churchill four silver wine coasters from herself and the Royal Family on his eightieth birthday and she sent him flowers on his ninetieth. According to her own decision, his funeral was a state one: the Churchill family on that cold winter's day of January 1965 were kept warm by the Queen's affection and her own carriages and rugs during the procession, complete with royal hot-water bottles.

The two greatest monarchs Churchill had served were both women, and it was appropriate that the most stirring hymn sung in St Paul's – the 'Battle Hymn of the Republic' – should have been written by a woman also, the American suffrage leader Julia Ward Howe, whose husband had ordered her to stay at home and stick to women's work. The Queen broke precedent in entering the Cathedral before the Churchill family and thus allowing them to occupy the places of honour – the last. When it came to unveiling the monument to Winston Churchill in Parliament Square on 1 November 1973, the Queen insisted that Clementine should pull the cord in the royal presence. 'For more than fifty eventful years,' she said, 'Lady Churchill was his deeply loved companion and I think it would be right, therefore, for her to unveil the statue of her husband.'

Whenever there is evidence of something being the Queen's own choice, not the result of advice or protocol, it always turns out to be exactly right.

There is a legend that Anthony Eden was not sent for by the Queen until the day after Churchill resigned, for a reason of royal prestige. It is true that the chronology might support some such assumption. Churchill's farewell dinner, as we have seen, took place on 4 April 1955; he resigned on the afternoon of the 5th and the Queen summoned Eden on the 6th. According to the story, Churchill had advised her not to appoint his successor until the next day in order to underline her royal prerogative of choice. The delay would suggest she was thinking about whom to send for; otherwise it might appear that Eden's succession was automatic, especially as he was Churchill's 'deputy prime minister'.

The 'delayed action' story has since been denied and in fact it is quite contrary to the Queen's character. Thanks to her father, she already had an unusually calm, confident attitude towards her constitutional rights and duties. The idea of her purposely delaying her summons to Eden as a show of power argues manœuvring and doubt. Moreover, the prerogative in 1955 was not a matter for discussion as it was to become in 1963. There was no need to act quickly or slowly, since Eden had no rivals. The night that passed between Churchill's resignation and Eden's appointment was not heavy with constitutional import, but just another night.

Something has already been said of the Suez adventure leading to Anthony Eden's downfall. A point not yet mentioned and not to be missed is the interior effect of that disaster on Queen Elizabeth II. It cannot have been anything less than traumatic. The point of a democratic monarch is to rejoice and to suffer with the people. But as the figurehead, a sensitive monarch will feel personally diminished when things go wrong in the international field. This was true of Queen Victoria. She suffered in her pride and in her heart over national rebuffs or defeats and could hardly look her numerous continental relatives in the face. Today the Queen has extremely few foreign relatives who occupy thrones. But in a sense the Commonwealth countries have become her comparable 'family' in whose eyes she naturally likes Britain to shine. In the next chapter we shall see how willingly she set out on her travels to erase the memory of Suez.

During that brief period when Anthony Eden served the Queen as prime minister (fifteen months), he is generally described in the biographies as 'tense' or 'intense'. Harold Wilson was to call him 'a great gentleman and a great tragedy'.

Part of the tragedy was due to his succeeding so late to the premiership. It is said that the Queen's father had intended, if he had lived, to use his royal prestige to bring about Churchill's retirement two years earlier, in 1953.[6] That would have given Eden a better start. As it was, Eden succeeded to the highest office with his health already vulnerable and his political past beginning to supersede, psychologically, his present. In 1938 he had been right not to appease Hitler; why, he asked himself, was he wrong not to appease Nasser now?

In the turmoil of Suez, opinions sometimes broke loose momentarily from their party moorings. Even Lord Attlee, for instance, the former socialist Prime Minister, was privately in one respect nearer to Anthony Eden than to many in his own party. He castigated the aggression in Parliament, but in fact believed that once launched, however wrongly, the troops should have gone forward to victory and the Canal. 'If you've broken the eggs,' he wrote to his brother, 'you should make the omelette.'[7] If Clarissa Eden, the Prime Minister's wife, could say, 'The Suez Canal is flowing through my drawing-room', we may be sure that the whole Red Sea was flowing through the Red Saloon at Buckingham Palace.

In Anthony Eden the Queen had to deal with a character totally unlike the ones who came before and after: the old Churchill still full of 'fun', the 'unflappable' Macmillan in his prime – neither the least bit 'intense'. This does not mean that the young Queen did not 'learn about people' from Anthony Eden, as she had always felt the need to do since her girlhood. Eden underlined the lesson her father had taught her about gallantry in misfortune. He resigned on 9 January 1957 after a breakdown in health, and the Queen came up from Sandringham to find a new Prime Minister. (Her press secretary announced that she had come up for shopping. The January sales?) Already a Knight of the Garter, she further honoured Sir Anthony Eden by creating him Earl of Avon. At the last he seemed to be bathed in the light of setting suns, a towering figure of nostalgia and romance.

The Queen's next two prime ministers can be seen positively as the eras of Macmillan and Home, or negatively as the non-era of Butler. It was the second aspect that subjected the Monarch and her prerogative to speculation and questioning, if not to criticism. There is little doubt that without the existence of R. A. Butler there would have been no problem, certainly not the first time. Macmillan would have 'emerged' as smoothly in 1957 as Eden did in 1955. There would have been no argument about royal 'consultations', nor would the Conservative method of producing a leader have been challenged as it was to be in 1963. Each time Butler was the unavoidable and unwilling cause of conflict.

The most brilliant 'ideas-man' in immediate post-war Conservative politics and an effective statesman – witness the 1944 Butler Education Act – Rab Butler was too good not to be prime minister ever, yet not sure enough of himself to be first choice at any one particular time. Fortunately from the Queen's point of view as a young, inexperienced sovereign in the first decade of her reign, she was frequently to have the benefit of his advice, despite his failure to become her first minister. She came to know well his charm, epigrammatic discourse and bland expression, masking the most *recherché* irony.

The only thing Elizabeth II may not have fully appreciated was Butler's overriding devotion to the idea of party – his Conservative Party. As one of the Queen's oldest friends has said:

> It is understood that party politics cannot enter in any way into the thoughts or activities of the Royal Family. Her Majesty never even *thinks* in these terms. It is against all her training and upbringing and has been completely bred out of her.[8]

Yet for Butler 'party' was the political ideal on whose altar he would willingly sacrifice his personal ambitions. He once told the author: 'The story of Sir Robert Peel splitting the Tory Party was for me the supremely unforgettable political lesson of history. It made an absolutely indelible impression. I could never do the same thing in the twentieth century, under any circumstances whatever.'[9] When writing his memoirs he chose the title *The Art of the Possible*, meaning the art of what was possible in politics today without breaking up the party. He was to go down twice in the cause, with bitterness perhaps on his tongue but with a Delphic smile on his face.

His close relationship with the Queen developed immediately after 'Suez', when he took over the prime ministerial duties temporarily from the sick Eden. In his own words, written many years later, he proceeded to clear up a mess not of his own making – 'I withdrew the troops, got money out of my old friend George Humphrey, the American Secretary of the Treasury, with which to repay our loans and debts, and restored the pound.'[10]

What was Butler's chagrin to discover early in 1957 (Eden having resigned and the premiership come under the party hammer) that the powerful Conservative 1922 Committee 'by subtle propaganda had been told that the withdrawal [from Suez] had been my fault'. In no sense was he to blame for Suez, he insisted. It was unfair, he told the author in the 1970s, that his career should have been tarnished by Suez in comparison with Macmillan's, who was far more involved. (According to Harold Wilson, however, Macmillan was 'last in first out'.) Rab was not even 'in on the initial contacts between the Israelis and the French on the Suez venture, as I was attending the Queen at the opening of a power station in the North of England'. His final admission was, 'I suffered much at this time';[11] and it seems highly unlikely that he did not avail himself of the Queen's quick sympathy for human distress.

At any rate, the Queen would always encourage him to talk, as he himself recollected. 'She would never give away an opinion early in the conversation,' said Butler to Robert Lacey, but would always ask first of all for his opinion and listen to it right through. Butler interpreted this as an example of the Queen's 'remarkable skill in not taking too much out of herself'. More likely it was her equally remarkable skill in letting her ministers unburden themselves, without their being aware of what she was doing.

Another original point about the Queen's character was made by Butler in the same interview with Robert Lacey:

When Butler stood in [for Eden] he was struck by the refined variety of gossip that Elizabeth II enjoyed. She seemed fascinated by Parliament – who was rising, who falling. 'Like all clever women she was very interested in personalities' and apart from the national interest, she enjoyed evaluating to what degree the Government had suffered a setback or had scored points in political terms. She appeared totally to appreciate the personal ambition inspiring the political animal, and was fascinated by the length one would go to secure his own advantage at the expense of another.[12]

Rab Butler's analysis reveals a keen interest on the part of the Queen in political gossip, not only as a duty but a pleasure. This trait should be contrasted with the Queen's distinct aversion to social gossip. She never encourages it, especially if it shows signs of becoming malicious. That she will study the weaknesses of the 'political animal', as distinct from the 'social animal', argues a genuine absorption in politics. A subtle picture is emerging of Queen Elizabeth II. She was no longer the Princess whose ambition was to live in the country with lots of horses and dogs; country life, however delightful, would never completely satisfy a woman who had begun to appreciate the intriguing nuances of the political game – a game that she herself must never play.

The contest between Rab Butler and Macmillan for the premiership in 1957 was the first occasion when it was suggested – though only retrospectively – that the Queen's prerogative might have been exercised more adroitly. At the time there was no obvious dissatisfaction with the Queen's part in the proceedings, only utter astonishment at the result.

As soon as Eden resigned, the Queen began her consultations with elder statesmen. These included Lord Chandos and Lord Waverley, and also Eden himself (contrary to the legend that she ignored him). Churchill advised her to take Harold Macmillan; this we know because Churchill unashamedly revealed the fact two years later. Some rather 'perfunctory' consultations with the party managers also took place.[13]

It was the sounding out of the Cabinet that really counted. Two more elder statesmen, Lord Salisbury and Lord Kilmuir, were to station themselves in the Privy Council office. Then Salisbury, with his aristocratic lisp, asked each cabinet minister in turn, 'Is it to be Wab or

Hawold?' while Kilmuir jotted down the replies. The operation today sounds more like a game of 'Oranges and Lemons' than a polling booth. Later the result was conveyed to Her Majesty. The Cabinet's vote had gone overwhelmingly to Harold.

This whole procedure recalls a famous prime ministerial crisis that occurred in 1827, when King George IV had to find a successor to Lord Liverpool. In despair he begged the Duke of Wellington to organise a vote by the Cabinet. Might they not *elect* their own leader? No, retorted the Duke; a vote would impair the royal prerogative to choose – 'the only personal act the King of England had to perform'. Let the Monarch make the choice. Similarly after the 1957 cabinet vote some people began to feel that the Queen's choice had been pre-empted by a close cabal of Tory aristocrats. In the final volume of his memoirs (1973) Macmillan himself was to write, 'There had been some feeling this procedure [of 1957] was too restrictive.'[14]

Meanwhile, in April 1957 not a single newspaper, with one exception, was confidently predicting Macmillan for prime minister. That exception was the London *Evening Standard* to which Randolph Churchill, Winston's son, contributed an inspired article. He had made his soundings on the telephone and got them right. But his correct prediction in no way lessened the shock of Macmillan's triumph next day. The present author happened to be in Piccadilly Circus when the posters appeared with 'It's Macmillan'. The surprise was so great that strangers exchanged comments.

The victor left home after lunch for the Palace. There was none of the flamboyance that might have been expected; the silence enjoined by protocol was strictly preserved by Macmillan. His wife Dorothy, however, guessed his destination after seeing him drive away in a tail-coat. At the Palace, he warned the Queen 'half in joke, half in earnest' that the new Government might not last more than six *weeks*. She quietly marked his words – and brought them up again, 'smilingly', when Macmillan resigned over six *years* later.[15]

In Macmillan the Queen had undoubtedly appointed someone acceptable to Parliament. That was her job and she had done it. If the Conservative Party did not yet possess a satisfactory method of conveying to her their wishes, it was not her responsibility. Indeed, if she had tried to improve their procedure she would have been exceeding her duty and risking the charge of party politicking. As one of her advisers was to say years later, 'The Sovereign's duty is to find a leader of the Government acceptable to Parliament – not to get mixed up in the leadership contests of the Conservative or any other party.'

She had therefore no reason not to enjoy the results of her choice – nearly seven years in partnership with a leader of incomparable panache, whose penetrating intellect did not in any way inhibit the emotional impulses of his 'ambiguous' nature – the adjective used by Anthony Sampson in his biography.

The Queen and Macmillan had many things in common, apart from her father and Macmillan having had the same doctor (Sir John, now Lord Richardson) and their Scottish descent, the latter with its by-product of Scottish 'carefulness'. When Macmillan's official telephone line was cut off by the Post Office as soon as he ceased to be prime minister, he asked his political adviser to telephone him, in order to save his having to pay 'a penny ha'penny a call'.[16] It was like the Queen's dog-lead.

Macmillan loved shooting and adored country-house visiting; he was a devoted father and grandfather. There were only two major interests that the Queen and her Prime Minister in no way shared: his reading and her racing.

Nor would she have quite got the hang of his doomwatch view of civilisation, bordering on Greek tragedy. The Queen's imagination was essentially practical, not the least haunted. When Macmillan said in 1950, 'We have not overthrown the divine right of kings to fall down for the divine right of experts'[17] – the Queen and even more her Consort would have been puzzled. They were on the side of the technocrats. But Macmillan's declaration of 7 February 1957, 'I propose . . . to follow the middle way', would have found an immediate response in Elizabeth II. A 'middle way' is always best for the monarchy.

Over television, too, there was some agreement. Where Macmillan saw it as an aid to 'Tory democracy', the Queen would use it to develop 'royal democracy'. They were both to have many of the same problems with the media. Macmillan's advisers were insistent that he should not be too 'mannered' or 'contrived'. Similarly the Queen would have to strike a balance between liveliness and dignity.

As working partners, both had an ineradicable layer of reserve but each enjoyed an atmosphere of gaiety, the Queen being partial, for instance, to hearing of people or places with curious names. They were equally quick, calm workers. Macmillan had pinned a quotation from *The Gondoliers* on the green baize door of the Cabinet Room at No. 10: 'Quiet, calm deliberation disentangles every knot.'[18] Their briefly expressed, succinct arguments left plenty of time during audiences for a human atmosphere to develop. The Queen's 'sympathetic' attitude on so many occasions was picked out with gratitude in Macmillan's diary, whether over the resignations of three of his ministers in 1958, or his failure in 'summitry' two years later. On this later occasion, after receiving 'a charming and sympathetic message' from the Queen, he wrote to her:

I hope I may say how heartened I was on my return to 10 Downing Street to receive the message . . . and I shall not conceal from Your Majesty the shock and disappointment which I have sustained.[19]

With a prime minister of Macmillan's up-and-down temperament, the Monarch's power to 'encourage' (here called 'hearten') was invaluable. As also was her aptitude for clearing the mind of this and every subsequent prime minister, by giving them the opportunity to summarise their views for her. Macmillan, for instance, wrote that he had summarised for Her Majesty on 3 April 1960 his negotiations with Eisenhower on Polaris. This forced him to clarify his ideas. The same goes for all royal audiences. In the words of A. J. P. Taylor:

In normal times the Queen has no important political duty except to give audience to the Prime Minister once a week. To make the Prime Minister explain himself is a useful task, often beyond the wit of Parliament to accomplish.[20]

Before each audience, the Queen was already aware of her prime minister's subjects for discussion, since he had sent her an informal agenda. (Subsequent premiers were to refine and develop this practice.) Macmillan in turn was permitted to sit and talk, not stand, which absolved him from addressing his sovereign as a public meeting. Queen Victoria complained of Gladstone treating her in this way; but he was forced to stand during audiences, unlike Disraeli from 1874 on. The privilege of being seated was later accorded to the aged Gladstone.

Elizabeth II's thoroughly competent mind was perhaps the factor that most often took Macmillan's breath away. 'She is astonishingly well informed on every detail,' he wrote on 3 February 1957, and again on 23 October, 'The Queen is not only very charming but incredibly well informed.' A few years later he was to register his surprise all over again: 'I was astonished at Her Majesty's grasp of all the details,' thinking of their common work on endless telegrams and despatches.[21]

Harold Macmillan's premiership was full of events that have become encapsulated in words and phrases. 'Suez' was lived down in Europe and the United States with the help of the Queen; 'Prosperity' took the stage at home, described in a phrase borrowed by the Prime Minister from the *Daily Express*, 'You have never had it so good'; the 'Wind of Change' was welcomed over Africa: the 'Swing of the Pendulum' was put out of action by Macmillan at the 1959 election. But Britain's entry into the Common Market was blocked by de Gaulle; 'little local difficulties' grew into the 'purge'; there was 'Vassall' and 'Profumo'.[22] Macmillan wrote a special letter to the Queen hoping these 'very distressing affairs' would appear as the 'irritations that her predecessors had to deal with when looking back on a very long and successful reign'. For sheer cloak-and-dagger melodrama, however, nothing was to touch the Prime Minister's exit at the end of his own reign.

The possibility of Macmillan's resignation had always formed part of his scenic gloom. This was when the unflappable 'Wondermac' would temporarily crumble. 'The PM needs increasingly to rest his legs,' wrote Harold Evans in 1960, his adviser on public relations (later Sir Harold, one of the last of the baronets). 'He had told the Queen that he might have to resign (apparently she did not react with the consternation he had expected).'[23] For the Queen was unflappable also. Then Macmillan's own unflappability reasserted itself. After cancelling a Covent Garden gala evening through ill health, he left London to shoot vigorously in Scotland.

Next year came a rumour from Tokyo that Macmillan had died from heart failure. In 1962 Evans was writing, 'Does Uncle Harold seriously contemplate . . . his own fall?' Uncle Harold had asked Selwyn Lloyd, his Chancellor of the Exchequer, 'Do you think the time has come for me to go?'[24]

An inept attempt to snub de Gaulle by cancelling Princess Margaret's visit to Paris in February 1963 aroused strong criticism. 'So we get some impetus for the rumours that are circulating about the desire for new leadership. But where,' asked Evans, 'is the Crown Prince?'[25] Evans's rhetorical question was another way of saying that there was no agreement on Macmillan's successor. Rab Butler's name was mentioned most often.

In October 1963, the leadership question suddenly came to a head.

The Conservative Party conference was due to open in the week beginning Monday the 7th. After many agonising reappraisals of his own situation – he did not sleep at all on the night of the 5th, endlessly going over his choice, 'to go or stay' – Macmillan had finally told his political friends on the opening day of the Conference that he would lead the party into the next election. He intended to tell the Cabinet so next day. But the jealous gods were listening. During the night that followed he was struck down by an even more agonising prostatic hypertrophy. This was the beginning of ten days that shook the Conservative Party.

After emergency medical treatment on the Tuesday morning, Macmillan managed to get through what turned out to be his last Cabinet meeting. That evening, soon after 9 pm, he was driven in his doctor's Jaguar to the King Edward VII Hospital where he would have an operation on Thursday. He remained calm except for deciding with haste to resign. And there was one throwaway remark to Evans, 'Perhaps I shall die.'

Next day, the 9th, a letter was drafted to catch the Balmoral courier, putting the Queen in the general picture. She was to telephone the hospital three times between the Thursday and Saturday, affording Macmillan his only satisfaction during that chaotic week. Meanwhile, still on the 9th, he summoned among others Lord Home, the Foreign Secretary and conference president, to his bedside.

Did Home think of taking on the leadership, and if not why not? was Macmillan's dramatic greeting. Home, having explained that he would be happier to remain at the Foreign Office, was entrusted with a message to be read out to the party conference next day, announcing Macmillan's resignation and looking forward to the selection of a successor by the 'customary processes'.[26]

As it happened, Macmillan's tumour was not malignant, he made an excellent recovery from the operation and within a fortnight was regretting his precipitate decision, as well he might. For his resignation plunged the party into a state of confusion at painful variance with its usual smooth 'custom and ceremony'.

'Uncle Harold' had decided in his own mind, and told Alec Home on the 9th, that short of himself, Home, the best prime minister they could have would be Lord Hailsham, the former Quintin Hogg. This was also the opinion of Oliver Poole, chairman of the powerful 1922 Committee. In any situation that could be exploited by brains and oratory, Quintin Hailsham was always at his best. He had become famous for ringing his bell when chairman of a previous party conference – ringing in the new spirit of confidence after the party's catastrophic defeat in 1945. Though his judgment might not be infallible, his 'calm in Cabinet', according to Home, showed that he was 'temperamentally of prime ministerial timber'.[27] Clearly Macmillan did not see Butler as a rival to Hailsham, even though it was Butler who now temporarily took charge of the Government – as in 1957. Butler had become politically 'always a bridesmaid, never the bride'.

Elizabeth II was not unused to cutting short a precious holiday at the call of duty; she returned to London. The conference delegates, however, were far from used to seeing a new leader emerge in the flashy razzmatazz of the media. 'Emergence' had previously possessed something of the monarchy's own mystique. If their leader could not be hereditary, at least he must succeed to No. 10 as if he had all along been a prince of the blood.

On the Thursday evening Hailsham declared that he would make himself available for the premiership. (Macmillan had noted the day before that if Hailsham were to be a 'competitor' he must act 'at once'.)[28] He would renounce his peerage, he said, and become plain Mr Hogg. But not quite plain enough; for a colourful supporting cast had been organised by Macmillan's son Maurice and son-in-law Julian Amery, not to mention Churchill's son Randolph, who pinned a 'Q.H.' badge on Butler's lapel. Though Butler

appeared at this stage still to be Hailsham's chief rival,
other candidates were emerging.

By Saturday the 12th Macmillan was thoroughly alarmed
by 'the large number of candidates' his resignation letter
had released from Pandora's box. He described Saturday as
a 'horrible day' because of the 'spasms' following his operation. The spasms were political as well as physical. 'I fear
that all kinds of intrigues and battles are going on about the
leadership of the party,' he lamented. The cartoonists got
busy. Five hands were shown by Illingworth grasping for
Macmillan's torch, while Cummings identified them as
Butler, Maudling, Hailsham, Heath and Macleod, respectively trying on the Prime Minister's cap, cardigan,
breeches, coat and shoes. Lord Home was not among
them.

It is often said that Home was drafted after all because
Hailsham had overplayed his hand, brandishing his baby
daughter on Blackpool television complete with baby food.
This was unjust. Hailsham's wife was in London when the
crisis broke at the conference. He needed to consult her
about his candidature; she came to Blackpool and the baby
had to come too.

It was not until Monday 14 October, when a Home lobby
had already built up at Blackpool, that Macmillan ordered
official 'soundings' of the party in all its dimensions. Next
day he sent the Queen an account of events from the 7th to
the 15th, to prevent 'mistakes or argument in the future'.
According to Harold Evans, 'the Home trend was clear' as
early as the 16th. Evans tried to give a hint of this to the
press, but the Butler lobby was so dominant that the press
did not take the tip. The next day Macmillan instructed
Evans to give Home's cause a 'push', with the result that the
Mail's early headlines were to support him.[29] It seems that
some lines had got crossed by the 17th, to Hailsham's
ultimate discomfiture.

Baby or no baby, it is probable that the 'customary
processes' would have selected Home in any case as being
more acceptable to the party pundits than either Hailsham

or Butler. Hailsham's backing was among the rank-and-file (sixty per cent) and Butler's among the MPS and what today would be called the 'wets' (forty per cent). Neither seemed quite right to the party managers. And so while Hailsham threw his hat into the ring and Butler merely 'put' his there, Home was to have his set upon his head.*

The Prime Minister's hat was set upon Alec Home's head by the Queen on the advice of Harold Macmillan. Besides 'soundings' having been taken of all ministers and MPS, all peers except backwoodsmen and all representatives of the National Union including candidates, cabinet voices had been counted by Lord Dilhorne, the Lord Chancellor. The voting was said by Macmillan to have worked out at: Home ten, Maudling four, Butler three, Hailsham two.[30] These figures were not to go unchallenged. Nor could the circumstances in which Macmillan gave his advice to the Queen be called anything but sensational.

Late on Thursday the 17th, there was a 'midnight assembly' (to quote Evans's words, with their pleasant gunpowderish tang) of ministerial malcontents at Enoch Powell's London house. It was agreed to demand a resounding of the Cabinet, when a new consensus in favour of Butler might well emerge. The *Daily Express*, getting wind of this, published a headline in its late editions of the 18th: 'I A.M. CABINET REVOLT'. The same thing was more sedately implied by *The Times*: 'THE QUEEN MAY SEND FOR MR BUTLER TODAY'.

Macmillan had to start the day 'very early' on Friday 18 October, for with the morning papers came two disquieting telephone calls. Home rang him at the hospital to say that he had been drafted to unify the party; his candidature being divisive, he would withdraw. Macmillan recalled him smartly to the colours, pooh-poohing the revolt as 'distasteful', an 'intrigue', an 'eighteenth-century' cabal, a 'putsch'. Simultaneously Butler was telephoning Dilhorne to suggest that he should make a reassessment of the cabinet voices.

* 'I certainly put my hat in the ring,' said Butler later.

But the voice from the hospital, when Dilhorne asked permission to do so, refused.

'This exchange [between Macmillan and Dilhorne] probably gave rise to subsequent stories that Macmillan had refused to take a telephone call from Rab. But no such call was made.'[31] Macmillan himself later said there were only two telephones on which Butler could have called him but did not; one by his bedside, the other at the end of the corridor, 'and how could I walk with a tube in my abdomen?'

Meanwhile, it had been already arranged the day before with the Palace that Macmillan's private secretary, Tim Bligh, should take the Prime Minister's written resignation to Elizabeth II on that Friday morning at 9.30, and that the Queen's acceptance of the resignation should be announced at 10.30 am. In fact Bligh set off half an hour late for the Palace, though the announcement was made at 10.30 am as planned. A story was none the less circulated that Macmillan had accelerated his announcement in order to scotch the putsch.

Now came the bizarre denouement. Queen Elizabeth II had decided to ask Macmillan's advice on his successor by driving to the hospital and sitting in an upright chair at his bedside. No doubt the sick Titan had been spruced up and moved temporarily to the board room. But he was still wearing pyjamas, a fact which foolish people later said was an insult to the Queen. He himself, on the contrary, was exhilarated as always to see his young sovereign.

She came in alone [he wrote] with a firm step and those brightly shining eyes which are her chief beauty. She seemed moved; so was I. I asked leave to read her a memorandum which I had written yesterday [Thursday the seventeenth] and brought up to date this morning. I said I was not strong enough to trust myself to speak without a text.[32]

But, speaking with a text, he made out his case for Alec Home. After all the 'customary processes' had been processed, Home was the party's '*preponderant first* choice'. Macmillan then returned his memorandum to its large envelope, asking that Her Majesty should keep it in the Royal Archives at Windsor as a true record of the advice he had given her – a sure sign that he regarded the situation as abnormal.

According to Macmillan: 'She expressed her gratitude and said she did not need and did not intend to seek any other advice but mine.' After further agreeing with him that Home was 'the most likely choice to get general support, as well as really the best and strongest character', she took her leave. The huge envelope, placed in the hands of Sir Michael Adeane at the door, made him look like the 'Frog Footman' in *Alice*, thought Macmillan; as for the Queen, she was and looked like, then and always, his ministering angel.

The royal visit to the hospital has been much criticised. Why did the Queen make it? Why not simply send the 'Frog Footman'? First and last, she went out of the kindness of her heart. He was ill, she a friend. As Macmillan said, they were both moved. Queens are encouraged to visit hospital beds with ordinary people in them. Why not with the prime minister?

It must be admitted, however, that such a scene could hardly be enacted today. For the Queen to go to Macmillan suggested, however erroneously, that she was in his hands. It was too much like Mohammed going to the mountain. Her authority has developed so greatly in the last twenty years that, if the need ever arose again, she would not hesitate to delegate her visit. In 1963, when the Altrincham criticisms were still vividly remembered, she may have felt it better to act in person, not through her allegedly 'tweedy' entourage.

On the other hand, if she wished to do a similar kindness today, she would be in a stronger position to do so.

Outside the unflappable precincts of the hospital room there was Conservative anger. Macmillan therefore advised the Queen to act 'with speed'. As soon as she returned to the Palace she sent for Home and offered him the premiership. Home, however, did not 'kiss hands' immediately (that is, accept), but said he would 'try' to form an administration.

According to Macmillan's account, it was he who advised the Queen '*not* to appoint Home as Prime Minister himself at his first audience, but to . . . entrust him with the task of forming an administration'. Both Home and Evans, however, agree in saying that it was Home from whom the suggestion came.[33]

In the event, neither Powell nor Macleod consented to serve in his administration; it was only through Butler's and Hailsham's opposite decision that the Queen's government could be carried on by Home at all. Powell deposited in his bank his account of the episode, accusing Macmillan of having given Her Majesty 'crucial information' that was inaccurate and thus having 'deprived the Queen of the exercise of her principal prerogative'. Macleod wrote his famous article in the *Spectator* on the 'Magic Circle' – a circle of Tory aristocrats who had allegedly acted against the party's democratic wishes – Lord Home against Mr Butler.

Two further points. There is no evidence that the Queen took no advice except Macmillan's. It was his own wording in his memoirs, *At the End of the Day*, that made it seem like that. The Queen may well have already sounded her usual reliable contacts, before she saw Macmillan. When *At the End of the Day* was published in 1973, Humphrey Berkeley, a former Tory MP, wrote angrily to *The Times* on 15 October: 'Mr Harold Macmillan has quite wrongly revealed that the Queen anyway wanted Lord Home to be Prime Minister to give a certificate of respectability to what occurred. I and many others resent the use of the Queen in this dubious episode.'

At the same time, though the Queen did indeed fulfil her duty by forming *a* government, it can be argued that she did not form the best one. In the days of the 'Magic Circle', the chances were that whoever she entrusted with the task would succeed, simply by being her nominee. A distinguished modern Conservative historian, Lord Blake, suggests that Butler too could have won the Queen's franchise, if he had stood firm and refused to serve under Home. He might even have won the 1964 election to boot, in which case 'the political history of Britain might have been different. . . .'[34] Blake implies that it would have been better.

Before moving on from Macmillan to Home, there remain a few other clues to the Queen's relations with her prime ministers, clues left by 'Uncle Harold'.

We know, for instance, that he ventured outside the strictly political sphere and advised the Queen on her forthcoming Christmas message in 1963. This of course was done mainly through the Queen's private secretary, Michael Adeane, and Macmillan's private secretary, Harold Evans. Macmillan's hope was to 'revitalise' the messages. It seemed at first that he was to be unsuccessful: 'Adeane had shown some resentment when the topic had first been broached on the telephone,' reported Evans. In a personal discussion, however, Adeane explained with great friendliness the difficulties involved:

> The Palace tries each year to get some freshness into the broadcast [said Adeane] and women have been drawn into the drafting but the limits are so circumscribing of course. Television has ruined the whole thing. The Queen is gay and relaxed beforehand but in front of the cameras she freezes and there is nothing to be done about it. One thing she won't have at any price – the idea of the family grouped round the fireside.[35]

The only comment necessary is that six years later, thanks to Prince Philip's encouragement, the Queen was to do just that – in the *Royal Family* film.

Macmillan has given a hint also of more relaxed relations with the Queen than either politics or television could create. He revealed to American journalists that when the astronaut John Glenn was space-orbiting, during the Tuesday audience, Her Majesty and the Prime Minister had listened on a transistor set, 'to the neglect of State business'.[36]

Elizabeth II's farewell letter to Harold Macmillan throws further light on her development. She described him as 'my guide and supporter through the mazes of international affairs and my instructor in many vital matters' regarding the constitution, politics and the social life of the people. No successor, 'however admirable', could be quite the same.[37]

Unlike Harold Macmillan, Lord Home did not dress up meticulously to go to the Palace. 'Heavens – in that suit!' exclaimed his wife Elizabeth when she heard on the radio how he had set off. Nor did he serve the Queen while still bearing his ancient and splendid title of 14th Earl of Home. He renounced his peerage, becoming Sir Alec Douglas-Home. For the Queen this was an instructive event. It had been her grandfather George V who established the rule of premiers-in-the-Commons, but Anthony Wedgwood-Benn (Tony Benn) who had brought about legislation for the renunciation of peerages only ten weeks before the crisis. There is an agreeable irony in the thought of King George and Tony Benn combining to make it possible for Lord Home to become prime minister.

From the start, Sir Alec Douglas-Home was probably more of a 'person' to Elizabeth II than any of her other prime ministers. Their Scottish families knew one another and Home had carried the Sword of State in Scotland in coronation year. At the time he had noticed how 'totally involved she was – how buoyed up'.[38] (Their Scots connection caused some people to suggest that it was responsible for the Queen's choice of Home over Butler. 'The Queen took no part whatever in choosing me,' says Home emphatically today.)

Like the Queen, he had always lived 'close to nature'. He

had watched as a child the stoat hypnotising the rabbit and was to write later: 'Such experiences were a salutary preparation for some of the shocks of life.'[39] Also like the Royal Family, he has had to argue about 'Blood Sports'. Home's philosphical answer is: 'This must be an individual decision. I must justify myself in heaven not here.' Then, as an afterthought, 'I'm not sure that football isn't a blood sport! Boxing certainly is. People must make up their own minds, whether royal or not.'[40] Prince Philip's defence relies on the close connection between conservation, culling and field sports. The same people often practise all three. The Queen's personal line is not to go hunting.

Home's understanding of the Queen as a person is also deeper than that of other prime ministers. He knows, for instance, intuitively what she feels about her private life, her home. 'She regards Windsor as her home,' he says, 'just like anyone else's home. It's hard for us to realize. She will move a chair to a new place saying that King George's or Queen Mary's place for it was here or there.'

The Tuesday discussions between the Queen and Sir Alec seem to have been unusually relaxed. 'Oh, ma'am, what did you think of de Gaulle?' To a straight question she would give a straight answer – her own opinion – and then move on to her next thought.

Home has personally noticed that the Queen is less formal in all her public appearances than her predecessors. 'I can't see Queen Mary on a Peckham walkabout!' The process, he believes, was begun by George VI marrying outside the Royal Family. He quotes Queen Elizabeth approvingly for saying 'We're all human', but adds:

> You've got to have a scarcity value if you're a monarch. You mustn't make the Queen an ordinary person. They've got the balance just about right. They divide up their year rather cleverly too. Balmoral is the big rest. But they've no wish to be away from the whole thing; just to have balance. The children of course keep them on the spot and up to date.[41]

Reverting to politics, Home discovered that the Queen had a gift for putting people at their ease. Commonwealth ministers, for instance, were more relaxed with her at dinner than they were with one another. She was friendly and informal and completely apolitical. 'She would never say a word about other ministers.'

Home agrees that she has formed her political ideas from Sir Henry Marten of Eton, who taught Home too. 'He did make us realize that statesmen had once been children like us. "Hullo, here he is!" Marten would say, going up to a portrait of Canning or Castlereagh. He was a dramatic, racy, enthusiastic teacher' – as indeed all the Queen's teachers seem to have been – 'and kept a tame raven in his study which occasionally nipped his ear. No, he did not take the raven with him to Windsor.'

The Queen and her prime ministers of the 'Magic Circle' era had tended to be more absorbed in the grandeurs and miseries of foreign affairs than in the mundanities of economics. This was true of Churchill, Eden, Macmillan and then Home. It was, if anything, rather convenient for the Queen that they should have this preference. Too pronounced an interest in economic affairs, unlike international problems at that date, could lead her into party politics and political controversy. But Home's throwaway, self-deprecating remark, 'I did my sums with match sticks', helped him to lose the 1964 election. Indeed he never concealed his dislike of economics, calling it the most 'inexact' of sciences, which had 'blunted the edge of oratory and wit'.[42]

In 1964 Elizabeth II was to have for the first time, in Harold Wilson, a prime minister who needed neither match sticks nor even a computer for his sums. His memory for figures equalled the Queen's for events. And with the end of the 'Magic Circle' the Queen would face four prime ministers in a row who had not been educated at public schools.

Meanwhile, Sir Alec Douglas-Home in his short year at the top had achieved a change in party organisation more radical than anything since Joseph Chamberlain's Birmingham 'caucus'. Home introduced machinery for choosing the Conservative Party leader by election instead of emergence. It was the end of that mysterious thing called 'customary processes' in one of its most arcane yet treasured forms. At least two of the 1963 candidates regretted its passing: Hailsham and Home himself. Alec Home wrote in his memoirs, 'the Magic Circle of selectors had almost everything to be said for it.'[43] But he added to the author, 'I could not ask anyone again to go through what I did. It was reported that the Whips had rigged the votes and jobbed the election in my favour.'*

Lord Hailsham also feels that the old ways were best:

> I did not myself agree with Alec's decision at the time. That is to say, I did not approve of his decision to change the system. I was interviewed by a BBC person who put to me this very point from the other angle. 'Why should not Members of Parliament do the voting, when the whole tendency is everywhere to consult the Party in the country?'
>
> I say, 'Not at all. It is the other way round. In the old system, the Party in the country was given a very considerable role, a much bigger role than now in the Conservative Party – and I think rightly.' In those days it would have been through Central Office and area organizers. Peers were also consulted through the Chief Whip. Feeling in the Party was ascertained better by that means.[44]

From the Queen's point of view the change could only be for the better. With both major parties electing their own leaders, all the previous creases in her prerogative have apparently been ironed out. No more embarrassing choices like that of 1963 which a Labour elder statesman was to describe as 'invidious'.[45]

Or could she be so sure? The situation was indeed to remain stable for twenty years. But twenty years is a very long time indeed in politics. The 1980s show signs again of

* In a television programme, *Elizabeth II: The First Thirty Years*, shown on 29 May 1983, Lord Home recalled the embarrassment that the old system could cause the Queen.

change. What was 'invidious' for the Queen in the 1960s may become inevitable or even interesting two decades later.

XV

'Our Mother is Coming!'

Between forty and fifty lands and islands were visited by
Elizabeth II in the 1960s, some of them twice over. Only
four of these visits were private. In the next decade, the
figures were over fifty official visits, fifteen of them state.
Audrey Russell, who has travelled for years with the
Queen, recording for the BBC, says: 'Nobody who has not
been on a royal tour can have the faintest idea of the utter
exhaustion.' Nevertheless, the Queen is an indefatigable
traveller. Most of her visits are to Commonwealth peoples,
and she sticks to them, in sickness and in health, because
she is wedded to the Commonwealth.

Past generations of historians would quote satirical journals such as *Punch* to give a special kind of emphasis. Today
the satirists are still at work and intrigued by the Queen's
feeling for the Commonwealth, which they see as 'the Big
White Mother in Buck House' holding that 'Nyerere and
Co. are absolutely the Bee's Knee'.

A tribute to the Queen's enthusiasm comes from the
lofty ambassadorial end of the scale also. Sir David Scott
'kissed hands' in London before his posting to Uganda as
High Commissioner in 1967:

> This turned out to be a friendly and intimate occasion at which
> the Queen as it were sets her personal seal on the appointment.
> In my experience these audiences have invariably demons-
> trated the extraordinary detailed professional knowledge which
> the Queen shows in diplomatic – and especially in Common-
> wealth – affairs.[1]

Her 'informed and sympathetic' discussions make sure that every ambassador invariably leaves 'encouraged and stimulated'.

The most interesting Commonwealth problem is what holds it together. The Queen might at first be surprised to learn that one of her late Commonwealth secretaries of state, Patrick Gordon Walker, drew attention to four links, without mentioning her name among them. The two 'outstanding links of affinity' he found in the English language and parliamentary democracy.[2] The latter he illustrated by the fact that Canada and Australia had both at times moved ahead of Britain: Canada in paying a salary to the Leader of the Opposition as early as 1905 and Australia in 1920, the 'Mother of Parliaments' not until 1937.

Gordon Walker's *The Commonwealth* was published in 1962, after Kwame Nkrumah had thrown the Ghanaian opposition into prison instead of paying them. Gordon Walker therefore argued that although parliamentary democracy was neither 'indispensable' nor its loss fatal to the Commonwealth, it would none the less 'affect its nature'. He predicted Ghana's later return to democracy – though not Kenya's resort to single-party government.

To language and democracy Gordon Walker added defence and economics. Since the war, however, there has no longer been a Commonwealth defensive system. Economic sympathy, despite the complication of Britain's new link with Europe, has recently been demonstrated by the Queen in person. In 1981 she presented the Victoria Dam as a gift from Britain to Sri Lanka.

The Queen's name is indeed implicit in Gordon Walker's thinking, for she is the personalised symbol of all that unifies the Commonwealth. Just as the crown helps to mark the distinction between the nation and the political parties – and does it more effectively than any elected president – so the Head of the Commonwealth helps to distinguish that august international body from the sum of its governments. There could in fact be an elected president of the Commonwealth. But the Queen – non-political, hereditary, neither voted for nor against, and permanent – is felt to do it better.

During the 1981 Commonwealth Conference at Melbourne, some of the delegates were asked privately what they themselves believed was the mortar between the bricks. The majority replied, 'The language and the Queen.' Some said, 'The Queen and the language.' Others added 'the law' as a third welder.

Mark Arnold-Foster, in the last *Guardian* column he wrote before he died, appointed five permanent guardians of Commonwealth unity:

> The more amiable parts of the British Commonwealth are held together still by five important institutions – cricket, the British legal system, commonsense, British universities, and the House of Windsor.[3]

Arnold-Forster added that the legal system in question was not seen to be British but 'seen to be fair'. The same goes for Elizabeth II on her travels. When the Canadians complained of her not having seen enough ordinary people, she saw many more next time.

Lord Home, when asked about Commonwealth bonds, replied with the non-dogmatic approach of the practical man:

> The Statute of Westminster is a kind of bond. It gives equality. But the essence of the Commonwealth is not bonds but being voluntary. Whenever countries become eligible they want to join. There's a very low casualty rate. They *know* we did our best, though we made mistakes. In any case, the Commonwealth can't *do* anything very much. The finance ministers meet twice a year, and are listened to by the International Bank. It's an influence in the world. And of course the Queen does a great deal to make it work.[4]

One of the Queen's later prime ministers, James Callaghan, pays tribute to the shrewdness of her judgment in assessing Commonwealth notabilities. This too helps to make it work:

She really does know much more about heads of Commonwealth [says Callaghan] than any prime minister does, because
she has travelled so much and over such a long period. She
really knows them, and about them. She has a great feeling for
the Commonwealth and she enjoys talking about it, encouraged by her private secretary of the day, Martin Charteris.[5]

Michael Stewart, however, an ex-Foreign Secretary
(now Lord Stewart), has related the Sovereign to the
Commonwealth in a more abstract way. He wrote in 1938:

The monarchy does not create Commonwealth unity – kinship
and common economic and defence interests are more powerful factors. It does, however, symbolize unity, focusing men's
affections and gratifying the strong human inclination to per-
sonify ideals and beliefs.[6]

Kinship is a rapidly diminishing factor in the new Commonwealth, though still significant at the time Stewart's
book first appeared. It is possible that today 'men's affections' for the Commonwealth are not 'focused' through the
Queen, but exist the other way round. Their affection for
the Queen spills over on to the Commonwealth of which
she is head.

One difference between the Queen's work abroad and her
work at home is that she can help a British government
while on her travels without appearing partisan. Occasionally there is a suspicious bark – as when Peter Shore
objected to her being supplied with a pro-Common Market
speech before Britain had joined – but not often.

It was after Suez that Elizabeth II first showed her
capacity to improve a ruffled international mood by paying
a state visit. At that date, 1957, her capacity was not great,
but over the years she has worked away at it, until twenty
years later she was being hailed as Britain's best ambassador.

Plenty of voices had demanded that Nehru should take
India out of the Commonwealth after Suez. Though Nehru

declined, calling it 'a retrograde step in the present world, to break down any link which exists between nations', nevertheless the crisis had been touch and go for the Commonwealth. There were foreign countries also to think of. Britain was fortunate to have an appealing young queen to send out like a dove from a battered ark.

A great step-up in the Queen's travels, especially her state visiting, therefore took place in 1957. After her return home from the first world tour in 1954 there had been only one journey abroad during the next year, a state visit to Norway. Again, one state visit in 1956 to Sweden; the rest private. But for 1957 there were four state visits: to Portugal, France (Britain's accomplice at Suez), Denmark and finally the United States and Canada. The 350th anniversary of the founding of Virginia had brought the Queen to America. After the ceremonies she went on to the British Embassy in Washington, whence Harold Caccia the ambassador sent an excited report home to 10 Downing Street: 'The Queen's visit has made a tremendous effect here. She has buried George III for good and all.' He was right, in so far as two years later Richard Daley, mayor of Chicago, welcomed King George III's descendant as if she were of the Irish royal line of Brian Boru – as indeed she was through her mother. 'Your Majesty,' he said as he presented Chicago to her in the form of his seven children, 'Chicago is yours.'

The Queen also spent from 12 to 16 October in Canada, to be followed in 1959 by a much longer and more significant Canadian tour. Meanwhile there was a state visit to the Netherlands in 1958; only two days, but interesting things always happened in Holland.

This time the 'custom and ceremony' of the grand English court looked like clashing with the more homely Dutch. Queen Juliana had abolished the curtsy. What would happen on the state visit? Should the Dutch court be ordered to curtsy to the English Queen but not to their own? Or to both? Or to neither? Common sense prevailed – the curtsy was left to the choice of those present.

Some curtsied, others did not. In sensible royal circles molehills are not made into mountains. Yet in America the curtsy was still to create mayhem as late as 1981. When Mrs Annenberg curtsied to Prince Charles, the press erupted with letters about the horrors of prostrating oneself as compared with the democratic dignity of an upright posture.

Elizabeth II's humanity was shown in her visit to the Ascher diamond factory at Amsterdam, owned by the family whose head had cloven the enormous Cullinan Diamond for King Edward VII.[7] The old man was still alive, surrounded by a crowd of jubilant descendants. Word had gone round the factory, and then round the Ascher family, that the Queen was wearing the brooch made from the famous stones. Old Ascher, it was said, had fainted with emotion after successfully cleaving the original diamond. Now he nearly fainted again. For the Queen was fiddling about with the brooch. She had taken it off. She had shown it to Queen Juliana. Now she had come over to him.

'You must see it.' Though almost blind the old man stood staring at the brooch and the young woman stood staring at him. It was a scene to remember – almost a case of *Nunc dimittis*.

The Queen's Canadian tour of 18 June to 1 August 1959, split by the flying visit to the United States on 6 July, was physically the most exacting of her reign. This was because she happened to be in the very early throes of her third pregnancy. Macmillan, her prime minister, probably realised how much she wanted this new baby and was extremely anxious about the visit. He put off a June election virtually for her sake. 'I was equally concerned about the strenuous character of the Queen's tour,' he wrote, 'and when the announcement of her pregnancy was made public on 7 August, while I shared the public pleasure, I was glad indeed to feel that she was safely home.'[8]

The Queen had felt awful but resolute. Hardly anyone was aware of her predicament, so there was no sympathy for her special endurance. At least she knew what to expect (unlike her daughter-in-law when expecting Prince William – 'Why did no one tell me you felt like this?'), but that did not mitigate the trials of a long hot crowded summer.

Rideau Hall, Canada's Government House in Ottawa, was famous for its airless atmosphere. In the days of a former Governor-General, Lord Tweedsmuir, the heat would cause people, says his son William Buchan, to talk like whimsical characters out of Chekhov. There is no press record of Elizabeth II holding inconsequential dialogues; only of her seeing a huge number of people. Her Canadian press secretary, indeed, had wanted to pare down the list. 'No,' said the Queen, 'I am not going out for a holiday but to work.'

She opened the St Lawrence Seaway, an occasion well worth her exertions. In Montreal a ball became so jampacked that the Queen and Prince Philip had to go home early; there was no room for them to dance, the whole floor, all the chairs and even tables being covered with people eager to see them. There was one innovation at the Governor-General's inauguration: they sang the national anthem, 'O Canada'. Elizabeth II was to become an expert on national anthems. When she visited Addis Ababa four years later, guests were supposed to gather under their own country's flag. Many did not know what their nation's new flag looked like, but the Queen did. 'She's been doing her homework,' said a member of her entourage. 'She knows the national anthems, too.'[9] The singing of 'O Canada' in 1959, however, had a special meaning: henceforth Canadian nationalism could not be ignored. Next year the Queen adopted a new personal standard for use in Canada and elsewhere to replace the old Royal Standard with its intensely British associations. It bore the monogram 'E'.

Within the next five years the Queen was to make – or be prepared to make – great sacrifices for the Commonwealth in which she so passionately believed. In a sense it was an inherited belief shared by all generations of the Royal Family and involving a mutual exchange between person and country. The Queen's mother had said that her Canadian tour of 1939 'made me'; while her son Charles was to say, 'Australia conquered my shyness.' But Elizabeth II's feelings for the Commonwealth were heightened by her special position. She had been called to be its head during a transitional period that was sometimes triumphant, often anxious, always exciting. 'Britain has lost an empire without finding a role,' was the double negative advanced by Dean Acheson. It was part of the Queen's mission to prove him wrong. Through the Commonwealth, indeed, British prestige in America could be restored.

Not all the Queen's governments felt equally strongly about the Commonwealth at every period of her reign. Many Conservatives have preferred the old Empire to what Macmillan called the 'New Commonwealth'. With Labour and Liberals it was vice versa. Harold Wilson records a moment when the rebuilt House of Commons was being ceremoniously opened after the war, attended by 'a great assembly of Speakers of the Commonwealth, black, white, yellow and brown, many wearing the traditional Westminster robes and wigs, others the colourful robes of their country', all united behind the Lord Chancellor and Mr Speaker by parliamentary democracy. So moved was the Labour Cabinet that 'there were few dry eyes'.[10] This was the sort of genuine emotion that drew the Queen to Wilson and Labour.

A progressive Conservative such as Rab Butler, on the other hand, could put into perspective his own and his sovereign's feeling for the inalienable connection between old and new. At his memorial service in Westminster Abbey, where Her Majesty was represented and Prince Charles was present, Butler's concept of the Commonwealth was recalled with admiration: 'A Commonwealth of independent nations, emerging out of an Empire purged from superiority of race and the false pride of dominion.'[11] Those words would exactly express the ideals of the Queen herself.

A few Conservatives who were dedicated to seeing Britain enter the European Economic Community might appear less wedded than the rest to a multi-racial Commonwealth. Most of them put the Commonwealth above the EEC, though Macmillan, the Queen's guide during the two fateful years of 1960 and 1961, would at least try to have it both ways. He believed that large was beautiful. The Commonwealth must be kept together if possible and Britain's power be supplemented by the EEC: 'The great majority [of Conservatives]', he wrote to the Queen in 1961, 'feel that our position in the Commonwealth, should we weaken industrially and economically, would ultimately fade away.'[12] Then the Common Market would give strength. The first serious sign of 'fading' had already appeared in South Africa.

Any trouble with South Africa was particularly poignant for the Queen. Her parents had loved the country and she herself, as Princess Elizabeth, had taken her twenty-first birthday vows of lifelong service in Cape Town. Thirteen years later, in 1960, the irrepressible need of the Afrikaners (Boers) to win their 'unfinished war' burst out again.

The timetable of events was sufficiently dramatic. On 20 January Dr Verwoerd, the South African Prime Minister, announced a forthcoming referendum on whether the Union should abandon the monarchical system and become a republic. This was followed on 3 February by Macmillan's 'Wind of Change' speech to Parliament in Cape Town, in which he pointed to the great wind of nationalism 'blowing through this continent'. Next day Dr Verwoerd amazed Macmillan by referring to 'a strong feeling in South Africa against recognizing the Queen as Head of the Commonwealth' – quite apart from her not being Queen of South Africa, if the referendum went against her. Macmillan considered Verwoerd's extreme republicanism 'not merely illiberal but definitely shabby'.[13] Surely South Africa could accept what India and so many other countries were prepared to do – recognise the Queen as head?

Home again, a cautious Macmillan said on television: 'I spoke of the wind of change . . . but that's not the same thing as a howling tempest. . . .' Ten days later, on 26 March, the howling tempest was to come indeed but not from the blacks. A tempest of police bullets at Sharpeville killed eighty-seven and wounded 170 black people.

Only six weeks after Sharpeville the Commonwealth Prime Ministers' Conference assembled at Windsor. The atmosphere was far from idyllic, even though the Queen now always made a point of inviting her worldwide 'family' to meet at Windsor, her family home, instead of Buckingham Palace, her 'office'. 'It was a splendid and moving opportunity,' wrote Macmillan of the first occasion in 1957, 'for the Head of the Commonwealth to welcome its leaders.'[14]

They assembled therefore at Windsor on 2 May 1960: Nkrumah of Ghana on his best behaviour, Nehru of India the great humane democrat, Ayub of Pakistan like an Anglo-Indian colonel, the hypersensitive Diefenbaker of Canada, the ultra-royalist Menzies of Australia, the Tunku of Malaya, Abu Bakar of Nigeria the 'new boy', and all the rest. During the informal talks before the official opening on the 4th, Diefenbaker put the cat among the pigeons by propounding racial equality within the Commonwealth. The Queen tried to cheer her guests with a superb dinner in the Waterloo Chamber, afterwards showing them round the State Apartments. She stayed with them until midnight and most of them enjoyed themselves. Macmillan, however, in his anxiety about the formal conference next day, had two critical thoughts: how tired he felt; and why did the Royal Family not live in these wonderful state apartments instead of in George IV's garish saloons?

Next day there were invitations to the Queen from the republics of India, Pakistan and Malaya to visit their countries. The Queen, wrote Macmillan in his diary, 'is rather pleased.' He himself was very pleased, for he hoped that this bonhomie would counteract the divisions introduced by Diefenbaker's statement. But no. Despite the good nature of Eric Louw, South Africa's representative, feelings against apartheid within the Commonwealth steadily

swelled. At one point, when Louw asked Diefenbaker what
Canada thought about it all, the latter replied like an angry
Dr Johnson, 'Nothing, sir.' And nothing permanent came
out of the conference to produce unanimity. It was true that
on the last day, Friday 13 May, a two-part formula was
evolved: non-intervention in the internal affairs of Commonwealth countries; and multi-racialism in the Commonwealth. It was the first time ever that multi-racialism was
formally declared. The Queen received an immediate report from her Prime Minister that registered qualified
relief: 'The official text is weak but it has the advantage of
being agreed.'[15]

The advantage was short-lived. In July the Queen heard
that South Africa's republican referendum would take
place in the autumn, despite Macmillan's plea for 'a breathing space'. There were to be no breathers in the next eight
months. On 5 October, 1,626,333 white South Africans
voted to abolish the monarchy by a majority of 74,580. No
black South Africans got a vote; if they had, it would
assuredly have gone to the Queen. In March 1961 Dr
Verwoerd, having brought South Africa out of the Queen's
'realms', was applying to remain in her Commonwealth.
But he would make not the slightest concession to the
democracy of race. No, he would accept no black high
commissioner in Pretoria. Yes, all black Commonwealth
officials would be segregated – though in superstar hotels.
In the end Verwoerd had to withdraw his application and
go home no longer a member of the Commonwealth. 'It
needn't have happened that year,' says Lord Home.
'Diefenbaker made it impossible to avoid a decision, and so
South Africa had to expel itself. But it would have happened in two years or so anyway.'[16]

However inevitable, this was a sad way for the Queen to
begin the 1960s of her reign. Fortunately, a renewed burst
of travel was to show her the Commonwealth in a more
heartening perspective. It was accepted that the new Afro-
Asian members, on attaining independence, would prob-

ably opt for republican systems. But would they be within
the Commonwealth or outside? No one guessed what an
imposing number of new members would apply to join the
multi-racial fraternity of which she was head. Writing in
1962, her shadow Foreign Secretary, Patrick Gordon Walker, predicted a membership rising to perhaps fourteen.
Today there are forty-seven, though admittedly many
member-countries are very small. But since no votes are
taken, that does not matter.

Nineteen sixty-one was to be a year in which the Queen
learnt much about the difference in the kind of public
opinion she would meet with, for instance, when on her
travels and when at home. In India it was taken for granted
that a tiger hunt would be laid on, but when the performance was about to be repeated in Nepal, Prince Philip was
found to have his trigger-finger swathed in bandages. Audrey Russell of the BBC boldly called it 'a diplomatic whit-
low'. It was another name for the effects of anti-blood sport
backlash from home. (Godfrey Talbot, also of the BBC,
made his inimitable Indian gaffe at this time, when he
described the Queen as being 'entwined' with her host on
an elephant's howdah. He had meant to say 'enshrined'.)

The tiger hunt furore formed part of that delicate royal
question, 'setting a good example'. Princess Anne, when
first off to boarding school, thought such an idea pompous
and 'ghastly'. Prince Philip, too, has said that the Royal
Family were there not to edify but to identify with, age with
age, youth with youth. Nevertheless they have set many
excellent examples, especially in the Commonwealth. On 9
February 1956 a leper settlement was visited by the Queen
and Prince Philip on the Oji River of Nigeria, the first to be
visited by a British sovereign, and there the royal couple
had each adopted financially a leper child. As they
approached, the Africans drummed out a welcome: 'Our
Mother is coming!'[17] There was no word for Queen on the
Oji.

In Sierra Leone Elizabeth II showed herself a most
popular queen by appearing everywhere in tiara and

jewels. At home they would have thought she had gone mad. But it was known that long ago in South Africa they had found the Royal Family's jewels disappointing and missed the flash of tiaras.

To be both a good guest and good host was a thing the Queen was learning during these years. Like many reserved people, she relaxed and unbent as a guest and was smiling and appreciative, but could still be stiff as a host. The charm and informality of her yacht *Britannia* encouraged her to entertain naturally, though parties in hotels were never easy. When not to smile was another thing to learn. Foreign males were apt to curtsy to her by mistake, especially when with their wives. An Anglican bishop once curtsied in New Zealand and a Roman Catholic layman genuflected in London.

These things were the froth on the surface of good queenship. Her visit to Ghana in June 1961 was a great trial and a great triumph; everything on the grand scale.

Ghana had become an independent republic within the Commonwealth in 1957, under Kwame Nkrumah. This clever, flamboyant African, educated by Western teachers at Makerere University, had nevertheless retained a few primitive habits. 'Is he fond of birds?' asked the Foreign Secretary, Lord Home, one day, seeing cages full of doves on the staircase of Nkrumah's home in Accra. No, he was only fond of their entrails, which he would always consult before making a flight. Nor was he exclusively devoted to parliamentary democracy, having recently put most of the opposition into prison, including Joseph Appiah, married to Peggy Cripps and therefore son-in-law of Sir Stafford Cripps the British Labour politician. Not unnaturally Nkrumah's political enemies were retaliating with violence. The deadly question for Macmillan's Cabinet was, could the Queen safely visit Ghana? No one expected her to be attacked personally. But if she rode in procession with Nkrumah she might share a bomb meant exclusively for her host.

The battle of opinions raged inside Parliament. There were many who were less than attracted by the prospect of risking their Queen's life for the sake of a black president reputedly in league with Russia. But this was just the point of the other side. Cancel the visit, and it would be tantamount to saying Ghana was not wanted in the Commonwealth. 'How silly I should look,' said Elizabeth II, 'if I was scared to visit Ghana and then Khrushchev went and had a good reception.' She had cancelled an earlier visit when expecting Prince Andrew.

After an audience, Macmillan told Harold Evans, 'She had been indignant . . . at the idea of having the trip called off. The House of Commons, she thought, should not show lack of moral fibre in this way.'[18] Macmillan had been lyrical, exclaiming to Evans, 'What a splendid girl she is.' He added: 'She took her Commonwealth responsibilities very seriously and rightly so, for the responsibilities of the UK monarchy had so shrunk that if you left it at that you might as well have a film star.' Macmillan was also to write out his account of this audience in his own diary.[19]

The Queen was due to fly out on 9 November. But a bomb five days before put the whole matter back in the melting-pot. The bomb blew off the legs of Nkrumah's statue in Accra. Though the legs were restored in twenty-four hours, it was not so easy to restore Parliament's confidence. So the Queen, resolute as ever, accepted a suggestion to 'try it on the dog'.[20] Her Commonwealth Secretary, Duncan Sandys, gallantly offered to fly out first and ride through Accra with Nkrumah. No bombs were thrown at them. Elizabeth II then followed on the appointed date.

Even now, however, there was a contretemps. A fog in London delayed her plane by five hours. She arrived at night instead of at teatime. As there was then no proper street lighting, her procession with Nkrumah was lit only by torches carried by young men running beside their car. The cheering spectators were all in darkness – a perfect invitation to gunmen. But none fired. For in the words of Audrey Russell of the BBC:

> They fell for her – went out of their minds for her – the people.
> She was the best protection Nkrumah had had for years. They
> were in that open car, but she didn't bat an eyelid – Nkrumah
> next to her. You just saw the Queen very calm, very poised –
> not smiling too much – just right.

There were still some dramatic moments. Whenever Kwame Nkrumah and the Queen were due to make a joint appearance, he would whip up excitement by having the cry raised ahead of him, 'Osagyfo is coming! Osagyfo is coming!' – Osagyfo being the Messiah in Ghanaian.[21] Sir Michael Adeane soon put a stop to this nonsense.

At the state banquet in the Ambassadors Hotel, half the top table was empty. The Opposition still had their names on the programme but some had been arrested and others had escaped. Several journalists, seeing the gaps, rushed up to the top table. (One of them, disconcerted at finding herself next to Prince Philip, rushed back to her place.) Nor was the Ambassadors Hotel the safest place for the Queen. People could look straight into it from the street. Fortunately they only looked.

A handsome, very self-possessed boy of seven, Kwame Appiah, son of the imprisoned Opposition leader, happened to be in Accra Hospital when the royal party visited it. With a little sleight of hand they were guided to Kwame Appiah's bedside. 'Well, last time I was here,' said Prince Philip firmly, 'I had luncheon with your mother. Give her my regards.' The big Kwame, who always carried a polo stick, slapped his own leg with annoyance. He knew who the small boy was.

On her departure, the people of Ghana not only heaped the Queen and her family with presents but gave her a booklet explaining 'The Symbolism of Ghana's State Gifts'. Her gold ear-rings, bangles, necklace and sandals all symbolised 'welcome home'. A crescent-shaped stool covered with gold leaf signified family affection, 'the warmth of a mother's embrace'. On Prince Charles's sandals was a design that said, 'Yese-agya, be like your good father', while Prince Andrew received a toy ivory tortoise and snail symbolising peace and the Ghanaian proverb, 'If the snail and the tortoise were left alone in the forest there would never be a gun-shot.'

After the Queen was safely home, Macmillan wrote in his diary:

> The Queen has been absolutely determined all through. She is grateful for MPs' and Press concern about her safety, but she is impatient of the attitude towards her to treat her as a *woman*, and a film star or mascot. She has indeed 'the heart and stomach of a man'.[22]

With this quotation from her great predecessor, Elizabeth II may be said to have become a true 'New Elizabethan'.

The next Canadian experience, in 1964, was as testing emotionally as 1959 had been physically. In the five years, Canadian nationalism, sharp-ended by Quebec separatism, had become conscious of its strength. The first ugly signs (not all the signs of nationalism were ugly by any means) were threats to the Queen's life.

As early as February 1964 the Queen received reports of violent political separatism in French Canada. Anonymous French separatists said they would not stop at assassination. Only months before, John F. Kennedy had been shot to death in Dallas, and security forces everywhere were keyed-up. They seemed to have cause in Canada. Asked whether Quebec would be another Dallas, Dr Marcel Chaput, a French separatist leader, told the press, 'It could.' In any case, if the Queen came to Quebec she would be shown that she was not welcome, and shown it 'brutally'.

By September the British press were on tenterhooks. 'THE QUEEN – MURDER PLOT PROBE' was announced by the *Daily Mirror* on 3 September in screaming headlines: '*We'll kill her on royal tour says Canadian killer gang.*' On the 15th

The Times explained to its alarmed readers that Mr Pearson the Canadian Prime Minister, in inviting Her Majesty to visit Quebec, was relying on a tradition 'that the French are even warmer to the throne than the English Canadians'. That tradition, said *The Times* nervously, was 'perhaps now eroded'.

As the departure date drew nearer, the press became gloomier. On 4 October the *Sunday Telegraph* ran a tale of Cuban-trained marxist terrorists encamped in Quebec forests, under the command of a guerrilla leader with the code name 'Le Gaspesian'; while their sympathisers were to be met in a certain Montreal bar. The *News of the World* reported 'a dark cloud of anger' hanging over 'the most challenging royal tour the Queen has ever faced', and the *Sunday Mirror* predicted that the Queen would be 'constantly exposed' to snipers. The *Daily Mail* on the Monday, however, quoted the Queen as saying the dangers were exaggerated. 'I am not worried about the visit and we are quite relaxed.'

Two steadfast characters were in fact on duty to meet the uproar, the Prime Minister Alec Douglas-Home and the Queen herself. It was known that the general threats of disturbance were not directed against the Queen personally, but against the Federal Government, her hosts. Arrangements for her flight on Monday 5 October proceeded calmly, the press describing her as 'serene and smiling' at take-off. She was still smiling in Prince Edward Island the same day, though few of the islanders saw her. Security had enthroned her inside a steel enclosure, crowned by barbed wire. The islanders were indignant at this slur on their loyalty, particularly after an American journalist revealed that he had been sent over from the States to write 'a tense piece' and was trying to get himself into the mood. Poor Mayor Gaudet of Charlottetown lamented that all this press nonsense had taken the bloom off the visit of 'a very wonderful lady'.[23]

Three successful days were in fact passed by the wonderful lady in Prince Edward Island. On 8 October she sailed away in *Britannia* towards the alleged danger zone, Quebec; between the Gaspe coast ('Le Gaspesian' territory?) and Anticosti Island into what the *Ottawa Citizen* called 'a beautiful sunset'. There were no serious 'incidents' however; *Britannia* and her destroyer escorts once had to make 'a fast shift of course' in order to avoid running down a fishing vessel, and on the Wednesday her gangplank shifted. But the Queen was not thrown into the sea and 'the Royal Navy is investigating'.

The story of the Saturday in Quebec was not a pretty one. Whereas Charlottetown had been festooned with bunting, Quebec's chief decorations were miles of wooden barriers painted yellow and stencilled over and over in black with the word 'POLICE'. By the Saturday morning the barriers had all been chained together, as if to remind the Quebecers of their own alleged enslavement to Ottawa. The Quebec Provincial Police were out everywhere in strength, breaking up groups and arresting suspicious characters.

Few would dare to watch the Queen when she came. Prince Philip, too, was in trouble with a jumpy police force. The Royal Canadian Mounted Police, it appeared, had noticed him 'playing with the window buttons' in the royal black limousine at Charlottetown. These buttons mechanically raised and lowered the shatter-proof glass windows. When he and the Queen were driving through a particularly dense throng of people, the Mounties would observe the Duke lowering the windows so that the people could get a clearer view of their royal visitors. They pleaded with the Household to make the Prince 'leave the buttons alone' – if not, 'the wires leading to the opening mechanisms would be severed'.

Even the journalists from outside were shocked by Quebec's state of siege. Everyone crossing the Quebec bridge was checked from the Friday to the Sunday, so that there were long traffic hold-ups and loud grumblings. It was one of the things Prince Philip particularly disliked – traffic being dislocated for a royal visit – as he had shown earlier by apologising for a traffic jam in Karachi.[24]

'This ancient walled capital,' wrote one reporter, 'today seems more like a fortress preparing for a siege than a city waiting to welcome its Queen.' The police were none too happy with the royal approach road to the fortress. After landing from *Britannia* at the Wolfe's Cove dock, the Queen would drive for over a mile under the frowning Heights of Abraham, before reaching the Legislative Buildings on the famous Plains above. It sometimes seemed as if she might be in greater danger than General Wolfe himself had been in 1759.

As it turned out, there were no bombs. But no rejoicing either. Silence reigned; or else the Queen was actually booed by small groups of people with banners declaring '*Québec aux Québecois*' or telling her to 'Go home!' – '*Chez vous!*' (How could she convince them that she was '*chez moi*' already? At home in her own French-Canadian realm?) The frantic activities of the helmeted provincial police did not help. They laid about themselves so freely with their long riot nightsticks that this 10 October went down in local history as 'the Saturday of the beatings-up'. Some alarmists believed that civil war was about to break out and split Canada in two. Perhaps the *Manchester Guardian* and *Daily Mirror* between them gave the most vivid picture of the personalised clash: the Queen showing 'regal annoyance, grim and unsmiling. And no wonder.' For her reception was 'silent, glum, glacial' in a city gripped by fear.[25]

Nevertheless, most Canadians realised that the intentions of even the most vocal demonstrators were limited. They were not against Elizabeth II as such. They simply wished to mark their fury at Ottawa's allegedly using the Queen to assert its own federal authority in Quebec, an authority that they fiercely repudiated.

The Queen's tour recovered its balance with two enthusiastic days in Ottawa. The *Winnipeg Free Press*, commenting on her 'ready smiles and an easy unaffected bearing', added by way of a new regal development:

What was most noticeable, however, was the sudden cocking of an eyebrow, the laughing shrug of a shoulder, and the sparkle in her eye as she met old Ottawa acquaintances. It was a return of the free and easy manner more usually associated with Prince Philip. . . .[26]

She sailed away on the 13th, leaving behind a series of bitter post-mortems, rather than healing memories of her address to the Quebec Legislature. She had spoken alternately in English and faultless French; she had boldly approved the singing of 'O Canada'; she had described the two civilisations as complementary and the role of French Canada as *'irremplaçable'*. She was not to return, except briefly, until 1970. Meanwhile, Prince Philip found it necessary to tell all Canadians in 1969 that the monarchy, unlike the French provinces, was not *'irremplaçable'*. He defined in his own language (so different from the pious hopes put into the Queen's mouth by Mr Pearson in 1964) the philosophy of a modern monarchy in a modern Commonwealth:

> The structure of any society [he began soberly] depends on the accepting by the community of that structure. The Monarchy exists in Canada for historical reasons, and it exists in the sense that it is a benefit, or was considered to be a benefit, to the country or to the nation.

Then, warming to the difficulties:

> If at any stage any nation decides that the system is unacceptable, then it is up to them to change it. I think it is a complete misconception to imagine that the Monarchy exists in the interests of the Monarch. It doesn't. It exists in the interests of the people.

Here the Duke characteristically implied that even less did it exist in the interests of the government, federal or otherwise. He ended on a robust man-to-man note:

> I think the important thing about it is that if at any stage people feel that it has no further part to play, then for goodness sake

let's end the thing on amicable terms without having a row about it.[27]

The Queen's state visit to Germany in 1965 was hardly less stirring then her tour of Canada. In one way at least the German visit caused more tension in herself, though only the closest observers noticed any change in her expression on either occasion.

Nineteen sixty-five was twenty years after the war ended – quite long enough, it might be thought, for bygones to be bygones and a state visit to seem natural. There were several factors, however, making for special interest. It was the first since 1913; two wars breaking out against the same country within twenty-five years of one another take longer to recover from than one (although Hitler was a psychopathic enemy, unlike the Kaiser), and Elizabeth II came of German stock. Not that any of these things caused her personal concern. She was used to German relatives. Her concern was of the opposite kind. Almost too much enthusiasm, too much excitement among the German people.

Michael Stewart, the Labour Foreign Secretary, accompanied her on this tour, though in these days of hard-worked ministers even the Sovereign could not have daily attendance. The minister flew out with her, stayed a few days, flew home and returned for the last of the ten days or so. 'In the old days,' recalled Stewart, 'it would have been a very leisurely ten days. The Foreign Secretary accompanied the Queen wherever she went – but you can't do that nowadays.'

Who invited her? That Stewart did not know. He had become Foreign Secretary only in 1964. A visit of such importance would have been arranged months if not years before. 'It would probably have been the German government,' he thought. 'Nobody hawks the Queen about.'

Stewart went on to describe the highlights of the visit. Indeed it was almost all highlights:

I remember on the first day a German official looking very gratified with the crowds in the streets, bigger than for de Gaulle. I think before that moment they would have been very nervous about the visit.

This nervousness on their part did not exactly convey itself to the Queen. I wouldn't have said that she was nervous but I did notice she didn't like one thing – and that was the passionate enthusiasm of the crowds in Berlin.

Berlin is a beleaguered city – feels itself as such – any notable visitor from outside is welcome. And now the Queen! The whole square filled with people and Willy Brandt, the mayor of Berlin, was there – he went out to meet her and the whole crowd began to chant 'Elizabeth – Elizabeth.' I think she thought this was a bit too much of a good thing – too reminiscent of ritual Nazi shouting. That was the only time I saw her perhaps at all put out.[28]

Willy Brandt of course soon quietened the crowd.

In 1965, the Queen was almost halfway through the first thirty years of her reign, but she had not entirely found her feet. Her dislike of that tremendous reception was an example of lingering wariness. A more experienced queen would not have worried about it so much. On the other hand, a less intelligent queen would not have made the connection between '*Sieg heil!*' and 'Elizabeth!'

The crowds went wild again when she bravely acknowledged her German descent. This showed not only maturity but also straightforwardness and common sense. She also had a genuine and deep interest in her family history. In Hanover she was shown a letter from a group of English magnates to George, Elector of Hanover: 'Queen Anne's dying. Come quick, certain persons want a Jacobite heir and not you.' The direct descendant of George I was riveted by that letter.

There was one other incident, trivial in itself but which reflected on the advantages of a royal head of state over a presidential one. On one of the days when Prince Philip was off on his special business – inspecting Hamburg harbour or what not – the procession was formed by the Queen in the first car and Michael Stewart as Foreign Secretary in the second.

> The crowds were as usual cheering the Queen wildly [said Stewart] and they thought at first the next car contained Prince Philip. I actually heard someone begin to call out 'Phil. . . .' and then whoever it was suddenly realized that whoever I was I wasn't the Duke of Edinburgh. Quite a number of them got it right, 'Stew-art, Stew-art.' But one or two thought I was the President of the German Republic. The car was speeding by and they were wondering who they would see – and one of the features of being a figurehead president is that you really fall between two stools. People rarely know who you are. They never know him the way they would know a governing president like Reagan or a crowned head like Elizabeth II.

At the end of it all, what do state visits to foreign powers accomplish? Stewart's view is positive:

> If the two governments are anxious to get on good terms with one another, a successful royal visit will certainly smooth the way. It won't overturn major obstacles – no amount of royal visits to Germany when Hitler was in power would have done any good.
> But they can smooth the way. For instance, Edward VII and the Entente Cordiale. If the interests of two countries are already coinciding, a royal visit can dispel what still stands in the way – which is usually prejudice and misunderstanding.[29]

Elizabeth II was nearly thirty-eight years old when her last child, Prince Edward, was born on 10 March 1964. Yet it was easy to think of her as 'the young Queen' still. She seemed extraordinarily youthful, with her bright complexion, light voice and elastic step. To see her spring on to the shore from a boat in Turkey on a fine autumn day in 1971 was to say she could not possibly be all of forty-five. Her playfulness with her children had increased rather than otherwise. She spent more time in the nursery. This was partly due to the retirement of Nanny Lightbody, a devoted surrogate mother of the old school who had brooked no interference in 'her' nursery. Mabel Anderson was now nanny to the two young princes. On her days off the Queen herself would baby-sit in the nursery, and if Andrew or Edward woke up it was she who would settle them to sleep again.

Biographers of Princess Elizabeth's four years as a young mother before she came to the throne rightly insist on the sacrosanctity of her morning half-hour and evening hour with her children. The question is never asked, Why not longer? Affairs of state did not then impinge too heavily. No heavier than they were to weigh on her daughter-in-law a generation later, who would certainly not be contented with so little of Prince William.

The answer is twofold. First, changes in the social atmosphere of all nurseries, royal included, where the permissive society has its own reflection however carefully filtered. The day of the autocratic nanny is over. Second, the Queen's changing temperament. Her early reticence allowed her to be 'terrorised' – if that is not too strong a word, but it has been used – whereas her later relaxation put her firmly in command. For sheer, carefree enjoyment Prince Edward was a greater gift than any of her three older children; while Peter Phillips outdoes all four. One need only compare the quiet mother showing her album to Andrew and Edward in the *Royal Family* film, made in 1969, with the grandmother, so obviously in charge when entertaining Peter at Royal Lodge in the additional *Royal Heritage*, 1980. But that is to anticipate.

Not only was 1964 the year of Prince Edward but also of Harold Wilson. This was the beginning of a new run of prime ministers, all of them roughly designated 'middle-class' if not lower, and as different as possible from the one Harrovian and three Etonians that the Queen had known hitherto.

Wilson likes to be remembered for the number of times he mentioned 'industry' and 'sales' on television, backed by the industrial awards promoted by Prince Philip and the Queen. The Queen's earnest enquiries about urban conditions, such as the famous back-to-back houses of Leeds, endeared her to him beyond all measure. Her enthusiasm increased his own interest in all these problems – a valuable variant of her right to 'encourage'.

The Queen's fondness for the first 'people's voice' of her reign was equally obvious and no more surprising. When the friendships between her grandfather George v and the Rt Hon. J. H. Thomas ('Jimmy' Thomas) and her father George vi and Ernest Bevin are remembered, there seems to be a natural affinity between the crown and those salty characters who rise to the top to serve it. Jimmy Thomas made George v laugh so much that he burst his stitches after an operation. The 'cheeky chappy' of the 1960s and 1970s, when he sat next to his sovereign at dinner, made her laugh with him without stopping.

Nevertheless middle age and by no means middling problems were creeping up on her. 'Rhodesia', which Wilson had seen as a problem of 'weeks rather than months', was to see out the 1970s and two more prime ministers, before it was finally solved in 1981. Finance became a headache for the Royal Family as it was for all who had once 'had it so good'. And in 1976, the Queen was to touch the fiftieth year of her age, and next year the twenty-fifth year of her reign. For all her youthful vitality, it would be against nature if she were not a subtly changed person, more commanding as well as more at ease.

Revaluations:
The 1970s

Changes leading to a new kind of stability – that was to be the Queen's experience in the 1970s. Each year brought its outstanding events for her which together were to make up a heterogeneous assortment with no apparent thread leading in any particular direction. There were the first official walkabouts; the first 'poking about' into the royal finances; the Silver Wedding and the death of the Duke of Windsor; the first of her children married and her first Commonwealth Conference attended outside Britain, a Britain that in the same year joined the Common Market; a serious contretemps over a governor-general, the first since 1925; the first woman prime minister; and alas the first member of the Royal Family to be murdered since the seventeenth century. All widely disparate events. Yet each one, whether tragic or joyful, was to form part of the monarchy's recognisably new mould.

A great deal has been made of Elizabeth II's innovation known as 'walkabouts', and rightly so. But a look into history makes them less revolutionary though no less interesting. Queen Victoria's immediate predecessor, her uncle William IV, walked about St James's Street so freely that his courtiers feared for his dignity if not his life; while so many inquisitive noses were pushed into Victoria's face on Brighton pier that she had to give up walking about there. Royal privacy may be dated from the moment when the Windsor crowds were no longer allowed to pack the

Terrace, strolling up and down under the castle windows, often face to face with the embarrassed Queen.

The widowed Victoria's later habits changed normal privacy into seclusion. This enabled the drives and race-course amblings of her son the Prince of Wales to seem, by contrast, almost as genial and jolly as his great-uncle William IV's walkabouts; his wife Alexandra also did some meticulously planned strolling among the people. Nothing much in the way of mixing was expected of George V, and indeed he led a leisurely life compared with his successors, with incomparably more shooting holidays and less work. He would have let off some surprised oaths at the sight of his granddaughter's patronage lists, home engagements and overseas visits for the 1970s.

At the same time, Elizabeth II's first walkabouts in New Zealand in March 1970 had their more immediate antecedents. We read of Edward VIII when Prince of Wales being 'surrounded and locked in by his father's [Indian] subjects, guarded by them a thousand times more wonderfully than if he had been enclosed by the finest Guards regiment in the world. . . .'[1] Admittedly the Prince was in a car, but the crowds who had burst the police barrier cut off the car from his escorts and forced his chauffeur to go at walking pace. The same sense of being protected by an enveloping crowd was felt by Queen Elizabeth (now the Queen Mother) when she walked about among a crowd of 10,000 Canadian veterans in 1939 and in South Africa, 1947.

The official dates, March 1970 in New Zealand and June 1970 in Coventry, for Elizabeth II's first walkabouts have not gone unchallenged. When the author cited 1970 in a *Sunday Telegraph* article on 'Thirty Years of Majesty' a correspondent wrote from Malta to enter a counter-claim:

Her Majesty made her first walkabout in Malta during the royal visit of November, 1967, when she walked along Valletta's main road, then Kingsway, now Republic Street, stopping to talk with the people who remembered her as a naval wife in Malta. . . .[2]

I do not doubt that the Queen enjoyed spontaneous walk-abouts in her old haunts, feeling almost as free again as she had been as a young princess. The success of those three or four days in Malta, indeed, may have inspired the later official début. New Zealand, as an outstandingly loyal member of the old Commonwealth, was a good location for the experiment.

Elaborate arrangements had to be made between the royal entourage and New Zealand security. It is said that when the experiments were repeated in Australia between 30 March and 3 May 1970, the Australian authorities were not so enthusiastic about shouldering their new responsibilities. Possibly, if the temperature of violence had been as high at this time as it is in the 1980s – Pope John Paul II and President Reagan both wounded in 1981 – the Queen and her advisers might have thought twice about taking new risks. For risks they are, and the Queen knows it. Yet just as the white 'popemobile', once it has appeared on the international scene, can never return permanently to garage, so the familiar figure in a straight coat with a small collar, a handbag over the left arm and the right hand ready for the children's posies – this picture of the Queen will never go back permanently into its portfolio.

At first the Queen and her advisers were disappointed that the photographers and editors did not live up to the new image. During a royal visit the papers would still concentrate on her inspections of worthy matrons and local councillors on the steps of their institutions, rather than the shoppers who had caught her eye down below. Today the message has been taken. The Queen will be photographed accepting two or three wild flowers from a child. The rest of the Royal Family follow her into the crowded streets, Prince Charles being seen on occasion with two but-tonholes, one on each side of his jacket.

The debit and credit accounts of walkabouts are quickly made up. Debits: harder on the Queen's feet and on her face, which must be a walking smile; if she stops smiling for a moment it is like a light switched off. More chances for the

feeble-minded to achieve notoriety by pretending violence.
More chances for terrorists. An end to the mystery of
someone who used to flash by, seen momentarily and for
ever remembered. Credits: the Queen and the people
know what each looks like, the sound of each other's
voices, accents. They are real to one another. She is
respected for the trouble she takes and time she spends.
Something new has caught on and become firmly rooted, a
rare thing in this kaleidoscopic world.

The Queen's overseas visits have always been the most
strenuous part of her work. In 1973 there was another big
jump forward on that front. During the previous year
Pierre Trudeau, Prime Minister of Canada, had invited the
Queen to attend the next year's Commonwealth Conference at Ottawa in person. No invitation could have been
more unexpected. It was quite on the cards for Mr Kosygin
to invite the Queen and Prince Philip to Moscow, which
indeed he did with unrelenting pressure at a Buckingham
Palace banquet, until he and his invitation were deflected
into the 'correct channels', after an sos from the Queen.
But Mr Trudeau! A French-Canadian by birth, at one time
he had not seemed averse to a republic. He might still want
one in due time. When asked in 1973 why he wanted the
Queen to visit, he replied with another question: 'Why
change a system when it works successfully?'[3]
    His action was in fact changing the system, though in a
monarchist direction. Hitherto the Queen had attended
only the conferences held in London, when the host would
be the British Prime Minister. To go to Ottawa meant that
the host would be Pierre Trudeau. The Queen would be
wearing her Canadian hat and her 'abroad' smile – often a
more relaxed smile than in Britain. Harold Macmillan had
once said: 'Everybody's so much nicer to you in other
countries than they are at home. At home you always have
to be a politician. When you're abroad you almost feel
yourself a statesman.'[4] At home the Queen always had to
be a senior civil servant. When abroad she could almost feel

herself a Gloriana – though far too modest to admit it.

She accepted Trudeau's invitation with alacrity immediately it was offered in 1972. On receiving this news, *The Times* commented: 'Trudeau certainly believes that the Commonwealth connection helps Canadians to think globally and not sectionally; and that the Commonwealth, by focusing attention on Ottawa, will help to preserve a Canadian identity distinct from the United States.'

By the same token, the Queen's attendance abroad – she was to attend every Commonwealth Conference following Ottawa – would help to preserve her Commonwealth identity distinct from the United Kingdom. For the Britishness of the Commonwealth has always been an ambivalent factor. Many would agree with the Australian Professor Miller 'that the Commonwealth, while no longer British in name, is British in inception and cannot be totally divorced from its imperial origins.' On the other hand, the 'Brits' in Canada for instance could be a controversial element. Whereas all other immigrants, wrote John Muggeridge in 1971, were forced to adjust, he as a 'Brit' was not. In an article called 'Why Those Brits Act Like Brits', Muggeridge explained:

> Change was thrust upon [the non-Brits] not only in the form of citizenship courses and English for New Canadians, but through day-to-day existence in a foreign country. They felt as well as spoke with a broken accent: we English get by as we are.[5]

In flying to Ottawa on 31 July 1973 and staying until 4 August for the conference, the Queen was acting less like a 'Brit' and more like the Head. The first Commonwealth Conference had been held in 1907 and for many years thereafter at irregular intervals, but always in Britain, with a 'Brit' prime minister in charge. For the first conference of her reign, chaired by Churchill in 1952, there were only eight countries present. Now the conferences are held regularly every two years or so and a Canadian, an Australian, a Tanzanian, a Nigerian, an Indian will be in charge. The whole idea of the conference has been stepped up, both by its regularity and diversity. And by the presence of its Head. In her turn she gains from the changes. 'Her position has been strengthened,' writes Michael Stewart, 'since Britain no longer controls it.'[6]

It is worth noting the view of a very 'Brit' prime minister, Mrs Margaret Thatcher, on this new situation as it affects both monarchy and Commonwealth:

> I think the Queen's presence at the Commonwealth Conference [says Mrs Thatcher] is a very positive factor in keeping the Commonwealth together. I cannot overstate its enormous significance. You get the continuity. They know the Queen. The Prime Ministers, who know her and see her, each and every one has a personal link which is of tremendous importance. I do not think the Commonwealth could be held together without the Queen. They know her concern.

Mrs Thatcher then illustrates how it worked soon after Belize achieved independence in 1981. The scene was a dinner:

> I had the Prime Minister of Belize next to me and he said he had never spoken to or dined with the Queen and what should he do? I said, 'You talk to her as one person to another, each in your own capacity – you as Prime Minister of Belize to her as Queen of Belize.'
> When I saw him afterwards, he had found it easier to talk than he had ever thought. He had found her knowledge fantastic – she knew of all the negotiations for the independence of Belize. I do not think anyone fully realizes the accumulation of experience she has.[7]

In regard to the Queen's 'accumulation of experience', it is clear that she does not rely wholly on her red despatch boxes, however assiduously studied. Before the Ottawa Conference of 1973, for instance, she had spent from 25 June to 5 July in Canada, flown home in between and returned to Canada on 31 July for five more days. In the words of a member of her entourage, 'She *feels* Canadian as well as *being* Queen of Canada partly because she has been all over it.' On this occasion she travelled 16,700 miles over Canada.

Sometimes she was meeting 'new Canadian citizens' of whom only a proportion could talk with her in English. 'What'll I say?' was the big worry, as each young workaday Canadian wondered what he or she had in common with a forty-seven-year-old monarch. 'I know you call her "Your Majesty",' said a housewife, 'but do you keep saying "Your Majesty" all the time?' Luckily, there was always one among them who knew the form, like Police Inspector Harding of Brampton, Ontario, who had come from Wales seven years before. 'I'm a royalist,' he said; 'I've always been a royalist.' Moreover there was often a high Canadian official to give them a preliminary lecture on why they of all people were meeting the Queen. The theme would be 'Canada's Cultural Diversity' and the lecturer would point out that no one wanted 'to pattern Canadians to a uniform mould of a model citizen'. Later on the Queen would rub in the same message. 'To become a Canadian citizen,' she said, 'implies a commitment to share the particular gifts of personality and culture, which the newcomer brings with him, with the rest of the family of Canadians.' They needed their diversity; and they needed the unity the Queen brought. That was her particular royal gift of 'personality and culture'.[8]

Becoming more 'political' than usual, she would answer the *Toronto Star*'s accusation that she represented only one element that had gone to make up modern Canada. She was 'Queen of Canada and of *all* Canadians', she retorted, not just of 'one or two ancestral strains'.

At other times it was not so serious. Mayor Walter Assef of Thunder Bay had the instincts of a vaudeville comedian. 'Prince Philip, Your Royal Highness, we're so pleased that you and your gracious wife could be here today.' Then Mr Assef turned to present the Duke with a painting of a loon (a diving bird). But he couldn't find it. 'Where's the loon?'

he shouted, and jigged on the platform until the painting was located. 'Oh, here it is – show it to Your Majesty.' Prince Philip laughed and slapped his knee while the Queen gave her widest grin.

The conference that followed a month later had its own pleasantries. President General Amin of Uganda sent a personal message to the Queen while she was in mid-Atlantic flying from London to Ottawa, requesting transport from Kampala and back and a bodyguard of Scots Guardsmen. It was not known whether they were to be fitted out in scarlet jackets and bearskins.

Of her own choice the Queen saw each one of the thirty-two Commonwealth representatives alone. It had been suggested that since they were now so many she might find it too tiring and prefer to meet them *en masse*; or to see only those alone whom she had not already met. But tête-à-têtes are best for the 'accumulation of experience', and today, with the number of members risen to forty-seven, she still sees them individually.

For her Christmas message of 1973 Elizabeth II included some television shots of a reception at Rideau Hall, Ottawa. They served a dual purpose. The public saw a broadly smiling Queen moving at ease among all those different peoples. It also saw men and women of note in the Commonwealth whose appearance and histories were far more familiar to the Queen than to their own neighbours in the receiving line or to the television audience. How many could distinguish the Minister of Western Samoa from the Vice-President of Zambia, each in a white jacket and black bow-tie? (The other pair thus smartly dressed were Pierre Trudeau and Edward Heath.) There had been a great effort at this conference to make it less of a 'public harangue' and more of 'an informal Cabinet meeting'.[9] Much of the success in this direction was due to the Queen's presence.

Meanwhile, the Queen's whistlestop Canadian tour of 1973 was described afterwards by Maurice Weaver, *Daily Telegraph* reporter, as 'less of a regal progress than a Royal hustings' – so 'punchy' were the Queen's speeches and so full of 'constitutional intent' her addresses.[10] She presented herself as the 'First Lady of the nation' with a specific and unique role to perform. Only forty-four per cent of the population were of British stock, and besides the 5,000,000 French-speaking Canadians there were growing numbers of Germans, Dutch, Ukrainians and Poles out West, Italians in the cities. The Queen seemed to admit that her sovereignty of Quebec was in doubt by overflying the region four times during the tour; indeed she had not toured Quebec since the demonstrations of 1964. Other signs that she would need all her force of character to maintain the Canadian monarchy were provided in various areas: the republican press dwelt on the expense of her tour; a vote of congratulation on Princess Anne's engagement was blocked in the Federal Parliament. Britain's entry into the Common Market was also a focal point for criticism; and, since Trudeau's political power had diminished, he was labelled an opportunist and 'instant monarchist'.

Nevertheless, the Queen's case as unifier was strengthened as well as weakened by outside events: the Watergate scandal suggested that a constitutional monarch may be a more principled head of state than a president; the very medley of ethnic strains required a historic figurehead; the Quebec Liberation Front had weakened somewhat since 1964; America's influence on nascent Canadian patriotism sometimes seemed too powerful, and at least Elizabeth II spelt behaviour with a 'u'. (John Muggeridge had written in 1971, 'At a "Keep-it-Canadian" teach-in the other day a political scientist proclaimed that whenever a Canadian spelled behaviour with a "u" he is helping to preserve his national identity.')

It was with justification that the Queen, wherever she went, predicted no end to her opportunities for service and pledged herself to carry on 'for my lifetime'.

The Governor-General who resided at Rideau Hall in 1973 was a gentleman of whom no reports, good or evil, travelled around the world. Two years later in Australia, however, the name of the Queen's Governor-General, Sir John Kerr, was to appear on every ticker-tape and to give a prodigious stir to the controversy between monarchists and republicans.

The story began when the Australian Labour Party, led by Gough Whitlam, won a general election on 2 December 1972. Unfortunately the original constitution of January 1901 had not been revised when the British House of Lords was reformed in 1911. Whereas the Lords were henceforth forbidden to interfere with the House of Commons over money bills, the Australian Senate, admittedly elected, was still empowered to thwart the will of their House of Representatives – which it did in 1975, threatening to cut off the Government's money supply. Kerr broke the deadlock by dismissing Whitlam on 11 November, appointing the Liberal Malcolm Fraser 'caretaker' and counting on him to win the election in 1976 – which he did. A 'cold civil war' erupted between those who were pro- and anti-Kerr, into which the Queen's majesty was dragged.

Hitherto Whitlam and the Labour leaders had been only 'long-term republicans', as it were; they thought an Australian republic would be declared in their children's time but not before. On his election, when Whitlam was asked by a British journalist whether he expected the Queen to remain Queen of Australia during his own lifetime, he answered 'Yes'. But after the *coup* of 11 November the tempo changed. (Among the older Australians the irony of the date – 11 November – did not go unnoticed. It was Armistice Day, when hostilities had ceased in an earlier war.) Kerr was denounced by the extreme Left as an agent of worldwide reaction, despite his appointment having been recommended to the Queen by Whitlam himself.

The London *Times*, in its alarm at the impetus given to republicanism, suggested that Kerr should be superseded by Prince Charles – truly a way of throwing the heir apparent in at the deep end. Elizabeth II received hundreds of letters asking her to dismiss Kerr, as Kerr had dismissed Whitlam; to all of which she replied that she was constitutionally precluded from 'interfering with His Excellency's tenure of office except upon the advice from the Australian Prime Minister' – and that prime minister was then Malcolm Fraser.

The author of a republican essay in a 'Penguin Special', *The Queen* (1977), prophesied that Australia would be a republic 'within ten years'.[11] At the time of writing that leaves only a few more years for Elizabeth II to remain Queen of Australia. Yet the signs are that provided she is not made a reluctant pawn in the party political game – always her blackest nightmare – Australia will find ways of establishing 'national identity' other than by electing a head of state from among the ex-party politicians. The new national anthem, for instance, chosen in place of 'God Save the Queen', has given some satisfaction; though there are Australians who prefer 'Waltzing Matilda' to the authorised 'Advance Australia Fair'. (The aggressive second verse of 'God Save the Queen' had itself been submitted to the cosmetic surgery of Lambeth Palace in the reign of George VI and the new second verse ran: 'Nor on this lane alone/But be God's mercies shown/From shore to shore/Lord, make the nations see/That men should brothers be/And form one family/The wide world o'er.') Perhaps the happiest thought lay in the Queen's popularity. Even the majority of republicans did not criticise her personally, conceding that she was 'hard-working and well-meaning'.

But that is to throw her into the shallow end, and keep her there. She wants more than that; to be a unifying head of the six Australian states, a romance to those of British stock and the symbol of one language, one law, one democratic rule to the ethnic immigrants.

It may be argued that the two 'Governor-General incidents' occurring at the beginning and end of a fifty-year period (1925 and 1975; the earlier occasion involving Canada and Governor-General Viscount Byng) were two too many. Should not the office be abolished? But that is to forget the unique information that the Queen obtains from these sources. Whereas ambassadors and high commissioners report to the Foreign Office as well as to the Queen, governors-general report back to her alone. 'The Crown gets its knowledge of what has been going on in the Commonwealth from the Governors-General, which the Prime Minister and Cabinet don't get. The Monarch has the opportunity of meeting on a wider basis members of the Commonwealth than the Prime Minister and members of the Cabinet,' says Edward Heath.[12] That is a major asset in her 'accumulation of experience'.

The premiership of Edward Heath will always be remembered for Britain's entry into the European Economic Community. At the time of Whitlam's election victory in 1972, the Australian people were said to have been 'bruised by the attempts of successive British Governments to enter the Common Market'.[13] The next year the attempt became achievement and presumably the 'bruised' Australian peoples – not to mention Canadians and New Zealanders – now felt battered. How did this change affect the Queen's work?

With her ardent devotion to the Commonwealth she probably could not be credited at first with more than ambivalent feelings. Harold Macmillan's well-informed biographer, Anthony Sampson, has stated forthrightly the effect on the Commonwealth of Macmillan's 1960s decision in favour of the Common Market. 'The negotiations, and the new climate they produced,' writes Sampson, 'turned Britain more firmly towards Europe; and the Commonwealth never loomed so large again.' Professor Mansergh confirms this, dating the Commonwealth's 'climax' from *before* Britain's entry into the EEC and the Commonwealth's 'disenchantment' from *after* Britain's entry.[14] Said *The Times*, 'Certainly Britain's entry into EEC will change both it and the Commonwealth.' The Queen cannot have particularly welcomed all this. Hugh Gaitskell had called it 'the end of a thousand years of British history'. A thousand years. That was also the lifespan of the British monarchy up to date. Was the monarchy also to be borne away on a rolling stream of change?

In her Christmas message of 1972, the Queen personally put the best possible face on the forthcoming economic alliance:

> The new links with Europe will not replace those with the Commonwealth [she said]. They cannot alter our historical and personal attachments with kinsmen and friends overseas. Old friends will not be lost; Britain will take her Commonwealth links into Europe with her.

There is a note of mingled nostalgia and defiance in those moving words. Indeed, the coincident dates of the Queen's Ottawa Conference and Heath's Common Market entry – both 1973 – were surely not unconnected. She was not going to miss a chance of putting the Commonwealth back in the headlines. Elizabeth II was none the less the spokes-woman for her government. Every public word she utters, it has been said, is put into her mouth by ministers. Even if that allows for some exaggeration – ministers will not inspire her views on vegetable marrows at the local harvest festival, for instance – the basic argument is correct. On a grave subject like the Common Market her spoken thoughts must be theirs.

But even here the ground is not quite firm. Illogically, a government that makes her utter controversial matter may be criticised by the Opposition, though everybody is supposed to know that the inflammable opinions are not the Queen's own. Peter Shore the Labour politician berated a Tory government in October 1972 for concocting a speech in which the Queen was made to congratulate President Heinemann of West Germany on the Common Market as 'a great achievement'. Shore advanced the view that the Queen must not be advised by her ministers to voice sentiments of 'acute controversy'. Yet every Queen's

Speech at the opening of Parliament is a nest of partisan vipers to the Opposition. It seems that the Queen's Speeches must not be used to give a neutral veneer to debatable issues. Her Speech from the Throne, however, makes no pretence of impartiality. It is simply an exercise in ministerial ventriloquism.

Three months after Shore's attack, the Queen and Prince Philip were booed by 300 young demonstrators when they arrived with Mr Heath at Covent Garden's opera house to celebrate Britain's joining the Common Market. The *Guardian* thought they 'seemed momentarily shaken' by the shouts of '*Sieg heil!*' though the Queen smiled and waved at the demonstrators as she left the opera house later. This time she was prepared.

Ten years afterwards, Edward Heath was asked whether Britain's entry into Europe could ever have any effect on the future prospects of the monarchy. Edward Heath is a strong royalist, a fact which bears on his reply:

> I see no reason why it should diminish the position of the monarchy. In so far as the monarchy itself depends on its own experience of life and events, both national and international, and as the monarchy has been in touch with European events during the period of the reign, then the monarchy can contribute more of its knowledge of Europe than it has done in the past. There would be an amplification of what it has always been doing.

In answer to a second question, as to whether the monarchy's continental relationships could help in this connection, Mr Heath said:

> It could work both ways. The fact that the Royal Family as a whole is in contact with a large number of the royal families of Europe could be helpful; provided the European royal families are really in touch with opinion in their own countries. If they are out of touch and out of date, then it could work the other way.[15]

Perhaps the best hope lies in a kind of royal 'natural selection', by which only those European families in fact survive or revive that are in touch and up to date.

The pace and scope of the Queen's work depends a good deal on the Prime Minister who occupies No. 10. In Edward Heath's perceptive words to the author:

> I don't think the royal prerogative 'to be consulted, to encourage and to warn' has lapsed, no. I think it depends on a Prime Minister how much he makes use of it, and encourages it himself. It has not lapsed at all – though there has been I suppose a narrowing down of the powers of the monarchy – the developments in the selection of party leaders, and so on.
>
> I believed in telling the Queen everything. There was always an agenda drawn up in agreement with the private secretary. She had it on a card on the table beside her to make sure that the items were covered, but I believed in telling her a good deal else of what was going on, which I hadn't mentioned to the private secretary, because I knew she would be interested. The discussion is always tête-à-tête, no notes taken. I don't know whether she writes it in a diary afterwards or not – short notes perhaps. No formal 'minutes' as it were. She talks about her own visits and what she has observed herself there. Reactions of different people. She gives you a lead.

Going back to her right to 'warn' and 'encourage' – does the Queen often say, 'I advise you not to do so-and-so?' Mr Heath replied, 'I don't think so today, no.' But he was emphatic on the 'encouragement.' 'The fact that she has all these years of experience, and is imperturbable, is a source of encouragement in itself.'[16]

What Edward Heath says about his own audiences probably goes to some extent for all four of the Queen's later prime ministers, though each would have had points of special contact which she would have been quick to develop. Edward Heath's music, carol-singing and sailing would appeal to more than one member of the Royal Family; and they would know that he had been brought up in an intensely royalist family of his own.

As a woman in her fifties, sometimes enlivened, sometimes beset with inevitable family problems, the Queen would have found reassurance and response in the avuncular figure of James Callaghan, somewhat older than herself; while Margaret Thatcher would form with her a duo working as remorselessly and unremittingly as only two women know how.

It is often suggested that the Queen got on best of all with Harold Wilson. Certainly they enjoyed one another's company, as Richard Crossman remarked in 1966: 'he's devoted to the Queen and is very proud that she likes his visits to her.'[17] Comparisons apart, Wilson has described in detail how he always looked forward to the annual weekend visit to Balmoral: the unusually relaxed atmosphere, the Queen's skill in cooking a perfect steak on an electrical barbecue after driving her prime minister out to one of the estate cottages in a shooting-brake. (There were no detectives around until after the kidnapping attempt on Princess Anne.) Wilson's wife Mary was to reflect the Queen's charm as an unshackled countrywoman in her Silver Jubilee poem:

> She notes a crumbling wall, an open gate;
> With countrywoman's eyes she views the scene;
> Yet, walking free upon her own estate –
> Still in her solitude, she is the Queen.

Another part of the royal ambience that Harold Wilson particularly liked was the appointment of bishops and clergy in the Church of England of which the Queen is head. It is the prime minister's duty to make recommendations to Her Majesty and Wilson looked forward to dealing with 'modest files' each weekend on this subject. Harold Macmillan used to lament that the Archbishop of Canterbury of his day, Dr Fisher, with whom he longed to hold pleasant religious colloquies, always 'reverted to politics'.[18] Harold Wilson was luckier. He found his ecclesiastical duties a peaceful oasis in the desert that most prime ministers inexorably make of their garden.

Wilson's sensitive feeling for the Queen's rights is well illustrated by the manner in which he left the premiership in 1976. First he warned the Queen's private secretary at Balmoral in September 1975 that he would resign six months later. Then he told the Queen at his weekly audience on 9 December that it would be on 11 March. Admittedly this well-documented resignation was intended to refute rumours that he had every sort of terminal illness – rumours which arose notwithstanding. One feels, however, that Wilson also wished to avoid giving the Queen the same sort of surprise as he was to give his Cabinet in March 1976.

There was a farewell dinner at 10 Downing Street on the 23rd, attended by the Queen, Prince Philip, the Cabinet and the Wilson family and friends. 'It was a happy and informal occasion,' wrote Wilson, jubilantly noting that though the Queen's car had been called for 10.30 she did not leave until a quarter to twelve.[19] He finally resigned on 29 March, pointing out with satisfaction that he had neither advised the Queen whom she should send for in his place, nor would the Queen have been obliged to accept his advice had she asked for it. (So the textbooks were mostly wrong.) All he did was to say that she already had the voting figures, which showed that Mr Callaghan had been elected leader of the Parliamentary Labour Party. Thus was the royal prerogative to appoint the prime minister preserved by Harold Wilson as far as possible.

James Callaghan was to hold the premiership for three years, until 1979. His memories of what he had been able to give the Queen, and she him, in no way conflicted with his prime ministerial colleagues' and yet were subtly different. He had no delusions but a mature philosophy. Of his audiences with the Queen he recalled:

I used to be 1 to 1½ hours, never less than 1 hour, unless both had dinner engagements – evening audiences always – no drink – that was the rule apparently – all treated the same. But each thinks he is treated in a much more friendly way than the one before! Though I'm sure that's not true. The Queen is more even-handed. What one gets is friendliness but not friendship.[20]

Queen Victoria could have explained that last strange but real fact about the Royal Family. It is part of the ethos that they cannot make friendships except with those of their own kind. (There are rare exceptions.) Yet such is their friendliness and perfection of good manners that those whom they meet come away with the agreeable illusion that an exotic new friendship has been formed.

Callaghan continued:

One gets a great deal of friendliness. And Prime Ministers also get a great deal of understanding of their problems – without the Queen sharing them, since she is outside politics. I think she weighs them up, but doesn't often offer advice. She listens. Of course she may have hinted at things, but only on the rarest occasions do I remember her ever saying, 'Why don't you do this, that or the other?' She is pretty detached on all that. But she's very interested in the political side – who's going up and who's going down. But not so passionate about MLR [Minimum Lending Rate]!

Asked further about her concern for domestic politics, Callaghan saw it in two ways:

The Queen has a deep sense of duty and responsibility in this area, and also sees it as a means of preserving the Royal Family institution. If her Prime Minister liked to give the Queen information and gossip about certain political characters, she would listen very attentively, for she has a real understanding of the value of a constitutional monarchy. I think she is absolutely right to be on the alert. I think the prestige of the monarchy could deteriorate if she didn't work so hard at it. Every monarch makes his or her own niche in people's minds and hearts, and this Queen has done that.[21]

Like everyone else who has served the Queen, Callaghan was struck by her attachment to the Commonwealth and knowledge of its chief figures. As a former shadow colonial secretary himself, he had known men like Nyerere, Kaunda and Kenyatta from their early days, but the Queen knows the whole range of Commonwealth first ministers better than any politician does, because she is so widely travelled.

On the subject of audiences, Callaghan was at pains to explain how informality would keep breaking in. No doubt, in theory every audience was carefully planned by the Queen's private secretary, Philip Moore, and Callaghan's opposite number Ken Stowe. At some point the Prime Minister might say to the Queen, 'Oh, I've got a topic to mention to you,' and they would both bring out their little cards, hers from her handbag, his from his pocket, on which three subjects for discussion would be typed each week. They might plunge into these topics for ten to fifteen minutes; the discussion being divided fifty-fifty or forty-sixty between the Queen and her prime minister.

Did she ever catch out Callaghan as she did Harold Wilson? Callaghan takes a more matter-of-fact view of all those telegrams they both read. She knows and he knows that neither can read every single one, 'but she never misses anything of importance'.

Most of the audience, however, could well be occupied with informal conversation about family or farming – how expensive hay was, or how silage was doing. (Callaghan has a farm in Sussex.) The informality would be greater at Windsor or Balmoral where the Queen's room was part of a family home, filled with photographs and all the things she has been dealing with that day. At Buckingham Palace it was 'more of a state room'. But even at Buckingham Palace informality would break out; Callaghan has been known to spend the greater part of an audience walking round the gardens with Her Majestry on a fine summer evening.

One last point about this most conscientious of monarchs. 'All her experiences are received,' says Callaghan. 'She has very little direct experience except in one field – horse-racing and breeding. She will tell you very frequently what somebody else has said to her about something; that is her means of judgment. She can't form her own judgment direct.'

But if her judgment on political problems and situations is 'received', her assessment of the monarchy at any given moment is intuitive, in her bones. 'She really knows about preserving the monarchy and about how to conduct herself on public occasions. When to step into the limelight and when to step out. She really is professional in her approach,' he adds fervently, 'and I admire her, and am very fond of her.'[22]

A professional, like everyone else, must put in a bill for expenses. Yet this simple fact can be relied on to provoke more excitement in Parliament, the media, the press, the student common rooms and campuses than almost any other similar event. The Queen's Civil List has involved two recent prime ministers in debates and legislation. It enabled her principal private secretary of the time, Michael Adeane, to put to use his historical skills by writing a classical analysis of her 'Life and Activities', which he presented to the Select Committee on the Civil List, 1971; he marginally up-dated it in 1981. (Lord Adeane got a First in History at Cambridge.) It has brought her principal opponent William Hamilton MP to fame and moderate fortune through his books, articles, radio and television programmes. He might be called a grace-and-favour republican or, in Harold Wilson's phrase, 'a benefitee of royalty'.

The first financial crisis of the reign broke in November 1969, thanks to an outspoken interview given by Prince Philip on the American *Meet the Press* TV programme. The Royal Family, he said, would 'go into the red' next year, not through bad housekeeping but a stagnant Civil List. Despite inflation, the Queen's allowance of £475,000 had not been raised for seventeen years – since her accession. On a following programme Prince Philip added with his usual flair for amusing the public, 'We may have to move into smaller premises.' Prince Philip has often acted as the Devil's Advocate Royal, putting up a case which needs making, though it would be unseemly on the Queen's own lips.

The impact of the American programme, reported in Britain, was immense. A countrywide sensation resulted. Wilson, addressing a packed House of Commons, promised to set up a Select Committee on the Civil List, having admitted that the royal reserves had run out and debts begun to accumulate in 1962. They had increased every year since. Indeed the Queen's 'annual grant' was now far short of outgoings, and by the end of 1970 'the Civil List over the reign as a whole would be in deficit'.

The Select Committee was set up in May 1971 by Edward Heath and reported at the end of the year. In 1972 a new Act of Parliament raised the Civil List to £980,000 (inflation pushed it up in 1979 to £3,317,000 and in 1982 to £4.2 million) and it was restructured in various ways. For instance, the Queen's Privy Purse became really private, instead of making certain confusing contributions to public expenses; while instead of the Queen having to apply dramatically to Parliament at irregular intervals, the Civil List would be adjusted annually and submitted to Parliament like any other department's budget. Meanwhile certain issues arose and were publicly argued which were to leave the problem of royal finances scarred for life – or, as others said, clarified and improved.

To begin with, what was the Civil List? From Harold Wilson's speech on 11 November 1969, it should have been crystal clear that it was a 'grant' or 'allowance' to cover the Queen's expenses as head of the state; in no way a 'wage' or 'pay' for her services. Yet those who should have known better, the press and television, for instance, mistakenly talked of the Queen asking for a 'pay-rise'. A left-wing journal like the *New Statesman* could be culpably misleading. In an article by R. H. S. Crossman entitled 'The Royal Tax-Avoiders', it not only made false references to the Queen's enormous 'pay-claim' and 'take-home cash' but also stated that the Queen's 'racing stables and polo ponies', not to mention yachts (in the plural), were 'kept going at full blast, at public expense'.[23] In fact, as every journalist knew, Prince Philip's private yacht *Bloodhound* had been run at his own expense and was now disposed of in order to economise, while the whole of the royal riding and racing establishments were paid for out of the Queen's private fortune.

Such misrepresentation, with its political animus, continued to stir up sporadic anti-royalism for many years afterwards. What was intended to be 'a peaceful disruption' of the Queen's visit to Stirling University because of its cost, turned into a demonstration in which the students took their bottles out of their mouths only to shout, 'Queen out!' They apologised afterwards for what was merely 'a typical boozy Glasgow party' and seemed to have admired the Queen's sang-froid. But it would not have happened at all without the stimulus of the Civil List fracas. As far afield as Washington DC, where a congressman wildly accused the United States Government of subsidising the Queen ('It is the American taxpayer who is getting crowned') and Vancouver, where the president of the students' union of British Columbia University attacked her in the *Vancouver Sun*, the knives were out against an 'extravagant' monarchy.

Even Michael Adeane's convincing evidence before the Select Committee was used against her. He had written of the 'burden' imposed by the great increase in her work – her accessibility, her mobility, the 200 letters on an average that reached her every day, the absence of any complete holiday or pensionable age. All this she undertook 'willingly', but it 'took its toll'.[24]

Then why, wrote an eager correspondent to the *Manchester Evening News*, does she not abdicate?

Harold Wilson's need to raise the Queen's grant again during his second administration gave Willie Hamilton MP another chance. Though the second reading was carried, despite Hamilton's eloquence, by 247 votes to sixteen and all the amendments to the Committee Stage defeated in under an hour, Hamilton took the opportunity to bring out his book *My Queen and I*; from his point of view a success. Three or four years later, when the Queen Mother was approaching eighty and the unfortunate Princess Margaret was ill and divorced, Hamilton declared it 'obscene' to spend £92,000 on the 'old lady', while Princess Margaret's allowance should be cut off altogether and used to support the Elizabeth Garrett Anderson Hospital. Hamilton's motion was defeated by 148 votes to 34 votes. He had made a gross tactical error in insulting the beloved Queen Mother.

Those who could answer back on the Queen's behalf did so. First there were the comparisons showing up the monarchy in a favourable light: comparisons with the cost of tranquillisers on the National Health, the opera at Covent Garden, the embassies, the American presidency (in which election and convention expenses should be counted), the Dutch and Scandinavian monarchies which were no cheaper in relation to their populations.

Then there were the romantic loyalists who wrote letters to the papers ending with words like, 'a replacement for the Queen and Royal Family? Never! For ever and ever. Amen.'

But the majority were those who were proud of their glamorous monarchy and did not believe that its lifestyle was extravagant. Prince Philip's modern ideas at Sandringham and Balmoral were approved of: the growing of blackcurrants and carrots for the market, the selling of pot-plants and tea-towels on open days.

Moreover many people were surprised to learn that most of the Queen's outlay went on staff wages, negotiated for the Royal Household by the Civil Service unions. People didn't want the ermine and velvet to be put away in mothballs as during the war. They didn't want royal economies to become sordid. Emanuel ('Manny') Shinwell, the veteran socialist, said, 'We can't have them going around in rags.' His slyly humorous voice was the perfect antidote to Hamilton's.

But even when this argument was won, there was a more subtle weapon at hand to confuse and change the issue.

The new argument turned on the fact that the Queen does not pay income tax, surtax or death duties. Prince Charles virtually taxes himself by handing back to the Treasury a proportion of his revenue from the Duchy of Cornwall, as does the Queen from the Duchy of Lancaster. (The rest of the Royal Family pay all normal taxes.) Hence the *New Statesman*'s slogan 'The Royal Tax-Avoiders'.

The tone was faintly venomous. But, without any venom, a number of Labour MPs, some of them on the Select Committee of 1971, advocated radical reform of the royal finances. In the interests of 'law and order' it was argued that the Queen should live within the ordinary laws of the land like everyone else, declare her private income to the taxman, pay her taxes to the Treasury – and receive whatever expense allowance was necessary for the job she did. Furthermore, the Palace should be tidily turned into a department of state, like the Ministry of the Environment or Defence, to be known as the Crown Department. The old system would be swept away.

Incidentally, the Select Committee had gone out of its way to report that rumours about the Queen's private fortune were totally unrealistic. Her visible treasures, such as the royal palaces, crown jewels, pictures and furniture, porcelain and plate, are all 'vested in the Sovereign and cannot be alienated' – in other words they are held in trust for the nation – while suggestions that 'the Queen owns private funds which may now run into £50 millions or more' are 'wildly exaggerated'.

Michael Stewart, who alone with Harold Wilson took the line of reform, defended his view in Parliament:

> I am not talking about the size of the [Queen's] bill. I am saying that immunity from tax exposes the Monarchy to unnecessary criticism . . . that this way of paying for the Monarchy by granting an inadequate Civil List, because the Queen does not have to pay income tax, is slovenly and an undignified way of going about the matter.

Asked about his views by the author ten years later, Lord Stewart maintained them, but perhaps with less fervour.

'What I dislike,' he repeated, 'was that we were asked to vote sums of money which obviously weren't enough and yet the Queen was able to make both ends meet – because she doesn't have to pay income tax. All these people she helps which aren't written down – Grace and Favour residences – this seemed to me a great muddle. . . . I had a feeling we ought to know definitely what is the total amount she gets from the public via Civil List or via not paying income tax. . . . If she paid income tax like everybody else we could then say, "We don't consider her private income at all when we decide what we give her for being Queen, any more than we consider whether a prime minister has a private income in settling his salary. Give her a proper salary, even on a lavish side, as there is no point in having a monarchy and stinting it. That would let us know where we are." '

'You don't think she should pay death duties, presumably?'

'I don't see why she shouldn't on her private income.'

'Then within a generation there would be a great danger of the historic royal houses being dispersed. What Prince Philip said in America about "moving into smaller premises" might really come true. Oil sheiks at Balmoral and Sandringham. . . . One quite appreciates your disliking the kind of muddled, vague mist which flows over the fringes of the whole affair. But should there not be some more overwhelming argument than tidiness, before one begins trying to improve, straighten out, rationalize an almost intangible thing like monarchy?'

'I must say it isn't something I would go to the stake on. . . .'[25] Nor, perhaps, even to the hustings.

The Queen has been lucky in her prime ministers during the 1970s, as she was in previous decades. All have been monarchists, though of different persuasions, none touched with what may be called Bennism.

The advent of Tony Benn to the premiership would probably mean that there had already been a fall in the royalist poll, which is said to be stable at around 70 to 75 per cent, though at the time of the Royal Wedding in 1981 it rose to 86 per cent. Harold Wilson told the author in 1980, 'Tony will never be leader. We should have to select someone the Queen could send for.' By 'we' he meant the Labour MPs. But since then the Labour leader has been chosen by an electoral college, in which MPs have only a minority vote.

By the end of the decade, however, the victorious Conservatives presented the Queen with something quite new and original in the way of premiers. Margaret Thatcher, the first woman ever to hold the office, came from the same kind of social background as Edward Heath, working her way from grammar school to Oxford University on a scholarship. Both were brought up in ardently royalist homes. But there the likeness ends. Whereas Mr Heath's feelings are as cool in expression as they are fervent within himself, Mrs Thatcher sees no reason to put a curb on her enthusiasms.

Not that the Queen and her prime minister have all their enthusiasms in common. Mrs Thatcher has a passionate interest, rare in the leaders of this country, in science and technology. She will spend five hours instead of the appointed two or three going round a computer factory and asking questions which show that she understands what is being said. This interest the Queen does not share. But they both love music and their families, and have total dedication to the work in hand. A *Times* expert on the monarchy, Alan Hamilton, once asked the author 'whether the fact that they are both women, and in some ways similar, might create friction?' A rumour about 'friction' seems to be going around, for Anthony Sampson in his *The Changing Anatomy of Britain* has recently written: 'The weekly meetings between the Queen and Mrs Thatcher – both of the same age – are dreaded by at least one of them.' He adds that the Queen is more 'matter of fact' and the Prime

Minister 'more like a Queen'.[26] Yet it would be hard to imagine a royalist such as Margaret Thatcher 'dreading' a visit to the Queen, or the imperturbable and today self-confident Queen 'dreading' any political visitor – except perhaps General Amin, who fortunately cancelled.

If I were a visitor to Mars or another planet [says Margaret Thatcher with mounting enthusiasm] and had to set up a constitutional system which was best for the people, for their personal lives to develop in their own way yet to live together, the system which I would set up would be a constitutional monarchy – a monarchy, an hereditary monarchy, wonderfully trained, in duty and in leadership, which understands example, which is always there, which is above politics, for which the whole nation has an affection and which is a symbol of patriotism. The whole thing is that through government after government the monarch remains. And the succession is assured. There is no substitute for this continuing factor. It gives a nation stability and assurance.

King George v and Queen Mary – I remember the Jubilee in 1935. I remember the affection of the whole people for them, and I think it must have been a revelation to them as to how much they were loved. When you are loved you give back.

Then there was the family responsibility of the Abdication – then we had the wonderful King George vi – we were so lucky – Royal Christmas broadcasts which I can remember all my life, 'The Man who stood at the Gate of the Year'. When he became King, it was not only himself but the whole Royal Family that meant so much.

Then after King George vi died, the love and loyalty of the whole nation went to the Queen Mother – a feeling which no other nation has. When Lord Mountbatten was murdered – it was terrible. We again remembered the Queen's family.

A constitutional monarchy excels all other forms of government and I would wish to set it up, if I had to advise a new country. It is the point of cohesion for a nation. It is not only a symbol of unity, but you respect and admire the monarch as well.[27]

As it happened, during the seven years before Margaret Thatcher took over there had been a remarkable number of 'cohesive' royal events of the kind she describes.

Not all unifying events are happy ones as Mrs Thatcher indicated in her mention of the Abdication and the death of Lord Mountbatten. The death of Edward Duke of Windsor on 28 May 1972 was in this category. Relations with the Windsors had always been a strain for Elizabeth II. On both sides of the family, at Paris and Windsor, there were bitter feelings that could never be entirely eradicated. In that sense, perhaps, they are a real organic family not a mere symbol. When James Pope-Hennessy, biographer of Queen Mary, visited the Duke of Windsor he found him still smouldering over the Duchess's treatment. Her name throughout the Windsors' house-telephone book was '*Son Altesse Royale*', a title King George VI had denied her. 'They treated me very shabbily,' said the Duke.[28] On the other side, the Queen Mother could never forget the horror of Abdication week. 'That last family dinner party was too awful,' she said to a friend years later, shuddering at the memory of her husband's agonies. 'Thank goodness I had flu and couldn't go.'

George VI had also been wounded by his brother's apparent callousness when he first visited Buckingham Palace after the Abdication. 'He seems very well,' wrote the King in his diary, '& not a bit worried . . . as to his behaviour in 1936.' But Michael Bloch, in his *The Duke of Windsor's War*, explains that the Duke did not mention the Abdication because his friend and adviser, Walter Monckton, had warned him to avoid anything controversial.[29] Misunderstandings as well as mistakes were responsible for the family estrangement. It was for Elizabeth II to heal the wounds as far as might be.

She invited the Duke to have a permanent private office in Buckingham Palace which greatly pleased him, and he and his wife attended the unveiling of Queen Mary's memorial plaque in 1962. Later the Queen met them in

France as her uncle and aunt, figures detached from the unmentionable past. She visited the Duke a week before his death on 28 May 1972, and invited his widow to stay at Buckingham Palace for the royal funeral at Frogmore on 5 June. The Queen had telegraphed condolences to the Duchess on the death of 'my uncle' and ended with the words, 'I am so glad that I was able to see him in Paris ten days ago.' In due course the Duchess herself will be buried by her husband's side in the cemetery laid out lovingly by Queen Victoria for her mother, Prince Albert and herself. The Duchess's Frogmore resting-place will not seem appropriate to the Royal Family but it is a point of honour.

Meanwhile the press were tempted to use the 'small figure' of the frail Duchess to beat them with, as if they were somehow responsible for her fragility. And in the constituencies the battle between republicans and monarchists was fought over her husband's body. 'Now, with sickening hypocrisy,' said Ian Mikardo MP at a dinner at Burton-on-Trent, 'they [the Royal Family] are falling over themselves to show to the corpse the charity which they denied to the man.' He predicted that these events would prove to be the end of the court. In a generation's time, we should have 'quietly got rid of the monarchy in the same way and for the same reason as we got rid of the crinoline, public executions and covers on piano legs.' In other words, because he considered the monarchy extravagant, heartless and prudish.

A third of that 'generation' has already passed, and there are no signs that the majority agree with Mikardo.

There were two other tragic losses to the family in that decade: Prince William of Gloucester in 1973 from a flying accident and Earl Mountbatten of Burma in 1979 from terrorist action which also caused the death of one of his twin grandsons, his son-in-law's mother Lady Brabourne, and a young Irish boat boy. In a poignant tribute to his great-uncle ('I adored him'), Prince Charles said in Westminster Abbey, 'I still cannot believe that I am standing here delivering an address about a man who, to me, always seemed reassuringly indestructible.'

It was the family that was indestructible, and the buoyant spirit of Dickie Mountbatten had had its large share in creating that family's strength.

Two intimate family occasions of the 1970s were the Queen and Prince Philip's silver wedding on 20 November 1972, followed by their only daughter's marriage on 14 November 1973. Each was less of a state flourish than might have been expected. The thin gauze of privacy that partly veiled both occasions must be put down to the Queen's own instincts. Prince Philip specifically absented himself from his daughter's pre-wedding arrangements. 'As you know, we have a wedding next week,' he told a lunch meeting in Perth, Australia. 'My being here is the best possible arrangement for a happy family relationship!' When a daughter was about to be married, the best possible place for a father to be was 'out of the way'. Jocularity apart, the reins were in the women's hands. At the time, Princess Anne's wedding seemed to be focused above all on 'naturalness'. But this naturalness must be seen in the light of later developments. It was only one aspect of the Queen's more and more determined struggle to maintain the emphasis on the second of the two words, 'Royal *Family*'.

Viewers who watched Princess Anne and Captain Mark Phillips, her fiancé, talking together on television the evening before their wedding were pleasantly surprised to find them 'very natural'.

The Queen had been 'very natural', reported the dressmakers at work on Princess Anne's trousseau. 'Don't mind me,' she said as she visited the fitting-room one day. Then, examining a piece of material, she asked her daughter, 'Will it wash?' Another case of 'Don't mind me' is reported by Ann Morrow. 'Once the head stable girl at Windsor,' she writes, 'briskly ordered an idler in the yard to fetch a bucket of water. When she looked round she was horrified to see the Queen obediently trotting towards her with a brimming pail.'[30]

Very naturally Princess Anne and Mark Phillips resented fallacious criticism of their honeymoon on the *Britannia*. The yacht took them to the Caribbean, where it waited to pick up the Queen and Prince Philip and carry them to New Zealand and Australia in spring 1974 – there was no extra expense involved. There were also objections to the couple's future house, criticisms that would not have arisen but for Civil List debates the year before.

Their courtship and marriage were the natural outcome of a consuming interest in common – riding and especially eventing. Princess Anne had won the European Championship in 1971 on Doublet: a 'family' horse originally bred by her mother as a polo pony for her father, but grown 'fat', as Prince Philip joked, through over-loving care. A statuette of Princess Anne on Doublet occupies a place of honour on her mother's desk.

Mark had been competing and winning in horse trials since 1967 and was a member of the British Olympic team in 1972. Anne won at the Combined Championship at Hickstead in 1973, the summer before her wedding.

The wedding, the Queen was at pains to explain, was not a state function but a family one. She asked for a day's holiday for all the children in the land – and was duly criticised by a few parents for causing 'inconvenience' and implying that modern children did not enjoy school. To mark the attempted simplicity, no kings and queens were invited, only princes and princesses. Whereas George v's only daughter, Princess Mary, had been attended by outside bridesmaids including Lady Elizabeth Bowes-Lyon, Elizabeth II's only daughter chose just two attendants, both from the family – her brother Prince Edward and cousin Sarah Armstrong-Jones. In any case this outspoken bride didn't want 'hordes of uncontrollable children'. She has been described as 'the Princess with a style for the times'.

Even so, the Sovereign's and Captain's Escorts, the sixteen trumpeters, the military bands, the Scottish State Coach and Glass Coach all reassured the cheering crowds that this wedding, if not a state one, was royal as well as 'family'. As one young man in the crowd was heard to say, 'It makes you feel proud of them and us.'

The Queen's silver wedding celebrations of the year before had also stressed the family wherever possible, though it was more difficult to avoid pomp and circumstance. Some people close to her believed she would secretly have preferred to celebrate entirely within the family, and she settled for a homely atmosphere, with smiles, wit and a walkabout.

She and Prince Philip entered Westminster Abbey smiling at each other. They had chosen the Abbey because they had been married there, though St Paul's would have held more people and perhaps generated more solemnity beneath its dome. At her accession Elizabeth II had been instructed, it was said, not to smile too much; to learn to look dignified. She had begun to unlearn that lesson where required. But one still had to be careful. Two good ladies had once seen her smiling as she came out of church. 'She ought to look serious,' they said.

A Guildhall luncheon or dinner was usually no joke. Everything would be in tune with the City's dignity. But on her silver wedding anniversary the Queen went all out to make the gold chains jingle with laughter on the mayoral chests. 'I think everyone will concede that today, of all occasions,' she said smiling widely herself, 'I should begin my speech with "My husband and I".' The Queen's hitherto sedate tone in delivering this royal cliché had been mercilessly mocked in the past; now the unexpected spice of wit amused everybody. Her final tribute to the nation's families, one of which she and Philip had begun to create twenty-five years before, was pithy rather than sentimental. She quoted the bishop who, when asked what he thought about sin, replied simply, 'I am against it.' If they asked for her view of family life she would say equally simply, 'I am for it.'*

---

* The full story of the 'bishop' was as follows: President Coolidge was once asked about a sermon to which he had just listened. 'What was it all about?' 'Sin.' 'What did he say about it?' 'He was agin it.'

After the dignitaries, the people. From the Guildhall to the Barbican was no distance in space but miles in spirit. For an hour the Queen and Prince Philip pursued their walkabout, cracking simple jokes, being photographed by small box cameras. Michael Adeane had pointed out the year before that one of the 'burdens' of sovereignty was always being watched. He made the royalty-watchers sound a bit like Orwell's 'Big Brother'. But on this day all the big brothers belonged to the family.

These family events, the silver jubilee of the Queen's wedding and Princess Anne's marriage, played their part in delineating the acceptable face of monarchy. In a sense, however, the occasions were a prelude to a weightier event, the Silver Jubilee of 1977. After her daughter's wedding and her own silver wedding, Elizabeth II would strive even more resolutely not to lose the family graces from a busy reign. After the Jubilee she would see in clearer perspective what sort of Queen she really was.

Under Paul's Dome:
1977–81

Suddenly she stood out. Before the Silver Jubilee it had always been the Queen and the Duke of Edinburgh, or the Queen and her family. This was in fact what she herself wanted. But during the Jubilee something happened which pushed her, willy-nilly, into a place out front.

Some of her most ardent admirers wished that her unique position as *the Queen* could be even more emphasised. Hugo Vickers, the young administrator of the Great Children's Party in Hyde Park two years later, was one:

> Yes, I wish the Queen could be alone more often. She is so good when she is alone. I always thought at the Silver Jubilee it would have been an inspiration to make the Queen walk alone, with Prince Philip and Prince Charles behind her because, whatever anybody says, she is the Queen and all rests finally on her shoulders. Prince Philip is a help, but constitutionally he isn't involved. I know she wouldn't want that because she likes to be with him. But if I had been her adviser . . . though I probably wouldn't have got away with it, that's what I would have tried for.[1]

This is a romantic young man's view. However, there have always been a few occasions when Elizabeth II was forced to ride or walk alone, thus underlining her status as Queen Regnant.

For instance, as head of the fighting services, she stands in front, alone at the Cenotaph. At Trooping the Colour she used to ride on ahead of all, a symbolically lonely figure, unsmiling because she was a soldier on duty. (After the firing of blanks at her in 1981, the Queen was escorted by four of the Household Cavalry down the Mall and rode alone only on the parade ground.) Another occasion was the Garter ceremony the next year. The Duke of Edinburgh was called away at the last moment to represent Britain at the funeral of the Saudi Arabian king, so that the Queen had to sweep down the hill from the Waterloo Chamber to St George's Chapel with no consort by her side. She looked even more regal than usual, just as a solitary ship in full sail, driven before the wind, looks more spectacular than two together. That same year, 1982, Prince Philip was away when she opened Parliament. Usually he is present to hold her hand aloft as she walks to her throne. This time, with her hands folded in front, she became an impressive, lone queen.

John Grigg (the former Lord Altrincham), a shrewd observer of royalty, linked the Queen's new prominence with the Silver Jubilee, though he did not explain why.

> The Queen, moreover, [he wrote three days before Prince Philip's sixtieth birthday in 1981] is clearly far more effective and confident than in the early years of her reign, and there is no longer any question . . . of her husband's having to carry the show. The Silver Jubilee was celebrated very much as a tribute to *her*, with incidental compliments paid to him, rather than as a tribute to their *joint* achievement.[2]

This observation, though true, does not affect the Queen's own life-long zest for building up joint achievements with her people, her husband and her children. She expressed it once and for all in her coming-of-age dedication to service: 'I shall not have the strength to carry out this resolution alone, unless you join with me, as I now invite you to do.' In that sentence lay the key to her character as Queen. Her ideal has always been one of shared experience. She is not interested in shining alone, but has directed all her energies to fostering mutual efforts and responses between the Royal Family and the people.

The Jubilee of 1977 and its aftermath were to demonstrate her new prominence; but at the same time to show her willingness to slip out of the limelight in favour of her family whenever there was an appropriate occasion.

The tone was set by the Queen during her pre-Jubilee Christmas broadcast of 1976. It was unusually sensitive to external events and people's feelings about them. She wanted her Silver Jubilee year 'to become a special one for people who find themselves the victims of human conflict': Catholics and Protestants in Northern Ireland, neighbours at home of different race and colour. She praised the Peace Movement in Northern Ireland and those working for better community relations. Old enemies could after all be reconciled, she insisted, remembering her own visit to America that summer. She had joined with the Americans in their bicentenary celebrations of independence. 'Who would have thought 200 years ago that a descendant of King George III could have taken part in these celebrations?' There was a final broad hint that, far from wishing to mark 1977 with lavish expenditure, she hoped above all for intangible offerings. 'The gift I would most value next year is that reconciliation should be found wherever it is needed. . . .'

Among private sorrows was the irreconcilable parting of Princess Margaret and Lord Snowdon in 1976. The Queen was 'naturally very sad', announced her press secretary Ronald Allison. 'There has been no pressure from the Queen on either Princess Margaret or Lord Snowdon to take any particular course.' They were divorced in 1978.

Modern royalty, if it is at all sensitive, must always look forward to major celebrations with a whiff of trepidation as well as joy, and the Silver Jubilee did not fail to provoke its share of criticism despite the Queen's overt appeals for modest celebrations. At its best the criticism took the form of, 'Let us live simply that others may simply live.' At its most petty, every royal function, even the State Opening of Parliament, was seen in terms of traffic congestion and loss of production. 'How many man hours are lost in London every time she does it? Why can't she open Parliament at night?'

The usual ideas of reforming royal taxation were burlesqued good-naturedly in *Punch*'s Silver Jubilee volume entitled *Punch and the Monarchy*. 'Can our Queen stay tax-free much longer? and what could she claim as expenses?' The Tax Inspector, after visiting the Palace, queries her sending birthday telegrams to centenarians – 'and a further 98 queries'.

The Silver Jubilee tours abroad were further opportunities for humour: an imaginary 'Pacific Diary' kept by the Queen revealed that she loathed jubilee mugs ('What Philip calls one silly mug put on another'); the Duke's backchat resulted in an offer of their own television show; public indifference had been a danger, but as a result of Philip and of 'Mr Willie Hamilton stirring up feeling in my favour', that danger had receded.[3]

The actual Jubilee tours began on 10 February and lasted until the end of March, then began again on 14 October and finished on 2 November – the celebrations in Britain, plus a Silver Jubilee review of the army in Germany, filling up the months in between. A total of 56,000 miles of smiles. 'Have you ever tried smiling continuously for even twelve miles?' a member of the Queen's Household asked Henry Miller of the *Daily Telegraph* in Barbados. There were places where it was hard to smile, for other reasons than facial fatigue. The Queen saw and lamented the age-old poverty behind much of the fresh paint. She knew that some of the peoples she visited considered monarchy irrelevant but they respected her for facing up to them and their facts so tirelessly.

She left Barbados to make a record flight home of three hours forty-five minutes in Concorde – she was founder-member of a 'jet-set' which had nothing to do with luxury playgrounds. It had been an extremely demanding year and she would not wish such an itinerary on any other woman. Nevertheless, she had undoubtedly drawn inspiration from it; particularly from the response of ordinary people to her pleas for unity. Even those who did not profess allegiance to her as monarch were loyal to the ideals she and her family represented – freedom and fairness.

One other fact was significant. Whereas her grandfather had been visited by heads of state during his Silver Jubilee, she had gone out to meet the people.

If the volume of letters received at the Palace meant anything, she had touched the feelings of thousands. Her Jubilee year's achievements were praised by over 100,000 people. On one day alone, around the peak period of London's festivities, 3,500 people had written to wish her well.

At home it was the simplest events that best celebrated Elizabeth II's first twenty-five years: the spontaneous street parties all over the country or the chain of bonfires started at Windsor by a monarch in a headscarf. The thing that Lady Airlie had noticed in her as a girl of not quite sixteen was more true of her at fifty-one. 'Although she was perfectly simple, modest and unselfconscious, she gave the impression of great personality.'[4]

It was the 'great personality' that the nation required her to show during the more solemn events of her Jubilee. On 4 May both Houses of Parliament presented loyal addresses to her in Westminster Hall. Since a Labour prime minister, James Callaghan, held office, the verbal tributes to Her Majesty's triumph fell from democratic socialist lips. After a fanfare of trumpets, the mace was covered and Peter Shore MP joined the Lord Great Chamberlain in escorting Her Majesty and HRH Prince Philip to their seats. Two Welshmen, Lord Elwyn-Jones and George Thomas, read the Lords' and Commons' loyal addresses.

In offering her thanks, the Queen emphasised the 'Constitutional Monarchy', the Commonwealth evolved from Empire, all the changes and challenges of twenty-five years – 'and, of course, there has also been television!' (laughter). Britain's many advantages the Queen saw not in power but in 'the basic stability of our institutions, our traditions of public service and concern for others, our family life and, above all, the freedom you have through the ages so fearlessly upheld'. These advantages were all rooted in the past. As the newest and 'perhaps one of the most significant decisions during my reign', the Queen boldly cited 'joining the European Economic Communities'. These views must for once have been the Queen's own, for her ministers could hardly expect to advise her on how to render them thanks.

After her thanks the trumpets sounded again, she passed out of the north door and the Members of Parliament, judges, diplomats and their spouses departed from a historic building, completed in 1099, that had survived fires, floods and fire-bombs – and would see all these dignitaries out. Because of fire precautions there was no heating. Nevertheless, on this chilly May morning the women honoured their monarch by dispensing with warm coats.

Just over a month later the Queen, Prince Philip and the Royal Family attended the Silver Jubilee Thanksgiving Service at St Paul's. All the panoply of state was focused on the magnificent carriage procession from the Palace to the Cathedral: the Queen and the Duke of Edinburgh in the State Coach, followed by the Irish State Coach, Queen Alexandra's State Coach, the Glass Coach and the State Landau. A carriage procession of the Royal Family preceded the Queen's carriage procession. As the Queen left Temple Bar a royal salute was fired from the Tower.

Meanwhile the congregation had been moving decorously into their places since 9.15 am when the doors of the Cathedral were opened. No boisterous cheers for all and sundry from the massed crowds, as there would be for Prince Charles's wedding in four years' time. In the nave and under Wren's stupendous dome the interplay of cool daylight, golden chandeliers, television dazzle and irreducible vistas of shadow gave a feeling of dramatic mystery.

The Order of Service – plain white with narrow red borders and a small golden 'E II R' on the cover – announced the object of the day with no flourish of verbal trumpets.

A Form of Prayer and Thanksgiving to Almighty God commemorating the blessings granted to THE QUEEN'S MOST EXCELLENT MAJESTY during the Twenty-Five Years of Her Majesty's Reign. St Paul's Cathedral Tuesday 7 June 1977 at 11.30 a.m.

The themes were continuity with the monarchy's past and confidence in its present. One hymn tune had been composed by Vaughan Williams for Elizabeth II's coronation, and the music of the anthem had been composed by Parry for the coronation of her great-grandparents. It was a thanksgiving for the monarchy as well as for the Queen. The first lesson declared that a day would come when every man should sit under his own vine and under his figtree; the second lesson, that the house built upon a rock would not fall. There were Scottish and Welsh and English traditional melodies, and a prayer that Elizabeth should 'always possess the hearts of her people'. Two verses only of 'God Save the Queen' were sung – no reference to knavish tricks or confounded politics under Paul's dome.*

The Queen did indeed 'possess the hearts of her people' when, after the service, she walked from St Paul's to the Guildhall for luncheon instead of going by car. Later, the Queen and Prince Philip drove forth, east and west and south and north, all over London, like Lars Porsena's messengers – except that they were messengers of goodwill not war. Concentrating in this year on the large centres of population, they visited thirty-six counties. Monarchy can

---

* When a jubilee cross had been dedicated to Queen Elizabeth II at Southwark Cathedral on 27 May, the present author was asked to write a new second verse to the National Anthem. Harry Bramma, Director of Music at Southwark, was responsible for the arrangement, and the words paid due attention to the false rhymes of the seventeenth-century original: 'Bind us in amity/Into one family/Under our Queen./Prosper her Commonwealth/All in good heart and health,/Linked by Elizabeth/Symbol and Queen.'

sometimes be an excuse for slush and tosh, but its special days and years are also traditionally the seed time for harvests that would otherwise go by default. Anything from nursing homes to dogs' homes had been laid at the feet of Queen Victoria. Elizabeth II's first twenty-five years were the occasion for Prince Charles to leave the Navy and head the Queen's Silver Jubilee Trust – 'to help the young to help others'.

By the time Jubilee year had run its course there was hardly a national sport, pastime, art or entertainment that had not been performed in honour of the Queen. Carnivals, youth festivals, ocean and river and cycling races, regattas, pop galas, steel bands, opera, concerts, plays; exhibitions of stamps, photographs, Fabergé, the Queen's Pictures; East End jubilees, even a Jubilee in celebration of other previous jubilees and so on *ad infinitum*.

There was another aspect of the Jubilee that involved the young. How far did the young understand the monarchy under which they lived? The Jubilee was a way to help the young to gain a better perception of their country, Britain. How necessary this was became clear after a piece of research among the boys of William Penn's (Junior) School, London. Asked what the Queen meant to them, their replies ranged from romantic royalist to embittered republican, but with little appreciation of her work. Though her 'representative' role was recognised in a loyal acrostic by young Ranjodh Singh, he surprisingly did not connect her with the Commonwealth: '*England* the queen repersants.'[5]

Paul Pitchley understood the respect due to her, explaining that if she came to dinner 'I would put some money in the meater so the lights would not go off half frow the dinner. . . .' He was well up in the idea of the Queen inspiring all sorts of improvements in the home and street: before her arrival he would do all the outstanding washing-up, sweep the floors, wash and paint inside and outside, make all the beds and tidy the bathroom.

Another essay entitled 'The Queen: Why I hate her' showed a significant mixture of prejudice and misunderstanding: 'I hate the Queen because she is a Snob who always goes around doing important things without a smile on her face. She always goes to meetings and always butts in on other people's Conversations.' So even walkabouts could be misunderstood?

But the most moving case of misapprehension surely came from Stephen Jones, who was struggling manfully to visualise the meaning of a monarch who reigned but did not rule. 'There she sits upon the throne. She does not rule over Britain in any way she just sits there every day. She just sits there every day not happily not sad just sitting there every day.'

These boys were too young to have learnt anything from the *Royal Family* film of 1969. But the *Royal Heritage* and *Queen's Garden* films of Jubilee year 1977 may have helped to break the sphinx-like spell for Stephen Jones.

Stephen, and all the other myriad Joneses, would see that *Royal Heritage*, officially 'The Story of Britain's Builders and Collectors', was very much the story of Elizabeth II herself. They would see the Queen enwrapped in archaic cocoons and at the same time bursting through into the light of a very modern day. At Holyroodhouse she was protected by a company of archers; at her coronation she had been protected by a bracelet worn by Charles II 'to embrace her with God's protection'. But at Windsor they would see the President of the Royal Academy, Sir Hugh Casson, redesigning rooms with contemporary furniture by Gordon Russell and a painting by the Australian Sidney Nolan, who was being introduced to Prince Philip. 'How did you get that squidgy, underwater effect?' asks Philip. 'With a windscreen wiper,' replies Noland. They would also see Prince Philip conducting the narrator, Huw Wheldon, past a dim corner. 'In this dark lobby are two pictures of mine,' says Philip. 'As it's dark, they can't be seen very well.' But in fact his bright colours and liberated technique, taught him by Edward Seago in Norfolk and the South Atlantic, light up the lobby remarkably.

They would see Queen Mary's Doll's House, presented to her in 1924 to show posterity how queens once lived, and furnished to taste. Kipling's poem 'If' was a favourite in her miniature library, and well it might be. 'If you can keep your head when all about you/Are losing theirs and blaming it on you.' She had to keep hers when George V, in one of his rages, was losing his head and being so rude that sometimes (as Lord Harewood recalls in his memoirs) the Queen, followed by her children, would rise from the dining-table and troop silently out of the room. They would contrast with this a domestic scene between Elizabeth II and her two-year-old grandson Peter Phillips in her own miniature house at Royal Lodge.

'Look in there first,' says the Queen firmly, as she stands at the door of the little house and Peter prepares to rush all over it. She is in a green suit with flat shoes and her handbag half open over her arm; he is in scarlet jeans. She directs him into the kitchen, where he gets a cup of tea 'for Granny'. Then, seeing the tiny grandfather clock, he opens the case and moves the hands, almost knocking it over. 'Careful, careful,' says his grandmother with an agonised look. 'Thank you,' smiling again when the clock settles. 'Is that the right time?' In close attendance is the 'custodian' of the house, the Queen's niece Lady Sarah Armstrong-Jones, an appropriate choice, for five years later Sarah will be librarian at Bedales School, wearing the official badge on her anorak. 'I love the library, for the peace and quiet you get there.'

The Queen and Peter leave the kitchen smiling conspiratorially at each other. He has succeeded in shutting the rolling-pin into the oven, to the applause of his grandmother. 'It's gone!'

Once upon a time the Joneses may have heard tell of 'a new Elizabethan age', to be ushered in by Elizabeth II's coronation. But *Royal Heritage* will have shown them that what she in fact brought about was a new 'Restoration' as

real as that of Charles II. The 'spirit of renewal' at the
Coronation meant a grand restoration of works of art.[6] A
portrait of King Henry VIII was not only cleaned but gar-
nished with a pair of his own hunting knives retrieved from
Italy and now laid out beneath it. The Department of the
Environment in collaboration with Sir Oliver Millar, Keeper of the Queen's Pictures, and Geoffrey de Bellaigue,
Surveyor of the Queen's Works of Art, started on their
mammoth task of cleaning and restoring anything from a
Van Dyck to a carved dragon, from suits of armour to
harpsichords.

King George V (but not George VI) had been against such
operations. Intensely possessive towards his pictures, he
felt that any changes, even cleaning, implied that his collection was not perfect. (In fact, the cleaning of a 'Rembrandt'
self-portrait showed that it was indeed imperfect, being a
forgery; but cleaning also showed that a hitherto question-
able self-portrait by Raphael – one of Prince Albert's treasures – was genuine.)

The contrast with George V's granddaughter was total.
Always receptive and 'advisable' – more so than any of her
predecessors – she had enhanced the royal collection by
the time of her Jubilee in three different areas: the private
apartments; the state rooms used for favoured visitors and
heads of state, and the state apartments open to the public.
Sir Oliver Millar wound up his book, *The Queen's Pictures*,
produced in Jubilee year, with the impressive words: 'More
and more people are enabled to enjoy more of the Queen's
pictures, and with fuller understanding than at any time in
their history.'[7] The new Queen's Gallery at Buckingham
Palace had already been mentioned. By 1977 there was a
small, reconstructed Holbein Room at Windsor, originally
set up by Prince Albert; in 1979 there was to be a new China
Museum, and in 1980 a new Museum of Old Master
drawings and watercolours. Every year something old becomes newly accessible, something new is added to the
total royal collection, and the Queen's policy of loans at
home and abroad is always being extended.

A Silver Jubilee train carried some of her royal works of art all across Australia. The Bahamas' gift of seashells appropriately hangs beside the family's swimming pool at Windsor below the terrace. Prince Charles, in the film, picks up a piece of Eskimo sculpture in the hall, revelling in its tactile qualities. 'That stone's got a musk ox or a bear inside.'

The Queen's personal possessions and those she holds in trust for the nation are not the only things to become more accessible in and after the Jubilee. She herself is more accessible. We Joneses see her in *Royal Heritage* exhibiting a glittering array of treasures with all the authority of a professional guide. 'You remember what I told you about that in the last room?' There is an air of assurance, of command. (Six years later, in Mexico, Anthony Carthew was to note that she chose to ride in the front of her touring car. Has she always secretly wanted to be a professional guide?) Information and anecdote are being poured out for our pleasure. The programme we have tuned into is entirely novel yet somehow familiar. Listen with Majesty.

That thought brings us back to the theme of this chapter: the effect of the Jubilee on the Queen's personality – not on her public image alone (though that too must change in correlation with her other changes) but in her individual self. Take for instance the film scene in the Royal Library at Windsor. There has been a dinner party for distinguished guests, Margaret Thatcher among others. Princess Margaret also is present, looking like a glowing seventeenth-century portrait, perfectly adapted to her surroundings. The Queen is simply dressed in buttercup yellow but she is every inch in charge. It is a tradition of the Royal Archives that she should show something appropriate to each of her guests after dinner. Sir Robin Mackworth-Young, the Royal Librarian and himself a musician, has found a manuscript of the ten-year-old Mozart for Mrs Thatcher, a bread roll dating from Queen Victoria's Diamond Jubilee for the manufacturer of Huntley & Palmer's biscuits, and for Bryan Forbes, the author, bookseller and film producer, a

Rowlandson cartoon of a bookshop. We have already had a glimpse of Prince Philip's private collection of cartoons, among them one of a letter marked OHMS arriving at the Palace. As he points it out, narrator Huw Wheldon smiles discreetly, that is, not too much.

The Queen is both smiling and serious as she entertains and instructs her guests. For she has come to terms at last with 'the smile', and it is no longer the enemy. During the next five years, between this anniversary and the thirtieth of her reign, she will show that she can afford to be as natural about the expression on her face as about the grey on her temples. When she smiles it will bubble from within herself like the voice of a natural singer; rather than coming from outside like someone trying to make music on a difficult instrument.

In a sense, the problem has been to stop living up to her wonderful mother. Elizabeth II has always known that she could never be Queen Elizabeth. She is too much her father's daughter. But with a smile as radiant as her mother's when it did appear, the difficulty was how not to switch it off, as if the money in schoolboy Paul Pitchley's 'meater' has suddenly run out. The answer was to let herself develop her natural firmness of character, give rein to the instinct to command, alongside which the smile might come – and often go – as seemed natural. It has been noticed that since the Jubilee she has issued all necessary orders with unusual decision. Never losing her temper like her grandfather or having a 'gnash' like her father, she will nevertheless put her foot down and say with all the insistence of Victoria herself: 'I will have that done.'

Yet one further link is necessary to attach the Queen's character to the Silver Jubilee. This time we must go back to George V looking for a resemblance rather than a contrast. 'I had no idea that I was so popular,' said the King after his Silver Jubilee. 'I am beginning to think they must really like me for myself.' But he did not live long enough for the new experience to work itself out in his character. His granddaughter was more fortunate. The manifest affection of her country and the Commonwealth broke down any remaining inhibitions, giving her the confidence to reign as the kind of queen nature had intended her to be.

When she was still a princess in her early twenties, the son of a bishop said: 'She's like a very healthy, sound, responsible prefect in a boarding school, marked out to be head girl.' A young woman might not dare or care to cultivate those qualities, even though they were natural to her. They sit exceedingly well on an experienced head of state.

The eightieth birthday of Queen Elizabeth the Queen Mother was the next event to be celebrated 'under Paul's dome'. The date, 4 August, was incongruously the same for her beginning in 1900 and the beginning of the First World War in 1914 – the one a bringer of so much happiness, the other the cause of untold misery. Yet it was while tending the wounded at Glamis that the young Elizabeth Bowes-Lyon first saw the need for what was to become her personal philosophy. As the congregation walked up the long nave of the Cathedral on 15 July 1980 (the date chosen for the service), and the television cameras swept in on behalf of those outside, a huge golden banner caught the eye. It was the prayer or acclamation of that inspired lady, Julian of Norwich: 'All shall be well, and all manner of things shall be well.'

In her family and with the people she knows and meets, Queen Elizabeth had helped to make those words come true. Prince Charles, her first and foremost grandchild, responded with a now famous panegyric:

> I can only admit from the very start that I am hopelessly biased and completely partisan. . . . Ever since I can remember my grandmother has been the most wonderful example of fun, laughter, warmth, infinite security. . . . For me she has always been one of those extraordinarily rare people whose touch can turn everything to gold. . . .[8]

The laughter that Charles put first of all was also the thing that came first to the minds of her daughters. When the birthday photograph of Queen Elizabeth and her two daughters was taken, Princess Margaret remembered: 'We three laughed all the time, even for that photograph. She could convulse us all with her imitations. There was that play, *Crown Matrimonial*, about the Abdication. I shall never forget her imitation of the actress imitating her!'

Her gift of mimicry was only part of a total gift for performance, which reached its height on that day of thanksgiving. Determined to make it entirely her mother's day, the Queen ordered the State Landau bringing Queen Elizabeth and Prince Charles to the Cathedral to occupy the place of honour in the procession – last. Arriving thus on the steps of St Paul's, Queen Elizabeth made the most of a dramatic moment. Instead of passing straight into the Cathedral, to progress up the nave beside the Queen, she halted, turned right round to face the enchanted crowd and waved with the grace and enthusiasm of a consummate actress who knew how to give her audience exactly what they wanted.

The address by Dr Runcie the Archbishop of Canterbury gave universal satisfaction: 'The Queen Mother has shown a human face,' he began. 'Royalty puts a human face on the operations of government.' After being ingeniously doctored by the press, his words have gone down to history as, 'The Queen Mother has shown the human face of Royalty.' It was indeed the most apt tribute to the woman who once said bitterly, in the days before television had brought royalty to the people, 'We are not supposed to be human.'

Only a year was to pass before another royal event came to ease the Queen's task – not by lightening the load of her work but by sharing the burden of her stardom. Her mother was a star in her own right, not just because she had once been Queen Consort and was now Queen Mother. Elizabeth II had not shown this particular quality, nor was it natural to her to strive for it. It was precisely as Queen, by being Queen, that she showed her star quality. The public loved this; but they wanted the other too. Now there arrived on the royal scene a teenage girl, Lady Diana Spencer, to shine in *her* own right. The occasional look of anxiety and strain began to pass from the Queen's face.

Prince Charles's future as a human being with a royal face was at last settled. There had been anxieties. Apart from his own admission to falling in and out of love 'on countless occasions' like a thirty-year-old teenager, there had always been enigmas and incongruities in his character. He wholeheartedly admired his mother for being, as he said, so 'wise and sensible'. But he also wanted to imitate his father's sharp-shooting, devil-may-care brilliance. As a young man of twenty-one, Prince Charles once confessed that he envied above all men of action and nothing would have given him more pleasure, had he been born a hundred years earlier, than to lead a cavalry charge. Since then polo, skiing, steeplechasing, diving, parachuting and commanding a minesweeper may or may not have been adequate substitutes for the vanished Light Brigade. Yet at the same time he is as sensitive as his mother, with layers of unexpressed feeling. When he speculated in *Royal Heritage* on what lay inside the Eskimo's stone – was it a musk ox or a bear? – one could not help asking, What lies inside *you*? His presence at the birth of his own son prompted a wonderful saying by this now fulfilled man. 'It is rather a grown-up thing, I found. Rather a shock to my system.'

The story of the young girl who made him grow up is now part of national legend, almost folklore. At least one fairy-tale seems to have woven itself into her life: the unconsidered youngest daughter who worked for her living in a Pimlico nursery school before winning the Prince. No one has made the mistake, however, of suggesting that Lady Diana's being a commoner was the crucial difference between herself and the Royal Family. In fact she and Prince Charles share the same blood, through King James I. Moreover Diana was descended five times from King Charles II: twice from Lucy Walter, twice from Louise de

Kéroualle and once from Barbara Villiers. No wonder the press with one voice called her pedigree 'impeccable', despite those peccadilloes of long ago.

No, the crucial difference between Prince Charles's mother and his future wife lay in their experience of childhood. Queen Elizabeth II grew up within an unbreakable family circle, a blessing she handed on to her own family. The future Queen Diana experienced the hazards of a broken home at the age of six. Yet she never failed to inspire and return affection, despite the experts' gloomy psyche-scans about the victims of broken homes. Her father, the 8th Earl Spencer, was tireless in singing his youngest daughter's praises on television; her mother, the Hon. Mrs Shand Kydd, had her to stay for romantic holidays on her second husband's Scottish island. Her boarding-school teachers were genuinely fond of the girl who 'tried hard', was kind to the younger children, had 'lots of common sense', won swimming and dancing cups but was never the slightest credit to them academically. Not that Diana ever wrote herself off as a dunce. Though she did not get a single 'O' Level, she knew enough to cut out and study a newspaper article on 'successful gifted failures'.[9]

Diana's success in forming happy relationships extended beyond her schooldays into working life. The children at the Young England Kindergarten gravitated to 'Miss Diana'; her three flatmates were so stoutly loyal that even the toughest press investigators were unable to dent their discretion; above all, her sisters Sarah and Jane encouraged her, Sarah 'acting Cupid', as she said, when in Jubilee Year she invited Prince Charles to shoot at the Spencers' family home of Althorp in Northamptonshire. Here Charles and Diana agreed they had met one another for the first time, 'in a ploughed field'.

This was not literally so, for during his Sandringham youth Diana was 'the girl next door'. Her home at Park House, less than half a mile from Sandringham, had a swimming pool in which the younger Princes would frolic;

Andrew in particular 'ganged up' with her. There were no memories of children's parties for Charles, though – he was at Gordonstoun while she was still in her buggy, and he was already a hero by the time she was a schoolgirl. Perhaps because his investiture occurred on her own eighth birthday – 1 July 1969 – she cut out a picture of him in his robes.

The course of true love might have broken with folklore and run as smooth as any royal lawn, but for the press. At Princess Margaret's fiftieth birthday ball, celebrated on 4 November at the Ritz, Lady Diana's presence stimulated much excitement and even more fiction. The *Sunday Mirror* concocted an article called 'Love in the Sidings'. Lady Diana was purported to have spent a night or nights on the royal train with Prince Charles, secreted in the West Country, following the Ritz ball. The article infuriated the Queen.

Not surprisingly Lady Diana, because she had not been brought up with royalty's unavoidable feelings of mingled fear and fascination for the press, was at first able to endure the initial harassments with consistent good humour, grace and charm. On their engagement day, 24 February 1981, Diana described herself on television as 'blissfully happy' and her fiancé as 'pretty amazing'; while Charles was 'amazed that she's been brave enough to take me on'. Did she feel equally brave about her future royal role? She replied to the interviewers, 'It's always nice when there are two of you and there's someone there to help you. . . . With Prince Charles beside me I can't go wrong.' And to her friends she said she felt for the first time in her life 'secure'.

It never crossed her mind that the harassment would not stop once they were engaged and married. Her biographer, Penny Junor, almost suggests that the frenzied press pursuit was Diana's own fault, for being so magnetic. 'Diana had an effect on the press and the British public that no one could ever have foreseen.'[10] True; except that in a sense the 'effect' was auto-induced. People felt they needed a Diana to help them through difficult times. If she had not existed they would have had to invent her.

Queen Elizabeth II may have seemed out of the picture for once, as the young couple stood together outside Buckingham Palace on their engagement day with the whole crowd focused on them. But the observant Charles saw that his mother was in fact in the picture, though in the background: the Queen was looking out of the window, but whenever the photographers glanced up at the Palace she would vanish from view.

The wedding was solemnised 'under Paul's dome' on 29 July 1981, the bride being twenty years and twenty-nine days old, the bridegroom well into his thirty-third year. Diana had never thought about the age gap and Charles was not concerned at all. 'I just feel you're only as old as you think you are. . . . Diana will certainly help keep me young.'

The bride had chosen five bridesmaids and two pages, the latter in naval uniforms of 1863, the date of the last wedding of a Prince of Wales. The girls' dresses might have come straight out of a Victorian *Keepsake* album. Winston and Clementine Churchill's five-year-old great-granddaughter Clementine Hambro was the youngest child. India Hicks, aged thirteen, granddaughter of Lord Mountbatten, assisted the indispensable Sarah Armstrong-Jones to keep what Princess Anne had once called 'hordes of uncontrollable children' in order. Actually the bride's twenty-five-foot train needed more disciplining than the children, not to mention the romantic taffeta wedding dress which had to be packed into the open coach with the Princess of Wales before the return journey began. According to royal custom, Prince Charles had no best man but his two brothers as 'supporters'. Why, though, did the Queen and her son choose St Paul's instead of Westminster Abbey where she and her parents had been so happily married?

It is sometimes said that the break with tradition was due to Diana's parents having been 'unhappily married' there. There were also Prince Charles's unhappy memories of

reading the lesson at his beloved greatuncle's memorial
service in the Abbey two years before. Mountbatten was
Charles's 'HGF', his 'Honorary Grand Father'. But this
explanation ignores the hymn chosen for the wedding, 'I
vow to thee my country' – Diana's favourite hymn but also
sung most poignantly at the Abbey in 1979. And she had
some of the new yellow roses named after Lord Mountbatten in her bouquet.

The choice of St Paul's was governed partly by practicali-
ties, but mainly by Prince Charles's own firm preference.
He had always loved St Paul's. Its enormous size enabled
him to organise a strikingly musical ceremony with three
orchestras, the Bach Choir and the Maori soprano Kiri Te
Kanawa raising the dome during the signing of the register.
The Cathedral's greater distance from the Palace meant
more people could line the route more comfortably. If
there were not enough soldiers to line the longer route,
'Well, stand them further apart,' said Charles.[11] So more
and more sleeping-bags were dragged into the Mall and up
Ludgate Hill, and Union Jacks appeared everywhere, on
children's jeans, on headgear, even painted on a few
faces.

It was a grand patriotic festival, partly focused on the heir
to the throne, partly on the bride's 'amazing' popular
interest, partly it must be confessed on the spice of danger.

The Queen had been shot at by those blanks on her way
to Trooping the Colour only the month before. Police were
instructed to face the people along the wedding route for
the first time in history, and the foreign television com-
panies kept on at their reporters to 'do their homework on
royal assassinations' and to 'get the story – be sure to get
the story' when the expected shots rang out. Their shiny
grey limousines lay around Hyde Park Corner like basking
sharks. But nothing happened. There is something about a
royal show which mysteriously reduces the crime rate on
the day to negligible figures instead of quadrupling it as
everyone expects. In the words Rebecca West wrote of the
Queen's wedding in 1947: 'People . . . are tired of evil, they

need to think of goodness.' And again of the royal scene in 1981: 'magnified images of ourselves . . . but better . . . ourselves behaving well'.[12]

Meanwhile the Queen was on the steps of St Paul's exchanging smiles with her friends, including Archbishop Runcie in his new silver cope. The subtle blue of her dress was described variously as sky, aquamarine and – inappropriately – ice. Prince Charles's postilions wore her racing colours, and the silver dressings on the horses' manes were from her silver wedding. The anthem, too, seemed to have been chosen with her in mind: 'Peace be within thy walls and plenteousness within thy palaces.'

The crowds outside St Paul's entered heartily into the marriage service, thanks to transistor radios, while 750,000,000 people watched it on television all over the world and 250,000,000 followed it on radios. When the bride was heard to say 'I will', there were loud cheers of relief, as if she might have said 'I won't.' When she pledged her troth to 'Philip Charles Arthur George' instead of to 'Charles Philip Arthur George', and when the bridegroom vowed to share *her* worldly goods instead of vice versa, there were more delighted cheers. Royalty had two human faces – both of them blushing.

After the service was over, the Queen stood absolutely still, serious and almost unblinking for the National Anthem. If the lines on her face showed, they inspired confidence not pity. She had seen life and understood. Her face lit up as the married couple passed down the aisle and she was the first to wave to them as they left St Paul's. Before the Royal Family appeared on the traditional balcony there were shouts of 'We want the Queen!' After they lined up it was found miraculously that the kissing did not have to stop. 'Kiss her!' shouted the merry throng beyond the Palace's gilt-topped railings, and for the first time in history the heir apparent gave his wife a public kiss on the balcony while the Royal Family looked on, at first with expressions of incredulity, and the crowd below went wild. After that it was only to be expected that the Queen herself should throw handfuls of rose petals and that the new Princess should kiss her impresarios, the Lord Chamberlain and his comptroller, at Waterloo Station in front of the cameras, after driving down the Mall in an open landau festooned by her princely brothers-in-law with blue balloons painted with the three silver feathers and carrying the traditional, heart-warming message of low comedy, 'Just Married'.

There were some among the television viewers who wondered afterwards why the Queen occasionally looked rather 'straight' during an event which she was known to have enjoyed with her whole heart. The answer lay in her natural modesty. This was *their* day. All eyes she assumed were fixed on *them*; when no one was thinking of *her*, why should she, a mother witnessing the sacrament of her son's marriage, contort her features into a senseless grin? Not that she was proof against the funny moments. Everyone saw the Queen dissolve into laughter when the energetic choirmaster knocked off a lampshade with his baton.

The Queen, like everyone else, was well aware that royal marriages could give the monarchy an almighty lift. The long-playing record of the wedding was 'Top of the Pops', the Princess of Wales was declared 'Woman of the Year', and the Prince 'Man of the Year'. A mini-Trog cartoon depicted a bewildered, jug-eared Prince answering a telephone call with the words, 'No, we DON'T want to put the show on the road.' Though the mission of Elizabeth II had always been to keep the show on the road, she had to think carefully about each royal event and judge it in its own context.

Questions had been asked, for instance, about the wedding as an amalgam of 'state' and 'family' functions. The Queen seemed to have aimed, as with her horses, at 'hybrid vigour'. There were no heralds to give it a special magnificence, though Charles would have liked it and the thirteen heralds would have loved it. But to the Queen this wedding, like her daughter's, was still a family occasion. There had in fact been no heralds at a royal wedding since Princess

Maud, daughter of Edward VII, married the future King Haakon of Norway in 1896.

Elizabeth II's reasons for her decision were valid but complex. Her nature inclined her to a family occasion. Her subjects, at least some of them, might be provoked by too much grandeur. There was a curious parallel between Queen Victoria's Golden Jubilee and the Royal Wedding. The Jubilee of 1887 had been sandwiched between two violent spasms of rioting in London, the second known as 'Bloody Sunday'. Elizabeth II had had her Brixton before her son's wedding: she did not want a 'Bloody Sunday' after it.

Three months before the wedding, Lambeth Council had already refused invitations to the royal garden party. William Hamilton MP could be relied on to point the contrast between the rise in unemployment and the British public's fall for 'phoney romance'. He predicted that 'the sky will be the limit' as regards royal wedding expenditure. It was the Queen's duty to prove him wrong, as indeed she did.

Nevertheless, there were whispers of republicanism on the day both at home and abroad. Clay Cross in Derbyshire planned but failed to stage a 'Republic Day' in its social club; 'Red Ken' Livingstone, the left-wing Chairman of the Greater London Council, while admiring the Queen as a hard worker, declined an invitation to St Paul's and got on with his own work; one coach party went to Boulogne, buying up anti-wedding souvenirs, and another went to Eire, singing anti-British songs; in Italy a left-wing newspaper reported the weddings of several Londoners on 29 July precisely because they were not Charles and Diana.[13] A state wedding might have set the spark to any inflammable material lying around.

Yet it was not easy to equate 250 choristers, a congregation of some 2,600 and 600,000 spectators on the route between the Palace and St Paul's with an intimate celebration by a family called Mountbatten-Windsor. Perhaps the only really intimate touch was provided by the bride as she arrived at the cathedral door and whispered, 'Is he here?' It is also said that Prince Charles greeted his bride in the Cathedral with the whispered words, 'You look beautiful,' to which she replied, 'Beautiful for you.'

In her balancing act between family and state, the Queen was inevitably forced into some curious postures. Since it was *family*, only foreign *royalties* were invited to the Palace to partake of the 255-pound cake at the wedding breakfast, non-royal heads of state being sent off to lunch with Margaret Thatcher at the Bank of England. This caused shock among many politicians, and also John Grigg, all of whom thought it wrong. But in so far as it was *state*, the Queen had to take her minister's advice that *Britannia* should pick the honeymooners off the Rock of Gibraltar. As a result the King and Queen of Spain refused to attend the wedding.

Sporadic republicanism at home was probably her least anxiety. Margaret Thatcher has described the number of British republicans as 'minute' and James Callaghan was emphatic that hardly anyone would object to the Royal Wedding on republican grounds. Certainly not the Labour Party. 'Why, when somebody wrote in *Labour Weekly* some weeks ago that it was time we got rid of the crown, there was a scurry to dissociate the Labour Party from such a terrible sentiment. The Labour Party says it would get rid of the House of Lords and courtiers by all means, but the crown – certainly not.'*[14]

The Queen must none the less take every possibility into account if she is to perform her task of preserving the monarchy, as she sees it. She must understand the changes that have already come, and may yet come. She must divine the real wishes of the people. She must appreciate the potential of her family and of her own character. Above all

* The popularity of the crown has increased in proportion as Elizabeth II has had to work with ordinary people, particularly in the making of television films. The team who made *The Queen's Garden* in 1977 were enchanted by her confidence and wit. At the end of shooting, one half-hour of film had to be cut. Which should it be? The Queen suggested: 'the *Planaria* eating the *Aseltus*, that shot by the lake of Hoglouse and Flatworm – sounds like a firm of solicitors!'

The first 'walkabout' during the royal tour of New Zealand, 23 March 1970. Walkabouts were probably the most popular innovation in the reign. (*Keystone*)

At Balmoral with some of her favourite labradors. (*Photo by Patrick Lichfield, Camera Press*)

The official photograph of the Queen and Prince Philip on the occasion of their silver wedding anniversary, 20 November 1972. There is no pomp; open-necked shirts are worn. (*Photo by Patrick Lichfield, Camera Press*)

Princess Anne's wedding to Captain Mark Phillips, 14 November 1973, with her bridesmaid Lady Sarah Armstrong-Jones, and her page Prince Edward. She did not want 'hordes of uncontrollable children'. (*Daily Telegraph*)

Giving prizes at the Windsor Horse Show. (*Photo by Serge Lemoine, BBC Hulton Picture Library*)

A Garter ceremony at Windsor Castle. (*Photo by Serge Lemoine, BBC Hulton Picture Library*)

The Queen and Prince Philip during the Silver Jubilee Service at St Paul's Cathedral, 7 June 1977. (*Photo by Serge Lemoine, BBC Hulton Picture Library*)

The Queen with her first grandson, Peter Phillips, 5 April 1978. (*Photo by Snowdon, Camera Press*)

Drinking coffee with His Highness Shaikh Khalifa Bin Hamad al Thani in Quatar, during their three-week tour of the Middle East, 21 February 1979. (*Keystone*)

An eightieth birthday portrait of the Queen Mother with her two daughters by Norman Parkinson, 4 August 1980. Princess Margaret recalls that they laughed and joked all the time the photographs were being taken. (*Camera Press*)

Prince Charles and Lady Diana Spencer with the Queen after the Privy Council had approved their engagement, 27 March 1981. The Queen has learnt to 'stand easy'. (*Press Association*)

The Queen reins in her startled mare Burmese after blank shots are fired at her during the Trooping the Colour ceremony, 13 June 1981. (*Syndication International*)

On the balcony at
Buckingham Palace,
after the Royal
Wedding, 29 June
1981. 'Kiss her!'
shouted the voices
from the crowd; and
he did. (*Keystone*)

The Queen greets
His Holiness Pope
John Paul II during
his historic visit to
England, 1982.
(*Photo by Walter
Castro, Camera
Press*)

The Christening of
Prince William in the
White Drawing-
Room at
Buckingham Palace,
4 August 1982.
(*Photo by Ron Bell,
Press Association*)

The Queen greets
Prince Andrew on
his return from the
Falklands. (*Photo by
Bryn Colton, Camera
Press*)

The Queen smiles at a reception during the Commonwealth
conference in Zambia, 12 September 1982. Kenneth Kaunda
who sits beside her is an old friend, and the Queen has
smoothed the way for Mrs Thatcher. (*Syndication International*)

Making a speech at the state dinner in San Francisco, 3 March
1983. The Queen's deadpan joke was about the weather.
(*Popperfoto*)

the monarchy must mean the same thing to her as to the nation. If all these things work out for her, then the golden banner that hung under Paul's dome may speak for the future of the whole royal system: 'All shall be well, and all manner of things shall be well.'

XVIII

'The System'

The meaning of monarchy is not a matter of linguistics, like 'the meaning of meaning'. It is rooted in history. Modern sovereignty can no more get away from its origins than the Commonwealth can get away from the Empire. Nor should either of them wish to.

As the days of Empire recede, they tend to be recalled with nostalgia instead of ridicule. At the first showing of Malcolm Muggeridge's film on the British Raj there was undisguised contempt for the pompous white man's cemetery, now in well-deserved ruins. Seen fifteen years later, it inspired a feeling of sadness, *lacrimae rerum*. Some of those old bones beneath the fallen angels had actually tried to do good, and often succeeded. When the Queen visited Sri Lanka the *Daily News*, in trying to explain her tumultuous reception by a country that had become a republic, boldly suggested that the Empire had done more good than evil.

The same would be true of constitutional monarchy. Its past is not only nostalgic but decorative. Kenneth Rose has warned us not to look too closely at the 'arcane' language in which monarchy is presented. Everything the Queen does, however odious to her, she is 'graciously pleased' to do. This is because our monarchy stretches back into a past when the sovereign's pleasure was law and '*le roi le veult*' meant what it said. Every time we read or hear archaic language we should congratulate ourselves. It reminds us that once we had absolute rulers – as other unfortunates still have – but that now our monarchy is constitutional.

Nevertheless, it may be asked whether the language of the court does not inevitably affect the minds of all who participate. In royal pronouncements four words are used where one would do. Does not this medieval habit eventually give the Queen and her court a langorous feeling that there is never any hurry since time has stood still? When the statutes of the Order of the British Empire were altered in 1970, it was pointed out on page one of the document that whereas the Queen's Royal Grandfather 'did institute, erect, constitute and create' this said Order of Knighthood, Her Majesty had the power of 'annulling, altering, augmenting, interpreting or dispensing with the same. . . .'

It may be retorted that a mere honour like the OBE does not impinge on the Queen's serious work. But the medieval miasma extends, says the Devil's Advocate, over the whole court. Look at their names; her comptroller spelt with a superfluous 'p'; her women-of-the-bedchamber (they never enter it); her more exalted ladies-in-waiting; her most exalted mistress of the robes; her equerries (where are their horses?); her lord-lieutenants (who in fact can be ladies but are still called lords – Lady Phillips, for instance, the Lord-Lieutenant of Greater London); her unpaid officials with purely nominal duties like the Queen's Watermen and Bargemaster, to be distinguished, as biographers royal are never tired of pointing out, from the Queen's Swankeeper who really does keep her swans. The Keeper of the Queen's Pictures is one person and the Surveyor of the Queen's Works of Art is another, as if pictures were not works of art, or a keeper was not a surveyor. And it seems only yesterday that the Sovereign had no press secretary whatever.

Of course even Parliament itself has its Black Rod. But Parliament has been criticised for being out of date, a 'talkshop not a workshop'.

Despite its archaic names the court stands on firm ground. If it ever became a department of state we can be sure of one thing: the numbers employed, recently reduced from

400 to 350, would be expanded and their pay increased. Today there is a good deal of voluntary effort which would perforce cease, and because the whole 'system' – which is how the court has come to speak of the royal set-up – operates on a shoe-string it has to be efficient. The word 'system' implies order and logic beneath the many archaisms and illogicalities.

Security is not part of 'the system' but entirely the responsibility of the police. Otherwise the above paragraph, in the light of the 1982 'intruder', might seem ironical.

Those who come to the Palace on business enter by the Privy Purse door, in the far north-east corner. The atmosphere is welcoming, at least as compared with most departments of state. The scarlet footmen greet you at the door as an old friend – which you probably are, since most researchers return more than once. During her engagement, Lady Diana Spencer blew in (literally, for her cape was flying in the wind) by the Privy Purse door, laughing and talking, to help with the wedding correspondence in Prince Charles's office. A footman kindly explained to the author, who witnessed this scene, that if Lady Diana had been wearing a hat the crowds behind the railings would have recognised her and cheered themselves hoarse. As it was, a hatless girl made no impression.

Meanwhile, visitors enter the small waiting-room, where various things tactfully remind them of the roaring world they have left behind: two morning papers laid on a side table: C. W. P. Frith's two fine Victorian tributes to the masses, *Departure Scene in Paddington Station* and *Life at the Seaside*.

Visitors have reacted differently to the atmosphere in the corridors, Basil Boothroyd finding it not unlike a cup final around Prince Philip's rooms, while Anthony Holden writes of mustiness and claustrophobia. The author found it easy to get lost, partly because one was always looking up at the pictures – Gladstone, Disraeli and, more relevantly, the Queen's four most recent principal private secretaries, painted for her by David Poole. Eager to discover the notorious 'tweediness', I found these four men immediately impressive: all out of a top drawer but not a tweedy one, or even the same one. Sir Alan Lascelles, the only straight reactionary among them (he resigned from the Reform Club when women were allowed to eat there), could have been an artist, having acquired with age a beard and good-humoured bohemian patina; Sir Michael (now Lord) Adeane, Eton, Cambridge and the Guards, looking every inch the clever cautious intellectual, was also in fact a painter; Sir Martin (Lord) Charteris, Eton and the KRRC and now Provost of Eton, enjoys sculpting and looked the archetypal professor with his half-moon glasses and quizzical expression though he had never been to a university; Sir Philip Moore, Cheltenham, Oxford and the Diplomatic Service, was once an international rugby player as his broad shoulders and smile seemed to indicate.

An unexpected tribute to the Queen's private office came from a Labour cabinet minister, Tony Crosland, in 1969. He had to make an all-day jaunt to Balmoral on being appointed Minister for the Environment, a new post which had created some confusion in Whitehall. 'The Queen unlike practically everyone else, turned out to be extremely well briefed.'[1]

One member of the court has noted that the wives in the Queen's entourage are often more 'cultural' than their husbands. If the husbands do not begin 'tweedy' they tend to get fond of shooting through their new opportunities. Only two major criticisms have been made recently: no top blacks (already mentioned) and no top women.

Anne Hawkins – now Mrs Michael Wall – was an assistant press secretary for many years until 1981, and was once suggested by some of the newspaper fraternity as a candidate for the job of press secretary. She herself, however, did not want the top job, especially after she married, preferring her day-to-day work with the press to a great deal of administration. Nor would she have wished to spend so much time away from home involved with overseas tours. (The press secretary very often has to do a 'recce', as well as the actual tour.) She felt that in any case she would not have been able to accompany the Queen on many of her overseas tours when a man is needed to cope with the large press party – almost wholly male and more than likely including 'paparazzi'-type foreign photographers – that covers such tours.

The press secretary, Michael Shea, is yet another change from the norm of thirty years ago: seconded from the Foreign Office, he writes best-selling thrillers under his own name, no longer under the pen-name of Michael Sinclair. Of the whole Household, his office is perhaps subject to the most harassment, as we shall see. Its most traditional activity, however, is not the 'Court Circular', as many people imagine. This is the province of the Master of the Household, who issues a brief record of the Royal Family's public engagements of the day before. *The Times* and *Daily Telegraph* set out what they are given each day. They may not be selective.

Mockery of the Court Circular's archaic language is not unknown. This is nothing new; *Punch* made its nineteenth-century readers laugh with a take-off of the Circular from Balmoral, including satirical references to Queen Victoria's favourite, John Brown. In 1972 the *Daily Mail* tried the same game, suggesting that both the presentation of a baby elephant to the Queen and an alleged little local difficulty Princess Anne had with her car should be announced in Court Circular language:

> Jumbo had the honour of being received by the Queen this morning and presented his letters of credence as Elephant Extraordinary and Plenipotentiary to the Court of St James's. . . . The Princess Anne made a tour of North Buckinghamshire in the vicinity of the M1 motorway last Saturday. A Thames Valley police patrol car was in attendance.

This is not the place to describe that part of the machinery of the Queen's Household which would be the same whoever occupied the throne. It is the changes in the system that are illuminating.

The most interesting change has come from the Lord Chamberlain himself, whose task it is to keep a general watch over this large institution – 'the system' or monarchy – and get some things and people changed where necessary. As Lord ('Kim') Cobbold put it, during a key year of the office, 1968, he hoped

> to help in bringing an ancient and venerable institution into more modern shape without losing tradition and 'mystery' or 'aura' (or whatever you call it), an objective always in the front of the Queen's and Prince Philip's minds.[2]

Lord Cobbold once described his position as being 'similar to that of a part-time chairman of a large company with a single active shareholder'.[3]

But since that 'single active shareholder' is Her Majesty the Queen, the 'company' must not continue to undertake any activities, however traditional, which might involve her in controversy. The Lord Chamberlain's position as theatre censor was a case in point.

From Elizabeth I's to Charles II's reign, theatre censorship had existed to protect the monarchy from abuse on the stage; in the eighteenth century Robert Walpole made its scope political and under Victoria it became moral. There were many reasons why, by 1968, theatre censorship was out of date: freedom of speech, for instance, or freedom of art. But in Lord Cobbold's view the overriding reason was that the censorship had become a danger to the monarchy, because its operations were carried out by the Queen's servant from the Palace of St James's. Plays had to be let through on the Queen's behalf which some people would consider offensive, while the banning of other works would make the Palace seem stuffy and behind the times. So this ancient office of theatre censor came to a timely end in 1968.

And the Queen? 'I am a traditionalist,' she always says;

but she is never unwilling to break a tradition when convinced of the necessity. Once convinced, she gives her full support. In the case of theatre censorship, it had been instituted four centuries earlier for the protection of a queen and was now terminated partly for the same reason.

Three other changes made by the Lord Chamberlain's office may be mentioned, all of them showing a movement towards a more 'open' monarchy. Royal servants were no longer appointed exclusively from a 'magic circle' of hereditary families but more and more from the outside. There was still an Adeane serving the Prince of Wales, but also a Ron Allison from the BBC, Michael Shea's predecessor in the press office. Medals and insignia could now be worn in the evening with dinner jackets instead of with the hitherto *de rigueur* white tie and tails, or, as in the old days, a thing called court dress. Invitations to garden parties were mainly 'once for all' treats for people who had served their community well, rather than 'over and over again' privileges for the same circles.

The lord-lieutenants and lieutenants of counties, who receive or represent the Queen at formal functions, are themselves today drawn from more representative backgrounds. The Labour Lord Rhodes regarded his high position as an opportunity to look after his Lancashire 'family' on Her Majesty's behalf. Lady Phillips, another Labour lord-lieutenant, takes enormous pride in presenting Her Majesty's medals to factory workers and others for good service: 'It is lovely to be able to say thank you to hundreds of ordinary people.' As the Queen and Prince Philip are so often at London functions, Norah Phillips could not attend them on every occasion. 'They are very considerate in letting me know well in advance if I will not be needed.'[4] Lord-lieutenancies, being military offices in origin, involve the wearing of swords, sword-knots, gloves, sashes, gorget patches, badges of rank and all the military trappings; although women are not required to wear any uniform whatever, not even a hat – just a single small badge of office.

The Queen's ladies-in-waiting tend to serve her, according to their rotas, for very many years, sometimes over thirty. In a sense the job was more interesting before Elizabeth II came to the throne. Instead of mainly looking after diplomats and visitors, writing personal letters, sending out (or refusing) photographs and so on, as now, the Princess's ladies-in-waiting would deal with everything, from a girl who wanted advice about removing facial hair (on which the Princess duly made enquiries and reported) to an angry provincial mayor who expected to ride in the mayoral car alone with his Princess, and not with a lady-in-waiting making three. In somewhat later days, riding in a car with the young Queen Elizabeth II was still quite a problem. The lady must not look grumpy, nor yet grin so widely as to focus attention on herself. A balanced half-smile had to be learnt.

One aspect of the role has not changed over the years. Thanks to the advice of Queen Elizabeth (now the Queen Mother) to a young lady-in-waiting that she should not remain 'mum' and uncommunicative with the Princess, ladies-in-waiting are frank and outspoken. After all, said Queen Elizabeth, they were her daughters' links with the outside world. Today, a few young men who have come to work temporarily at the Palace may be too nervous or diffident to speak out, no one else. Though the women can become a bit 'holy' from long association with royalty, the best of them, including the wives of members of the Household, have minds and interests of their own and, though unshakeably discreet, speak when they do speak with originality and freshness.

None of this, however, constitutes major change. Queen Mary had clever ladies-in-waiting in Lady Airlie and Lady Cynthia Colville; Lady Ponsonby, wife of Queen Victoria's private secretary, was a woman of distinction. The duties of the Queen's Household, though traditional, are not mysterious but systematically tabulated and written down. There is nothing of an 'unwritten constitution' about the Household.

Unlike the Queen in Parliament. Her remaining constitutional prerogatives are chronically in dispute, unwritten
and operating in a 'grey' area.

The Sovereign's prerogatives are mysterious, if not part of
the royal mystique. There is the right to be consulted,
agreed. But was Elizabeth II 'consulted' over Suez? Some
writers believe that the royal prerogative includes the right
'to know'. If so, did the Sovereign, between 1967 and 1980,
know that her brilliant Keeper of the Queen's Pictures,
Anthony Blunt, had confessed to espionage? In this case
we can be sure that the few people who know whether Her
Majesty knew or not will not tell.

But the genuine mysteries of the royal prerogative are far
surpassed by the popular confusions. In the 1960s, for
instance, there were still many people in the United Kingdom and the Commonwealth who believed that the Queen
personally took political action. Lord Blake has quoted an
opinion poll of 1966 in which the majority stated that if the
Queen and her ministers disagreed, the Queen should and
would prevail. In the same year Kenneth Rose reported the
white Rhodesians as being angry with the Queen for referring in her speeches from the throne to their 'illegal regime'. They refused to draw a distinction between the views
of Her Majesty on the crisis – whatever they might be –
and of her ministers. Three years later, according to a *New
Society* poll taken among children, they thought the Queen
not the Prime Minister ran the country.[5]

Egregious errors apart, there still seems to be room in
every decade for differences of informed opinion on the
key question: Is it possible for the Queen ever to become
personally and constitutionally involved in a political
crisis? The problem is focused on two situations, a dissolution and a 'hung' parliament. In the 1960s Sir Harold
Nicolson envisaged a prime minister deciding to prolong
Parliament's life for fifty years – in other words becoming a dictator – and the Queen rightly calling a general election, in accordance with her Coronation Oath to

govern according to the 'laws and customs' of the realm.[6]

In the 1970s, with the two-party system still reasonably intact, it was usual for socialist writers to reply to the key question with a resounding no. Patrick Gordon Walker, as we saw, remained confident that all the Queen had to do, even in the case of a hopelessly 'hung' parliament, was to go on sending her potential ministers back to their political wheeling and dealing until they eventually came up with the person who could form a government. Michael Stewart would have agreed at that date: and even in the early 1980s, when politics are in flux, he still feels that the Monarch by hook or by crook must keep out.

'You might very well have an occasion,' he says, 'when the Monarch's judgment proved to be more felicitous than that of any politician. But if that encouraged monarchs to think they could go on doing that kind of thing, I think one of them would come a cropper sooner or later. And the monarchy can't afford to do that.'[7]

Even in the 1970s there were two consecutive occasions when this constitutional plain-sailing seemed to run on the rocks.

After the first indecisive general election of 1974, the enemies of the Conservative Prime Minister, Edward Heath, criticised him bitterly for his 'pig-headedness' in not going at once to the Palace with his resignation, but instead spending a long weekend trying fruitlessly to form an alliance with Jeremy Thorpe and his Liberals.[8] The election figures were Labour (Wilson) 301, Conservatives (Heath) 296, Liberals and others 37. In fact Heath's procedure was right and constitutional, as his immediate successor, the Labour leader Harold Wilson, pointed out.

It was Wilson who might have set Her Majesty the problem which so many people now expect to dominate the coming years. Having formed a minority government, Wilson was urged by some members of his party to hold a second general election at once, after duly applying to the Queen for a dissolution. 'Let him do so at his peril!' cried threatening voices on the media, thus perhaps themselves infringing the Queen's prerogative, as Wilson came to believe later.[9] The then hypothetical question for the monarchy was, would the Sovereign have been justified in refusing a second dissolution in the interests of the country's stability? In the event Harold Wilson did not put the Queen to the test but managed to carry on with his minority government until the autumn, when a second general election gave him a small working majority. (He had been helped to carry on by tactful Tory abstentions.) The constitution was seen to be working satisfactorily also. But today no one knows what would have happened if Wilson had come to Her Majesty like a hungry Oliver Twist, after only three or four months, asking for more polling and a chance to win more votes.

Edward Heath has called this 'a grey area':

> The one grey area which seems to exist is if a prime minister with a majority – a narrow majority, as happened in 1974 – is defeated early on and demands a further election. Is the Queen obliged to give it him?
>
> Opinions vary on this. Very much on the basis that it is impossible to lay down a doctrine that if it is six months minus a day after an election she ought not to, and if it is a full six months after the election, she is compelled to. So it does leave an element of discretion.[10]

Lord Hailsham, twice Lord Chancellor, thinks that 'it isn't impossible for the Queen to be involved', but 'the object of every right-minded person obviously must be to reduce the possibility to a minimum, and I think it has been reduced almost to a minimum.'[11]

Michael Stewart, too, subscribes to a 'grey area' surrounding a 'hung' parliament, though perhaps a rather greyer area than Lord Hailsham pictures:

> Suppose at the next election Mrs Thatcher was beaten and it is uncertain whether Roy Jenkins, David Steel or Tony Benn ought to have a go. . . . The Queen has got to choose, and apply her own judgment as to which of these is going to be able to

form a government. If she did do that, nobody could blame her, because she could not do anything else until we have sorted this out a bit more, and know what the rules are. That is always the British Constitution – you make up the rules as you go.[12]

Stewart was bearing in mind the political event of 1981 which was to sharpen the edge to arguments about the Queen's prerogative. This was the rise of the new Social Democratic Party soon to form the 'Alliance' with the Liberals. Obviously the existence of three or four major parties would reduce the chances of a clear-cut election result and increase the incidence of 'hung' parliaments, thus introducing abnormal 'greyness' into the Queen's spectrum.

Added to this is the fact that the Alliance has declared for proportional representation, a sure way of complicating the Queen's duty to appoint a prime minister. Coalitions and bargaining between numerous small parties are rarely absent under such a system. Nor is there anything monstrous about minority opinion being thus democratically expressed. Nevertheless, it will take longer for the Queen to pick out the one dominant star from such a large, inviting galaxy. Harold Wilson has said that 'British democracy stood still' while Heath was negotiating with Thorpe;[13] more agitatedly, David Watt wrote: 'What does the British Constitution say about coalitions? Who governs the country while the lengthy shenanigans are going on? What are the rules of the game?'[14]

In the rising tempo, Sir John Colville remembered his days serving Churchill and argued positively that the Queen can refuse a dissolution 'should an alternative government be available in the existing Parliament'[15] – thus depriving the shenaniganists of their fun; while Alan Watkins didn't care about the constitutional arguments for dissolution, he simply thought Her Majesty 'might not take kindly to her people being bothered by an election'[16] if a government merely wanted to cash in on a mid-term success. (He was thinking of the Falklands victory.)

More soberly, Lord Stewart and Lord Hailsham give
contrary examples from abroad: Stewart thinks proportional representation will work if the country wants it,
without straining the Queen's prerogative: 'I remember the
Dutch minister once saying to me, "I do not yet know who
my colleagues are." The British constitution writes itself as
it goes along.'[17]

From Italy, Lord Hailsham takes the cautionary tale of
unfortunate heads of state forming new governments on an
average of every eight months. 'Queen Elizabeth II would
have to have consultations with the leaders of the parties,'
he adds, 'and try to persuade combinations to form coalitions. This would inevitably involve her taking an active
part which could be made the subject of criticism.'[18]

Finally, there is Margaret Thatcher, the first British
woman prime minister, who considers proportional representation little short of immoral:

> I am not an advocate of Proportional Representation. I have
> seen too much of it on the Continent. Splinter party after
> splinter party. They go into an election saying 'I stand for this, I
> will do this.' After the election they compromise on everything
> they have promised. It is the most awful horse-trading I have
> ever seen. I despise it.

Mrs Thatcher then comes on to the results of proportional
representation:

> People are afraid to give a lead, and if there is one danger for
> democracy it is 'followership' instead of leadership. The job of
> politicians is to say, 'I am here to have a larger vision – I believe
> in what I am saying. You can choose whether you follow it – I
> will accept your judgments but I will not resign from my duty to
> give a judgment – ever.'

Of the probable effect of proportional representation on
the Queen's prerogative, Mrs Thatcher says:

It means the Queen has an extremely difficult job. Look at Queen Beatrix of Holland. She can't form a government. She calls someone to do so and they can't. So then she calls for someone else and then she gets two people trying to form a government. There is uncertainty which spreads through a whole community and the government which becomes a government doesn't stand for anything.

As for the wider effects:

Just supposing you were a tyrant (and tyrants have been born throughout history) you would choose that time to move – in the interregnum. When we had the last European conference at Lancaster House in November [1981] they were just forming a government in Belgium. It had taken them since their election in May. . . . I am here with a strong majority behind me.[19]

Yet the expert psephologist, David Butler, believes it unlikely that Britain's present first-past-the-post system will 'see the century out'.[20] It is equally unlikely that the Queen will not do so. But by then her long experience and gift for rapid work should enable the white smoke to rise from Buckingham Palace within a reasonable time. And the danger of a tyrant seizing power in the interregnum seems no more imminent than that of Antichrist taking over in Rome while the cardinals are electing a pope.

An intruder in the Queen's Palace was noted in the first chapter of this book. An intruder on the Queen's prerogative made his appearance a few months later. In August 1982 Tony Benn MP wrote in the left-wing magazine *New Socialist* that the crown's only two remaining prerogatives – the right to dissolve Parliament before its full term and to appoint a prime minister – should be abolished. Four months later Benn added that in the event of proportional representation producing a 'hung' parliament, 'We will move from first past the post to first past the Crown.' Though strenuously opposed to such a race, Benn hastened to absolve himself of crown-baiting. 'I have a deep contempt,' he wrote, 'for those who confine their comments on our constitution to cheap sniping at the Royal Family.' It was therefore not 'sniping' when, in March 1983, Benn mounted a pulpit and demanded the 'liberation' of the Church of England from the Queen and the State by an act of disestablishment.[21]

Benn had earlier cited the case of the Governor-General of Australia who terminated Gough Whitlam's premiership in 1975. To avoid a repetition of such behaviour by the crown's representatives, Benn proposed that the Speaker of the House of Commons should take over the Queen's prerogatives.

This procedure has already been adopted in Sweden but has given less than complete satisfaction. In Denmark the job is done by an *informateur*. Why Benn should think a parliamentary Speaker, who had been a member of a political party, would be more impartial than the Queen, who had not, remains unexplained. And indeed Benn later insisted that he was not impugning the impartiality of the Queen. How does he explain his *démarche* in favour of the Speaker? Perhaps a case of British parliamentarianism suffering from one of its periodic fits of swelled head.

Benn's proposal may have sprung from another event of 1981, as significant as the rise of the Social Democratic Party and indeed partly responsible for its birth. This was the special Wembley conference in January at which the Labour Party voted to change the method of selecting its leader. Instead of being elected by the votes of Members of Parliament, he or she would in future be chosen by an electoral college, 40 per cent of the vote going to trades unions, 30 per cent to constituency parties and 30 per cent to MPS.

Immediately heated arguments broke out. In answer to those left-wingers who gloried in the prospect of the Prime Minister being virtually elected by the unions and perhaps 'recalled' by them, Peter Jay replied in *The Times*: 'The Labour Party conference can change and has changed the Party's constitution; but it cannot and has not changed the

British constitution[22] – by which the Queen appoints the Prime Minister. Tony Benn's new proposal may have been another move in this game.

Benn in turn has been answered by Norman St John-Stevas, the fallen Conservative minister who, to adapt Wolsey, serves his Queen even better than he served his 'Blessed Margaret'. He flew to the Queen's defence, asserting her proven impartiality and calling Benn's proposals 'ill thought out, unconstitutional and dangerous'.[23] It is true that without her powers of dissolving Parliament and appointing a prime minister, the Queen's prestige and therefore usefulness as a national head and stabiliser in time of crisis would be greatly reduced.

The Benn 'reforms' are unlikely ever to become law or a brand of extreme Labourism to recommend itself to the electors. 'Multi-party government, however,' writes Vernon Bogdanov, 'is more than likely in the future and politicians should begin in earnest to work out its effect on one essential part of the constitution – the monarchy.'[24]

The Queen in her Household, the Queen in Parliament, the Queen on the screen; many people would feel that the press and media provide monarchy's most crucial test. No one should expect the Queen to see eye to eye with a free popular press, but unless there is some common ground 'the system' will not get its verdict of 'all is well'.

In judging its success, we must first clear out of the way certain run-of-the-mill contingencies which will always cause hiccups but not give the Palace a seizure.

The republican foreign press, for instance, is paranoid in its obsession with royalty. Last century a Swiss newspaper had Queen Victoria married to John Brown and this century *France Dimanche* had Elizabeth II's marriage at an end, because she was disastrously disfigured by chicken-pox. No one is surprised when French freelance journalists are arrested for trespassing in the grounds of the Wales's Gloucestershire home, Highgrove.

There are also minor contretemps during foreign tours,

such as the Queen's visit to King Hassan of Morocco in October 1980. The King's concern with security (800 guests had been bombed and 100 of them killed at his birthday celebration nine years before) led him to keep the Queen waiting for her lunch until 3.40 one boiling afternoon. Though the Queen enjoyed the banquet on the last day, the press and media were chiefly concerned to feature her looking anxiously at her watch at 3.35. The suggestion was that the Sultan had been deliberately rude. 'Queen in Rage over Snub', said the *Sun*.

If the media want the monarchy to use its magic on foreign countries they should keep a sense of proportion – and humour. In this respect the Palace is more sensible than the press. When King Hassan and his whole family were dining on *Britannia*, a lady-in-waiting asked the eldest of the small princes, aged ten, if he liked the sea. Straightening his miniature dinner jacket the child informed her, 'I am the Commander of the Fleet!' She did not blink.

The real perils arise when events like jubilees or royal weddings capture the public imagination and so tempt the press into major extravagances. After her Silver Jubilee tour of Australia, the Queen had to rebuke the press for wildly exaggerating minor republican demonstrations. A thin card bearing the words 'Independence for Australia' had been thrown into the royal car; next morning it became the kind of heavy 'placard' which might have concussed the Queen. Among an enthusiastic crowd of 3,000 the only worthwhile incident was apparently a dozen people shouting 'Go home, Pommy Queen!' This is press coverage in the sense that clouds cover the sun. An American magazine, having researched Australian republicanism, found that the monarchy's popularity had dropped only a half of one per cent in the past decade.

However, it is the marriage of the Prince and Princess of Wales that provides the *locus classicus* on this subject.

The public could see for themselves Lady Diana Spencer being hounded by the press while still a schoolteacher: nervously stalling her car, covering her face with her hands as she hurried to school but once there, with a child in each hand, apparently forgetting to cover her elegant legs with anything but a see-through skirt. (In fact this last coup was a 'paint job'; they had painted in the legs.) Her public admired her unfailing good temper but not the press's boorishness, against which her mother, Frances Shand Kydd, was the first to protest openly, in *The Times*. 'May I ask the editors of Fleet Street, whether, in the execution of their jobs, they consider it necessary or fair to harass my daughter daily, from dawn till well after dusk?' This was early December 1980. A month later Prince Charles took the opportunity at Sandringham to wish their editors 'a peculiarly nasty' New Year.

The next big brush with editors looked like giving Prince Charles 'a peculiarly nasty spring'. While in Australia his telephone calls to Lady Diana and the Queen were said to have been tapped, put on tape, 'dropped' into the 'lap' of the British journalist Simon Regan (author of *The Clown Prince*), and passed to the West German women's magazine, *Die Aktuelle*. Temporary injunctions were granted to Prince Charles and Lady Diana against publication in Germany or Britain. (Too late in Germany. No '*skandal*' only '*liebe*', reported the *Aktuelle* sadly.) Meanwhile it turned out, as many suspected, that this mish-mash of 'lovey-dovey' exchanges and anti-Australian politics were 'phoney' – the appropriate word. In its 'Side Lines' column the *Daily Express* pointed out that on the alleged 'tapes' Prince Charles was made to call Australian premier Malcolm Fraser the Prime Minister of New Zealand![25]

News of the 'tapes' broke at the beginning of May. The date is relevant to the Queen's deteriorating relations with the press. For while the 'tapes' furore was still on, Mrs Doreen and Mr Jack Hill, mother and father of Jacqueline Hill, thirteenth and last victim of Peter Sutcliffe (the 'Yorkshire Ripper'), included a letter to the Queen in their campaign against newspapers who had offered large sums to Sutcliffe's near relatives for 'exclusive stories'. The Queen responded with unusual fervour. 'I am commanded by Her Majesty the Queen,' wrote her assistant private secretary William Heseltine, 'to . . . begin by offering to you both Her Majesty's very heartfelt sympathy at the tragic death of your daughter.' The royal letter went on to express 'a sense of distaste' at the *Daily Mail*'s proposal, 'if true', to pay members of Sutcliffe's family 'substantial sums' for their stories. (The *Mail* later admitted that it paid Sutcliffe's father £5,000.) The letter ended by expressing the conviction that 'all right-minded people' would share in Her Majesty's distaste.

It is doubtful if the Queen would have thus plunged into a denunciation of 'cheque-book journalism', as applied to the relatives of criminals, but for her seething anger over the 'tapes' and the public's clear sympathy with the Royal Family. Her deeply felt letter to Mrs Hill met with wide approval. The majority believed she was right to speak out; it would do good, and the Press Council would now look into the affair.

Nevertheless, the ensuing acrimonious press debate on 'cheque-book journalism' showed how careful the monarchy must be about public expressions of private opinion. David English, editor of the *Mail*, took umbrage at being singled out for royal rebuke and won the support of some colleagues even on rival newspapers. Other journalists, such as Mervyn Jones in the *Listener*, showed their qualified disapproval by criticising the English of William Heseltine: 'His letter to Mr and Mrs Hill starts off with a superfluous "very" in "very heartfelt sympathy"; either an emotion is felt in the heart or it's not.' Auberon Waugh abandoned a first impulse to pillory the Queen in *Private Eye* for picking on the *Mail* in favour of castigating her in the *Spectator* for 'hitching a free ride on any indignation which Mrs Hill's tragic loss may generate for her cause'. Even among sober circles most loyal to the Queen there were some startled reactions, half dubious, half admiring. 'This is a precedent! The first time she's ever spoken like this on a *moral* question.'

Fortunately any doubts about the Queen's embarking on a new unscheduled role were quickly dispelled by a hilariously successful meeting with the media at Buckingham Palace. It was 8 December 1981. The Princess of Wales had been under the impression that once she was married the press photographers would lay off and allow her reasonable privacy. Not at all. When she could not even venture outside Highgrove to buy sweets without being assaulted by intrusive lenses, she began to feel 'totally beleaguered'.

Twenty-five years earlier the Queen had summoned the press to Buckingham Palace and appealed to them not to give her young son Charles that 'beleaguered' feeling. Now she was to go into action again, for her pregnant daughter-in-law.

Through Michael Shea her press secretary she invited the whole gamut of the national press and media, editors of daily and Sunday newspapers, the Press Association, television and radio news. After Shea had told them about the Queen's 'increasing concern', the group adjourned to an informal meeting with the Queen herself. Suddenly they all realised that this was no longer an apparently tongue-tied woman but one who had become articulate through pent-up feelings at last released. 'Why can't the Princess send a servant to buy her fruit gums?' asked the editor of the *News of the World*. 'That's the most pompous thing I have ever heard,' said Her Majesty, to the spontaneous applause of twenty other editors.

The Queen had tempered her sharpness with a smile; nevertheless her unerring choice of the word 'pompous' – a real silver bullet against which no Fleet Street operator was proof – became a climacteric in her reign. When the next confrontation occurred, between the Royal Family and the *Sun* and *Daily Star* (the editor of the *Sun* had not accepted the invitation to the Palace in 1981), there was no doubt whatever as to where public sympathy lay. Their long lens had followed the Prince and Princess of Wales to a beach in the Bahamas in February 1982, where they were spending ten days' holiday; the Princess in a bikini and also in her sixth month of pregnancy. On the 18th, photographs of the Princess appeared in both papers, one caption being, 'Bahamas Mama'. In response to Michael Shea's protest that the Queen and Royal Family were 'very very upset', both papers apologised – if that is the word. 'Sorry Diana!' said the *Star*. 'If we have upset you, we are deeply sorry. . . . Our interest was out of a deep affection for the Royal couple. We were so pleased to see Diana enjoying herself so freely on the beach that we thought our readers would want to share her joy. . . .' Hypocrisy could hardly go further; so little was the long lens interested in the Princess's 'joy' compared with her bikini; or interested in her bikini compared with what the Victorians would have called her 'interesting condition'.

'The system' depends for smooth working on amicable relations between the Royal Household and the Fourth Estate. This is recognised by both sides. On 10 February 1982, a week before the *Sun* and *Star* disappeared behind the clouds, the Press Club invited the heir to the throne to their centenary banquet. He accepted; and made a witty speech declaring his firm faith in a free press, in marriage, in pregnant husbands and in God. But the Royal Family's marriage with the press, up to the 'fruit gums' affair, had been becoming shaky. Six weeks before Prince Charles's speech to the press, Princess Anne had replied brusquely on television to a charge of being unco-operative with journalists: 'I don't do stunts. I don't go for them anyway. Why should I do it to please their editors?' Over a period, the Queen and the Princess of Wales had been concerned for their privacy. It had become a subject of consummate importance. The 'fruit gums' affair merely focused attention on what had been building up for a long time. Increasingly, the telephoto lens had affected the attitude of the monarchy to the media. It might have been a dangerous trend.

Then, after twenty-five years, came another Buckingham Palace press conference which defused the situation.

Everyone hoped that tension would not build up to a peak again at least for another twenty-five years. And that the press's need for 'stories' and the Queen's need for 'privacy' would meet on what was after all the common ground of monarchy's need to be kept in the public eye.

Such hopes were premature. On a quiet Tuesday morning in February 1983, while the Queen was away on her second state visit to Mexico, the *Sun* newspaper suddenly startled its unsuspecting readers with what it proudly called an 'amazing' article. It was displayed under the headlines: 'QUEEN KOO'S* ROMPS AT THE PALACE. ANOTHER AMAZING SUN EXCLUSIVE'. Yet another 'amazing' exclusive was intended to hit the headlines the next day, but the second article never got beyond its trailer: '*When barefoot Di buttered my toast.*' (The toast of Kieran Kenny, 'author' and kitchen storeman at the Palace, aged twenty.) The Queen's deputy treasurer sought and was granted an injunction against the *Sun* and asked for damages. For despite the Royal Family's traditional avoidance of resort to the courts, there was one precedent for legal action. In 1849 Prince Albert had successfully used the courts to prevent publication of some sketches by himself and Queen Victoria on grounds of 'breach of confidence'. Since the storeman had also given an undertaking not to publish, he too could be claimed to be in breach of confidence. Again the *Sun* professed itself 'amazed'; but it had to agree terms and pay £4,000 to charity in lieu of damages. Would this affair at last prove the grand deterrent?

Meanwhile, Elizabeth II had reigned for over thirty years. It is time to see how chance and change had dealt with the two ultimates in a constitutional monarchy: the 'magic' that it generates and the magician who must cast the spell.

---

* The actress Miss Koo Stark, friend of Prince Andrew.

XIX

The Spell

Over the present reign, the British monarchy has collected a meritorious list of honorary titles. It has been called a working, mobile, flying, modern, representative, democratic, parliamentary, unifying monarchy; an ancient institution with a human face; a family monarchy. Alternatively it is decried as an antiquated relic, costly, labour-intensive, wasteful, snobbish, class-ridden, irrelevant. But there is more to it than appears in those confrontations.

People see the monarchy as a thing that is real and exists, yet somehow has not been entirely fabricated by themselves. Chance, or the element of chance in a hereditary monarchy, paradoxically confers strength, making it seem to reach out into a world beyond the institutional microchips. A hereditary monarchy's continuity with history brings it something apart from the here and now, linking it to the nation's immaterial needs.

For the most part the British system rightly depends on the vote. The monarchy, however, was not conceived in a ballot-box, born of a referendum, nor did it suffer under a reselection committee. It has been with the nation, for better and for worse, for a thousand years; and though such a period in the sight of eternity is 'but as yesterday', in human terms this long span brings a sense of timelessness that stirs the heart and imagination.

Again paradoxically, because it has worked so long it still works. And because it is not quite rational, not wholly logical, nor even fully intelligible to itself or to us, it can become the national focus for service and chivalry as well as fantasy and dreams. In a word, like few other institutions, it can be loved.

Of course it would be perfectly possible to have an inexpensive elected head of state and to pay him or her no more than a prime minister's salary. Things like state visits would come cheaper too, since fewer foreigners would want to visit or be visited. In laying out millions on the monarchy the public is paying partly for a unique product – magic.

The mysterious side of monarchy is something that interests the British quite extraordinarily, the British Royal Family not excluded. Every kind of opinion has been expressed about it. 'Something as curious as the monarchy,' said Prince Charles to Anthony Sampson, 'won't survive unless you take account of people's attitudes. . . . After all, if people don't want it, they won't have it.' What exactly did Prince Charles mean by 'curious'? Was it a modest way of describing the monarchy's magic? Anthony Sampson himself believes that it has the magic of survival.[1]

David Wood, on the contrary, applauds because the Royal Family have 'surrendered all mystery' by the calculated exposure of their 'human ordinariness' on television: 'It is an astonishing non-stuffy achievement.'[2] Nicholas Wapshott speaks of 'the demystification of royalty'[3] as an accomplished fact. Charles Douglas-Home, however, thinks that the mystery not only remains but is heightened by a modern paradox. If the Queen is ever forced to use her prerogative, he writes, she may never use 'that last tiny atom of power' again – like a bee that stings once and then dies. The existence of this prerogative 'both adds magic to the mystery and threatens to destroy it'.[4]

Less subtle examples of the royal magic abound. There are all those millions of people who are said to have dreamt at least once of the Queen. There was Sir Harry Secombe receiving his knighthood. He said afterwards, 'When the Queen smiled I could have climbed Everest.' Or Bill Beaumont, retired captain of the Lions, 'intensely proud' to be given the OBE by the Queen 'on behalf of all the English players. . . . I could hardly believe my ears when the Queen said how nice it was to see me again, as if I were quite a regular little visitor to the Palace.'[5] Or Virginia Wade being handed her Wimbledon tennis trophy by Her Majesty – the cheering so loud that Virginia couldn't hear what the Queen was saying, 'but it was just great to see her lips moving'. Or Adrian Moorhouse the young breast-stroke champion winning a gold medal for England because his Queen was watching. 'Over the last fifteen metres I kept saying to myself "You've got to win for the Queen." She gave me inspiration.'

Besides inspiration the magic can dispense nervous anxi-ety. There was the housekeeper in Gloucestershire who answered the door-bell, unexpectedly, to Prince Charles – and fainted. There was Lady Diana Cooper who at first did not recognise the 'nice little woman' to whom she was chatting at the concert to celebrate Sir Robert Mayer's one hundredth birthday; and when she did realise who it was she blurted out, 'Oh, ma'am. Please, ma'am. I'm so sorry, ma'am – I didn't recognise you without your crown.' To which Ma'am replied pleasantly, 'I thought it was Sir Robert's night, not mine.'[6] Or Kingsley Martin and Sir Hugh Casson both independently noticing that everybody 'changes gear' when in the presence of royalty.[7] Or Casson also commenting on the 'punctuality angst – endemic to royal occasions', which gets all guests to Windsor half an hour early and leaves them parked under the trees waiting among the rabbits.[8] Or even the magnificent Lord Chancel-lor trembling at the opening of Parliament. 'Is it emotion or fear or tension?' asked Richard Crossman. 'I don't know, but for more than half an hour he stands trembling before the Queen arrives.'[9]

The magic can work equally well on a sophisticated new generation. A young couple who had distinguished them-selves in literature and the arts were invited for dinner and the night to Windsor Castle. 'We did not arrive in a particularly royal mood,' they said afterwards, but they were to find it all overwhelming. 'The whole Royal Family were present, the Queen talked to everyone for exactly the same number of minutes and the courtiers were superbly efficient, polite and welcoming.' They left in ecstasy. And this despite the usual misunderstandings and mishaps. The husband had discussed the sport of coaching with the Duke of Edinburgh, the visitor thinking they were on to the vehicles and the Duke still talking about the horses. 'You have to consider the bite,' said one. 'And of course the springs and brake,' said the other. Then they both burst out laughing. The wife found her clothes had been kindly unpacked for her before dinner and her rather tatty 'plunge' bra to wear with her new evening dress taken away – 'to be washed or burnt?' she wondered – so she and her husband had each to grip her ordinary bra in both hands and tear it down to make a 'plunge'.

A great deal of mutual pride goes into the making of the magic. There is the nation's pride in their royal family and the family's pride in the nation. A lady in a train picked up a copy of the *Mirror* lying on the seat. There were photographs of the Queen and President Reagan on the front page, the President announcing that it was his special ambition to be visited by Elizabeth II, in 1983. The lady passed the picture to the author, a stranger, with the ringing words: '*Our* Queen!'

Vice versa, the Prince and Princess of Wales drew inspiration from the people's response to their magic: 'Our wedding was quite extraordinary as far as we were concerned,' said the Prince. 'It made us both extraordinarily proud to be British.'

Not all the people's responses to the magic were conscious. The choice of wedding presents for Charles and Diana provided examples of something deeper. Among the thousands of beautiful and useful things displayed for charity at St James's Palace – the Herend porcelain, the library ladder, the video cassette recorder, the pair of bellows – was a fair sprinkling of quite different gifts.

Decorated eggs, Welsh wooden love spoons, a grain of rice in a silver box, corn dollies, models and pictures of mice and rabbits, some in bridal attire. Fertility symbols have always been a potent part of magic.

There are other things that have customarily gone to make up royal magic, most of them unchanged for decades: the crown jewels, processions, pageantry. Street pageantry is almost its old self today, since the Clean Air Act of 1956 produced buildings again worthy of being beflagged.

The royal yacht *Britannia* should be recognised for its magic, as well as for its usefulness on tours – it has already carried the Queen and Prince Philip over 600,000 miles and assured her 'rest between some fairly merciless demands' and 'murderous' schedules, as Susan Crosland wrote[10] – or as a potential hospital ship or on NATO manoeuvres. Prince Philip's perceptive private secretary, Lord Rupert Nevill (who died alas in July 1982), once described the impact of *Britannia* on Commonwealth crowds:

> The dramatic effect is enormous of the Royal Yacht slowly leaving port with thousands of people watching the Queen go and cheering. This has a stupendous influence which a take-off from an air terminal could not touch. People love to watch the great ship sailing away and come in their thousands.
>
> Her Majesty is able to entertain members of the Commonwealth she is visiting, on board the yacht, in a way she could not do in a hotel or Government House. She can dine 60 people on board and hold a reception for 250. The whole thing is very agreeable and the Commonwealth love it.

Its interior was most recently designed by Sir Hugh Casson in 'restrained "English country house style" '.[11]

The young Queen broke a bottle of Empire wine on the yacht's young bows in 1953, and since then its value to the Commonwealth has far exceeded today's annual £1.25 million spent on its crew and upkeep, and the original £2,000,000 plus £10,000,000 for refits. Tiny islands such as Nauru and Tuvalu, with populations of a few thousands, which are none the less members of the Commonwealth, could never be visited by their Queen – 'Mrs Gwin' as they greeted her in Tuvalu – but for *Britannia*. Altogether the grace and comfort and efficiency of yachts somehow symbolise royalty even in countries where magic is not at a premium. King Haakon of Norway was presented with the yacht *Norge* on his seventy-fifth birthday by a grateful people. It was the thing he had always wanted most.

The honours system undoubtedly partakes of the magic, though it does not cast its spell evenly over the nation; some people are immune, others bewitched. As the 'fount of honour', King Edward VII said he did not want the fountain to become a pump. George V succeeded in stopping the flow in individual cases, and critics of the present set-up have sometimes wondered why the Queen did not 'put her foot down' over unpopular creations. But she would have to step exceedingly delicately in questioning a prime ministerial recommendation. For this reason Philip Howard, in his book on the British monarchy, suggested that it would be an improvement 'to remove honours from the hands of the Prime Minister and entrust them to someone above politics like the Monarch, with checks and safeguards to ensure impartiality'.

Others have criticised the decision not to create hereditary titles, initiated by Wilson and followed by Heath, Callaghan and Thatcher – until 1983. It was objected in the 1970s that without the support of an hereditary aristocracy the hereditary monarchy would crumble.[12] Ten years later, with the hereditary aristocracy entirely dependent on its own reproductive powers, the hereditary monarchy seemed more buoyant than ever. It was even said that the monarchy was the only British institution that was working exactly as it was intended to work. 'If there were a Queen's party,' wrote Peregrine Worsthorne during the silly season of 1981, 'it would sweep the country. This is quite new. Nothing like it has been seen in this country in modern times.'[13] Be that as it may, the magic of honours conferred by a sovereign has never been better stated than by

Malcolm Muggeridge in his article of 1957, reprinted in 1981.

> If the honours were conferred by a president or a prime minister the odds are that they would lose some of their allure. The worthy alderman kneels ecstatically with creaking joints before the Queen to receive the accolade; the aged party hack finds one more canter in him when it is a question of being elevated to the peerage by Her Majesty in person.[14]

Changelessness and continuity are aspects of the magic which have to adapt themselves to that other prerequisite of monarchy: keeping up to date. One of the Queen's friends has seen no changes in 'the big things' over the last thirty years. 'Things are still done in basically the same way. One thing, for instance, will always make the Palace different from any other home in Britain, the existence of servants.'

Andrew Duncan in his *The Reality of Monarchy* pilloried the system for being 'out of date' and suggested a few 'short-notice visits' to factories, hospitals and housing estates, and less protocol.[15] By a coincidence his book was published in 1970, the very year in which the Queen went on her first walkabout in England. The Queen and Prince Philip regard their walkabouts as the turning-point of the reign, if a 'pedestrian' one.

Changes are going on even in the most traditional areas: trappings such as carpets and bunting for the welcome of kings, even kings from the Arabian Nights countries, are today recycled.

What could be more traditional than a royal wedding? Coronations, jubilees, funerals, weddings are all material for the display of 'custom and ceremony'. Yet on 29 July 1981 the bride wore her veil to the wedding covering her face and did not promise to 'obey'; ten-and-a-half months later she was giving birth to her son in St Mary's Hospital, Paddington – the first future king to be born within sound of a railway terminal. The baby's nanny will not wear a uniform ('Good grief, no!') and the father drove his family home from the hospital. All three, father, mother and son, later flew together to Balmoral, thus breaking the security protocol of 'separate planes'.

Shortly before his fiftieth birthday Prince Philip asked his biographer, Basil Boothroyd, a pertinent question. 'Did greater knowledge of the Sovereign mean less mystery?' Boothroyd was too much surprised by such a query coming from such a questioner to think up an answer. Kenneth Rose, however, answered it epigrammatically some two years later. 'The Queen has come to Coronation Street and something of the magic has departed.'[16]

But here again there are conflicting views. Sir Roy Strong believes that the monarchy is being headed in the direction of 'hyperadulation, a very serious one'. Twenty years ago Kingsley Martin was complaining, 'the Queen is not allowed to wear a crown, nothing less than a halo will suffice'.[17] Then along comes Professor Edmund Leach in 1981 saying, 'On the contrary, there is no point in having a Crown at all unless it has a halo.'[18] Admittedly a halo is not the same thing as mystique. It implies moral leadership. But moral leadership is part of the magic. If we ever had 'one bad sovereign, or glaringly incompetent ruler', wrote a modern prime minister Robert Menzies, 'the monarchy would hardly survive'.[19]

There is yet another way for the Royal Family to look at this question. Now that they have 'come to Coronation Street', it is up to them to find some element of magic in their new surroundings. Walkabouts must not mean boredom. Nor do they. Princess Anne has put the point at its barest. 'Some engagements are more interesting than others – but never boring,' she said; 'there is always at least one individual to make it interesting.'[20]

Today it is a point of honour with the Royal Family to discover interest in every situation that faces them. To the Queen Mother it comes as naturally as breathing. The Queen and her daughter have worked at it. As a result there has been, so to speak, a transfer of magic. Some of the

magic may have departed from the monarchy, but it is
reflected back from Coronation Street through the Queen
herself.

A touch of loneliness or remoteness has always been part of
the mystique – something that is impressive and moving
for us, the spectators, but formidable for them. Sir John
Betjeman celebrated Prince Charles's investiture with
these words:

> You knelt a boy, you rose a man,
> And thus your lonelier life began.

Fortunately the Prince's wedding twelve years later in St
Paul's enabled Sir John to show in a new ode how royal
loneliness can be made bearable.

> The scene is changed, the outlook cleared.
> The loneliness has disappeared
> And all of those assembled there
> Are joyful in the love you share.[21]

In fact a royal family constantly increasing through marriages and births has always been the safe antidote to
loneliness and also a part of the magic in its own right. The
birth of Prince William* Arthur Philip Louis of Wales,
second in line to the throne, on 21 June 1982, and his
christening on his great-grandmother's eighty-second
birthday, was a case in point. The traditional euphoria, not
to say hysteria of the crowd over the royal birth (one
teenager managed not only to kiss Charles's cheek outside
the hospital but to leave lipstick on it), was balanced by
William Hamilton's affectionately satirical comment on the

---

* Some journalists succumbed to the apparent joke that the last King
William was nicknamed 'Silly Billy'. The joke was against them. In fact it
was they who were the silly billies, for 'Silly Billy' was the Duke of
Gloucester (1776–1834), King William IV's brother-in-law, who married
Princess Mary.

baby's name: 'I think it is a very lovely name and I am sure they had me in mind when they chose it.' And a group of Labour MPs marked what to them was no doubt the Century of the Common Baby by signing a Commons motion of congratulations to the parents of a baby born in Goole on the same day as Prince William.

The royal baby's christening took place in the Music Room of Buckingham Palace, where his father had been christened before him, wearing the same historic robe of Honiton lace. The Queen and her family then gathered in the gold and blue Drawing Room, where the baby's lusty cries were stilled only after his grandmother and great-grandmother had signalled in despair for his mother. The Princess of Wales gave him her little finger to suck. No other finger would do.

The Queen Mother, dressed all in blue like the Queen, had earlier mounted an upturned flower-pot on the balcony of Clarence House the better to wave to the crowds on her birthday morning. She was shown on television in April greeting the white-coated butchers at Smithfield – a small figure in perpetual motion, laughing, gesticulating, turning this way and that, determined to collect them all into her own particular magic circle.

The whole day's television was a lesson in the Royal Family's special characteristics: continuity (four generations present at the christening); universality (operating in the Meat Market as well as the Drawing Room); and democracy. For that same evening Lord Home was to tell viewers about a question he had once put to an absolute monarch, the Shah of Iran. 'Why did you take so much on yourself?' he asked. The Shah replied: 'But who could I trust?' That is not a problem for Elizabeth II.

It was to Kensington Palace that Prince Charles had driven his wife and son from St Mary's Hospital, for a far from lonely homecoming. Their relatives rushed out to welcome them waving handkerchiefs, towels, anything they could lay hands on. Then Princess Margaret, the Kents and the rest all went round to the Gloucesters. 'Never has there been such a party,' said the jubilant Princess Margaret.

Anyone who was looking for an example of daylight being let into the magic circle would find it in Prince Richard of Gloucester. A shy second son who was catapulted into the royal dukedom by the tragic death of his elder brother William, Prince Richard had made the most of his early freedom. He married a Danish commoner, Birgitte van Deurs, whom he had met at Cambridge, practised as an architect and sat as the Queen's representative with the British Museum trustees. It was while carrying out this latter duty that he showed how much daylight had crept in. Arriving in Northumberland Avenue for a meeting of the trustees, he asked the receptionist which floor it was on. The receptionist glanced at the crash-helmeted young man who had thundered up on a motor-cycle with his papers in his pillion bag. 'Second floor,' she said. A fellow trustee overheard and, knowing she had made a mistake, corrected her. 'It's on the seventh floor.' The receptionist looked at them both severely and repeated, 'Second floor. Second floor for dispatch riders.'

The 'Kensington Palace set' is a descendant, so to speak, of the 'Marlborough House set' of the last century; except that the Prince of Wales's 'fast set' of those days did not meet with his mother's approval, whereas Elizabeth II has shown her approval through her generosity with apartments.

The Queen must be seen, as in the great royal photographic portraits, flanked by families of cousins. Everything that these cousins do counts, in the sense that they too are part of the extended Royal Family. When one of them wins a scholarship it is one up to the monarchy. When another gets divorced it may be one down; alternatively, it may ease the monarchy along the pot-holed road of adaptation to twentieth-century mores.

It would be inhuman if there were not one or two members of a richly varied Royal Family who seemed sometimes to prefer daylight to magic. Both Princess Margaret and Princess Anne have announced their children's exemption from 'the system' in words that suggest little regret. Princess Margaret's spokesman said of her daughter Lady Sarah: 'She will not undertake public engagements or take on official duties. She is an entirely private person and not a member of the Royal Family.' And Princess Anne's remark on television about her children has already been noted: 'I doubt if the next generation [of Princess Anne's own family] will be involved at all.'[22]

With the 'inner' Royal Family now standing probably at eleven rather than fifteen, Elizabeth II still goes out of her way to cultivate the growing outer circle – witness her huge family parties at Christmas. King George VI's 'Royal Firm' has become Elizabeth II's 'multinational'; quite literally, for the delightful Duchess of Gloucester and the striking, Bohemian-born Marie-Christine von Reibnitz, now Princess Michael of Kent, have reintroduced continental blood, which used to be so prolific in the Royal Family but had not been replenished since Princess Elizabeth married Prince Philip of Greece.

It is relevant to look at the European monarchies and their state of play, and to ask how far the existence – or non-existence – of other royal families affects the magic of the British monarchy. The European game was perhaps at its lowest ebb in 1943, when Prince Paul and Princess Olga of Yugoslavia were driven into final and irretrievable exile. True, Greece had a king, Constantine II, from 1964 to 1967, but after that it seemed that no European monarchy would survive further south than Belgium and Luxembourg, apart from the tiny principalities of Liechtenstein and Monaco. The national habitat of crowned heads would in future be a physically cold climate.

Then came the death of the Spanish dictator General Franco in 1975. Suddenly there was a democracy and a king again in Spain, the second largest European country which also possessed Mediterranean coastlines. The succession of Juan Carlos I to the long-empty Spanish throne gave a boost to royalist stock. It had been a grim reminder of the past when the six kings and queens who attended Lord Mountbatten's memorial service in 1979 turned out to be exiles all: King Simeon of Bulgaria, King Umberto of Italy, King Michael and Queen Anne of Romania, King Constantine and Queen Anne-Marie of the Hellenes. An extension of 'the system' again in southern Europe was no disadvantage to Elizabeth II. Especially as the new king was a liberal interested in social progress and showing to the outside world the right mixture of 'dignity and informality'. That the restoration of the Spanish monarchy meant also the restoration of democracy showed that royalty could bring off a striking double coup. Not only that, but it was the Spanish king's firmness and prestige which was largely responsible for defeating the military coup in 1981.

Europe's royal families are not only interrelated by blood but also through ideas. There have always been close relations between the Scandinavian and British houses, and there is a tendency to make comparisons which are stimulating. As early as 1908 King Edward VII sent a warning message to his daughter Queen Maud of Norway: if she and her husband King Haakon insisted on travelling by tramway they would destroy the royal mystique. (He was wrong in implying that there was only one kind of mystique, the British brand.)

On the other side, the idiosyncrasies of foreign democratic monarchies are not always relevant or congenial to the British version. In Spain King Juan Carlos attends his government's cabinet meetings, a thing that has not happened in England since the century before last. In Sweden since 1977 the King has lost his right to appoint prime ministers, having already gained the privilege of paying income tax. A new subject for discussion has been started through Sweden also: should not the crown go to the first-born irrespective of sex?

Crown Princess Victoria, born in 1977, will eventually succeed to the Swedish throne, despite the birth of a brother, Prince Philip, in 1979. The beginnings of a debate on this subject in Britain were cut off by the birth of Prince William of Wales. This put an end to the effective argument, at least for a generation. But if it ever started up again, two things are clear: Sweden would be cited in evidence on one side and Elizabeth II, as a self-confessed traditionalist, would feel strongly on the other. The result of a 'Swedish' victory might affect other families, not only the royal line. After inheritance by the first-born male had disappeared, inheritance by primogeniture could go too, estates being equally divided among all the children; then, it might be argued, the estates themselves would be broken up, by which time the British monarchy would be in any case as unlikely to survive as an ice cube in the Red Sea.

The present arguments for and against the 'Swedish' solution are nicely balanced. For: natural justice, the tonic effects of any change, the success of former British queens, the fact that it is easier to be a popular queen in the modern climate than a popular king. Against: the Bagehot warning against 'poking about' the monarchy, the debilitating effects of any change on something so steeped in tradition as the monarchy, the fact that in a democratic age 'one reform' will lead to another. Peregrine Worsthorne once wrote of the monarchy in this context: 'In its past is its future.' Deface its past and it has no future.

Holland is another democratic monarchy whose charms could prove dangerously seductive. There is no religious coronation service but a secular investiture in a church. This, though moving, does not build up the mystery. Moreover two queens of the Netherlands have recently abdicated in favour of a daughter. In 1948 Queen Wilhelmina, who had reigned for fifty years, took as her model the Emperor Charles V who abdicated after a tempestuous reign of thirty-seven years because he no longer possessed 'enterprise and energy'. (Her anti-model, so to speak, was King Gustav of Sweden whom she said she did not wish to emulate in hanging on.) Again in June 1980 there was an abdication, that of Queen Juliana in favour of her daughter, the progressive Queen Beatrix – who proved popular on her state visit to Britain in 1982.

Abdication is still a sinister word in British mythology. It happened once in 1936 and there is a strong national wish for 'never again'. Even without any sinister connotation, 'abdication' brings royalty into the world of civil servants, where it simply means retirement on a pension – an excellent step when convenient but lacking any magic whatever; whereas the Queen's accumulated years of uninterrupted work, with no document-free holidays, are already different enough from the norm to possess something akin to magic.

The arguments from Edward VII to a future Charles III are invalid. It is said that Edward's long frustrating wait for his mother to die damaged his life and reign. On the contrary, had Victoria abdicated, say in 1880, Edward VII's reign would not have been better than it was; rather worse, because his sensual appetites at forty were more vigorous and ungovernable than at sixty. King Edward was an unintellectual man, though a shrewd diplomat. Prince Charles is a conscientious intellectual, deeply in love (Edward never was) and full of good ideas for his family (we do not hear of Edward ever having any). There is every reason why a popular young Prince and Princess of Wales should gradually take over some of the tours and visits; none why a respected and loved Queen, full of health, experience and accumulated wisdom should abdicate.

Abdication is never discussed at the Palace. 'It is simply not on the agenda.' May it never reach an agenda which could only turn out to be a blue-print for royal presidency.

No one who has ever watched the Queen walking round a room full of people will forget the extraordinary way a group changes as she approaches. Some groups are struck dumb by tension. Others become animated; then, as she moves away, the excitement fades and they return to normal. It is as if the beam of a lighthouse were circling round the room. As long as that beam still plays over a crowd there is no need to ask whether the mystique of monarchy works.

The spell is there to be used. But it is a woman not a witch who must use it. Clearly something of the old mystique has diminished, depending as it did on physical remoteness. Walkabouts and television have brought the Queen into the streets and living-rooms. This, however, while reducing the Queen's mysteriousness, has caused a transference rather than a destruction of interest. For it has compelled the Royal Family to discover a kind of magic in ordinary people. The Queen Mother has always spontaneously felt this magic of the ordinary and her descendants are quick-witted enough to pick it up from her.

In another way the mystique seems to have transferred itself psychologically into the Queen's personality. Her own reticence is an essential part of it. Thus the mystique is today attached to the very character of the Monarch rather than to outward symbols, like rare public appearances or communication only with top people. This makes the mystery in a way more powerful. Lady Cynthia Colville once wrote that though the mystique had decreased, people were just as loyal.[23] One might add, just as much in awe.

Any particular change in the quality of the mystique of course depends on the character of one particular monarch. A different monarch with a more outgoing or extrovert temperament would lose the special mystery of reticence. If Queen Elizabeth the Queen Mother had happened to be queen regnant her magic would have been totally different.

Not that reticence forms more than the ambience of Elizabeth II's character. Within that limiting or, if you will, enhancing factor, she was born with and has cultivated many other distinguishing traits that have affected the style of her reign. In the end everything from 'the system' to the 'magic' comes back to the Queen herself.

The Queen

Courage is the Queen's hallmark. On disembarking from *Britannia* at Sullom Voe to inaugurate the new Shetlands oil complex on 9 May 1981, she could have avoided the real danger of terrorists by stepping straight into a 'bullet-proof bubble'. But not even fast cars taking evasive action, far less bubbles, were her style, as the Palace pointed out: 'We don't live in a society where the Queen drives along at 90 m.p.h. in a blacked-out limousine.'

She rejected the idea of a specially proofed 'Trooping cloak'. She was not going to become, as it were, an untouchable. Prince Philip, in one somewhat cryptic remark, seems to have suggested that anti-terrorist measures actually caused terrorism. 'If it hadn't been for the security,' he said to Boothroyd, 'Kennedy wouldn't have been shot.'[1]

Going back twenty years from Sullom Voe, Harold Macmillan in his 1961 diary put Elizabeth II's attitude, as he saw it, once for all:

> If she were pressed too hard and if Government and people here are determined to restrict her activity (including taking reasonably acceptable risks) I think she might be tempted to throw in her hand. She does *not* enjoy 'society'. She likes her horses. But she loves her duty and means to be a queen and not a puppet.[2]

The Queen's own courage has always enabled her to sympathise with the heroism and tragedies of her people, whether at Aberfan or Mousehole or the Falklands. Photographs of her in prayer during the Falklands war showed that a face set in deeply grave lines can be exceptionally queenly. On the other hand, during the hymns at the Thanksgiving Service there was a change from remoteness to participation: the Queen was seen on television singing with her whole heart and soul.

Again, her own reticence has made her sensitive to the reserves and hesitations of others. She said one day to a young lady-in-waiting: 'I hear that you would like me to be your baby's godmother, but being who I am, you don't like to ask me. There's nothing I should like more.'

In the very early days her unassertive temperament made her an acquiescent, mechanical speaker. There seemed nothing for it but to accept every speech that was given to her and deliver it. But all the time she was developing her own opinions; and though today she continues to read every speech, she will often object, 'I can't possibly say that,' and introduce a new thought or change something around. She still tends to be monosyllabic on occasion. An 'Oh', or 'Oh, really', is known to mean, 'no more on that subject, please.' Journalists have sometimes pitied her for her oft-repeated comment, 'How interesting.' But these trite words more often give pleasure than not – even to journalists. One woman journalist recounted with great gratification how the Queen had said 'How very interesting' twice over when told that her son, also a journalist, had learnt to ride both an elephant and an oil-rig.[3]

Those who are not satisfied with 'How interesting' or 'Well done', can, by using their own imagination, give the Queen a chance to converse at greater length. If only half the story, for instance, is told her about any particular person or object presented to her, the Queen is exceptionally quick at picking up the clues and eliciting the other half of the story for herself.

Many elements of formality once thought to be the *sine qua non* of majesty are gradually being eliminated from royal dialogues. Guests at garden parties have noticed that the Queen no longer insists on introducing every subject herself. At the Queen's Christmas broadcast in 1981, her exchanges with the disabled car-owners invited to the Palace were remarkably natural. After an initial 'ma'am', the talk flowed merrily, unpunctuated by protocol.

The Queen's quickness in picking up facts about people is matched by her speed in performing her formal royal functions. She will invest from 140 to 160 people with honours at a time, yet will speak to each individually without any impression of being hurried. She gets quickly through the paper-work at her weekly audiences, leaving her prime ministers plenty of time to clear their minds on special matters – one of the unique uses of a monarch. A monarch is the best of weekly catalysts.

One journalist remarked on the Queen's 'firm level gaze', which seemed to say 'I've done my boxes – have you done yours?' Thoroughness in her reading and natural attentiveness combine to make her a formidable observer of the political, administrative and social scene. During the troubles over the Rhodesian Unilateral Declaration of Independence the rebel Prime Minister Ian Smith tried to miss out on a reception at the Palace by ensconcing himself at the Hyde Park Hotel for a quiet steak. The Queen noticed his absence and he was fetched by an equerry.

In one great department of state, a mistake was made in drafting by the Executive Officer which was overlooked by the higher Executive Officer, the Assistant Secretary of State and the Secretary of State himself. It was only when the document reached the Queen for her signature that the mistake was noticed and rectified. It came back bearing a manuscript correction in the royal hand.

In large crowds the Queen will observe and remember individuals. 'Her eyes are everywhere', wrote Avril Mollison who accompanied her on the Tuvalu (South Pacific) tour in 1982, 'and she has a disconcerting habit of noticing everything. One local dignitary, on being presented at a state banquet, was told, "I've seen you twice today in the crowd."'[4]

We saw that in youth she had no great interest in clothes

and no innate dress sense, but she and Diana Spencer shared a quality of extreme tidiness as children. It has been left to the Queen's daughter-in-law to do the trend-setting in fashion. Neither Prince Charles nor Prince Edward show special concern with clothes, and in this they are like their mother. It is remembered that Princess Elizabeth disapproved of the so-called New Look. 'Possibly if she had had a French maid as a dresser instead of Bobo,' says a friend, 'she would have been smarter – but not so serene.' As it is, she and Bobo will simply put on her tiara after dinner, when necessary, with never any of that fuss and fume over hairdressers that so often go with 'First Ladies'. The Queen can none the less achieve successful results when she wants to make a particular point. In being photographed with her Yeoman Warders she chose a red ior her dress that must have been dyed exactly to match theirs.

The Queen's aim is to be recognised rather than copied. Hence her custom of wearing a hat in a hatless crowd. Ann Morrow tells an amusing anecdote of the Queen's satisfaction when recognition takes place. She had popped down to the village shop at Sandringham wearing a headscarf and anorak, when a fellow customer stopped her and said: 'Excuse me, but you do look like the Queen.' 'How very reassuring,' replied the Queen with a smile.

Her shoes are chosen for elegance and comfort, and she has worked out over the years a way of standing that is least hard on the feet, and which she solicitously relayed to Susan Crosland, sparkling American wife of her Foreign Secretary, Anthony Crosland, in 1976: ' "One plants one's feet apart like this," said Her Majesty, hoisting skirt above ankles to demonstrate. "Always keep them parallel. Make sure your weight is evenly distributed. That's all there is to it." '[5] This sensible stance is now second nature to the Queen, so that when photographed with Charles and Diana after the Privy Council confirmed their engagement the Queen was shown standing with feet planted apart and parallel, while Lady Diana's feet were close together, with toes turned out in a ballet dancer's position. One knew which would tire first.

'That's all there is to it.' Those half-dozen words might well be taken as the Queen's practical philosophy. One of the Queen's strengths is to know what she means to do and to do it without fuss. It is a far cry from the child worried at night because she could not arrange her shoes under her chair – *exactly parallel*.

Mrs Crosland and her husband accompanied the Queen and Prince Philip on the royal visit to the United States for the Independence bicentenary. Susan Crosland said afterwards, 'I have never experienced anything so arduous.' Not so royalty. 'The Queen never faltered in the day's walkabout under a remorseless sun, crowds stretching out their arms to her.'

This was the more remarkable since Elizabeth II is a 'cool weather' queen. Because of her fair skin and tendency to sinusitis (her only health problem) a 'remorseless sun' is peculiarly trying for her. She believes in homeopathic medicine for treatment of this trouble. As an essentially northern queen, she is not tempted to buy a villa or vineyard in Italy, like her fellow royalty Queen Beatrix of the Netherlands. Indeed Elizabeth II is exceptionally home-loving. No mountain looks more beautiful to her than Mt Lochnagar, no climate suits her better than Balmoral's, and no country is better for walking eleven Welsh corgis than Scotland.

Susan Crosland had the fun of seeing this cool Queen in action both at the French Embassy in London and on board *Britannia*, as well as in Washington. At the embassy in a heatwave the Queen lost a battle for fresh air only because the French President M. Giscard d'Estaing was an honoured guest. The Queen got the window behind her open fully, but just for a moment. M. le Président had it lowered again, for fear of a *courant d'air*, to within four inches of the sill. The French enjoyed their visit immensely but were puzzled by the British mixture of 'informality' (fresh air) with military pomp.[6]

In a force nine gale, the Queen remained upright on *Britannia* as long as anyone, though twice, as she tried to get through the sliding door of the drawing-room, *Britannia* heaved and sent it sliding to a close. 'Wheeeeeeee,' said the Queen each time. Susan Crosland recalled an incident the next day:

> When we foregathered in the drawing-room before lunch complexions were better than the evening before. 'I have *never* seen so many grey and grim faces round a dinner table,' said the Queen. She paused. 'Philip was not at all well.' She paused. 'I'm glad to say.' She giggled. I'd forgotten her Consort is an Admiral of the Fleet.[7]

Like all her family, particularly her father, the Queen is an adept at the dry joke. She greeted one of Prince Charles's girl-friends, who had arrived at Windsor Castle for lunch, with the words, 'Did you find it all right?' And when her resilient mother, after recovering from an illness, announced, 'I'm going to live to a hundred,' the Queen replied, 'Then it'll be Charles who'll send you your centenarian telegram' – by then a 'telemessage'.

Occasions like investitures and privy councils are fertile fields for both mystique and mishaps, the latter of which the Queen takes with good humour, as her father did before her. The day when, in her reign, one man was presented with two Orders so that she had none to give the next in line, was paralleled by the day in George vi's reign when a distinguished legal figure was accidentally invested with a position in the Duchy of Cornwall as well as the Duchy of Lancaster. Second time round the King said, 'You seem to be in great demand.'[8]

There is a misconceived idea that the Queen looks black with rage when ludicrous gaffes are made – as they frequently are – by privy councillors. This was true of Queen Victoria but not of Elizabeth ii. In 1892 Victoria's Liberal council disgraced itself by members falling on their knees as they entered her room and then, instead of rising and walking across to kneel again and kiss her hand, they crawled up to her on hands and knees. She wrote angrily in her journal: 'A motley crew to behold.'[9]

When the same thing happened to Elizabeth II at Balmoral, and a privy councillor knocked a book off a table during his travels 'on knee' instead of on foot, the Queen could barely stifle her laughter. But Sir Edward Bridges, in charge of operations, thought she looked 'blackly furious'. After the lamentable show was over he 'crept back' to apologise to her. 'I'm terribly sorry.'

'You know, I nearly laughed.' Suddenly Bridges realised that she had looked so black in the face because she was trying to stop herself laughing.

This story was recounted to Richard Crossman the Labour politician, and relayed by him in his famous *Diaries*. As Lord President of the Council himself, it was his duty to read aloud to the Queen the fifty or sixty Orders in Council, with three other ministers standing beside him. At every pause Her Majesty would say 'Agreed'. The ritual took about two-and-a-half minutes. Crossman at first criticised the procedure on two counts: its 'mumbo-jumbo' and waste of time, especially when the council was at Balmoral. Why could not the Queen come south – 'but it's *lèse majesté* to suggest it' – or why could not the Queen and Lord President do the job between them? At this stage it did not occur to Crossman that ministers might actually wish to keep in personal touch with their sovereign. Over the years, however, Crossman himself was tamed and charmed by the Queen, as these extracts from his *Diaries* show.[10]

October 1964. Crossman kissed hands on his appointment as a privy councillor. He wrote:

We drove to the Palace and there stood about until we entered a great drawing-room. At the other end was this little woman with a beautiful waist, and she had to stand with her hand on the table for forty minutes while we went through this rigmarole. We were uneasy, she was uneasy. Then at the end informality broke out and she said: 'You all moved backwards very nicely,' and we all laughed. And then she pressed a bell and we all left her.

August 1966. During July Crossman, while dining at the country home of Lord Porchester, the Queen's great friend, had brashly inveighed against the monarchy and the 'snobbish' and 'dreary' court. Next month he found himself unexpectedly at the Palace. The Queen immediately said, 'Ah, Lord Porchester was telling me about you.'

'I never expected this,' said Crossman with one of his endearingly rueful smiles. Afterwards he reflected how 'very clever' it had been of the Queen to mention his gaffe straight away. 'I found it was perfectly simple and straight-forward to get on with her. Indeed she puts one at ease immediately and we were able to chat about other things fairly happily.' (Among the 'other things' would be the Queen's corgis *versus* the Crossmans' poodle, farming or Prince Charles's education.) 'And then in the actual recep-tion,' continued Crossman, 'George Brown [Foreign Secretary] took over and was as familiar and cosy with her – "my dear" and such nonsense – as any one could possibly be.'

September 1966. Conversation faltered, because the Queen and her minister were both thinking, 'Oh dear, are we boring each other?' Nevertheless, she had 'a lovely laugh' and was 'a really very spontaneous person'.

September 1967. Annual one-day visit to Balmoral. Crossman wrote:

> If this is necessary to the magic of monarchy, I accept it as fair enough. But surely there must be a limit to which busy Minis-ters are compelled to sacrifice their time to suit royal private engagements. It's only fair to add, however, that I am pretty certain that the Queen herself knows nothing about all this [juggling with Ministers' dates] and it's all a matter between endless courtiers.

November 1967. His last private audience in the *Diaries*. The barriers were down. He talked about her delivery of the Queen's Speech and how 'excited' he had been by her 'tiny pause' before announcing a diminution of the Lords' powers. What he would really like, he said, would be to compose a speech for her one day that could be delivered properly. 'We were really having a very cosy little chat [shades of George Brown] when she pressed the button and brought the others in.'

Little, lovely, clever, spontaneous – this robust 'lefty' had found her all these things. If it was not a case of magic, there was certainly magnetism.

Along with the Queen's laughter and pleasant sense of the ridiculous, goes her common sense. One American diplomat has called her 'street smart' and said he's 'learnt a lot from her'.[11] Many observers, among them President Reagan, have noticed that she was 'down-to-earth'. It was perhaps not the best metaphor for him to choose, however, for when he rode at Windsor with the Queen in 1982 neither of them wore hard hats. They were severely reprimanded by viewers for their down-to-earth risk.

All these characteristics were inherent in the Queen: her courage, sense of duty, reticence allied to spontaneity, speed and precision, gift of observation, personal attractiveness, tough good health, shrewdness, humour. Other qualities she has cultivated during the thirty years of her reign.

Prince Charles once said that everything worthwhile has to be 'worked at', from marriage to the Commonwealth. The Queen has herself worked at both these things and each now stands out in the new dimension she has brought to it. First, there is the whole family idea in the present monarchy; second, the Queen's contribution to affairs abroad, beginning of course with the Commonwealth.

The best witness in the first field of action is again Prince Charles. He said of his parents' marriage in 1975: 'I hope I will be as lucky as my parents, who have been so happy.' When Diana's pregnancy was announced, Charles remembered his wedding day. He remembered standing at his window after the long, exciting hours were over, and thinking, 'Some day I may be able to tell my children what I feel now.' In him the family idea had already been firmly inculcated, not least by his mother.

The Queen's happy marriage depends as so often on a union of opposites. She is reserved, Prince Philip is an initiator; where she is cautious, he is audacious. In whatever walk of life he had been born, he would have got to the top. If fate had decreed that she should have been born in the tweed instead of the purple, she would have remained a charming and contented woman, probably at the centre of a thriving village. The Queen's energy is tireless but she is always on an even keel; her consort is a speed-boat with bows half out of the water. When things go wrong on tours, the Queen endures, he explodes.

Sir Hugh Casson pays tribute to his 'sharp . . . brisk opening' of a committee and his 'skateboard' tour of an exhibition.[12] Ten years ago, Prince Philip said of the energy crisis that 'nuclear fusion would release the energy-equivalent of 2,500 gallons of petrol from one gram of a hydrogen isotope contained in eight gallons of water'. Prince Philip can do it without nuclear fusion.

A man of ideas who speaks spontaneously without much recourse to notes will always let slip a few phrases he regrets – for example, his unfortunate remark in Scotland about the unemployed wasting their leisure. His wife and his entourage understand this and have no wish for a very honest person to be emasculated. What is exasperating for the Queen is to hear him or others of her family blamed for mistakes they have not made. For instance, his much publicised 'near miss' mid-flight aircraft collision in 1981. He was not at the controls, his plane being one of the Queen's Flight; the plane was in the correct position and the Boeing was five minutes early. Another example, Princess Anne watching bullocks being mauled to death by tigers – total fiction.

Prince Philip's personal reply to the anti-blood sports people has, over the years, been streamlined into two sentences: 'I don't hunt – I shoot. If you don't shoot stags in Scotland you get over-population.' His World Wildlife Fund is not to save the species cow from being eaten for beef but to prevent the extinction of threatened species.

Prince Philip's love for horses is quite different from the Queen's. Hers is based on intimate understanding, his includes comic misunderstandings. He finds 'the mentality' of horses 'sometimes difficult to fathom', as when they seem to say, 'Yes, we've been ridden across this water but we are not pulling this carriage across it.' He also refers to 'incomprehensible equine thought processes'.[13]

Like the Queen, he has emerged with a deepened character in recent years. The first sign was in 1973, when he presented Mother Teresa of Calcutta with the Templeton Prize for Progress in Religion, describing her work as 'tactical compassion' and saying: 'It is in the lives of such people that the nature and influence of God is to be recognized.' Nine years later he was publishing a selection of his philosophical addresses delivered under the aegis of the Dean of Windsor and entitled *A Question of Balance*. The Duke of Edinburgh himself seems to be achieving the balance required of Plato's 'philosopher-consort'.

At the same time, the Queen's younger children have shown themselves impressive additions to the 'Royal Firm', Prince Edward teaching for two terms in a New Zealand school and Prince Andrew establishing the traditional connection between the monarch and the people in time of war. Prince Andrew's performance in the Falklands task force on HMS *Invincible*, where his Sea King helicopter was used as a decoy for an Exocet missile, proved to be an irresistible mixture of the heroic and the human. A hero, as he lay on the deck enduring 'the most lonely feeling in the world' and trying to 'think positively'. Human, when back from the South Atlantic, he called for the deeply missed pint of fresh milk and waved an uninhibited farewell to his comrades at Portsmouth. A holiday on Mustique seemed the necessary antidote to so much horror.

The Queen on the quayside was seen to wipe away a tear as she welcomed her heroes home.

Prince Charles has always been beset by an active conscience as he admitted in an interview with Peter Osnos of the *Washington Post*: 'I suffer from the constant battering that my conscience gets as to what I can try and do to help, if you know what I mean.'[14] He has had to look deeper into himself since Prince Andrew's exploits. 'In some ways, I envy my brother being able to go and do what he did in the South Atlantic, because I never had that chance to test myself. It's terribly important to see how you react, to be tested.'[15] That particular brand of self-doubt is a function of being the sovereign's eldest son. Edward Prince of Wales, later Edward VIII, knew it well. In Prince Charles's case, it represents a clash between the primitive instinct of the crown-wearer to be also the sword-bearer, and his realisation that he must find other ways of self-testing.

Fortunately for the Queen, the conflict in the case of a woman is never so extreme. If she cannot go out to meet danger she can and does show regal courage when danger comes to her.

An alphabet of 'The Greatest' was recently published by the *Sunday Times Magazine* in honour of its 1001st number. Q was for Queen Elizabeth II, sandwiched between P for Publisher Carmen Callil and R for Runner Steve Ovett. The Q caption picked out three things to explain Her Majesty's selection: so much dignity in presiding over the dissolution of the Empire 'that Commonwealth is still not quite an empty concept'; the unexpected demonstrations of loyalty at her Silver Jubilee; and the 'unrivalled interest' aroused by her and her family all over the world.

If the formulation of this tribute is somewhat negative, it is none the worse for that. The words 'not quite empty' and 'unexpected' convey what the Queen has been up against. Her signing of the proclamation of Canada's final independence on 18 April 1982 was an example. She had to be prepared for the absence of Quebec and the presence of some anti-Trudeau demonstrators, as well as some ill-informed views in Canadian magazines. The British writer Tim Heald complained that the Queen should have 'pursued the Canadian connection with more obvious relish, but . . . royal preference seems always to have been for Australia.'[16] Yet the Queen has visited Canada more often in her reign than Australia (twelve times to nine by 1982). Despite all this, the atmosphere she created at Canada's independence was radiant. 'The Constitution of Canada has come home,' said Pierre Trudeau. The Queen of Canada felt she had too.

In Africa the Queen's familiarity with political personalities enabled her to be not only a figurehead but a moving spirit in negotiations. It is generally known that her friendship with Kenneth Kaunda of Zambia smoothed the path of the Lusaka Commonwealth Conference in 1979. This in turn 'ensured the progress of the [1980] Lancaster House talks on the future of Rhodesia, a feat which Mrs Thatcher alone would not have been able to accomplish.'[17] In 1983 Kenneth Kaunda was to say on television: 'She *minds* about people; that is why she is so great.' What may not be so well known is how the Queen worked to accomplish her Commonwealth ends, through frankness, humanity and fairness.

When the Queen arrived in Lusaka, two days before Margaret Thatcher, she found that the Bantu press were violently anti-British over Rhodesia. She said: 'Kenneth, I've known you and Julius Nyerere longer than anyone else here. I don't want to get involved in the politics of Rhodesia. But do you want this conference to fail before it even starts? Don't you think it would be only fair to sit down?' Overnight the press changed round. 'We don't agree with Mrs Thatcher,' they said, 'but we do believe it's our duty to sit down and talk.'[18]

In fact the Queen is much better at talking to West African politicians than to Welsh miners; she has known the Africans all by name over a long period.

After the Lusaka Conference was over, a white Zimbabwean, Richard Acton, said in London to the Queen, 'We have the impression, Ma'am, that Buckingham Palace played an enormous part in the successful outcome.'

'A little,' the Queen replied, smiling.

Lord Home is another who has personally experienced her benign effect on the Commonwealth:

All the Commonwealth Prime Ministers that I saw at the Commonwealth dinners melted with the Queen, from Nkrumah to Trudeau. She knew all about their countries, which is a good start, and she always understood the scale of the problems involved in independence.[19]

Finally, an example of her scrupulous fairness between party politicians. On Zimbabwe Independence Day a high official said to her, 'What a superb job Lord Carrington has done.'

'Yes, indeed. But we mustn't forget that it was David Owen [the previous Foreign Secretary] who put it all in train.'

The official knew this was true and admired her all the more for recognising it.[20]

The 'unrivalled' world interest shown in the Queen and her family ranges from the touching to the bizarre. The Mexican crowds who turned out in 1975 for her state visit took even their President's breath away and he joked, 'I only ordered half a million!' The crowds were rewarded by her never missing an engagement despite unloading troubles in rough seas. Their 'chopper' which was to fly them from *Britannia* to Mexico City got overheated while making innumerable journeys back and forth in pouring rain and high winds, so that they had to wait for another one. But the Queen was determined not to let down the thousands of schoolchildren waiting for her. In the words of one of those who accompanied her, 'Our Royal Family would die rather than let people down.' The Queen was to be tested again some eight years later in storm-battered California. Her resolve was unchanged: to carry out each programme *in full*. Indeed she positively likes things to go wrong, within reason, welcoming a challenge. The cascading waters in California she found 'rather exciting and delightful', said Michael Shea. 'So much of the Queen's life is timed down to the last second that sometimes it's quite enjoyable when things go astray.' But she was horrified when her three American security men died in a car accident on the treacherous rainswept road.

The same friend who went with her to Mexico can never remember her getting rattled, hurried or fussed except once – marginally. This was flying through an electric storm over the Sahara, and then her slight agitation, as the lightning flashed along the wings, was not for herself but for the pilot who, in an emergency, would have nowhere to land.

The bizarre aspect of royal interest was shown in a fictional American movie of the royal romance in which an attractive actress with huge round black eyes played Lady Diana; another actress, who would have played a Daughter of the American Revolution admirably, impersonated the daughter of Lord Strathmore; and a team of American actors manfully struggled to impart British stiffness to their upper lips.

Elizabeth II was once called 'very well read', in the literal sense that she read all her state papers every day and the *Daily Telegraph* right through. In fact she hardly reads at all for pleasure. ('The Queen has a surplus of reading,' says Princess Margaret.) She deliberately leaves the strong stuff in literature to Prince Philip. Let *him* take the chair for Marshall McLuhan speaking on 'The Future of the Book' and make what he can of sentences like, 'If the book can be sent anywhere . . . the paradoxical electric reversal is that it is *the sender who is* sent. This flip, *or chiasmus* of form and function occurs at the level of instant speed, and is characteristic of telephone and radio and video alike.'[21] When the Queen attended a poetry reading devised to celebrate the 150th anniversary of the Royal Society of Literature, they pleased her with things like Betjeman's 'Beside the Seaside', Yeats's 'Prayer for My Daughter' and Raleigh's 'To the Queen'.

The Queen goes very little to concerts or theatres and does not embroider chair seats like her father or paint like Charles or pot like Andrew. When she comes into her own room she does not turn on the music. She concentrates for her pleasures on the subject she has mastered completely – horse-racing and breeding.

Nevertheless, the arts have been so much a pleasure to royalty in the past that they are still part of the royal image today.

Of three kings who cultivated the decorative arts, Charles II and George IV had a taste for the grand, George III for the domestic. Elizabeth II is nearer to George III, while her consort's taste can be baroque. He designed a bronze 'tulip' fountain for the Windsor terrace garden (the garden redesigned by the Queen and himself) which admirably matched the topiary work. Whenever she has acquired a magnificent work of art it has been to fill a gap in the royal collection; as for example Hogarth's portrait of George II and his family.

Royal portraiture has moved away at last from the Renaissance tradition of magnificence to something nearer to realism, and Elizabeth II with it. Her chosen artist, however, Pietro Annigoni, is more poetic than Prince Charles's chosen portraitist, Bryan Organ. Nor has she yet been painted by Organ, though her sister Princess Margaret was – with two lovely eyes, one very blurred and one very bright, as if signifying something deep; Sir Roy Strong has called the work 'a lonely flirtation with the present'.

The 'Blue Annigoni' (1954) of the young Queen delighted her public, especially its gentle dignity conveyed by the dark blue Garter robe against a contrasting spring landscape. 'I had to try to get into the portrait,' said Annigoni, 'the feeling of being close to the people, yet very much alone.' The 'Red Annigoni' (1970) was less popular, in so far as the stiff red mantle of the Order of the British Empire turned the Queen into a red pyramid, while the background of strange earth and sky seemed to belong to outer space. It may have been Annigoni's sadness at the death of his wife that led him to emphasise the stress lines in a face he had not seen for sixteen years. Yet she was not sad but made lively conversation in French during the sittings.[22]

Bryan Organ's twin portraits of Prince Charles and Lady Diana gave much satisfaction to the sitters, both for the informality of the idea and for its result. Charles wanted a new, relaxed impression to accord with his own view of himself. However, Organ tried to show the future king torn in two directions – himself an ordinary person out of the limelight, and a bit worried; was he equipped for his role, the role he would have to play? A small Union Jack hoisted behind on the polo ground seemed both to encourage and to threaten.

Sir Roy Strong and John Hayes applauded this portrait for getting away from the 'heroic' royal tradition; a *Standard* reader called it 'a jaundiced lump of clay'. With both portraits it is possible to admire the likenesses while instinctively looking for the symbolism. Then the doubts creep in. If the blank green fence behind Charles and the closed door behind Diana symbolise anything, they are perhaps things best ignored.

But in fact Bryan Organ at forty-six has abandoned the kind of abstractions he used so effectively in the Lincoln's Inn portrait of Princess Margaret and has turned more and more to visual realities. A simple person, he wandered around Windsor polo ground until he found what seemed a suitable background, the high green fence. Prince Charles enthusiastically agreed.

There is a mental vision of the Queen that has captured the imagination of journalists and others. A woman sits in front of the television with her shoes off, having her solitary dinner on a tray while her husband is away on some function of his own. She is lonely, pathetic – and a fiction.

The grain of truth in the vision springs from the known

reticence of the Queen's character, which is all too easily translated into loneliness. Annigoni made the same unjustified leap when he saw her standing at the window of the Yellow Drawing Room with streams of people and cars passing up and down the Mall below her. 'I often wonder who all those people are,' she told him, 'and what they think of the Palace.' The sensitive artist at once saw her as 'a prisoner of the Palace'.

It is true that Elizabeth II feels a freer woman in the country than in the Palace. She does not depend on or react to people as her mother does. She likes to be told things about her friends and their families but does not ask questions.

> She's got her ear to the ground [says one of these friends] but never passes on gossip and has no favourites in the Household, though great friends like Patrick Plunket [who died]. She does not think of herself as in any 'set', certainly not a rich jet set. She is humble and will come into a room not expecting to make any effect. No one could be more unself-conscious – sitting for her portrait, whatever she is doing, never self-conscious. She thinks of herself as an ordinary person.[23]

A quiet evening at home (interrupted of course by the red boxes) should have conveyed serenity not loneliness; and the people in the Mall were a fraction of all those whom the Queen had to wonder about, worry about, think about, dream about, in order to weld them eventually into the loyal supporters of monarchy. It has been said that one change in today's monarchy concerns the loyalty of the people. Two or three generations ago kings took loyalty for granted. This queen has had to work for it.

She has not failed. On the thirtieth anniversary of her reign, the two major critics of her first decade were questioned again. Grigg's new article in the press was entitled by his sub-editor 'Marvellous Ma'am, but if I might suggest . . .' – less gush from the media and less stuffiness in the Household.[24]

The Queen might legitimately answer that the House-

hold *is* less stuffy. 'Everyone round this table is an Eto-
nian,' Prince Philip once said crossly. Now it is not so at all.
As for tweediness, the Household is getting less and less
tweedy as the years pass. No one belongs to the 'huntin',
shootin', fishin' set'. Some of them *become* a little tweedy if
they find that they are good shots or good at fishing. But
they are not engaged for that reason.

   Muggeridge said in reply to questions in 1982:

> The point is that the dangerous things – like regarding the
> monarchy as an ersatz religion – she has corrected it herself,
> whether unconsciously or consciously. We saw it all in the
> Cawston [*Royal Family*] film and loved her – the way she was
> told a gorilla was coming to visit her and he did! She did it all so
> nicely. The TV and other personnel concerned in making that
> programme were expecting all sorts of protocol but were de-
> lighted to find she very naturally and very spontaneously played
> her part.[25]

In answer to the question, could Muggeridge name one
change he would like to see comparable to the 'stuffiness'
criticised by Grigg, he added: 'I would like to have seen her
refuse to put her sign manual to the Abortion Bill!' But
that, he realised, would have created uproar, revolution;
and he didn't want to get rid of her.

   The idea of a constitutional monarch giving a moral lead
is fraught with difficulties, particularly in an age that asks,
What is morality? The meeting of Pope John Paul II and
Elizabeth II in Buckingham Palace on 28 May 1982 was
shown on television and made a deep impression. The
scene was in primary colours, the Queen in blue, the carpet
red, the room cream and gold. For forty-five minutes the
Pope spoke with her alone, no doubt on primary subjects,
peace and reconciliation. The Falklands war against Catholic Argentina was not yet over. In April the Argentines had
chanted, '*Se siente, se siente, La Riente esta caliente*' – 'We
feel it, we sense it, we know it well, For the Queen it's
getting hot as hell!' They failed to understand the meaning
of a constitutional monarch and saw the Queen as an

Anglo-Saxon General Galtieri. At the end of their talk the Pope said to the Queen, 'God bless your son.'

Whether or not Elizabeth II speaks her mind on any particular occasion, the nation is fully aware of her standards and deeply felt religious beliefs. After thirty years she is intuitively understood and whole-heartedly respected. Against the hurly-burly of national life her thoughts have become a kind of ideal voice-over, no less moving and effective for being often unspoken.

Queen Elizabeth II always leads a double life, her own and the country's – ours. This is not peculiar to her. In every royal person there is a private person trying to keep in. But with Elizabeth II the contrast between the royal and the private is particularly strong. In private she is witty, laughing and spontaneous, though not so spontaneous as her mother, who only has to hear of a new plan to say, 'Let's do it.' The Queen thinks things over. She would not have made such a totally supportive queen consort as her mother. Her spontaneity in her own home is none the less great enough for friends and members of her Household often to forget whom they are addressing. That can never happen to her in public. There will always be a dichotomy. The question is whether it will be successful in both parts.

Writing in 1964, Christopher Hibbert took a subfusc view of the dualism. He saw 'an uneasy compromise' between the court's attempt to present the Queen as human and their determination not to 'let light in on magic', in Bagehot's phrase. The result, Hibbert felt, was that the Queen made her 'regular but fleeting appearances on the pages of the world's newspapers and magazines in the guise of a hybrid, never wholly real nor ever truly magical.'[26] The Queen would not be alarmed by that word hybrid. What might have been true twenty years ago, has been transformed by the 'hybrid vigour' of her double life, enhanced by the impact of television. But if today she is wholly real and truly magical, that is not because the two sides of her life, public and private, have become one. Never the twain shall meet.

It was her father, that intensely private person, who was the sovereign, while her outgoing mother was his consort, his pledged and devoted supporter. Nature had already given the child Lilibet more of her father's than her mother's temperament, and when the laws of primogeniture gave Elizabeth II his royal status also, she went on to model herself on him.

As the younger generation begin to take on more of the travel and subsidiary royal functions while the Queen reserves herself for the pomp and circumstance, the two sides of her nature will not come closer together. It will be only on television that we see her carefree side, the side known to her grandchildren Peter and Zara, William and whoever comes next. When a gracious symbol of the nation's unity is actually watched riding along the Mall in a glittering coach, it will be the Queen.

Nevertheless, every personality must have its ultimate cohesion. With Elizabeth II it is found in something the nation has long recognised but cannot put a name to: total dedication that gives a lead without crudely 'setting an example'; a rare kind of goodness that is yet within reach of every human being.

Bibliography

All published in London unless otherwise stated

Airlie, Mabell, Countess of, *Thatched with Gold*, 1962
Alexandra of Jugoslavia, *Prince Philip: A Family Portrait*, 1949
Alice, Princess, Countess of Athlone, *For My Grandchildren*, 1965,
    reprinted 1979
Alice, Princess, Duchess of Gloucester, *Memoirs*, 1983
Altrincham, Lord, *see* Grigg, John
Aronson, Theo, *Royal Ambassadors: British Royalties in Southern
    Africa 1860–1947*, Cape Town, 1975
    Princess Alice, 1981
Asquith, Lady Cynthia, *The King's Daughters*, 1937
    Weekly Illustrated magazine, article, 4 April 1953
Attlee, C. R., *As It Happened*, 1956
Avon, Earl of, *The Memoirs of Sir Anthony Eden: Full Circle*, 1960
    Facing the Dictators, 1962
Bagehot, Walter, *The English Constitution*, first edition, 1867
Balfour, Neil and Mackay, Sally, *Paul of Yugoslavia: Britain's Maligned
    Friend*, 1980
Beaton, Cecil, *Diaries: The Strenuous Years 1948–1955*, 1973
    'The Official Portrait', *Happy and Glorious*, ed. Colin Ford, 1977
Beaumont, Bill, *Thanks to Rugby: An Autobiography*, 1982
Beaverbrook, Lord, *The Abdication of King Edward VIII*, ed. A. J. P.
    Taylor, 1966
Birkenhead, Lord, *Walter Monckton*, 1969
Blake, Robert, 'The Queen and the Constitution', *The Queen*, 1977
Bloch, Michael, *The Duke of Windsor's War*, 1982
Bogdanor, Vernon, *Multi-Party Politics and the Constitution*,
    Cambridge, 1983
Boothroyd, Basil, *Philip: An Informal Biography*, 1971
Boys of William Penn School, 'The Queen's Subjects', *The Queen*, 1977
Brittain, Vera, *Chronicles of Youth: War Diary 1913–1917*, 1981
Bryan, Joseph, *Holiday* magazine, articles, 1956
Buchan, William, *John Buchan: A Memoir*, 1982
Burrow, J. W., *A Liberal Descent*, 1981
Butler, R. A., *The Memoirs of Lord Butler: The Art of the Possible*, 1971
    The Art of Memory: Friends in Perspective, 1982

Campbell, Judith, *Elizabeth and Philip*, 1972
   Anne and Mark, 1975
   The Queen, 1977
Casson, Hugh, *Diary*, 1981
Cathcart, Helen, *Her Majesty*, 1962
   The Queen Mother, 1965
Cawston, Richard, 'The Royal Family Film', *Happy and Glorious*, ed.
   Colin Ford, 1977
Channon, Sir Henry, *Chips: The Diaries of Sir Henry Channon*, ed.
   Robert Rhodes James, 1967
Churchill, Randolph S., *They Serve the Queen*, 1953
Clark, Brigadier Stanley, *Palace Diary*, 1958
Clear, Celia, *Royal Children: From 1840 to 1980*, 1981
Clynes, J. R., *Memoirs Vol. II, 1924–1937*, 1937
Colville, Lady Cynthia, *Crowded Life: An Autobiography*, 1963
Cooke, Colin, *The Life of Sir Richard Stafford Cripps*, 1957
Cooper, Lady Diana, *The Light of Common Day*, 1959, reprinted 1979
Cooper, Duff, *Old Men Forget*, 1953
Crawford, Marion, *The Little Princesses*, 1950
Crosland, Susan, *Tony Crosland*, 1982
Crossman, Richard, *The Diaries of a Cabinet Minister: Vol. I. Minister of
   Housing 1964–1966*, 1975
   *Vol. II. Lord President of the Council and Leader of the House of
   Commons 1966–1968*, 1976
Curling, Bill, *All the Queen's Horses*, 1975
Dalton, Hugh, *The Fateful Years: 1931–1945*, 1957
   High Tide and After: 1945–1960, 1962
Day, J. Wentworth, *The Queen Mother's Story*, 1967, 1969
Donaldson, Frances, *Edward VIII*, 1974
   King George and Queen Elizabeth, 1977
Duncan, Andrew, *The Reality of Monarchy*, 1970
Eden, Sir Anthony, *see* Avon, Earl of
Edgar, Donald, *The Queen's Children*, 1978
Edinburgh, HRH the Duke of, *Prince Philip Speaks: Selected Speeches
   1956–1959*, ed. Richard Ollard, 1960
   A Question of Balance, 1982
Evans, Harold, *Downing Street Diary: The Macmillan Years 1957–1963*,
   1981
Fisher, Graham and Heather, *Elizabeth Queen and Mother*, 1964
Fitch, Inspector Herbert T., *Memoirs of a Royal Detective*, 1936
Frere, James A., *The British Monarchy at Home*, 1963
Frewin, Leslie, *Royal Silver Anniversary Book*, 1972
Fyfe, David Maxwell, *Political Adventure: The Memoirs of the Earl of
   Kilmuir*, 1964
Glendinning, Victoria, *Edith Sitwell: A Unicorn among Lions*, 1981
Grigg, John (Lord Altrincham), article, *National and English Review*,
   August 1957

Hailsham, Quintin (Lord), *The Dilemma of Democracy*, 1978
Hamilton, William, MP, *My Queen and I*, 1975
  'The Case against the Monarchy', *The Queen*, 1977
Hancock, W. K., *Survey of British Commonwealth Affairs*, Vol. 1,
    Oxford, 1937
Hardinge, Lady (Helen), *Loyal to Three Kings: A Memoir of Sir
    Alexander Hardinge 1920–1943*, 1967
Harewood, George, Earl of, *The Tongs and the Bones: The Memoirs of
    Lord Harewood*, 1981
Harris, Kenneth, *Attlee*, 1982
Hibbert, Christopher, *The Court at Windsor: A Domestic History*, 1964
  *The Court of St James's: The Monarch at Work from Victoria to
    Elizabeth II*, 1979
Holden, Anthony, *Charles, Prince of Wales*, 1979
  Their Royal Highnesses: The Prince and Princess of Wales, 1981
Home, Sir Alec Douglas-Home, Lord Home, *The Way the Wind Blows*,
    1976
Horne, Donald, 'The Queen as Queen of Australia', *The Queen*, 1977
Hough, Richard, *Mountbatten: Hero of our Time*, 1980
Howard, Philip, *The British Monarchy in the Twentieth Century*, 1977
Hudson, Derek, *Kensington Palace*, 1968
Hunter, Ian, *Malcolm Muggeridge: A Life*, 1980
Hyde, H. Montgomery, 'Dear Mrs Simpson', article, *Harper's & Queen*,
    1980
Inglis, Brian, *The Abdication*, 1966
Iwi, Edward, 'Mountbatten-Windsor', *The Law Journal*, 18 March 1960
Jenkins, Roy, *Asquith*, 1964
Jennings, Sir Ivor, *The Queen's Government*, 1954
Jones, Thomas, *Whitehall Diary: Vol. I. 1916–1925; Vol. II. 1926–1930*,
    ed. Keith Middlemas, Oxford, 1969
Judd, Denis, *Prince Philip: A Biography*, 1980
  King George VI 1895–1952, 1982
Junor, Penny, *Diana Princess of Wales*, 1982
Kilmuir, *see* Fyfe, David Maxwell
*King George VI to His People: 1936–1951 Select Broadcasts and
    Speeches*, 1952
Lacey, Robert, *Majesty: Elizabeth II and the House of Windsor*, 1977
  Princess, 1981
Laird, Dorothy, *How the Queen Reigns*, 1959
  Queen Elizabeth the Queen Mother, 1966
Liversidge, Douglas, *Queen Elizabeth II and the British Monarchy
    Today*, 1974
Longford, Elizabeth, *The Royal House of Windsor*, 1974
  'The Monarchy through Six Reigns', *Happy and Glorious*, ed. Colin
    Ford, 1977
  'The Role of the Prince Consort', *Burke's Guide to the British
    Monarchy*, 1977

'Personal Styles in Twentieth Century Monarchy', *The Queen*, 1977
The Queen Mother, 1981
Mackenzie, Compton, *The Windsor Tapestry*, 1938
Macmillan, Harold, *Tides of Fortune 1945–1955*, 1969
  Riding the Storm 1956–1959, 1971
  Pointing the Way 1959–1961, 1972
  At the End of the Day 1961–1963, 1973
McLachlan, Donald, *In the Chair: Barrington-Ward of The Times*, 1971
Mansergh, Nicholas, *Survey of British Commonwealth Affairs* Vol. I,
  Oxford, 1952
  Vol. II, Oxford, 1953
  The Commonwealth Experience, 1969
Marie-Louise, Princess, *My Memories of Six Reigns*, 1956
Marquand, David, *Ramsay MacDonald*, 1977
Martin, Kingsley, *The Crown and the Establishment*, 1962
Massey, Vincent, *What's Passed is Prologue*, 1963
Masters, Brian, *Dreams about HM the Queen and Other Members of the
  Royal Family*, 1972
Menzies, Sir Robert, *Afternoon Light: Some Memories of Men and
  Events*, 1967
Millar, Oliver, *The Queen's Pictures*, 1977
  Catalogue of *Van Dyck in England*, National Portrait Gallery, 1982
  Catalogue of *Kings and Queens*, The Queen's Gallery, 1983
Miller, J. D. B., *Survey of Commonwealth Affairs*, 1974
Montgomery-Massingberd, Hugh, ed. *Burke's Guide to the British
  Monarchy*, 1977
Morrah, Dermot, *The Work of the Queen*, 1958
Morrison, Herbert, *An Autobiography*, 1960
Morrow, Ann, *The Queen*, 1983
Mountbatten: Eighty Years in Pictures, 1979
Muggeridge, Malcolm, *Like It Was: The Diaries of Malcolm Muggeridge*,
  ed. John Bright-Holmes, 1981
  Article, *New Statesman*, 1955, reprinted *Listener* 1981; *Saturday
  Evening Post*, 1957
Nicolson, Harold, *King George V*, 1952
  Monarchy, 1962
  Diaries and Letters 1945–1962, ed. Nigel Nicolson, 1968
Oaksey, John (Lord), 'The Queen's Horses', *The Queen*, 1977
Ormond, Richard, 'The Face of Monarchy', *Happy and Glorious*, ed.
  Colin Ford, 1977
Petrie, Sir Charles, *Guards Magazine*, Summer 1972
Plumb, J. H., 'Royal Residences', *The Queen*, 1977
Plumb, J. H., and Wheldon, Huw, *Royal Heritage: The Reign of
  Elizabeth II*, 1981
Pope-Hennessy, James, *Queen Mary*, 1959
  A Lonely Business: A Self-Portrait of James Pope-Hennessy, ed. Peter
  Quennell, 1981

Pope-Hennessy, Una, *Agnes Strickland: Biographer of the Queens of England*, 1940

Powell, Violet, *Five out of Six*, 1960

Punch and the Monarchy, ed. William Davis, 1977

Rose, Kenneth, *King George V*, 1983

St James's Palace, *Catalogue of Wedding Gifts to HRH Princess Elizabeth*, 1947

Souvenir Catalogue of the Royal Wedding Gifts, 1981

Sampson, Anthony, *Macmillan: A Study in Ambiguity*, 1979

The Changing Anatomy of Britain, 1982

St John-Stevas, Norman, *Walter Bagehot*, 1959

Scott, Sir David, *Ambassador in Black and White: Thirty Years of Changing Africa*, 1981

Select Committee on the Civil List, HMSO, 22 November 1971

Soames, Mary, *Clementine*, 1979

Stewart, Michael, *The British Approach to Politics*, 1938, 1965

Talbot, Godfrey, *Ten Seconds from Now*, 1973

The Country Life Book of Queen Elizabeth the Queen Mother, 1978

Townsend, Peter, *Time and Chance: An Autobiography*, 1978

Turner, Clare Forbes, 'The Name Mountbatten-Windsor', *Genealogists' Magazine*, Vol. 17, No. 3, September 1973

Vickers, Hugo, 'Twenty-five Years a Queen', *Burke's Guide to the British Monarchy*, 1977

Debrett's Book of the Royal Wedding, 1981

Wales, HRH the Prince of, *The Old Man of Lochnagar*, 1980

Walker, Eric Sherbrooke, *Treetops Hotel*, 1962

Walker, Patrick Gordon (Lord Gordon-Walker), *The Commonwealth*, 1962

The Cabinet, 1970

Warwick, Christopher, *Two Centuries of Royal Weddings*, 1980

Princess Margaret, 1983

Watson, Francis, *Dawson of Penn*, 1950

Wheeler-Bennett, Sir John, *King George VI: His Life and Reign*, 1958

Wilson, Sir Harold, *The Labour Government 1964–1970: A Personal Record*, 1971

The Governance of Britain, 1976

A Prime Minister on Prime Ministers, 1977

Final Term: The Labour Government 1974–1976, 1979

Windsor, Duchess of, *The Heart has its Reasons*, 1956

Windsor, HRH the Duke of, *A King's Story: The Memoirs of HRH the Duke of Windsor*, 1951

Ziegler, Philip, *Crown and People*, 1978

Reference Notes

Chapter I   Today

1 Table-talk with Harold Macmillan and others
2 Harold Nicolson, *Diaries and Letters 1945–1962*, 4 November 1952
3 Sir Henry Channon, *Chips: The Diaries of Sir Henry Channon*, 25 September 1953
4 Michael Jamieson, 'An American Actress at Balmoral 1893', *Theatre Research International*
5 Theo Aronson, *Princess Alice*, p. 43
6 Memoirs of Princess Alice, Duchess of Gloucester, p. 105
7 Henry Hallam, *Views on the State of Europe during the Middle Ages*, 1818

Chapter II   The World of Her Birth: 1900–26

1 Private information
2 Sir John Wheeler-Bennett, *King George VI: His Life and Reign*, p. 140
3 Walter Bagehot, 'The Monarchy', *The English Constitution*, p. 57
4 Ibid., p. 75
5 Ibid., pp. 78, 32
6 Ibid., p. 83
7 Ibid., p. 103
8 Lord David Cecil, 'Staying with Margot', *Observer*, 19 December 1981
9 Roy Jenkins, *Asquith*, App. B, p. 543
10 Hancock, *Survey of British Commonwealth Affairs*, Vol. I, p. 58
11 Erskine Childers, President of Ireland, letter to the author, 31 August 1973
12 J. Wentworth Day, *The Queen Mother's Story*, p. 143
13 Wheeler-Bennett, p. 28
14 Ibid., p. 18
15 Ibid., p. 150
16 Ibid., pp. 150–1
17 Lord Harewood, *The Tongs and the Bones*, p. 103
18 W. B. Yeats, 'A Prayer for My Daughter', June 1919
19 Francis Watson, *Dawson of Penn*, p. 285, 9 March 1936
20 Thomas Jones, *Whitehall Diary*, Vol. I, p. 76
21 Ibid., p. 260

Chapter III   'Innocence and Beauty Born': 1926–30

1 Violet Powell, *Five out of Six*, p. 51
2 James Pope-Hennessy, *Queen Mary*, p. 159
3 Wheeler-Bennett, p. 209
4 Lady Cynthia Colville, *Crowded Life: An Autobiography*, p. 127
5 Dermot Morrah, *The Work of the Queen*, p. 11
6 Jones, Vol. II, pp. 5–6 and p. 38
7 Vincent Massey, *What's Passed is Prologue*, pp. 116–17

8 Wheeler-Bennett, p. 755
9 Ibid., p. 215
10 Ibid., p. 216; Celia Clear, *Royal Children: From 1840 to 1980*, p. 96
11 Pope-Hennessy, *Queen Mary*, p. 346
12 Wheeler-Bennett, p. 247
13 *News Chronicle*, 22 August 1930
14 J. R. Clynes, *Memoirs Vol. II, 1924–1937*, p. 178
15 Clear, p. 98
16 Lady Cynthia Asquith, *Weekly Illustrated*, 4 April 1953

Chapter IV 'A Golden Age': 1931–5
1 Wheeler-Bennett, p. 263
2 Quintin Hailsham, *The Dilemma of Democracy*, pp. 144–5
3 David Marquand, *Ramsay MacDonald*, pp. 635–6
4 Harold Nicolson, *King George V*, pp. 483 and 471
5 Compton Mackenzie, *The Windsor Tapestry*, p. 405
6 Marion Crawford, *The Little Princesses*, pp. 9 and 12
7 Christopher Warwick, *Princess Margaret*, p. 14
8 Inspector Herbert T. Fitch, *Memoirs of a Royal Detective*, p. 123
9 Crawford, p. 16
10 Ibid.
11 Ibid., p. 17
12 Powell, p. 50
13 Crawford, p. 22
14 Colin Cooke, *The Life of Sir Richard Stafford Cripps*, pp. 159–60
15 Earl of Avon, *Facing the Dictators*, pp. 51–2
16 Vera Brittain, *Chronicles of Youth: War Diary 1913–1917*, 11 December 1913
17 Princess Marie-Louise, *My Memories of Six Reigns*, p. 193;

Nicolson, *King George V*, p. 525
18 Harewood, p. 17
19 Aronson, *Princess Alice*, p. 186

Chapter V The Year of Three Kings: 1936
1 Duchess of Windsor, *The Heart has its Reasons*, p. 225
2 Mabell Airlie, *Thatched with Gold*, pp. 196–7
3 Ibid., p. 198
4 Crawford, p. 28
5 *Standard*, 29 March 1982
6 Robert Lacey, *Majesty*, p. 75; private information
7 Mrs William Ladd, formerly Vicomtesse de Bellaigue, to the author
8 Hugo Vickers, *Burke's Guide*, p. 21
9 Pope-Hennessy, *Queen Mary*, p. 569
10 Helen Hardinge, *Loyal to Three Kings: A Memoir of Sir Alexander Hardinge 1920–1943*, p. 112
11 Wheeler-Bennett, p. 268
12 Crawford, p. 38
13 Avon, *Facing the Dictators*, p. 410; Lord Beaverbrook, *The Abdication of King Edward VIII*, p. 80
14 Lady Cynthia Asquith, *The King's Daughters*, p. 96
15 Sir Charles Petrie, *Guards Magazine*, Summer 1972
16 C. R. Attlee, *As It Happened*, p. 86; Hugh Dalton, *The Fateful Years: 1931–1945*, p. 113; Lord Birkenhead, *Walter Monckton*, p. 127
17 Bagehot, p. 79; Nicholas Mansergh, *Survey of British Commonwealth Affairs*, Vol. I, p. 186
18 Hardinge, p. 174
19 H. Montgomery Hyde, 'Dear Mrs Simpson', *Harper's & Queen*, June 1980; Mollie

Woolnough, *New York Journal*, 26 October 1936 and 'Tribute to a Gentleman', New York, December 1936

Chapter VI Bred to be Queen: 1937–9

1 Harewood, p. 17; Windsor, *The Heart has its Reasons*, p. 300
2 Pope-Hennessy, *Queen Mary*, p. 585
3 Massey, p. 252
4 Airlie, p. 202
5 Crawford, p. 43
6 Princess Margaret, *Desert Island Discs*, 'Castaway of the Year', 3 April 1981
7 Crawford, p. 41
8 Donald McLachlan, *In the Chair: Barrington-Ward of The Times*, p. 127; William Buchan, *John Buchan: A Memoir*, p. 222
9 Duff Cooper, *Old Men Forget*, p. 194
10 Channon, 11 August 1937
11 Pope-Hennessy, *Queen Mary*, p. 594
12 Theo Aronson, *Royal Ambassadors: British Royalties in Southern Africa 1860–1947*, pp. 89–90
13 Wheeler-Bennett, p. 372
14 Crawford, p. 59
15 HRH the Duke of Edinburgh, *A Question of Balance*, p. 24
16 Basil Boothroyd, *Philip: An Informal Biography*, p. 136

Chapter VII The Windsor Fortress: 1940–45

1 Crawford, p. 54
2 Ibid., p. 62
3 Wheeler-Bennett, p. 749
4 Ibid., p. 438
5 Ibid., p. 446
6 Aronson, *Princess Alice*, p. 212

7 Pope-Hennessy, *Queen Mary*, p. 596
8 Princess Margaret, *Desert Island Discs*, 'Castaway of the Year', 3 April 1981
9 Crawford, pp. 71–2
10 Wheeler-Bennett, p. 470
11 Boothroyd, p. 137; Crawford, p. 86; Denis Judd, *Prince Philip: A Biography*, p. 104; Wheeler-Bennett, p. 230
12 Dorothy Laird, *How the Queen Reigns*, p. 161
13 Princess Alice, Countess of Athlone, *For My Grandchildren*, p. 260
14 Airlie, p. 219
15 Neil Balfour and Sally Mackay, *Paul of Yugoslavia: Britain's Maligned Friend*, p. 285
16 Harewood, p. 74
17 Mrs William Ladd, formerly Vicomtesse de Bellaigue, to the author
18 Lady Pamela Hicks to the author
19 Wheeler-Bennett, p. 592
20 Crawford, p. 89
21 Airlie, p. 225
22 Elizabeth Longford, 'cloistered', *The Royal House of Windsor*, p. 208; Lacey, 'secluded' and 'purdah', *Majesty*, pp. 135 and 143
23 Crawford, pp. 85 and 87
24 Mrs William Ladd, formerly Vicomtesse de Bellaigue, to the author
25 Wheeler-Bennett, p. 626
26 Mrs William Ladd, formerly Vicomtesse de Bellaigue, to the author
27 Pope-Hennessy, *Queen Mary*, p. 609

Chapter VIII 'Us Four' – and Philip: 1945–7

1 Cecil Beaton, 'The Official Portrait', *Happy and Glorious*, p. 97

2 Wheeler-Bennett, p. 654
3 Mary Soames, *Clementine*, p. 366
4 Wheeler-Bennett, p. 627
5 Sir Harold Wilson, *A Prime Minister on Prime Ministers*, p. 263
6 Wheeler-Bennett, p. 638; Kenneth Harris, *Attlee*, p. 264; Dalton, *High Tide and After: 1945–1960*, p. 8
7 Kingsley Martin, *The Crown and the Establishment*, p. 78
8 Patrick Gordon Walker, *The Cabinet*, p. 78
9 Pope-Hennessy, *A Lonely Business*, p. 176
10 Airlie, p. 228
11 Boothroyd, p. 24
12 Wheeler-Bennett, p. 749; Judd, *King George VI*, p. 230
13 Pope-Hennessy, *Queen Mary*, p. 615
14 Warwick, *Princess Margaret*, p. 142
15 Aronson, *Royal Ambassadors*, p. 110; Helen Cathcart, *The Queen Mother*, p. 183
16 Aronson, ibid., p. 119
17 Private information
18 Aronson, op. cit., p. 102
19 Hope Dyson and Charles Tennyson (eds), *Dear and Honoured Lady: The Correspondence of Queen Victoria and Alfred Tennyson*, p. 27
20 Pope-Hennessy, *Queen Mary*, p. 615
21 Lady Margaret Colville to the author
22 Sir John Colville to the author
23 Wheeler-Bennett, p. 716n
24 Malcolm Muggeridge, *Like It Was: The Diaries of Malcolm Muggeridge*, 1 December 1949, p. 362
25 Private information
26 Airlie, p. 230
27 Soames, pp. 309 and 404
28 Anne Sharpley, *Standard*, 29 July 1981. She had reported the royal wedding on 20 November 1947
29 Wheeler-Bennett, pp. 754–5

Chapter IX Interlude for Living: 1948–51

1 Sir John Colville to the author
2 Muggeridge, *Like It Was*, 14 November 1948, p. 308
3 Anthony Holden, *Charles, Prince of Wales*, p. 53, letter from Princess Elizabeth to her former music teacher, Mabel (Goosey) Lander
4 Pope-Hennessy, *Queen Mary*, p. 616
5 Holden, op. cit., p. 53
6 Channon, 26 October 1948
7 Ibid., 18 June 1949
8 Christopher Thorne, reviewing R. F. Holland, *Britain and the Commonwealth Alliance*, *Times Literary Supplement*, 1982
9 Boothroyd, p. 106
10 Wheeler-Bennett, p. 740
11 Boothroyd, p. 145
12 Private information
13 Wheeler-Bennett, p. 775
14 Channon, 15 June 1950
15 *Daily Mail*, 16 August 1950
16 James A. Frere, *The British Monarchy at Home*, p. 139
17 Wheeler-Bennett, p. 801
18 Wilson, *The Governance of Britain*, p. 22
19 Wilson, *A Prime Minister on Prime Ministers*, p. 294
20 Massey, p. 459
21 Wheeler-Bennett, p. 744
22 Gist of letter from Sir Stafford Cripps to John Colville, c. 1947
23 Lady Pamela Hicks to the author; Eric Sherbrooke Walker, 'HM the Queen at Treetops', *Treetops Hotel*, pp. 102–13
24 Duff Hart-Davis to the author

Chapter X The 'New Elizabethans': 1952–3

1 Eric Sherbrooke Walker, op. cit.
2 Private information
3 Lady Pamela Hicks to the author
4 Ibid.
5 Avon, *Full Circle*, p. 40
6 Massey, pp. 459–60
7 Pope-Hennessy, *Queen Mary*, p. 619
8 Pope-Hennessy, *A Lonely Business*, p. 190
9 Ibid.
10 Author's recollection
11 Airlie, p. 236
12 Victoria Glendinning, *Edith Sitwell: A Unicorn among Lions*, p. 299
13 Private information
14 Paul Johnson, *Now!*, 8 February 1980
15 Peter Townsend, *Time and Chance: An Autobiography*, p. 197
16 Warwick, *Princess Margaret*, p. 59
17 Ibid., p. 60
18 Sir John Colville to the author
19 Boothroyd, p. 49
20 Ibid., p. 50
21 J. Bryan III, 'The Duke of Edinburgh', *Holiday* magazine, May 1956
22 Boothroyd, 'Prince Philip', *The Times*, 10 June 1981
23 Edward Iwi, 'Mountbatten-Windsor', *The Law Journal*, 18 March 1960; Longford, *The Royal House of Windsor*, pp. 228–9
24 Private information
25 Sir Arthur Bryant to the author
26 Judith Campbell, *The Queen*, p. 70; Mansergh, *Survey*, Vol. II, p. 420
27 A. L. Rowse, 'Queen Elizabeth I and Today', 14th Clayesmore Lecture, Clayesmore School, Dorset, 3 March 1982
28 Channon, 11 February 1952
29 Frere, p. 165
30 Malcolm McEwen, *Daily Worker*, 30 May 1953
31 Soames, p. 274
32 Lacey, *Majesty*, p. 190
33 A. J. P. Taylor, Introduction to *Punch and the Monarchy* (1977), p. 18
34 Alistair Forbes, 'After the Royal Wedding', *Books and Bookmen*, October 1981; Morrah, p. 128
35 Lord Pakenham on the Coronation, *Manchester Guardian*, 12 June 1953

Chapter XI 'Uphill All the Way?': 1954–7

1 Mansergh, Vol. II, p. 421
2 Bryan, *Holiday* magazine, July 1956
3 Lady Pamela Hicks to the author
4 Godfrey Talbot, *Ten Seconds from Now*; Ursula Banbury, letter to *The Times*, December 1980
5 Soames, p. 404
6 Herbert Morrison, *An Autobiography*, p. 248; Wilson, speech, 23 March 1976
7 Sir Robert Menzies, *Afternoon Light: Some Memories of Men and Events*, p. 93
8 Sir John Colville to the author
9 Princess Margaret, *Desert Island Discs*, 'Castaway of the Year', 3 April 1981
10 Pope-Hennessy, *A Lonely Business*, p. 242
11 Harewood, p. 218
12 Lacey, *Majesty*, p. 238
13 Graham and Heather Fisher, *Elizabeth Queen and Mother*, p. 138
14 Lord Altrincham (Grigg), *National and English Review*, August 1957

15 *Saturday Evening Post*, 19 October 1957; *New Statesman*, 1955, reprinted in *Listener*, 26 March 1981; Ian Hunter, *Malcolm Muggeridge: A Life*, pp. 198–200

16 John Osborne, *Encounter*, October 1957

Chapter XII The Sport of Queens

1 Harewood, p. 18
2 John Oaksey, 'The Queen's Horses', *The Queen*, p. 132
3 Bill Curling, *All The Queen's Horses*, p. 18
4 Ibid., p. 17
5 Lord Porchester to the author
6 Curling, p. 30
7 Oaksey, p. 137
8 Curling, p. 33
9 Oaksey, p. 139
10 Curling, p. 43
11 Ibid., p. 72
12 Ibid., p. 112
13 Private information
14 Curling, p. 123
15 Lord Porchester to the Eton Equestrian Society
16 Lord Porchester to the author
17 Woodrow Wyatt to the author

Chapter XIII A Family in the 1960s

1 Iwi, op. cit.
2 HRH the Prince of Wales, *The Old Man of Lochnagar*
3 Ibid.
4 Frere, p. 170
5 Una Pope-Hennessy, *Agnes Strickland: Biographer of the Queens of England*, p. 85
6 Private information; Bill Beaumont, *Thanks to Rugby: An Autobiography*, pp. 198–9
7 Philip Howard, *The British Monarchy in the Twentieth Century*, p. 115
8 Nicolson, *Diaries and Letters*, 26 December 1957

9 Holden, *Charles, Prince of Wales*, p. 136
10 Prince Charles in radio interview with Jack de Manio, 1 March 1969
11 Holden, op. cit., p. 142
12 Ibid., p. 134
13 Information given to the author for an article in Princess Anne's Wedding Programme, sold in aid of King George VI's Jubilee Fund
14 Bagehot, p. 86
15 Private information

Chapter XIV The Queen and the Magic Circle: 1952–64

1 Kenneth Rose, 'Twenty-five Years On', *Sunday Telegraph*, 30 January 1977
2 Soames, p. 437
3 Kenneth Rose, op. cit.
4 Soames, p. 452
5 Donald McLachlan, *Daily Telegraph*, 21 April 1955
6 Judd, *King George VI*, p. 247
7 Harris, p. 547
8 Private letter
9 Lord Butler to the author
10 R. A. Butler, *The Art of Memory: Friends in Perspective*, p. 101
11 Ibid.; and conversation with the author
12 Lacey, *Majesty*, p. 243
13 Wilson, *A Prime Minister on Prime Ministers*, p. 314
14 David Maxwell Fyfe, *Political Adventure: The Memoirs of the Earl of Kilmuir*, p. 285; Macmillan, *At the End of the Day 1961–1963*, p. 509; Lacey, *Majesty*, pp. 241–2
15 Macmillan, *Riding the Storm 1956–1959*, p. 185
16 Harold Evans, *Downing Street Diary: The Macmillan Years 1957–1963*, p. 302

17 Anthony Sampson, *Macmillan: A Study in Ambiguity*, p. 88
18 Evans, pp. 22 and 42
19 Macmillan, *Pointing the Way 1959–1961*, p. 213
20 Ibid., p. 253; A. J. P. Taylor, *Punch and the Monarchy*, p. 18
21 Macmillan, *Riding the Storm*, pp. 189 and 344
22 Macmillan, *At the End of the Day*, p. 445
23 Evans, 23 October 1960
24 Ibid., 10 February 1963
25 Ibid.
26 Macmillan, *At the End of the Day*, p. 503
27 Lord Home, *The Way the Wind Blows*, p. 183; Lord Home to the author
28 Macmillan, op. cit.; Evans, 13 October 1963, p. 298
29 Evans, ibid., pp. 299–300
30 Macmillan, op. cit., p. 514
31 Ibid.; Evans, op. cit., p. 300
32 Macmillan, ibid., p. 515 *et seq.*
33 Ibid., p. 513; Evans, op. cit., p. 301; Home, p. 185
34 Lord Blake, review of *Rab: An English Life* by Patrick Cosgrave, *Times Literary Supplement*, 15 May 1981
35 Evans, 2 June 1963, p. 270
36 Ibid., 25 February 1962, p. 187
37 Macmillan, op. cit.
38 Lord Home to the author
39 Home, p. 13
40 Lord Home to the author
41 Ibid.
42 Home, p. 50
43 Ibid., p. 218
44 Lord Hailsham to the author
45 Lord Stewart to the author

Chapter XV 'Our Mother is Coming!'

1 Sir David Scott, *Ambassador in Black and White*, p. 138
2 Walker, *The Commonwealth*, p. 203
3 Mark Arnold-Forster, *Guardian*, 26 November 1981
4 Lord Home to the author
5 James Callaghan MP to the author
6 Michael Stewart, *The British Approach to Politics*, pp. 277–9
7 Audrey Russell to the author
8 Macmillan, *Riding the Storm*, p. 746
9 Buchan, p. 226; Leslie Frewin, *Royal Silver Anniversary Book*, p. 133
10 Wilson, *A Prime Minister on Prime Ministers*, p. 279
11 Rev. Harry Williams, CR, at Lord Butler's memorial service, 5 April 1982
12 Macmillan, *At the End of the Day*, p. 27
13 Macmillan, *Pointing the Way*, p. 154
14 Macmillan, *Riding the Storm*, p. 376
15 Macmillan, *Pointing the Way*, p. 177
16 Lord Home to the author
17 Audrey Russell to the author
18 Evans, 18 November 1961
19 Macmillan, *Pointing the Way*, p. 472
20 *Annual Register*, 1961
21 Audrey Russell to the author
22 Macmillan, op. cit.
23 *Ottawa Citizen*, 5 October 1964
24 Alexandra of Jugoslavia, *Prince Philip: A Family Portrait*, p. 215
25 Hella Pick, *Manchester Guardian*, 12 October 1964
26 *Winnipeg Free Press*, 13 October 1964
27 Prince Philip, reported in *The Times*, 20 October 1969
28 Lord Stewart to the author
29 Ibid.

Chapter XVI
Revaluations: The 1970s

1 Fitch, p. 181
2 J. A. Mizzi, letter to *Sunday Telegraph*, 7 February 1982
3 Douglas Liversidge, *Queen Elizabeth II and the British Monarchy Today*, p. 107
4 Sampson, *Macmillan*, p. 138
5 John Muggeridge, *Saturday Night*, April 1971
6 Stewart, p. 280
7 Mrs Margaret Thatcher MP to the author
8 Reports in *Globe* and *Mail*, 30 June and 4 July 1973
9 Robert Carvel, *Evening Standard*, 31 July 1973
10 Maurice Weaver, *Daily Telegraph*, 7 July 1973
11 Donald Horne, *The Queen*, p. 46
12 Edward Heath MP to the author
13 Sir Alexander Down to British journalist Geoffrey Parkhouse, 1973
14 Sampson, *Macmillan*, pp. 223–4; Mansergh, *The Commonwealth Experience*, Chapter 13, 'The Climax of Commonwealth and the Dawn of Disenchantment'
15 Edward Heath MP to the author
16 Ibid.
17 Richard Crossman, *The Diaries of a Cabinet Minister: Vol. II*, December 1966, p. 160
18 Wilson, *The Governance of Britain*, p. 108; Macmillan, *Riding the Storm*, p. 344
19 Wilson, *The Final Term*, pp. 236 and 239
20 James Callaghan MP to the author
21 Ibid.
22 Ibid.
23 Richard Crossman, 'The Royal Tax-Avoiders', *New Statesman*, 28 May 1971
24 Sir Michael Adeane's evidence to the Select Committee on the Civil List, 1971
25 Lord Stewart to the author
26 Sampson, *The Changing Anatomy of Britain*, p. 6
27 Mrs Margaret Thatcher MP to the author
28 Pope-Hennessy, *A Lonely Business*, pp. 212 and 218
29 Michael Bloch, *The Duke of Windsor's War*, p. 21
30 *Daily Express*, 16 June 1981; Ann Morrow, *The Queen*, pp. 217–18

Chapter XVII Under
Paul's Dome: 1977–81

1 Hugo Vickers to the author
2 John Grigg, *Observer*, 7 July 1981
3 *Punch and the Monarchy*, pp. 87, 96–7 and 152
4 Airlie, p. 219
5 Boys of William Penn (Junior) School, *The Queen*, p. 186
6 J. H. Plumb and Huw Wheldon, *Royal Heritage: The Reign of Elizabeth II*, p. 206
7 Oliver Millar, *The Queen's Pictures*, p. 223
8 Godfrey Talbot, *The Country Life Book of Queen Elizabeth the Queen Mother*, Introduction by the Prince of Wales
9 Penny Junor, *Diana Princess of Wales*, p. 68; Alison Miller, *Sunday Times Magazine*, 5 July 1981
10 Junor, p. 129
11 Ibid., p. 168
12 Rebecca West, quoted by *Telegraph Sunday Magazine*, 1981 from an article in 1947; *Guardian*, 25 July 1981
13 Massimo Justi, *Il Settimanale*, quoted in *International Daily News*, 7 August 1981

14 James Callaghan MP to the author

Chapter XVIII 'The System'

1 Susan Crosland, *Tony Crosland*, p. 208
2 Notes by Lord Cobbold on his evidence to the House of Commons Committee on the Lord Chamberlain and Censorship, 1968; Lord Cobbold's notes for the author, July 1982
3 Lord Cobbold to the author
4 Lady (Norah) Phillips to the author
5 Robert Blake, *The Queen*, p. 13; Kenneth Rose, *Sunday Telegraph*, 15 May 1966
6 Nicolson, *Monarchy*, p. 299
7 Lord Stewart to the author
8 David Watt, *The Times*, 11 December 1981
9 Sir Harold Wilson MP to the author
10 Edward Heath MP to the author
11 Lord Hailsham to the author
12 Lord Stewart to the author
13 Sir Harold Wilson MP, 'The Girl I Saw Become Queen', *The Times*, 6 February 1982
14 David Watt, *The Times*, 11 December 1981
15 Sir John Colville, letter to *The Times*, 2 February 1982
16 Alan Watkins, *Observer*, 4 July 1982
17 Lord Stewart to the author
18 Lord Hailsham to the author
19 Mrs Margaret Thatcher MP to the author
20 David Butler, *The Times*, 23 July 1982
21 Tony Benn MP to the Parliamentary Press Gallery, 1 December 1982; *Guardian*, 2 December 1982 and 3 March 1983
22 Peter Jay, 'Memo to the Labour Party: Prime Ministers are chosen by the Queen', *The Times*, 2 February 1981
23 Norman St John-Stevas, press statement, 27 August 1982
24 Vernon Bogdanor, 'The Royal Right to Refuse', *Guardian*, 28 August 1982; Bogdanor, *Multi-Party Politics and the Constitution*
25 Junor, p. 149; *Daily Express*, 12 May 1981

Chapter XIX The Spell

1 Sampson, *The Changing Anatomy of Britain*, p. 13
2 David Wood, *The Times*, 20 April 1981
3 Nicholas Wapshott, *The Times*, 21 July 1982
4 Charles Douglas-Home, 'Royal Wedding', *The Times*, 28 July 1981
5 Beaumont, p. 200
6 Lady Diana Cooper, *Robert Morley's Second Book of Bricks*, p. 48
7 Martin, p. 16; Hugh Casson, *Diary*, 24 July 1980, p. 88
8 Casson, 21 December 1980, p. 173
9 Crossman, Vol. II, p. 544
10 Crosland, pp. 344 and 346
11 Ann Morrow, 'Britannia', *Majesty* magazine, 29 July 1981
12 Howard, p. 28; Angus Maude, 'Do You Wish to Undermine the Throne, Mr Heath?', *Sunday Express*, 20 December 1970
13 Peregrine Worsthorne, *Sunday Telegraph*, 2 August 1981
14 Malcolm Muggeridge, *The Listener*, 26 March 1981
15 Andrew Duncan, *The Reality of Monarchy*, p. 326
16 Boothroyd, p. 223; Kenneth Rose, 'Twenty-five Years On', *Sunday Telegraph*, 30 January 1977
17 Martin, p. 16
18 Edmund Leach, *New Statesman*, 24 July 1981

19 Menzies, p. 256
20 Princess Anne, television interview, 23 December 1981
21 Odes by the Poet Laureate on the Prince of Wales's Investiture, 1969, and Wedding, 1981
22 Princess Anne, op. cit.
23 Colville, p. 133

Chapter XX   The Queen

1 Basil Boothroyd, 'The Prince I came to know rather well', *The Times*, 10 June 1981
2 Macmillan, *Pointing the Way*, 13 November 1961, p. 471
3 Rose Hillmore, 'Royal Reminiscences', BBC, 4 August 1975
4 Avril Mollison, *Sunday Express Magazine*, November 1982
5 Crosland, p. 346
6 Ibid., p. 343
7 Ibid., p. 346
8 Private information
9 Longford, *Victoria R.I.*, p. 520
10 Crossman, Vol. II, p. 44
11 Sampson, *The Changing Anatomy of Britain*, p. 4
12 Casson, 19 and 20 February 1980, pp. 26–7

13 HRH the Duke of Edinburgh, 'The Joys of Horse Power', *Telegraph Sunday Magazine*, 25 April 1982
14 Interview of Prince Charles with Peter Osnos, *Washington Post*, reprinted in *Guardian*, 30 August 1982
15 *Guardian*, 28 September 1982
16 Tim Heald, 'A Job Well Done', *Toronto Star, Today Magazine*, 6 February 1982
17 Alan Hamilton, *The Times*, 1 February 1982
18 Private information
19 Richard Acton to the author; Lord Home to the author
20 Private information
21 Seminar on 'Do Books Matter?', National Film Theatre, 27 April 1972
22 Michael Mifsud, 'A Tale of Two Portraits', *Majesty* magazine, November 1980
23 Private information
24 Grigg, *Standard*, 4 February 1982
25 Malcolm Muggeridge to the author
26 Christopher Hibbert, *The Court at Windsor: A Domestic History*, p. 293

Index